LANGUAGE BROKERING IN IMMIGRANT FAMILIES

Language Brokering in Immigrant Families: Theories and Contexts brings together an international group of researchers to share their findings on language brokering— when immigrant children translate for their parents and other adults. Given the large amount of immigration occurring worldwide, it is important to understand how language brokering may support children's and families' acculturation to new countries. The chapter authors include overviews of the existing literature, insights from multiple disciplines, the potential benefits and drawbacks to language brokering, and the contexts that may influence children, adolescents, and emerging adults who language broker. With the latest findings, the authors theorize on how language brokering may function and the outcomes for those who do so.

Robert S. Weisskirch, MSW, Ph.D. is a Professor of Human Development in the Liberal Studies Department at California State University, Monterey Bay.

LANGUAGE BROKERING IN IMMIGRANT FAMILIES

Theories and Contexts

Edited by
Robert S. Weisskirch

NEW YORK AND LONDON

First published 2017
by Routledge
711 Third Avenue, New York, NY 10017

and by Routledge
2 Park Square, Milton Park, Abingdon, Oxon, OX14 4RN

Routledge is an imprint of the Taylor & Francis Group, an informa business

© 2017 Taylor & Francis

Library of Congress Cataloging-in-Publication Data
A catalog record for this book has been requested

ISBN: 978-1-138-18511-1 (hbk)
ISBN: 978-1-138-18514-2 (pbk)
ISBN: 978-1-315-64471-4 (ebk)

Typeset in Bembo
by Apex CoVantage, LLC

To Paige,
who opened her heart and makes home home
and
To Dr. Sylvia A. Alva,
who walked across the hall and shared an article she thought
I would find interesting. I did and appreciate your mentorship.

CONTENTS

PART IV
Parents' Roles and Emerging Adult Language Brokers   **245**

ABOUT THE CONTRIBUTORS

Tony Cline, Ph.D. is a member of the Educational Psychology Group at University College London (UCL) and contributes to its Professional Doctorate for experienced Educational Psychologists. He initially worked in inner city and suburban areas around London as an educational psychologist. Subsequently, he moved into higher education, where he has led professional training in Educational Psychology at UCL and headed the Department of Psychology at the University of Luton before returning to UCL to take up his present post in September 2004. His publications have covered a wide range of subjects, including child language brokering, the education of bilingual children, psychological assessment, dyslexia, and selective mutism. He is co-author of the textbook, *Special Educational Needs, Inclusion and Diversity*.

Meghan Corella is an Assistant Professor in the Department of Language and Literacy Education at the University of British Columbia. Her research interests include academic language, multiple literacies, language assessment, language brokering, and racial humor. She earned a Ph.D. in Education from the University of California, Santa Barbara and a B.A. in Spanish Literary and Cultural Studies from Occidental College. She has experienced the role of language broker in the context of cross-cultural interactions among American and Ecuadorian family members.

Catherine L. Costigan, Ph.D. is an Associate Professor and Director of Clinical Training in the Department of Psychology at the University of Victoria. She obtained a M.A. and Ph.D. in Clinical Psychology from Michigan State University, completed a pre-doctoral Clinical Internship with the Institute for Juvenile Research at the University of Illinois, Chicago, and a post-doctoral research fellowship at the University of Washington. Her research focuses on understanding how families navigate challenging circumstances, including families raising children who have intellectual disabilities and families undergoing cultural changes associated with immigration. Some of her recent research has focused on understanding the ways in which immigrant parents support the identity development of their adolescents; understanding how acculturation processes influence the ability of immigrant mothers and fathers to co-parent together effectively; and understanding relationship dynamics such as language brokering that affect the psychological development of youth.

Sarah Crafter, Ph.D. is a Senior Lecturer in the Department of Psychology at the Open University in the UK. She has a Ph.D. in Cultural Psychology and Human Development and her theoretical and conceptual interests are grounded in sociocultural theory, transitions, critical or contested ideas of "normative" development, and cultural identity development. Her work with child language brokers grew out of broader interest in the constructions or representations of childhood in culturally diverse settings.

Guida de Abreu, B.Sc., M.Sc., Ph.D. is a Professor in Cultural Psychology at Oxford Brookes University. She earned a Ph.D. from the University of Cambridge. Her research interests focus on the impact of sociocultural contexts in learning and identity development. Her research explores young people's experiences of key aspects of their lives, such as the relationship between home and school mathematics, being an immigrant or minority student, acting as a language broker, acting as a young carer, and living with a chronic illness. This work includes the perspectives of teachers and parents. Her first culture and language is Portuguese. She directed the first large-scale research project with Portuguese students in schools in England and Jersey, where language brokering emerged as part of the children and young people's life in Britain (commissioned by the Portuguese Department of Education, 2000–2003).

Lisa M. Dorner, Ph.D. is an Associate Professor of Educational Policy in the Department of Educational Leadership and Policy Analysis at the University of Missouri-Columbia. Having earned a Ph.D. and M.A. in Human Development and Social Policy from Northwestern University, she continues to be interested in the intersections between human lives, development, and the implementation of educational policies, particularly for Spanish-speaking immigrants in the United States. Her interests in brokering and bilingual/dual-language education come from her own transcultural experiences working as an English instructor in the city colleges of Chicago and in junior high and high schools in Niigata, Japan.

Valerie C. Flores-Lamb, Ph.D. is currently a full-time faculty member at Grand Canyon University in the College of Doctoral Studies for Psychology. Her research program centers around finding ways to improve the academic achievement of Latino/a American students across the span of development. In particular, she has focused on Latino/a students' language brokering, executive functions, mental health, and their father involvement, with the use of self-report, behavioral, and neuroscience methodologies. At Loyola University Chicago, she earned a Ph.D. and M.A. in Developmental Psychology and a B.S. in Psychology. She is a third-generation Mexican American whose drive to augment the quality of education for Latino/as is fueled by her experience teaching low-income Mexican American second graders in her native state of Arizona.

Eva Gjorgieva is a research technician in the Neurology Department at Northwestern University. Her research interests include language brokering, executive functions, and cognitive development, with an integration of neuroscience methodologies. She earned a B.S. in Psychology from Loyola University Chicago and plans to pursue a Ph.D. in Neuroscience. She is a Macedonian immigrant, who grew up frequently language brokering for her parents, earning the unofficial title of "Family Secretary."

Shu-Sha Angie Guan, Ph.D. is an Assistant Professor in the Department of Child and Adolescent Development at California State University, Northridge. Her research focuses on how social contexts (e.g., culture, digital media, relationships) affect mental and physical well-being, especially among ethnic minority and immigrant adolescents and young adults. She earned her B.A. in Psychology at the University of California, Berkeley and Ph.D. in Psychology from the University of California, Los Angeles. She was born in China and immigrated with her family to Los Angeles at the age of 2. Her childhood work as a language broker for her parents and extended family taught her about the rewards of reciprocity and inspired her first research project in graduate school.

Lisa M. Guntzviller, M.A., Ph.D. is an Assistant Professor in the Communication Department at the University of Illinois at Urbana-Champaign. Her research interests focus on interpersonal communication in health and family contexts, specifically examining individual and dyadic perceptions of complex interactions, such as language brokering. Both her Ph.D. and M.A. are from Purdue University in Interpersonal Communication. Her dissertation explored communication processes during brokering in Mexican-heritage adolescents and their mothers. Her B.A. is in Mathematics and Communication from Aquinas College, Michigan. She has acted as a Spanish-English informal interpreter in the United States and Central America, and married into a multilingual family in which brokering frequently occurs.

Josephine M. Hua, Ph.D. earned her doctorate in Clinical Psychology at the University of Victoria. She obtained her B.Sc. in Psychology at the University of

British Columbia, her M.Sc. in Clinical Psychology at the University of Victoria, and completed a pre-doctoral clinical residency in Clinical Health Psychology within the Faculty of Medicine of the University of Manitoba. Her research interests focus on risk and resilience factors related to child and youth adjustment and family relationships, including the acculturation of immigrant families. Her masters and doctoral research more specifically focuses on relations among language brokering, psychological adjustment, and the quality of parent-adolescent relationships. The daughter of immigrant Chinese parents, Josephine first became interested in the language brokering process when she worked as a literacy program coordinator and often witnessed the dynamics of language brokering between children, parents, and grandparents.

Jennifer A. Kam, Ph.D. is an Associate Professor in the Department of Communication at the University of California, Santa Barbara. Her research interests include identifying interpersonal protective resources that can attenuate the effects that culturally related stressors have on adverse academic, relational, and health outcomes. Her work primarily focuses on immigration and ethnic minority issues such as language brokering, fear of deportation, separation/reunification, and perceived discrimination. She earned a Ph.D. in Communication from Pennsylvania State University, a M.A. in Communication from San Diego State University, and a B.A. in Communication and English from the University of California, Davis. She is the daughter and granddaughter of Chinese immigrants, and both her father and mother language brokered for their parents.

Su Yeong Kim, Ph.D. is an Associate Professor of Human Development and Family Sciences at the University of Texas at Austin. Her research interests include the role of cultural and family contexts that shape the development of adolescents in immigrant and minority families in the United States. She received her Ph.D. in Human Development from the University of California, Davis and a B.A. in Psychology and a B.S. in Business Administration from the University of Southern California. As the principal investigator of NSF CAREER (BCS-0956123) and NIH grants (R03 HD060045), she was able to collect longitudinal data on more than 600 Mexico-origin middle school language brokers and their mothers and fathers in the Austin, Texas area.

Jenny Kurman, Ph.D. is a Professor of Psychology at the University of Haifa, Israel. Her research interests evolve around culture, focusing on the way self and personality interact with culture. She studies various aspects of minorities in Israel, with role reversal and filial responsibilities children assume in their families upon immigration as a main component of this line of research. She received a Ph.D. in Psychology and an M.A. in Clinical-Educational Psychology from the University of Haifa, and a B.A. in Psychology from Tel Aviv University.

Jin Sook Lee, Ph.D. is a Professor of Education in the Gevirtz Graduate School of Education at the University of California, Santa Barbara. Her research interests focus on sociocultural aspects of heritage and English language practice, maintenance, and development in immigrant families. She earned her Ph.D. in Education from Stanford University, and an M.A. in Linguistics and a B.A. in English Literature from Yonsei University in Seoul, Korea. She is the daughter of Korean immigrants and has had extensive experience language brokering for her parents and community elders during her childhood in the United States.

Andrea Michel, Ph.D. is research associate in the Department of Developmental Psychology at the University of Jena, Germany. Her research interests focus on adolescent development, including immigrant adolescents' language brokering, psychological adaptation, and autonomy. She earned her diploma (German M.Sc. equivalent) and Ph.D. in Psychology from the University of Jena, Germany. During her academic career she also worked at the University of Leipzig, Germany, where she was involved in a research project investigating the effects of child maltreatment in childhood and adolescence. Having grown up in one of the areas with the largest and most diverse immigrant populations in Germany, she experienced language brokering second-hand in several of her (immigrant) friends.

Afaf Nash, Ph.D. is a lecturer in the Middle East Studies Program in Dornsife College of Letters, Arts, and Sciences at the University of Southern California. Her research interests focus on language brokering, heritage language, Arab immigration, sociolinguistics, conversation analysis, institutional discourse, and Arabic literature and linguistics. She earned a Ph.D. in Applied Linguistics from the University of California, Los Angeles, a M.A. in Linguistics from California State University Fullerton, and a B.A. in English Literature from the University of Baghdad, Iraq. She emigrated to the United States during the Iraqi-American coalition war and has helped her parents, siblings, and many relatives to move to and settle in the United States. She often performs language brokering for her parents, mostly during medical visits.

Lindsay O'Dell, B.Sc., Ph.D. is Director of Post Graduate Studies in the Faculty of Health and Social Care at the Open University, UK. Her research focus is on children, young people, and families who are in some way "different" including child language brokers, children with autism, children with ADHD, and young carers. She is currently Chair of the Psychology of Women Section of the British Psychological Society and co-editor of the journal *Children & Society*.

Olga Oznobishin, Ph.D. is a Research Associate in the Department of Psychology at the University of Haifa, Israel. Her research interests include parenting and parent-child relationships within immigrant families, with a special focus on role reversal, language brokering, and intergenerational transmission of family relationships. She received a Ph.D. in Psychology, an M.A. in Clinical-Education Psychology, and a B.A. in Psychology and Special Education from the University of Haifa. She immigrated to Israel from Russia as an adolescent and experienced language brokering for her parents.

Evangelia Prokopiou, B.A., M.Sc., Ph.D. is a lecturer of psychology in the Faculty of Health and Society at the University of Northampton, UK. Her research interests focus on the Psychology of Culture and Human Development, and more specifically on the construction of identities in culturally diverse contexts; the impact of immigration on cultural identity development of children, adolescents, and adults; identity development in community/supplementary schools; constructions of childhood (including unaccompanied asylum seekers and language brokers); and the impact of cultural change on family, community, and identity.

Vanessa R. Rainey, Ph.D. is an Assistant Professor of Psychology in the Psychology Department at the University of West Florida. She earned her Ph.D., with an emphasis on Developmental Psychology and Statistics, from Loyola University, Chicago. It is during this time that she developed an interest in working with unique, inner-city child populations. Her research interests have focused on language development and executive function development, particularly in bilingual populations such as language brokers. She has most recently been investigating these areas using neuroscience techniques.

Yishan Shen, Ph.D. is an Assistant Professor in the Department of Family and Child Development at Texas State University. Her research interests center on how culture-specific processes (such as language brokering and acculturation) and culture-general factors (such as family socioeconomic status) conjointly influence youth development in immigrant families. She received a Ph.D. and an M.A. in Human Development and Family Sciences from the University of Texas at Austin, and a B.S. in Psychology and a B.S. in Space Physics from Peking University in China. She grew up as an ethnic Korean in China and observed language brokering behaviors of her peers for their parents with limited fluency in Mandarin Chinese.

Cynthia Stohl, Ph.D. is a Professor in the Department of Communication at the University of California, Santa Barbara and an Honorary Professor at the University of Arhus School of Business and Social Sciences in Denmark. A leading expert in globalization, networks, and organizational participatory processes, she has explored the brokering role of non-governmental organizations within the international human rights community. Her most recent work addresses global organizing, collective action, and corporate social responsibility in the digital media environment. She earned her Ph.D. and M.A. from Purdue University.

Kelsey E. Tilton has a B.S. in Applied Learning and Development from the University of Texas at Austin. She plans to continue her education towards a B.S. in Nursing, and afterwards, a graduate degree in an advanced nursing practice, specializing in maternal and child health. A native of South Texas, her upbringing along the United States–Mexico border allowed her to experience language brokering through her peers, community, and most notably within the education system.

Peter F. Titzmann, Ph.D. is a Professor of Developmental Psychology at the Leibniz Universität Hannover, Germany. During his academic career he worked at the University of York, UK; the Friedrich-Schiller University Jena, Germany; the University of Zurich, Switzerland; and the University of Education Weingarten, Germany. His general research interests relate to the interplay between normative development and migration-related adaptation among adolescents with immigrant backgrounds. He investigated this interplay in various developmental outcomes, such as experiences of stress, delinquent behavior, friendships, autonomy development, and changes in the family hierarchy and family interaction. He first encountered the topic of language brokering during focus group interviews conducted in preparation of his Ph.D., and this has accompanied his research ever since.

Robert S. Weisskirch, M.S.W., Ph.D. is a Professor of Human Development in the Liberal Studies Department at California State University, Monterey Bay. His research interests focus on language brokering, ethnic identity, acculturation and immigrant issues, how technology affects relationships, and the pedagogy of human development. He earned a Ph.D. in Human Development from the University of California, Davis, a M.S.W. degree from San Diego State University, and a B.A. in Psychology from the University of California, Irvine. He is the son of Argentine immigrants and has experienced language brokering for his grandparents and other relatives, as well as others in the community.

INTRODUCTION

Robert S. Weisskirch

This book brings together contemporary researchers who study language brokering from broad fields, using a variety of methods, and with a focus on diverse populations. Interest in studying language brokering has grown in the last two decades, perhaps in reflection of the growing migration patterns occurring throughout the world. In 2015, 243 million individuals resided in a different country than the one in which they were born (United Nations, 2015). In addition, ethnic minority immigrants are moving to broader geographical areas within developed countries than in the past. For example, between 2000 and 2014 in the United States, states that have not typically been destinations for immigrant populations—Tennessee, Kentucky, Wyoming, North Dakota, and South Carolina—saw the largest percent growth of immigrant population (Zong & Batalova, 2016). Given these recent waves of immigration, it is no wonder that researchers, practitioners, interventionists, and others have become interested in language brokering as a phenomenon.

In talking with anyone from an immigrant background, it is nearly impossible to find someone who has not had any experience with language brokering for parents, other relatives, or members of the community. In addition, in discussions about language brokering, there is a large amount of speculation and conjecture about language brokering. For some, there is a pervasive negative perspective on language brokering—that children should not and should never have to broker for their parents or have to deal with "adult" situations and circumstances. This attitude, however, may negate the reality of the immigrant situation that parents and families need language brokers in order to survive in their new culture. There is also a perspective that language brokering can be positive for children—helping them maintain the heritage language, learning about their culture, extending their knowledge about the host culture, and providing cognitively complex situations that may enhance development. There is also a perspective that language brokering may also be relatively neutral: It is just part of being bilingual, and part of one's role in the family as others may have other roles, chores, or responsibilities. This book addresses some of these perspectives, but, like many areas of science, there is no single answer.

The research in this volume goes beyond simplistic findings that indicate if language brokering has beneficent, detrimental, or neutral outcomes for children, parents, and family. These contemporary researchers have brought together their latest findings and thinking about language brokering from their own research-based experience. The idea for this book was to have each chapter's authors comment on how their findings could contribute to overall theory about language brokering as elucidated in Chapter 14, "Future Directions for Language Brokering Research." It is my hope that the culminating chapter provides direction and fodder for the next wave of research on language brokering.

I am particularly proud of the diversity of authors from the United States, Canada, the UK, Germany, and Israel who were willing to contribute chapters to this volume. Given that immigration has been increasing globally, insights into how language brokering may be occurring in countries that have long-standing histories of receiving immigrants may be instructional for countries that have not traditionally had such concerns with immigrant acculturation. In addition, the diversity of the findings allows for potential formulation of theoretical ideas about what may be occurring with language brokering.

The order of the chapters begins with frameworks of language brokering. Weisskirch (Chapter 1) provides a developmental perspective to language brokering during childhood, adolescence, and emerging adulthood. He applies Piagetian and Eriksonian theory to what the language brokering literature has found across the pertinent stages in the lifespan. Kam, Guntzviller, and Stohl (Chapter 2) look at language brokering from a Communication perspective. They discuss how theories from the Communication field apply to language brokering but also transcend disciplines by looking at language brokering as a communicative act. The authors present ways of understanding how the communication of language brokering may influence the outcomes for the child and parents. Shen, Tilton, and Kim (Chapter 3) provide a review of dimensions of language brokering and their effects on multiple domains. They organize the review into the socioemotional, behavioral, academic, relational, cultural, parental mediators, and moderators to the outcomes of language brokering. Taken together, these three chapters provide broad, interdisciplinary views of developmental issues in language brokering, how language brokering can be understood through a communication lens, and what is known about language brokering, which provide key frameworks for the rest of the book.

The next section broadly focuses on family dynamics. Titzmann and Michel's chapter (Chapter 4) on ethnic Germans from the former Soviet Union and their return to Germany provides insights on an unique circumstance. They incorporate acculturation theory and family perspectives to understand how the immigrant youth experience obligations to engage in brokering and how that affects psychological functioning. Similarly, Oznobishin and Kurman (Chapter 5) present findings on immigrant adolescents from the former Soviet Union in Israel who experience language brokering as burdensome and as negative for family relationships. The authors note that the pressure in Israeli society to assimilate as well as loss in status upon immigration may explain the findings. Nash (Chapter 6) presents qualitative findings on Arab American emerging adults and their experiences with language brokering in the United States, and with confronting anti-Arab and anti-Muslim discriminations both in public and at home. These findings elucidate how brokers' navigate discrimination when language brokering and shed light on the current circumstances of a growing immigrant population. Hua and Costigan (Chapter 7) investigate how Chinese Canadian teens' psychological adjustment relates to language brokering, focusing on for whom they broker (i.e., mother or father), using self-determination theory. They find that parental autonomy-supportive contexts aligned with positive feeling towards language brokering. The differing samples in these four chapters helps to present how family dynamics may influence how language brokers experience their work.

The next set of chapters focuses on applied contexts and settings. Guan (Chapter 8) presents findings on how immigrant adolescents use the Internet to support their language brokering. She employs mixed methods by using a quantitative survey and analyzing those results as well as presenting qualitative case studies of interviews of minority youth and their experiences. In Chapter 9, de Abreu and O'Dell provide an overview of the literature on child language brokers in health care settings in the UK, including how practitioners and others react to child language brokers. Rainey, Flores-Lamb, and Gjorgieva (Chapter 10) investigate how findings from neuroscience may apply to language brokers and to individuals when language brokering. They provide insights on areas of the brain and functioning that may be active or involved in bilingualism and, particularly, when language brokering. In Chapter 11, Crafter, Cline, and Prokopiou provide evidence for how former language brokers and teachers in the UK view their language brokering and the language brokering experiences of their students. Lee and Corella Morales, in Chapter 12, provide a unique perspective by looking at parents' interactions with their children and examining how parents provide support for their child language broker and, in fact, act as language brokers for their children to aid comprehension of concepts and vocabulary. Dorner (Chapter 13) investigates how language brokering is experienced by emerging adults. She explains the framework of emerging adulthood and how it applies to language brokering. She provides examples from interviews with well-experienced language brokers who now have become emerging adults and discusses how that life stage interacts with language brokering work. In Chapter 14, Weisskirch provides some ideas about the direction of research on language brokering. He focuses on issues of measurement, methodology, and theorizing on how language brokering may be understood in a broader developmental, social, familial, and cultural context.

It is anticipated that readers might walk away from this volume with more questions than answers. Given that immigration experiences, family dynamics, and cultural issues vary broadly across groups, it is not possible to come to a single conclusion. Instead, the chapters of this book should spawn greater and more creative thinking on the topic and, hopefully, provide insights for those who work with and develop programs for immigrants and ethnic minorities and their families.

References

United Nations. (2015). Population facts No. 2015/2. Retrieved from www.un.org/en/development/desa/population/migration/publications/wallchart/docs/Migration WallChart2015.pdf

Zong, J., & Batalova, J. (2016, April). Frequently requested statistics on immigrants and immigration in the United States. Migration Policy Institute. Retrieved from www.migrationpolicy.org/article/frequently requested-statistics-immigrants-and-immigration-united-states#Immigrant Population Change over Time

PART I

Frameworks of Language Brokering

1

A DEVELOPMENTAL PERSPECTIVE ON LANGUAGE BROKERING

Robert S. Weisskirch

Introduction

Language brokering has been defined as the process whereby children interpret from one language to another for parents and other adults (Tse, 1996b). Many children who speak and understand more than one language may begin language brokering as children but may continue to engage in the practice through adolescence and into adulthood (Valdes, 2003; Weisskirch, 2006; Weisskirch, et al., 2011). The experience of language brokering may affect children, adolescents, emerging adults, and adults differently because of the unique characteristics of each developmental period and because of the varying role of parents in language brokering during each of these periods.

Contexts of Language Brokering

Language brokering occurs in a wide range of locations, situations, with a range of items requiring translation.[1] In the past, language brokers have reported translating in a variety of places (e.g., medical offices, social service offices, immigration offices, schools, and parental worksites), with a diversity of items (e.g., rental agreements, immigration forms, notes from school, insurance documents, bills), and in many types of settings and situations (e.g., hospital emergency rooms, parent-teacher conferences, parent's workplace, on the phone, and in stores) that may require sophisticated conceptual understanding linguistically, culturally, and conceptually (Acoach & Webb, 2004; Morales & Hanson, 2005; Orellana, Dorner, & Pulido, 2003).

Language brokering for parents within a family merits specific discussion. In families, parents typically hold a position of power and authority. However, when youth language broker for parents, it may alter typical and expected patterns of authority. Parents may feel less able to direct the family with the outside world and feel diminished in their role as parents and, possibly, personally as individuals, in consequence (Oznobishin & Kurman, 2009; Titzmann, 2012). However, there is growing evidence that parental interactions with child language brokers may shape the outcome for all parties involved. That is, parents who provide a supportive relationship in which to provide language brokering tend to have children who report positive outcomes (Shen, Kim, Wang, & Chao, 2014; Weisskirch, 2007; Wu & Kim, 2009). In contrast, parents who are less positive (i.e., demanding, place undue expectations, etc.) have child language brokers who report more negative experiences with language brokering (Hua & Costigan, 2012; Love & Buriel, 2007; Weisskirch, 2007). How parents frame language brokering tasks for their children may be an extension of their general parenting style, a new pattern of behavior in response to their language deficit, or even both. Since parents strongly influence developmental outcomes for children, how parents interact with and respond to their children when language brokering may have immediate and cumulative effects. Further, how language brokers view language brokering may be perceived by them as an extension of their parent-child relationship. Hence, in language brokering, the family environment and parent-child relationships intersect distinctively with developmental processes for children, adolescents, and emerging adults.

The family lifecycle may also affect the experience of language brokering. McGoldrick and Shibusawa (2012) asserted that there are developmental times in which the family relationships are closer and inward-focused toward the family, and times in which they are more distant, expansive, and outward-focused. For example, when children are infants, families across generations may be closer, given the focus on family building. When children are adolescents, the relationships may be more distant. Adolescents' attentions are focused outside the family, parents (typically in their 40s) are engaging in some reevaluation of their lives, and grandparents may be preparing for retirement. During the children-as-adolescents cycle of the family, inserting language brokering may further place the family system in disequilibrium.

In the family lifecycle, researchers asserted that unpredictable stressors such as immigration may disrupt the family system. Falicov (2012) further noted that immigrants to the United States experience loss, mourning, and grief related to immigration similar to those experiencing the death of loved ones. The loss continues to "reach forward to shape future generations born in the new land" (p. 301). However, Falicov indicated that immigrating families become resilient, use their resources (such as language brokering), and can reorganize relationships to become adaptive and thrive in the host country.

Given that immigration is an unpredictable life event (even if the immigration was planned), in order to adapt to the host country families may need to use their assets, which include language brokering among other adaptive acculturative processes (Berry, 2003). Most often, language brokering occurs in immigrant families, where cultural expectations may differ from the host countries. Many of the immigrants are leaving countries with collectivist cultural origins and moving to countries where the culture is more individualistic, such as the United States, UK, Canada, Germany, and Israel (Hofstede, 1980; Triandis, 1995). The cultural shift in the host country also may contribute to how youth experience language brokering.

Individuals from collectivist societies tend to favor their in-groups—such as family, tribe, clan, or nation—and shape their behaviors to support the group norm or expectations. Individuals from individualistic societies support the notion that individuals are autonomous and independent from their in-groups and favor personal goals over group goals, shaping behaviors to support achievement of their own goals (Triandis, 2001). For parents from collectivist cultural backgrounds, their beliefs may be that one sacrifices one's own goals for the betterment of the family. Carrying this belief into the language brokering situation, parents may expect their children to cease their own activities and step into the position to help the parents and the family unit as whole by language brokering. Youth, with greater exposure in an individualistic society like the United States, UK, Germany, etc., than their parents, may want to focus their time and efforts on their own activities and may not fully understand, or perhaps empathize with, why their parents cannot be more independent in their dealings. This lack of understanding may be developmental in that the children or adolescents may not be fully able to take other perspectives, and it may also be a lack of cultural socialization in that the children or adolescents may not have been taught how to think and behave in a manner consistent with the collectivist heritage background.

Indeed, language brokering may support family ethnic socialization in which parents and others provide guidance (e.g., explicitly teaching, commenting on behavior, using a heritage language use, etc.) on beliefs and behaviors that are valued with the ethnic group of origin (Huynh & Fuligni, 2008). Many ethnic minority individuals are taught about their ethnic heritage and about how to cope with discrimination. Language brokering may be a vehicle by which parents engage in cultural socialization by encouraging heritage language use, learning cultural customs, and providing enculturation of values (Hughes, Rodriguez, Smith, Johnson, Stevenson, & Spicer, 2006). Indeed, Wu and Kim (2009) indicated that when Chinese American youth are more Chinese oriented they feel a sense of efficacy in brokering for parents. Further, Weisskirch et al. (2011) found greater support for cultural values of origin among frequent college student language brokers in comparison to non–language brokering co-ethnic college students. Similarly, Cila and LaLonde (2015) reported a significant association between the number of items translated and heritage value orientation among a sample of South Asian Canadian college students. There is some evidence that individuals gain a greater understanding of their heritage culture through language brokering, which may, in turn, contribute to positive individual development as well.

Language Development in Children

Theories support the notion that humans evolved to develop language (Dunbar, 1993). Research has found that children *in utero* react to external sounds. Shortly after birth, infants will prefer the sounds of their mother's voice over others (DeCasper & Fifer, 1980). Infants through the first year and beyond gradually attune their discrimination of the sounds of the language(s) to which they are exposed (Werker, 1989). Children within the first 2 years move from producing sounds to forming words and small phrases to learning several words a day (Tamis-Lemonda, Bornstein, Kahana-Kalman, Baumwell, & Cyphers, 1998). By the time children are 6 years old, they may have as many as 14,000 words in their vocabulary (Clark, 1993). For children who grow up bilingual, the same is true. Bialystok, Craik, Green, and Gollan (2009) noted that "Bilingual language acquisition is as effortless, efficient, and successful as monolingual acquisition" (p. 90). Given their developing language abilities, children can readily acquire a second language (or more) from being in an environment where the languages are used.

Within immigrant families, however, full bilingualism may not be achieved. For children who immigrate to the United States, the level of bilingualism may depend on the age of arrival and exposure to English. Those children who arrive at older ages (e.g., close to or at adolescence) may retain nativity in the first language. Children who arrive at younger ages may lack exposure to in-depth heritage language learning due to insufficient opportunities for heritage language retention, and they may shift quickly to English dominance (Suárez-Orozco, Abo-Zena, & Marks, 2015). For children who grow up in a two-language household but are not immigrants themselves, there may be dominance in one language over the other. In addition, because English is the language of instruction in school, children may develop an English-dominant academic vocabulary with a home-life vocabulary focused on the heritage language. Although these speakers of two languages may have some understanding of both languages, their level of bilingualism may be incomplete.

Children and Language Brokering

Although full bilingualism may not be achieved, language brokering may begin early in life. There are some qualitative and case studies of immigrant children to provide evidence that children serve as language brokers as soon as they acquire the host language (e.g., Guo, 2014; McQuillan & Tse, 1995; Vasquez, Pease-Alvarez, & Shannon, 1994). In retrospective qualitative and case studies of immigrant adolescents and adults, many participants indicate that they have engaged in language brokering since childhood (e.g., Valdes, 2003). A few studies report that participants indicate beginning to language broker between 8 and 12 years old, on average (Chao, 2001; Cila & LaLonde, 2015; McQuillan & Tse, 1995; Tse, 1995, 1996a) and within 1 to 3 years of arrival in the United States (Tse, 1995, 1996b).

Given the average of when children begin language brokering as reported in the research literature, the subsequent section will focus on this developmental period.

Children in Middle Childhood and Language Brokering

According to Piagetian theory, children between roughly ages 7 to 11 are in the stage of Concrete Operational Thought. In this stage of development, children are able to successfully "conserve" mass, weight, volume, and area on classic Piagetian conservation tasks—which means that children can hold at least two different conceptual ideas in their minds at the same time when performing a task. Guo (2014) provided an example of an 8-year-old Chinese immigrant boy to the UK who in overhearing a conversation between the parent and a researcher in Mandarin about the pine trees in the garden interjected that the pine trees are called *conifers*, using the English word because it was a word he did not know in Mandarin. His ability to recognize the class inclusion of pine trees as a kind of conifer—let alone following the conversation in Mandarin and responding with the English concept—is characteristic of children in the Concrete Operational Thought stage. At this stage, children can engage in transformational thought where they can mentally reverse mental actions (Piaget, 1953). Children also move away from egocentrism and are better able to see things from others' perspectives, given their experience interacting with others (Piaget, 1928). However, they lack some abilities to engage with abstract concepts and thoughts, and they may be limited in their ability to engage in scientific processes.

Applied to language brokering situations, children at this age may find themselves able to understand the languages for translation but may struggle with a limited vocabulary and incomplete conceptual understanding. They may reshape the discussion of topics in a way that fits with their vocabulary and understanding of the text or communication. For example, in one study, Hai, a 7-year-old Chinese immigrant to Britain, explained to his mother about wearing a poppy for Remembrance Day in commemoration of those who served in military battles. He explained, mostly in Mandarin, that "In the trench, there is Yuk mud, nothing grows but only poppy grows, and poppy is pretty" (Guo, 2014, p. 82). Hai's understanding of why poppies are worn demonstrated partial understanding, as may be characteristic of a child language broker in the stage of Concrete Operational Thought. Further, children at this stage, may try to advance their understanding through the interaction as best they can. Vasquez et al. (1994) gave an example of a Latina language brokering child, Leti, who in a chiropractor's office with her mother fails to translate accurately but becomes aware of how she can choose what gets translated. Further along in her narrative, Leti explained that her mother went to a specialist for women in another town to address her abdominal pain. The doctor replied with a specialist—a gastroenterologist. Leti acquiesced that the doctor's assumption was correct because she did not know the term "gastroenterologist." Later, she did not know the word *matriz* (uterus), in Spanish or its

English equivalent and substituted "stomach" because that was how her mother had referred to the area that was causing pain. This example may be emblematic of the newly developed cognitive skills that children in the Concrete Operational Thought stage are able to do—manipulate the vocabulary and concepts to present their understanding, despite the imprecision or inaccuracy. In addition, because of her developmental level, she may not fully have grasped the outcome that the doctor was incorrect in his understanding of the kind of medical specialist. Further, she did not recognize the limitation in her vocabulary, did not have the cognitive abilities yet to realize that her understanding and translation were inaccurate, and did not know to ask for clarification, which may be typical of children in Concrete Operational Thought.

According to Eriksonian theory, children from ages 6 to 12 are in the Industry versus Inferiority stage of ego development. At this stage, children should be able to resolve the central psychosocial task by being productive and feeling competent in their ability to perform in their school work and other tasks given to them. They gain mastery of "tools" to help them complete tasks competently. These tools include language and cognitive abilities to help them interact with broader social contexts like schools and neighborhoods. Children who do not resolve the developmental turning point (what Erikson called a "crisis") successfully or completely may feel that they are not competent and are unable to produce work products that meet the demands of the adults and society around them. As a consequence, they may give up, not try hard at tasks, and develop a sense of antipathy towards work.

The resolution of the Industry versus Inferiority stage may apply directly to children's experiences with language brokering. In language brokering, children are thrust into larger social contexts, beyond the family, and have to interact with others when they translate. For many, the activity of successfully translating may lead to feeling industrious, in an Eriksonian sense, in that a challenging task was completed with competence. Indeed, Weisskirch (2005), among a sample of 55 Latino/a sixth graders (mean age = 11.72 years), found that they generally felt positively about translating for others. Those children who were low in acculturation felt more positively about translating, but also more obliged to participate in language brokering. Given that the feedback for translating successfully is typically received in the moment of translation, it is likely that, over time, children who are successful may develop ongoing feelings of competence and mastery that may contribute to resolving this stage of psychosocial development. However, children who may not have adequate vocabulary or conceptual understanding of the topics, who receive inadequate or negative feedback, or who do not feel productive in their language brokering work may develop a sense of inferiority in their abilities to accomplish tasks.

As noted earlier, the way parents and other adults frame the language brokering work that children engage in may shape outcomes for the children. Parents who provide children with positive feedback about translating or who provide praise for the work tend to have children report more positive outcomes. At the same time, parents who are negative, create a stressful environment, or make the work burdensome, have children who indicate negative experiences when language brokering. This notion that the context shapes the children's development is consistent with Eriksonian theory. Since language brokering may be a primary bridge for children from immigrant families to interact with the outside society, the expectations and influences from the psychosocial environment may have a direct impact on the child's development as well as successful resolution of the Industry versus Inferiority stage.

Accordingly, Weisskirch and Alva (2002) found that, among a small sample of Latino/a fifth graders who language broker (mean age = 10.53 years), more translating was associated with greater acculturative stress. The total amount of brokering was also associated with less comfort when translating. The connection between frequency of brokering and more acculturative stress and less comfort may be illustrative of how the interactions during language brokering may support successful or unsuccessful resolution of the central crisis of the Industry versus Inferiority stage. Less comfort and more acculturative stress may be manifestations of "inferiority" for these children. Hamachek (1988) noted that people who successfully develop a sense of industry adopt implicit attitudes of being a good learner, being excited by producing, and working hard to succeed. Accordingly, Orellana, Reynolds, Dorner, and Meza (2003) gave an example of a diary entry from a child, Amanda, who indicated that her family received a letter from the IRS and noted "The paragraph said things about taxes I don't remember exactly but I told her what it said. I felt good because I knew all the words" (p. 21). Here, she indicated feeling good about her task—contributing to her sense of industry as well. Moreover, Dorner, Orellana, and Li-Grining (2007) found that, among the 280 Latino/a fifth and sixth graders in their sample, frequency of language brokering was associated positively with reading scores on standardized tests. This finding may indicate that the sense of industry one develops by language brokering may further transfer to academic tasks as well. For language brokers, the successful resolution of this stage may emerge through positive feedback or perceptions of competence in their language brokering work.

Adolescents and Language Brokering

In Eriksonian theory, adolescents are at a psychosocial stage where they must come to a resolution on their identities and answer the question, "Who am I?" Identity exploration and commitment are central processes for later identity consolidation. The exploration and commitment may encompass domains such as ethnicity, sexuality, religious views, occupation, and ideology, among others. Moreover, adolescents strive for greater autonomy and independence from parents and families, and may want to spend more time with friends and romantic partners as part of this identity search process. They also may become more aware of social conflicts and demands, creating a sense of confusion. The outcome of this stage, Erikson noted, is ego strength, fidelity—being true to the self (Erikson, 1968).

Adolescents who language broker may incorporate their role as language brokers into the larger notion of who they are and their evolving personal identities. Translating for parents and other adults may just be part of whom they are and whom they will continue to become. Orellana (2009) recorded a teenaged Latino language brokering boy saying, "If I'm gonna help my mom with something I'm just gonna do it because my mom does her job and I just do my job to help" (p. 113). In describing the roles in the family, the boy is also explaining how helping his mother by language brokering is part of his role in the family and part of who he is. Similarly, Degener (2010) describes a 13-year-old Lebanese émigré to Germany who noted that "I am by now used to it [language brokering], because it happened several times already" (p. 355). She went on to describe language brokering as a neutral, natural activity for her, causing little distress. For this girl, being a language broker had already become integrated into her sense of who she is—her identity. Corona et al. (2012) also found a recurrent theme among the young US Latino/a adolescents in their sample, that language brokering was just a normal part of their everyday lives, indicating that language brokering may already be incorporated into their identities.

Ethnic identity, a component of personal identity, may be particularly salient for adolescent language brokers, given their close immigrant ties. Heritage language retention has been associated with greater ethnic identity and family cohesion (Oh & Fuligni, 2010). Moreover, Weisskirch (2005) found that, among the Latino/a early adolescents in his US sample, ethnic identity was associated with frequency of language brokering. Specifically, he found that positive feelings about language brokering predicted ethnic identity. In contrast, Martinez, McClure, and Eddy (2009) found that Latino/a youth in families with high demand for language brokering had less of a sense of ethnic belonging and affirmation in comparison to youth in families with low demand. Their finding may indicate that youth with less English-proficient parents were grappling with figuring out who they are in terms of their ethnic identities, given that their language brokering activities require them to present their ethnic affiliation each time they broker. It could be that, in those language brokering situations, the youth may have to "show" their ethnicity each time they have to interpret from Spanish to English, when they may prefer to "blend in" or be less obvious to others in who they are. For some, there may be a contribution of language brokering to the developing ethnic identity as well as the overall personal identity.

From a Piagetian perspective, in adolescence, individuals move into the stage of Formal Operational Thought where they can understand abstract ideas like justice and equity. With this capacity for hypothetical thought, adolescents may develop a sense of idealism and utopianism, constructing ideas about creating a better world. In addition, they can engage in scientific thought and manipulate several ideas simultaneously in their minds. Supporting the connection between language brokering and advances in cognition, Buriel, Perez, DeMent, Chavez, and Moran (1998) found that the amount of language brokering was predictive of academic performance among ninth and 10th grade Latino/a students. Further, in formal operational thought, adolescents develop a flexibility of thought that allows them to adapt their thinking to a broader range of tasks than in the past. They also develop skills that allow for metacognition, thinking about their thinking. Dorner, Orellana, and Jimenez (2008) described a Latina adolescent language broker who was struggling to figure out a language brokering task and said "I just did it different ways. Then I figured it out; then I remember a few things; then I would just put them all together. They [the parents] would figure it out, too." Here, the adolescent is demonstrating her problem-solving abilities that have emerged in adolescence, but also metacognitive abilities to think about her thinking in that episode. Adolescents, in this stage, develop the ability to take their enhanced thinking skills and apply them to practical, work-oriented tasks where these thinking skills can be honed for utility. However, these skills may need greater practice. Villanueva and Buriel (2010) found that, among a sample of young Latina, language brokering adolescents, participants continued to report problems with vocabulary knowledge and comprehension problems in both English and Spanish. Furthermore, in this stage, adolescents develop a sense of mental maturity in understanding the world. It is not surprising, then, that adolescent language brokers demonstrate advanced skills at language brokering and may move towards independent decision-making for the parents and the family.

Having these advanced cognitive abilities and skills may come with negative outcomes. For example, Hua and Costigan (2012) found that the Chinese Canadian adolescents in their sample had more conflict with parents when they language brokered frequently. In addition, adolescents demonstrated more internalizing symptoms and lower self-esteem when they perceived their parents as more psychologically controlling. The authors surmised that the teens may be placing some perceived pressure on themselves to perform well, which may relate to the negative outcomes. The ability to perceive that there is pressure on them to perform well as a language broker requires complex reasoning that comes in the stage of Formal Operational Thought. Further, Walsh, Shulman, Bar-On, and Tsur (2006) found that former Soviet Union immigrant adolescents to Israel reported greater "parentification" than non-immigrant teens. However, the authors noted that this parentification may be the result of immigrant teens needing to communicate on behalf of the parents and the family, and having exposure to sensitive issues in their parents' lives. Titzmann (2012) also found that ethnic German adolescents from the former Soviet Union returning to Germany indicated greater parentification, which was related to better-self efficacy and lower levels of emotional exhaustion. He noted that "most likely, taking on instrumental adult-like responsibilities within the family develops adolescents' social and cognitive skills, which in turn help the adolescent in coping with every demands and challenges" (p. 889). From the outside, an adolescent being "parentified" may seem negative—but it may, in practicality, be adaptive for the circumstances and may be syntonic with the autonomy-seeking of adolescence.

The growing cognitive capacities in adolescence may bring greater awareness of the outcomes of the language brokering situation and the ability to assert oneself as a decision-maker. Orellana (2009) described a teenaged Latino boy, Nova, who "realized that is was easier for him to just speak to people in English than it was for him either to translate for his mother (an act that marked the family as immigrants) or to request a Spanish speaker" (p. 113). His realization demonstrates a sophisticated level of cognition in that he conceives of the potential outcome (and acts accordingly). The newly developed thinking may also support the autonomy in interactions on behalf of parents because the youth may comprehend the outcome. In one study of East Indian adolescents in Britain, one adolescent noted that "Sometimes the English person asks for your parents, but you know they're not going to be able to speak English, so you just pretend they're not in, and answer yourself" (Kaur & Mills, 1993, p. 115). The advancement of more sophisticated and complex ways of thinking in the stage of Formal Operational Thought continues as adolescents move toward adulthood.

Emerging Adults and Language Brokering

In 2000, Arnett proposed a new life stage called emerging adulthood. He cited evidence that youth between roughly ages 18 to 25 (sometimes to age 30) feel "in-between" being adolescents and being full-fledged adults. He noted that youth today are more likely to be in college or other post-secondary training, which limits their complete movement into adulthood because of some sense of financial and emotional dependence on parents and well as personal feelings of transience. Arnett (2004) described emerging adulthood as the age of identity explorations, the age of instability (e.g., financially or occupationally), the self-focused age, the age of feeling in-between, and the age of possibilities.

Identity exploration typically emerges through love and work before making long-lasting choices. That is, the consolidation of identity may not be concluded until sometime in one's 20s (Schwartz, Côte, & Arnett, 2005). The age of instability refers to the number of life changes that may occur at this time in residence, living situations, and romantic relationships, as well as educational training (e.g., changing one's college major). The self-focused age begins about the time when youth gain independence by moving away from parents' homes and/or establishing a more independent lifestyle than during adolescence. They are less reliant on parents and move towards acquiring skills and knowledge for life as adults, without many of the long-term responsibilities of adulthood. Youth, at this time, feel "in-between" in that they do not subjectively feel fully like adults but also do not feel like adolescents. Emerging adulthood as an age of possibilities refers to a sense of optimism about life choices and that one's future has not yet been decided.

Oftentimes, youth have great hopes and expectations about what life may hold for them. All these aspects comprise the developmental stage of emerging adulthood.

For emerging adult language brokers, the ongoing consolidation of their identities, the self-focused nature of this stage, and the feeling that they are in an age of possibilities specifically may influence the brokers' experience of language brokering. Given that their identities are still being consolidated, ongoing responsibilities to language broker for family members may contribute to how they view themselves and develop their identities. For some, being a language broker helping parents and other family members may just be who they are. Guan, Nash, and Orellana (2016) presented an Asian American college student language broker who described his ethnic identity. He said, "I am not completely Asian or American. Phenotypically I am—still look Asian, but I was born in America, like the mannerism of America, that's probably why I call myself Asian-American" (p. 160). The authors surmised that the language brokering experiences may reinforce both ethnic and American identities, which may prompt an opportunity to reflect on identity for consolidation. Moreover, Weisskirch et al. (2011) found that ethnic identity was significantly higher for college students who frequently language broker in comparison to both infrequent language brokers and co-ethnic college students who do not language broker. The experience of language brokering may align with the central identity issues of emerging adulthood.

Language brokering responsibilities may clash with the self-focused nature of emerging adulthood. That is, youth may want to be focused on themselves and building their self-directed experiences toward what they envision is needed for their adult lives. Instead, obligations to language broker pull them out of their focus on their selves and may force them to focus on the needs of their parents, family, and others. Sy (2006) found that Latina college students experienced more school-related stress when they engaged in more language brokering. Guan, Nash, and Orellana (2016) also reported an incident where a female 18-year-old Mexican American language broker was forced to translate in meeting with her mother and a lawyer. The woman was not there to provide translation, but emotional support, and felt she had to step in, uncomfortably, when the mother did not understand the communication. Despite the obligation to translate, this is not to say that all emerging adult language brokers are reluctant and resistant to respond to parents' requests for translation but rather that being solicited to do so may create some internal and external conflict within the family. Further, the emerging adults' sense that they are in an age of possibilities may be discordant with the needs of parents who need language brokering support. For example, among a sample of Mexican American emerging adult language brokers, Weisskirch (2013) found that frequency of language brokering was negatively associated with ethnic society immersion and family obligation, which may indicate that the more they have to language broker the less connected they feel to heritage culture and family-oriented values. In that study, lack of parental support predicted a sense of burden when language brokering. Given that emerging adults see that there are many choices for them in life, they may be less empathetic to parents who may be fixed in their language skills and in desire to improve their skills, and continue to require language brokering. The emerging adult language brokers' optimism about what the future may hold may be disrupted by the reality of their parents' needs, which may not appear to be changing at the same pace as their own lives. At the same time, emerging adults may work to prepare parents for impending life changes that come in emerging adulthood by supporting parents' independence, preparing a younger sibling to take over language brokering responsibilities, or reserving only certain language brokering tasks for themselves.

Erikson proposed that youth, after adolescence, move into a stage of Intimacy versus Isolation where youth must resolve a crisis around establishing intimate relationships with others or risk isolation from others and loneliness. At this stage, youth move beyond using their interactions to form a personal identity; once that identity is formed, they are able to develop deeper relationships with others and, in particular, romantic partners. Youth, at this time, are also able to support their rights and beliefs against those that may be in opposition or are psychologically threatening. They also come to understand that relationships require commitments that include compromise and sacrifices from both partners. Paul, Poole, and Jakubowyc (1998) found that college students who had failed to achieve intimacy early in their college years also had diminished psychological well-being at the end of the academic year. Hamacheck (1990) also noted that individuals who develop intimacy have implicit attitudes that include feelings of contentment with themselves and others, that others can generally be trusted, and that mutual interdependence can bolster resiliency.

For emerging adult language brokers, resolving the crisis in Intimacy versus Isolation involves establishing more intimate relationships with others. Although most theorizing and research tends to focus on romantic relationships, Eriksonian theory provides the flexibility to include the notion that emerging adults may also deepen their skills in intimacy with their familial relationships as well. That is, as emerging adults, they may shift their relationship with their parents to be more on an adult-like plane, and, likely, a deeper level of intimacy. The cumulative experience of language brokering in childhood, adolescence, and emerging adulthood may bring about greater understanding of parents. Given that the prerequisite for successful resolution of Intimacy versus Isolation is the formation of an identity, for language brokers, personal identity is likely to include elements of who they are as language brokers. Once that personal identity, inclusive of being a language broker, is consolidated in emerging adulthood, the individual may have even closer relationships with parents. On a similar vein, in a sample of college students from immigrant families, Guan, Greenfield, and Orellana (2014) found that brokering for parents related to greater transcultural perspective-taking and empathic concern related to brokering for others. These findings may indicate how brokering may help develop skills for better relationships with parents and

TABLE 1.1 Elements of Developmental Theories Applied to Language Brokering

Ages	Piagetian Theory	Eriksonian Theory	Arnett's Theory	Language Brokering (LB)
7–11	**Concrete Operational Thought** • Manipulation of two ideas in mind simultaneously • Increase in perspective-taking • Limited in understanding abstraction and scientific processes	**Industry vs. Inferiority** • Need to feel productive and competent in tasks • Mastery of tools (like language) to complete tasks	N/A	• Understanding complexity of concepts in two languages • Beginning control of meaning to be favorable or within comprehension limits • Limited vocabulary and conceptual understanding • Limited metacognition • Feeling positively about completing LB tasks successfully • Sensitive to parents' positive and negative interactions when LB • Limited skills may yield stressful experiences
12–18	**Formal Operational Thought** • Understanding of abstract and hypothetical concepts • Can engage in scientific thought • Can manipulate several ideas simultaneously • Can take multiple perspectives • Increase in metacognition	**Identity vs. Role Confusion** • Explore and commit to identity • Greater autonomy from parents • Greater awareness of social conflicts and demands	N/A	• Identity incorporates role as language broker • LB contributes to ethnic identity • Understanding of potential consequences of LB situation • Managing communication to yield a positive outcome • Acting autonomously from parents • Perception of pressure to perform well • Limits to vocabulary and comprehension
18–25	**Formal Operational Thought** • Increases in cognitive development acquired in adolescence	**Intimacy vs. Isolation** • With a formed identity, consolidation of identity continues • Intimate, deeper relationships with others • Mutual interdependence with others	**Emerging Adulthood** • Age of identity explorations • Age of instability • Self-focused age • Feeling in-between • Age of possibilities	• Consolidation of identity through LB • LB tasks clash with self-focused activities • LB obligation discordant with youth sense of life possibilities • More intimate relationships with parents • Increase in empathy and perspective-taking • Greater proficiency in LB

Note: LB = language brokering.

with others. From an Eriksonian perspective, then, for emerging adult language brokers, the resolution of intimacy and forming deeper relationships may be the outgrowth of their cumulative language brokering experiences.

A Developmental Perspective

Fundamentally, a developmental perspective to understanding language brokering focuses on individual growth and development across developmental domains, over time, and within contexts. This chapter presents the aspects of the familial and cultural contexts to be considered as well as some developmental theories applied to language brokering. Piagetian theory helps to provide a framework for understanding children's cognitive development and how that development can support or hinder children's and adolescents' abilities to successfully engage in language brokering. Generally, once individuals reach adolescence, Piagetian theory neglects to continue to explicitly describe further cognitive development into late adolescence and emerging adulthood. The theory supports that higher reasoning and better abilities with scientific reasoning continue to develop through adolescence and into adulthood. Indeed, there is some evidence that there may be a cognitive shift in emerging adulthood, which may allow for more sophisticated thinking (Labouvie-Vief, 2006). This idea coupled with the evidence from neuroscience that areas in the brain responsible for judgment and reasoning do not finish maturing until the early 20s may support language brokers' increasing proficiency in language brokering as they move into adulthood (Mills, Goddings, Clasen, Giedd, & Blakemore, 2014).

Eriksonian theory also applies to the development of language brokers to provide a framework of the central psychosocial developmental turning points (also known as "crises") that may occur during the period from childhood through emerging adulthood. Eriksonian theory supports the notion that individual development occurs in relation to the demands of the outside world. In childhood, individual development is fueled by industrious acts; in adolescence, by resolving one's identity; and in emerging adulthood, by forming more intimate relationships with others. The existing language brokering literature provides some evidence of how these elements may manifest when individuals engage in language brokering.

Contribution to Theory

Accounting for the developmental periods of language brokers is critical to better understanding language brokering. For the most part, the language brokering research literature neglects to include a clear developmental framework for the research. Most of the research focuses on one age group or a contrast between two age groups. Even when there are longitudinal studies, there is little discussion of differences or changes due to developmental periods or developmental abilities.

Adding a developmental perspective to the research is important to highlight findings that may extend beyond being an artifact of a developmental period. For example, Rainey, Flores, Morrison, David, and Silton (2014) reported that college students who retrospectively reported starting to language broker between ages 9 to 13 indicated greater anxiety as emerging adults in comparison to those who began brokering at older ages. With a developmental lens, for example, the anxiety may be the outcome of tasks that were beyond the students' cognitive development (a la Piaget) accumulating over time or, perhaps, language brokering experiences during that age range did not allow for feelings of accomplishment and productivity (a la Erikson), leaving students to doubt their abilities. Since individual development continues to unfold as children, adolescents, and emerging adults are language brokering, it may be important to recognize the influence that development may have on the outcomes and experiences with language brokering.

Note

1 I recognize that there are practical and conceptual distinctions between and within "interpreting" and "translating," but for the purpose of this chapter, I am using them both interchangeably to indicate when one person converts language and meaning from one language to another.

References

Acoach, C. L., & Webb, L. M. (2004). The influence of language brokering on Hispanic teenagers' acculturation, academic performance, and nonverbal decoding skills: A preliminary study. *The Howard Journal of Communications, 15*, 1–19.

Arnett, J. J. (2000). Emerging adulthood: A theory of development from the late teens through the twenties. *American Psychologist, 55*(5), 469–480. doi:10.1037/0003-066X.55.5.469

Arnett, J. J. (2004). *Emerging adulthood: The winding road from the late teens through the twenties.* New York, NY: Oxford University Press.

Berry, J. W. (2003). Conceptual approaches to acculturation. In K. M. Chun, P. Balls Organista, & G. Marín (Eds.), *Acculturation: Advances in theory, measurement, and applied research* (pp. 17–37). Washington, DC: American Psychological Association. doi:10.1037/10472–004

Bialystok, E., Craik, F. M., Green, D. W., & Gollan, T. H. (2009). Bilingual minds. *Psychological Science in the Public Interest, 10*, 89–129. doi:10.1177/1529100610387084

Buriel, R., Perez, W., DeMent, T. L., Chavez, D. V., & Moran, V. R. (1998). The relationship of language brokering to academic performance, biculturalism, and self-efficacy among Latino adolescents. *Hispanic Journal of Behavioral Sciences, 20*, 283–297. doi:10.1177/07399863980203001

Chao, R. K. (2001, April). The role of children's linguistic brokering among immigrant Chinese and Mexican families. In V. Tseng (Chair), *Families of color: Developmental issues in contemporary sociohistorical context.* Paper presented at the meeting of the Society for Research on Child Development, Minneapolis, MN.

Cila, J., & Lalonde, R. N. (2015). Language brokering, acculturation, and empowerment: Evidence from South Asian Canadian young adults. *Journal of Multilingual & Multicultural Development, 36*, 498–512. doi:10.1080/01434632.2014.953540

Clark, E. V. (1993). *The lexicon in acquisition*. New York, NY: Cambridge University Press. doi:10.1017/CBO9780511554377

Corona, R., Stevens, L. F., Halfond, R. W., Shaffer, C. M., Reid-Quiñones, K., & Gonzalez, T. (2012). A qualitative analysis of what Latino parents and adolescents think and feel about language brokering. *Journal of Child and Family Studies, 21*, 788–798. doi:10.1007/s10826-011-9536-2

DeCasper, A. J., & Fifer, W. P. (1980). Of human bonding: Newborns prefer their mothers' voices. *Science, 208*, 1174–1176.

Degener, J. L. (2010). "Sometimes my mother does not understand, then I need to translate:" Child and youth language brokering in Berlin-Neukölln (Germany). *MediAzioni, 10*. Retrieved from http://mediazioni.sitlec.unibo.it

Dorner, L. M., Orellana, M. F., & Jiménez, R. (2008). "It's one of those things that you do to help the family": Language brokering and the development of immigrant adolescents. *Journal of Adolescent Research, 23*, 515–543. doi:10.1177/0743558408317563

Dorner, L. M., Orellana, M. F., & Li-Grining, C. P. (2007). "I helped my mom," and it helped me: Translating the skills of language brokers into improved standardized test scores. *American Journal of Education, 113*, 451–478. doi:10.1086/512740

Dunbar, R. M. (1993). Coevolution of neocortical size, group size and language in humans. *Behavioral and Brain Sciences, 16*, 681–735. doi:10.1017/S0140525X00032325

Erikson, E. H. (1968). *Identity, youth, and crisis*. New York, NY: Norton.

Falicov, C. J. (2012). Immigrant family processes: A multidimensional framework. In F. Walsh & F. Walsh (Eds.), *Normal family processes: Growing diversity and complexity* (pp. 297–323). New York, NY: Guilford Press.

Guan, S. A., Greenfield, P. M., & Orellana, M. F. (2014). Translating into understanding: Language brokering and prosocial development in emerging adults from immigrant families. *Journal of Adolescent Research, 29*, 331–355. doi:10.1177/0743558413520223

Guan, S. A., Nash, A., & Orellana, M. F. (2016). Cultural and social processes of language brokering among Arab, Asian, and Latin immigrants. *Journal of Multilingual & Multicultural Development, 37*, 150–166. doi:10.1080/01434632.2015.1044997

Guo, Z. (2014). *Young children as intercultural mediators: Mandarin-speaking Chinese families in Britain*. Bristol, UK: Multilingual Matters.

Hamachek, D. E. (1988). Evaluating self-concept and ego development within Erikson's psychosocial framework: A formulation. *Journal of Counseling & Development, 66*, 354–360. doi:10.1002/j.1556–6676.1988.tb00886.x

Hamachek, D. E. (1990). Evaluating self-concept and ego status in Erikson's last three psychosocial stages. *Journal of Counseling & Development, 68*, 677–683. doi:10.1002/j.1556–6676.1990.tb01436.x

Hofstede, G. (1980). *Culture's consequences: International differences in work-related issues*. Beverly Hills, CA: Sage.

Hua, J. M., & Costigan, C. L. (2012). The familial context of adolescent language brokering within immigrant Chinese families in Canada. *Journal of Youth and Adolescence, 41*, 894–906. doi:10.1007/s10964-011-9682-2

Hughes, D., Rodriguez, J., Smith, E. P., Johnson, D. J., Stevenson, H. C., & Spicer, P. (2006). Parents' ethnic-racial socialization practices: A review of research and directions for future study. *Developmental Psychology, 42*, 747–770. doi:10.1037/0012–1649.42.5.747

Huynh, V. W., & Fuligni, A. J. (2008). Ethnic socialization and the academic adjustment of adolescents from Mexican, Chinese, and European backgrounds. *Developmental Psychology, 44*, 1202–1208. doi:10.1037/0012–1649.44.4.1202

Kaur, S., & Mills, R. (1993). Children as interpreters. In R. W. Mills & J. Mills (Eds.), *Bilingualism in the primary school: A handbook for teachers* (pp. 113–125). London, UK: Routledge.

Labouvie-Vief, G. (2006). Emerging structures of adult thought. In J. J. Arnett & J. L. Tanner (Eds.), *Emerging adults in America: Coming of age in the 21st century* (pp. 59–84). Washington, DC: American Psychological Association. doi:10.1037/11381–003

Love, J. A., & Buriel, R. (2007). Language brokering, autonomy, parent-child bonding, biculturalism, and depression: A study of Mexican American adolescents from immigrant families. *Hispanic Journal of Behavioral Sciences, 29*, 472–491.

McGoldrick, M., & Shibusawa, T. (2012). The family life cycle. In F. Walsh (Ed.), *Normal family processes: Growing diversity and complexity* (pp. 375–398). New York, NY: Guilford Press.

McQuillan, J., & Tse, L. (1995). Child language brokering in linguistic minority communities: Effects on cultural interaction, cognition, and literacy. *Language and Education, 9*, 195–215.

Martinez, C. R., McClure, H. H., & Eddy, J. M. (2009). Language brokering contexts and behavioral and emotional adjustment among Latino parents and adolescents. *Journal of Early Adolescence, 29*, 71–98.

Mills, K. L., Goddings, A., Clasen, L. S., Giedd, J. N., & Blakemore, S. (2014). The developmental mismatch in structural brain maturation during adolescence. *Developmental Neuroscience, 36*, 147–160. doi:10.1159/000362328

Morales, A., & Hanson, W. E. (2005). Language brokering: An integrative review of the literature. *Hispanic Journal of the Behavioral Sciences, 27*, 471–503.

Oh, J. S., & Fuligni, A. J. (2010). The role of heritage language development in the ethnic identity and family relationships of adolescents from immigrant backgrounds. *Social Development, 19*, 202–220. doi:10.1111/j.1467–9507.2008.00530.x

Orellana, M. F. (2009). *Translating childhoods: Immigrant youth, language, and culture.* Piscataway, NJ: Rutgers University Press.

Orellana, M. F., Dorner, L., & Pulido, L. (2003). Accessing assets: Immigrant youth's work as family translators or "para-phrasers". *Social Problems, 50*, 505–524.

Orellana, M. F., Reynolds, J., Dorner, L., & Meza, M. (2003). In other words: Translating or "para-phrasing" as a family literacy practice in immigrant households. *Reading Research Quarterly, 38*, 12–34. doi:10.1598/RRQ.38.1.2

Oznobishin, O., & Kurman, J. (2009). Parent–child role reversal and psychological adjustment among immigrant youth in Israel. *Journal of Family Psychology, 23*, 405–415. doi:10.1037/a0015811

Paul, E. L., Poole, A., & Jakubowyc, N. (1998). Intimacy development and romantic status: Implications for adjustment to the college transition. *Journal of College Student Development, 39*, 75–86.

Piaget, J. (1928). *Judgment and reasoning of the child.* New York, NY: Harcourt Brace Jovanovich.

Piaget, J. (1953). *Logic and psychology.* Manchester, UK: Manchester University Press.

Rainey, V. R., Flores, V., Morrison, R. G., David, E., & Silton, R. L. (2014). Mental health risk factors associated with childhood language brokering. *Journal of Multilingual & Multicultural Development, 35*, 463–478. doi:10.1080/01434632.2013.870180

Schwartz, S. J., Côté, J. E., & Arnett, J. J. (2005). Identity and agency in emerging adulthood: Two developmental routes in the individualization process. *Youth & Society, 37*, 201–229. doi:10.1177/0044118X05275965

Shen, Y., Kim, S. Y., Wang, Y., & Chao, R. K. (2014). Language brokering and adjustment among Chinese and Korean American adolescents: A moderated mediation model of perceived maternal sacrifice, respect for the mother, and mother—child open communication. *Asian American Journal of Psychology*, 5, 86–95. doi:10.1037/a0035203

Suárez-Orozco, C., Abo-Zena, M. M., & Marks, A. K. (2015). *Transitions: The development of children of immigrants*. New York, NY: New York University Press.

Sy, S. R. (2006). Family and work influences on the transition to college among Latina adolescents. *Hispanic Journal of Behavioral Sciences*, 28, 368–386. doi:10.1177/0739986306290372

Tamis-Lemonda, C. S., Bornstein, M. H., Kahana-Kalman, R., Baumwell, L., & Cyphers, L. (1998). Predicting variation in the timing of language milestones in the second year: An events history approach. *Journal of Child Language*, 25, 675–700. doi:10.1017/S0305000998003572

Titzmann, P. F. (2012). Growing up too soon? Parentification among immigrant and native adolescents in Germany. *Journal of Youth and Adolescence*, 41, 880–893. doi:10.1007/s10964-011-9711-1

Triandis, H. C. (1995). *Individualism & collectivism*. Boulder, CO: Westview Press.

Triandis, H. C. (2001). Individualism-collectivism and personality. *Journal of Personality*, 69, 907–924. doi:10.1111/1467–6494.696169

Tse, L. (1995). Language brokering among Latino adolescents: Prevalence, attitudes, and school performance. *Hispanic Journal of Behavioral Sciences*, 17, 180–193.

Tse, L. (1996a). Language brokering in linguistic minority communities: The case of Chinese- and Vietnamese-American students. *The Bilingual Research Journal*, 20, 485–498.

Tse, L. (1996b). Who decides?: The effects of language brokering on home-school communication. *The Journal of Educational Issues of Language Minority Studies*, 16, 225–235.

Valdés, G. (2003). *Expanding definitions of giftedness: The case of young interpreters from immigrant countries*. Mahwah, NJ: Lawrence Erlbaum.

Vasquez, O. A., Pease-Alvarez, L., & Shannon, S. M. (1994). *Pushing boundaries: Language and culture in a Mexicano community*. Cambridge, UK: Cambridge University Press.

Villanueva, C. M., & Buriel, R. (2010). Speaking on behalf of others: A qualitative study of the perceptions and feelings of adolescent Latina language brokers. *Journal of Social Issues*, 66, 197–210. doi:10.1111/j.1540–4560.2009.01640.x

Walsh, S., Shulman, S., Bar-On, Z., & Tsur, A. (2006). The role of parentification and family climate in adaptation among immigrant adolescents in Israel. *Journal of Research on Adolescence*, 16, 321–350. doi:10.1111/j.1532–7795.2006.00134.x

Weisskirch, R. S. (2005). The relationship of language brokering to ethnic identity for Latino early adolescents. *Hispanic Journal of Behavioral Sciences*, 27, 286–299. doi:10.1177/0739986305277931

Weisskirch, R. S. (2006). Emotional aspects of language brokering among Mexican American adults. *Journal of Multilingual & Multicultural Development*, 27, 332–343. doi:10.2167/jmmd421.1

Weisskirch, R. S. (2007). Feelings about language brokering and family relations among Mexican American early adolescents. *Journal of Early Adolescence*, 27, 545–561.

Weisskirch, R. S. (2013). Family relationships, self-esteem, and self-efficacy among language brokering Mexican American emerging adults. *Journal of Child and Family Studies*, 22, 1147–1155. doi:10.1007/s10826–012–9678-x

Weisskirch, R. S., & Alva, S. A. (2002). Language brokering and the acculturation of Latino children. *Hispanic Journal of Behavioral Sciences*, 24, 369–378. doi:10.1177/0739986302024003007

Weisskirch, R. S., Kim, S., Zamboanga, B. L., Schwartz, S. J., Bersamin, M., & Umaña-Taylor, A. J. (2011). Cultural influences for college student language brokers. *Cultural Diversity and Ethnic Minority Psychology, 17*, 43–51. doi:10.1037/a0021665

Werker, J. F. (1989). Becoming a native listener. *American Scientist, 77*, 54–59.

Wu, N., & Kim, S. Y. (2009). Chinese American adolescents' perceptions of the language brokering experience as a sense of burden and sense of efficacy. *Journal of Youth and Adolescence, 38*, 703–718.

2

NEW APPROACHES TO STUDYING LANGUAGE BROKERING FROM A COMMUNICATION PERSPECTIVE

Jennifer A. Kam, Lisa M. Guntzviller, and Cynthia Stohl

Introduction

To date, most of the research on language brokering has come from fields of Psychology, Education, Human Development and Family Studies, Linguistics, and Sociology. Despite the fact that language brokering, in and of itself, requires communication to occur—only recently has the field of Communication begun investigating language brokering. Past research has made great contributions to the understanding of language brokering as a complex and multidimensional process that affects the well-being of many immigrant families throughout the world. From such research, we know that language brokers—"individuals with little to no formal training who act as linguistic and cultural intermediaries for two or more parties, both of whom are from different cultural backgrounds"—may experience both positive and negative academic, relational, and health outcomes (Kam & Lazarevic, 2014a, p. 1995). For example, findings from both qualitative studies (e.g., semi-structured interviews and focus groups) and quantitative studies (e.g., surveys) revealed that language brokering was associated with higher standardized reading test scores (Dorner, Orellana, & Li-Grining, 2007), greater respect for family and parent-child closeness (Chao, 2006; Tilghman-Osborne, Bámaca-Colbert, Witherspoon, Wadsworth, & Hecht, 2015), and higher rates of depressive symptoms and substance use (Love & Buriel, 2007; Martinez, McClure, & Eddy, 2009). Within the past decade, a large body of research on language brokering has emerged, all of which has come to the same conclusion: Language brokering can lead to both positive and negative outcomes, *depending on a number of complex, contextual factors* such as cultural values, beliefs, and norms; the quality of family communication and relationships; individual and relational goals; and the environment in which brokering occurs (Dorner, Orellana, & Jiménez, 2008; Guntzviller, 2015,

2016; Hua & Costigan, 2012; Jones, Trickett, & Birman, 2012; Kam & Lazarevic, 2014a, 2014b; Oznobishin & Kurman, 2009; Roche, Lambert, Ghazarian, & Little, 2015; Weisskirch, 2013; Wu & Kim, 2009).

An acculturation-stress-resilience framework (Kam, Castro, & Wang, 2015; Kam & Lazarevic, 2014a; Umaña-Taylor & Updegraff, 2007; Umaña-Taylor, Updegraff, & Gonzales-Backen, 2011) provides a large overarching theoretical perspective that focuses our attention on the conditions under which language brokering is positively or negatively related to various academic, relational, and health outcomes. This framework stems from Umaña-Taylor and colleagues' work on US Latino/a adolescents, suggesting that ethnic minorities may experience culturally related stressors that place them at risk for depressive symptoms, low self-esteem, poor academic performance, and problem behaviors. Culturally related stressors refer to adverse experiences (e.g., fear of deportation, separation from family, perceived discrimination, and under some circumstances, language broker-ing) that stem from ethnic minority status, ethnic identification processes, cul-tural orientations, and/or acculturation (Umaña-Taylor, 2003; Umaña-Taylor & Updegraff, 2007; Umaña-Taylor et al., 2011). Although ethnic minorities might be at risk for negative relational, academic, and health outcomes, Umaña-Taylor and colleagues (2007, 2011) posit that they may be resilient against culturally related stressors when they have certain protective factors (e.g., supportive parent-ing, familistic values, ethnic pride).

Although language brokering may be an important contribution to family functioning that is perceived as "normal" or "natural" among immigrant com-munities (Dorner et al., 2008), the acculturation-stress-resilience framework sug-' gests that brokering may, at times, function as a stressor that can lead to negative academic, relational, and health outcomes. Linguistically and culturally mediating for family members may be particularly stressful when young language brokers lack the necessary linguistic vocabulary to translate, feel overwhelming pressure to help their family succeed in their new environment, and feel nervous or embar-rassed about translating (Kam, 2011; Tse, 1996). Language brokers, however, may have certain resources that serve as protective factors and may make them resilient to the stressful nature of brokering, and even lead to positive outcomes (Kam & Lazarevic, 2014b). Given the potentially negative and positive outcomes of lan-guage brokering, the current chapter focuses on five theoretical frameworks that shed light on the conditions under which language brokering, rooted in accul-turation processes, may function as a stressor, as well as a protective factor that may lead to positive outcomes. Although many theoretical perspectives exist that can be applied to language brokering, the present chapter utilizes a conceptu-alization of language brokering that is rooted in interpersonal communication to provide a new way of thinking about language brokering that can comple-ment past research findings rooted in fields of Psychology, Education, Human Development and Family Studies, Linguistics, and Sociology. An interpersonal -communication-based conceptualization of language brokering emphasizes five key social interaction theories that have the potential to make great contributions to the understanding of language brokering, but that still have not been widely considered in relation to this phenomenon. The five frameworks are (a) the theory of planned behavior and focus theory of normative conduct, (b) communal coping, (c) multiple goals theories, (d) privacy management, and (e) organizational brokering and social networks.

An Interpersonal Communication Conceptualization of Language Brokering

Interpersonal communication refers to "a complex, situated social process in which people who have established a communicative relationship exchange messages in an effort to generate shared meanings and to accomplish social goals" (Burleson, 2010, p. 151). Kam and Lazarevic (2014b) applied this definition of interpersonal communication to explicate the social interaction that occurs during language brokering. More specifically, they argued that language brokering, a form of interpersonal communication, comprises simultaneous and *complex processes* that involve the cognitive interpretation of messages, the creation of messages, and the coordination of interactions. When language brokering, young members of immigrant families must quickly assign meaning (i.e., cognitive interpretation) to the verbal and nonverbal messages that they receive from both their own family member(s) and people from the new environment. They must encode messages (i.e., creation of messages) that can create shared meaning between the participating parties, while simultaneously managing the ongoing flow of information exchange between parties (i.e., interaction coordination).

In addition to being a complex process, language brokering also is a situated and social one, meaning that language brokering transpires between two or more parties (i.e., *social*) and is contextually influenced (i.e., *situated*). Burleson (2010) referred to contextual influences that involve the physical environment, relationship between parties, and cultural backgrounds of the parties. Consistent with the acculturation–stress–resilience framework, language brokering's associations with academic, relational, and health outcomes depend on a number of moderating contextual factors (see Shen, Tilton, & Kim, Chapter 3 in this volume). With respect to physical contextual influences, one study found that Latino/a adolescents felt the medical context was the most challenging in which to broker (Corona et al., 2012). Another study found that brokering in the school was the most challenging for a sample of US Latino/a adolescent brokers (Villanueva & Buriel, 2010). Other studies revealed that relational contextual influences relate to outcomes. For example, Hua and Costigan (2012) found that language brokering frequency was related to adverse psychological health for Chinese Canadian adolescents who scored high in parental psychological control. This observation emphasizes the importance of relational contextual influences on the outcome of language brokering. Cultural contextual influences also were apparent in Hua

and Costigan's study: They found the same positive association between brokering frequency and adverse psychological health for adolescents who scored high
in family obligation values, which are values common in collectivist cultures. In
short, the conceptualization of language brokering as an interpersonal communication process emphasizes the importance of considering contextual factors that
influence language brokering outcomes.

Finally, Burleson (2010) defined interpersonal communication process as *functional*. Kam and Lazarevic (2014b) described the functional nature of language
brokering, stating that each party involved in the brokering process has certain
relational, instrumental, and identity goals that they want satisfied during the
language brokering exchange. While engaging in the language brokering interaction, the individuals must manage their relational goals, such as maintaining
parent-child, teacher-student, and physician–patient relationships. Further, they
must manage their instrumental goals, which may include the need to understand
what the other party is communicating, thereby leading to the fulfillment of other
instrumental goals (e.g., paying a bill, learning how one's child is performing in
school, receiving a prescription). Identity goals refer to motivations to maintain or
enhance one's self-esteem and self-concept. Several studies on language brokering (e.g., Kam & Lazarveic, 2014a; Niehaus & Kumpiene, 2014; Weisskirch, 2013;
Wu & Kim, 2009) have considered how brokering is related to self-esteem and
self-concept, as well as how one's self-efficacy might lead to better language brokering experiences, all of which are rooted in identity goals.

In sum, according to Kam and Lazarevic (2014b), language brokering is an
interpersonal communication process that involves a contextually influenced,
complex process (i.e., a series of interdependent message processing, production,
and coordination acts), occurring between two or more parties who each have
relational, instrumental, and identity goals that they manage throughout the interaction. Given this conceptualization, the next sections introduce five theoretical
perspectives commonly used or rooted in the Communication discipline that
emphasize a particular aspect of the interpersonal communication conceptualization of language brokering. These theories are (1) theory of planned behavior and
a focus theory of normative conduct, (2) communal coping, (3) multiple goals
theories, (4) communication privacy management theory, and (5) organizational
brokering and social networks. With these five perspectives, we introduce new
ways of thinking about language brokering, as well as new suggestions for future
research.

Theory of Planned Behavior and Focus Theory of Normative Conduct

Interpersonal communication emphasizes the contextual influences that are at
play when two (or more) individuals exchange ideas. Kam and Lazarevic (2014a)
combined the theory of planned behavior (TPB; Ajzen, 1991) and a focus theory

of normative conduct (FTNC; Cialdini, Reno, & Kallgren, 1990) to understand how language brokering relates to psychological health outcomes and risky behaviors, depending on a number of contextual factors rooted in norms, feelings, and efficacy. TPB and FTNC have been widely used to explain why people engage in certain behaviors, concentrating specifically on persuasion in the areas of academic-, health-, environment-, and safety-related behaviors (Cialdini et al., 1990; Guo et al., 2007).

In particular, TPB posits that individuals are more likely to develop intentions to engage in a particular behavior when they have favorable *attitudes* (i.e., positive valence of the behavior), *subjective norms* (i.e., the perception that important others think one should engage in the behavior), and *perceived behavioral control* (i.e., feeling confident in one's ability to enact the behavior). Similar to TPB, FTNC identifies factors that increase the likelihood of engaging in a behavior, but FTNC focuses particularly on norms. FTNC states that individuals are more likely to engage in a behavior when they have more favorable *injunctive norms* (i.e., equivalent to subjective norms) and *descriptive norms* (i.e., the perception that others engage in the behavior). Later, Elek, Miller–Day, and Hecht (2006) added *personal norms*, which refer to the perception that one should engage in the behavior. TPB and FTNC are theories intended to explain why individuals are motivated to engage in a particular behavior, which can be used to explicate why young members of immigrant families engage in language brokering. One of the key assumptions, however, of TPB is that the behavior is of the individuals' volitional control, that the behavior is voluntary (Ajzen, 1991). Language brokering occurs because family members lack familiarity with the new environment's mainstream language and culture. They need assistance from language brokers to successfully function in the new environment; hence, the behavior may not be as voluntary as other behaviors that have been examined using TPB and FTNC (e.g., substance use, exercise, recycling).

Despite the potentially involuntary nature of language brokering, the brokering literature parallels TPB and FTNC. In particular, TPB and FTNC identify specific psychological beliefs (e.g., attitudes, norms, and efficacy) that, if in favor of a certain behavior, will likely motivate individuals to carry out the actual behavior. Kam and Lazarevic (2014a, 2014b) drew from TPB and FTNC, postulating that when young members of immigrant families maintain such favorable psychological beliefs about language brokering, they may not only be more likely to engage in the behavior, but they may be more likely to engage in the behavior with ease. Thus, such favorable psychological beliefs may protect young language brokers against the potentially stressful nature of this form of interpersonal communication. With positive perceptions of language brokering, young members of immigrant families may be less likely to experience negative academic, relational, and health outcomes, and may be more likely to experience positive outcomes instead. Moreover, past language brokering research (e.g., Kam & Lazarevic, 2014a; Weisskirch, 2013; Wu & Kim, 2009) has identified positive and negative brokering feelings, norms, and efficacy as important components for language brokers, but the combination of TPB and FTNC provides an overall theoretical framework that can explain how all three types of beliefs work together to create a positive brokering environment.

Past Research on TPB and FTNC

To test the utility of TPB and FTNC, Kam and Lazarevic (2014a) utilized self-reported longitudinal survey data from 234 Latino/a sixth through eighth grade students to examine a moderation model (i.e., $X \rightarrow Y$ depends on M). They posited that the indirect effects of language brokering on substance use and other risky behaviors through depressive symptoms and family-based acculturation stress would be attenuated or amplified based on the language brokers' brokering feelings, brokering norms, and brokering efficacy. The moderation model yielded several important findings. When Latino/a early adolescents scored high in *brokering efficacy* (i.e., they felt confident in their ability to broker), the positive association between language brokering for parents and family-based acculturation stress (and in turn, alcohol use) was not significant; however, that association was significant for Latino/a early adolescents that scored low in brokering efficacy. Similarly, when Latino/a early adolescents scored high in descriptive brokering norms (i.e., thought their peers brokered often), the positive association between language brokering for parents and depressive symptoms was not significant; however, that positive association was marginally significant for early adolescents who scored low in descriptive brokering norms. Finally, for Latino/a early adolescents who scored high in brokering as a burden (i.e., the perception that brokering prevents them from engaging in other activities), the positive association between brokering for parents and family-based acculturation stress was significant (and in turn, family-based acculturation stress was related to an increase in alcohol and marijuana use), although that positive association was not significant for Latino/a early adolescents who scored low in brokering as a burden. In sum, Kam and Lazarevic utilized TPB and FTNC to identify specific contextual psychological factors (norms and efficacy) that have the potential to function as protective factors for language brokers, while also pointing to one contextual psychological factor (brokering as a burden) that may place brokers at risk for adverse mental health outcomes and engaging in substance use.

Future Research Directions

Because TPB and FTNC garnered support in Kam and Lazarevic's (2014a) study, the significant moderation that they found shed light on a promising area of research with respect to language brokering. Not only do TPB and FTNC warrant further testing, given that only one empirical study has been conducted, but researchers interested in language brokering may consider several ways to extend past research. First, because the term *brokering feelings* is commonly used in the language brokering literature, Kam and Lazarevic used *brokering feelings* as a substitute for the TPB component, *attitudes*. Nevertheless, studies that have considered attitudes traditionally measure this component by assessing the extent to which participants find a particular behavior good or bad and beneficial or harmful. Attitudes are based on the outcome expectancies that individuals have regarding the behavior—whether they believe positive or negative outcomes will occur from engaging in the behavior. Language brokering researchers, however, often use Tse's (1996) measure of brokering feelings, which assesses the extent to which participants like to broker, feel good about themselves when brokering, feel nervous about brokering, or feel embarrassed when brokering. Positive feelings and attitudes are likely to result in an overall favorable impression of language brokering that can make brokering feel less stressful and burdensome. Thus, research on language brokering may benefit from incorporating traditional measures of attitudes in addition to feelings.

Another area of future research would be to examine how feelings, attitudes, norms, and efficacy interact with each other to predict language brokering outcomes. For example, can favorable brokering attitudes (outcome expectancies) attenuate the negative effects of feeling nervous or embarrassed? If this is the case, the more nervous and embarrassed young members of immigrant families are about brokering, the more likely they may be to develop psychological distress. If, however, they believe that brokering will yield high payoffs (positive outcome expectancies), the association between negative brokering feelings and psychological distress may be weaker than when young members of immigrant families believe that brokering yields little payoff. Thus, language brokering researchers may consider the interactions between attitudes, norms, and efficacy to determine whether certain beliefs carry more weight. The results from such pursuits can inform the design of school-based, family-based, and therapy-based culturally grounded programs for immigrant families.

Communal Coping

In addition to the stress perspective, the parentification perspective has been widely discussed among language brokering researchers. The parentification perspective suggests that brokering places young members of immigrant families at risk for prematurely adopting adult responsibilities (Roche et al., 2015). More recent research, however, suggests that language brokers and their family members work together as a team, maintaining clear understanding of adult-child roles (Dorner et al., 2008; Katz, 2010). Given the social aspect of language brokering as an interpersonal communication process that can involve more than two people, communal coping (Lyons, Mickelson, Sullivan, & Coyne, 1998) is a theoretical framework that naturally complements the idea that family members work together as a team when language brokering.

More specifically, communal coping identifies ways in which individuals deal with stressful experiences, focusing particularly on coping that is shared among a group of people (Afifi, Hutchinson, & Krouse, 2006). Communal coping refers to instances when a group of people (e.g., family members) perceives the stressor as its shared problem and its shared responsibility to resolve the problem (i.e., "our problem, our responsibility"; Lyons et al., 1998). Communal coping is comprised of *appraisal* and *action*. Appraisal refers to the cognitive assessment of the adverse experience and whether the appraisal is shared among group members. *Action* refers to the cognitive and behavioral acts that people engage in to deal with the adverse experience (Lyons et al., 1998). By contrast, *individual coping* refers to the perception that the stressor as the person's individual problem and responsibility to resolve (i.e., "my problem, my responsibility"). Social support occurs when an individual perceives the stressor as a shared problem, but the individual's responsibility to manage it (i.e., "our problem, my responsibility"). Lastly, social support seeking takes place when an individual perceives the stressor as his/her problem, but the responsibility of the group to resolve (i.e., "my problem, our responsibility").

As an extension of Lyons et al.'s (1998) theoretical model of communal coping, Afifi et al. (2006) later argued that another type of individual coping exists. An individual can perceive the stressor as his/her problem, the group's shared responsibility, and the other's responsibility (i.e., "your responsibility, my problem, and our responsibility"). Afifi and colleagues also emphasized the importance of considering how the type of stressor and context influence communal coping, and argued for a communicative approach to studying communal coping, representing it as a dynamic and transactional process between members of a social group. Thus, social group members such as families engaging in communal coping might be more likely to use "we" language instead of "I" or "you" language. Although communal coping may not always be beneficial, the theory suggests that the collaborative and synergistic nature of communal coping may create a more resilient environment for dealing with adverse experiences.

Past Research on Communal Coping

To our knowledge, communal coping has not been used as a theoretical framework for studying language brokering, although it has been applied to many other contexts. For example, Afifi, Felix, and Afifi (2012) considered the protective nature of communal coping among adults who were residents of a small city that experienced three large wildfires over a 5-month period. They found that communal coping may have played a protective role against psychological distress for residents who evacuated their homes. More specifically, among evacuated residents, uncertainty about their home was negatively associated with their mental health for those who scored low to moderate in communal coping; however, this negative association was not significant for evacuated residents with high communal coping. They found a similar pattern with respect to uncertainty about personal safety. In addition to the work of Afifi and colleagues, Rohrbaugh et al. (2012) evaluated a communal-coping-based smoking cessation program for tobacco users who suffered from a heart or lung problem. Rohrbaugh and colleagues found that the use of communal coping language ("we-talk") among couples was related to smoking cessation among individual tobacco users. In short, the research on communal coping suggests promising results for its buffering effects, although it is important to note that there social groups or dyads may also use unhealthy coping strategies. Such nuances may serve as the impetus for future research, particularly with respect to language brokering.

Future Research Directions

Communal coping may be a useful tool for understanding how some family members work together during the language brokering interaction, and it may help researchers predict when language brokering, a potential stressor, may not be associated with negative health outcomes (Kam & Lazarevic, 2014b). One important step necessary to incorporate a communal coping perspective is the development of measures to operationalize communal coping among immigrant family members who experience language brokering. Past research often refers to a family working together, but can members from the mainstream cultural environment (e.g., teachers or physicians) perceive the experience as communal coping ("our problem, our responsibility")? Although communal coping may not always be beneficial, working together as a group to solve a problem and appraising it as a shared problem may lead to more positive brokering experiences. Moreover, given that qualitative data suggests some language brokering adolescents felt discriminated against while brokering (Dorner et al., 2008), it is possible that if the language brokering adolescents and the members of the mainstream cultural environment perceive brokering as their shared problem and responsibility, they may be less likely to perceive or engage in discrimination.

The aforementioned research questions emphasize the importance of also collecting data on perceptions of communal coping from multiple perspectives (e.g., language broker, family member, and members of the new environment) to determine whether discrepancies exist in perceptions of communal coping. Language brokering researchers may identify factors that lead each party to appraise the experience as their shared problem and their shared responsibility, while also determining how variations in such perceptions affect their subsequent behaviors.

Multiple Goals Theories

Conceptualizing language brokering as an interpersonal process highlights the strategic and purposeful nature of brokering, and thus the relevance of multiple interaction goals—desired end states that require communication to achieve

(Wilson, 2002). Guntzviller (2016) demonstrated that both language brokers and their mothers have interaction goals specific to language brokering. However, interaction goals can conflict, making situations like language brokering complex and difficult to navigate communicatively (Wilson, 2002).

Multiple goals theories (Caughlin, 2010) represent interaction goals as a dyadic communication process. For a single communicative interaction, both individuals have multiple, potentially conflicting goals they want to fulfill during their communicative exchange; therefore, recognition and prioritization of interaction goals shape individuals' verbal and nonverbal messages. The exchange of verbal and nonverbal messages influences individuals' *goal perceptions* (of both their own goals and their partner's goals), and in turn, goal perceptions affect individuals' interpretations of messages, which drives their overall evaluation and satisfaction with the conversation. This process is mutually influential among the parties participating in the communicative exchange, such that partner goals and partner messages will influence each individual. Caughlin (2010) noted that relationship research would benefit from focusing on (a) how goals shape messages, (b) how varying recognition and successful pursuit of situationally relevant goals shape communication quality, and (c) how own and partner goal perceptions moderate the impact of messages on conversation evaluations.

Multiple goal theory (Caughlin, 2010) also posits that interaction goal research need not be limited to a single conversation. For example, relational partners who frequently engage in a certain type of communication (e.g., mother and children who engage in language brokering) will, over time, develop *goal tendencies*—typical interaction goals that are specific to that type of communication exchange (e.g., language brokering). Multiple goals theories predict that, similar to how interaction goals influence conversation communication quality, perceptions of goal tendencies impact perceptions of relational communication quality, including relational satisfaction. Likewise, individual's perceptions of goal tendencies ascribe meaning across conversations, thus driving the link between myriad communicative messages and relational quality. Hence, examining goal tendencies is an ideal framework for language brokering scholars; Orellana and colleagues (2003) note that the cumulative effects of language brokering over time may provide greater insight into participant consequences than one specific brokering interaction.

Past Research on Multiple Goals

Work applying multiple goals theories to language brokering has mainly been conducted by Guntzviller (2015, 2016). In particular, Guntzviller (2016) examined a typology of interaction goals relevant to language brokering in 100 mother-child Mexican-heritage dyads who frequently engaged in brokering. Children reported their own brokering goal tendencies across interactions (i.e., respect the mother, respect the English speaker, alter messages to save face, act American, and act Latino/a), and mothers reported their own goal tendencies (i.e., instrumental brokering goal and support child goal). Children also reported perceptions of mother goal tendencies and vice versa. As proposed by multiple goals theories, mother-child dyads perceived multiple important goal tendencies for themselves and for their partner, although mother and child perceptions of the same goal were often not aligned.

Guntzviller (2015) then tested the assertion that mother and child brokering goal perceptions would relate to mother-child relational satisfaction. Overall, mother relational satisfaction associated with mother goal perceptions (of her own and child goal tendencies) and child relational satisfaction associated with child goal perceptions (of the child's own and mother goal tendencies). For example, the more mothers reported their goal tendency to support the child during brokering, the more satisfied mothers were with the mother-child relationship. Children also reported greater mother-child relational satisfaction when they perceived that their mother believed it is important to support her child. Interactions between mother and child perceptions of the same goal (e.g., child reports and mother perceptions of the child alter message goals) were also associated with relational satisfaction (Guntzviller, 2015).

Future Research Directions

Multiple goals theories have the potential to guide language brokering researchers to better understand brokering communication, mother and child perceptions of brokering interactions, and the mother-child relationship as influenced by frequent brokering. As Guntzviller (2016) identified that both children and mothers pursue multiple, potentially conflicting, brokering interaction goals, researchers could examine message strategies that are more or less successful in managing these goals simultaneously. For example, how do children successfully manage the goals of acting American and acting Latino/a simultaneously? Guntzviller's (2015) work provides initial support for the connection between brokering goal perceptions and relational satisfaction, and could be expanded to examine other relational contexts (e.g., father-child, or child-English-speaker) and for other family types (e.g., Asian heritage). Understanding brokering goal perceptions and ways in which mother and child goal perceptions might misalign could offer interventions to both improve brokering communication (i.e., through help recognizing and successfully managing multiple goals) and parent-child relationships. Furthermore, studies may be conducted to examine how members from the new environment (e.g., a physician or a teacher) perceive their own goals and goals of others' (e.g., a patient who primarily speaks another language), while engaging in language brokering interactions. Such information may provide insight into families' abilities to form and cultivate productive relationships with members from the new environment.

Communication Privacy Management Theory

Researchers have asserted that children (including pre-adolescent, adolescent, and emerging adult children) who language broker may learn private information that is not developmentally appropriate for them (e.g., family financial troubles), which may cause them undue stress and concern (Roche et al., 2015). Privacy issues abound in language brokering, highlighting one type of complex process inherent to this form of interpersonal communication. For example, children may learn information about the parents or family when brokering (e.g., parent health or family finances), then they must decide what information to share with the parents (e.g., feelings about brokering) and may have to work with their parent(s) to decide what information they should share with other family members (e.g., siblings may not be told about parent employment difficulties). Additionally, parents and child must manage what information they share with members from the new environment (e.g., disclosing parent citizenship documentation status to a health care provider; Katz, 2014). For example, when Cohen, Moran-Ellis, and Smaje (1999) interviewed general practitioners (GPs) in London to learn about their views on language brokering, Cohen et al. found that several GPs thought certain topics (e.g., mother's period) were taboo to discuss with the young language brokers, particularly sons who brokered for mothers. These challenges to information sharing during language brokering can be understood with communication privacy management (CPM) theory (Katz, 2014).

CPM theory focuses on how private information is disclosed and managed within dyads, families, or groups (Petronio, 2002). CPM is predicated on the dialectic tension between privacy and disclosure: Family members have the need to be connected while simultaneously retaining individual autonomy. Disclosure decisions are based on this dialectical tension (Petronio, 2002). Privacy management happens both within families (e.g., children deciding what information to disclosure to their parent when language brokering) and between families and outsiders (e.g., families deciding what information to share with non-family members when brokering). Individuals want to control their own private information (i.e. *privacy ownership*), but disclosing to another allows that person *co-ownership*, as both parties then have the ability (and responsibility) to manage confidentiality. To manage this tension, individuals and families create implicit and explicit *privacy rules* to dictate how their private information should be managed. Privacy rules may be based on various criteria, such as cultural factors, motivations for privacy or disclosure, context, risk factors, and gendered expectations. Privacy rules create boundaries for information flow and disclosure, although boundaries may vary in permeability. CPM posits that explicitly stated, shared privacy rules lead to more successful boundary management and adherence to privacy rules. However, privacy rules may be intentionally or unintentionally violated, particularly when those rules are ambiguous, creating *boundary turbulence*. Boundary turbulence may also occur when a confidant did not want to learn the private information, and that confidant experiences a privacy dilemma between respecting the privacy rules and disclosing the information.

Past Research on Communication Privacy Management

Language brokering researchers have not explicitly used a CPM framework, although some CPM studies align with language brokering scenarios. For example, Petronio, Sargent, Andea, Reganis, and Cichocki (2004) interviewed 123 informal health care advocates—family and friends who attend health care visits with a patient—to examine how advocates managed privacy boundaries during and after medical interactions. Some advocates were also linguistic translators. Advocates functioned as *privacy spanners*, bringing private information from one boundary (advocate-patient privacy boundary) into another (patient-physician privacy boundary). Advocates reported facing privacy dilemmas between maintaining patient privacy about information intentionally or unintentionally not disclosed to the physician and revealing this information for the sake of patient health. Advocates chose to clarify, correct, or refute patient information when they felt patient well-being was at stake. Patient responses to these advocate disclosures varied from being grateful to embarrassed or upset. Physicians also treated advocates as sources of information, and direct physician-to-advocate questioning shifted privacy and disclosure dynamics, as patients became the third party and advocates were no longer choosing whether to act as a privacy spanner. Petronio et al. noted that linguistic translators saw privacy spanning as useful because the translators could assist in communicating patient information. Nevertheless, translators faced unique dilemmas: For example, bad news disclosure, which is a burden placed on the physician in the patient-physician privacy boundary, was transferred to the translating advocate. Advocates acting as translators may not be prepared to be the source of such a disclosure. Advocates also became co-owners of the patient's medical information, and these responsibilities often came with patient assumptions that advocates would participate in decision-making. Translators were not always prepared for decision-making or co-ownership responsibilities, and both patients and advocates were, at times, unprepared to give/receive private disclosures required in a medical context.

Future Research Directions

The application of a CPM framework to better understand brokering interactions and consequences is an area ripe for study. Little is known about the creation and management of privacy rules during brokering, although research suggests that both parent and child may attempt to regulate disclosures (e.g., a son decides not to ask his mother about her sexual history during a medical exam; Green, Free, Bhavnani, & Newman, 2005). How parents create and manage privacy rules with their children, and the explicit or implicit discussion of boundary rules for brokering-related disclosures are important to examine. For example, Hall and Sham (2007) found that children brokering in parent–teacher conferences may inaccurately relay information to maintain personal privacy and to maintain positive impressions. Such privacy management may affect the success of the language brokering exchange; whether goals are met; and the academic, relational, and health outcomes of all involved parties.

Family management of boundaries and boundary turbulence may also function to increase acculturation stress or to mitigate the impact of stress on the child and family. Children may become unwilling confidants, and may intentionally or unintentionally break family privacy rules with varying consequences for the family. For example, Baptiste (1993) described a disclosure and boundary turbulence challenge in a Costa Rican family in which the younger son learned that his father earned less than his older brother during brokering interactions. The younger son told the older son this information against his father's wishes, which upset the father, threatened the father's masculinity, and gave the older son leverage to pressure the family to move back to Costa Rica. Thus, it is possible that parents may attempt to maintain familial power structures or decrease child stress by denying children co-ownership responsibilities outside of brokering contexts. CPM provides a lens for examining disclosure dilemmas inherent to brokering, which ultimately, can affect the well-being of the child and the family.

Organizational Brokering and Social Networks

Brokering has long been a central construct in the study of organizational and community networks in Sociology, Management, and Communication Studies (Burt, 1992). Although this literature is grounded in macro processes of competition and cooperation, the relational dynamics are quite similar to those described in earlier sections of this chapter and offer useful insights for new directions in the study of language brokering in immigrant families.

In terms of network theory, a broker is an individual who serves as a bridge between otherwise disconnected segments or cliques. Similar to language brokering, organizational brokers mediate between two or more parties, which includes conflict resolution between the parties and spreading resources among the parties (Cornwell, 2009). Burt (1997) described gaps in the network (i.e., gaps between two or more segments) as structural holes and argued that filling a structural hole represents "an opportunity to broker the flow of information between people and control the form of projects that bring together people from opposite sides of the hole" (p. 340). Just as language brokering can have both positive and negative effects on the language broker and the larger family system, research in organizations and communities finds mixed effects for brokering at both the micro (personal) and macro (i.e., groups, organizations, communities) levels.

Georg Simmel defined a broker, in broad terms, as *tertius gaudens*, literally, "the third who benefits" (Simmel, 1922). Further, from a micro perspective, when brokers provide a unique link between disparate groups they personally gain a competitive advantage over others in three ways: (a) access, (b) timing, and (c) referrals. *Access* refers to receiving and/or having valuable pieces of information and perspectives as well as being the one who knows who can use the information most effectively. *Timing* indicates the ability to get information earlier than others in the network, making the broker's information and his/her external relationships highly valuable to others. *Referrals* address the advantages a broker gains in terms of legitimacy and access to others contacts (Burt, 2001). Empirical studies have shown that in the workplace brokers tend to receive better performance evaluations and are more highly compensated than peers (Mehra, Kilduff, & Brass, 2001), have higher and earlier rates of promotion and status (Gabby & Zuckerman, 1998), and are more likely to have better and more creative and innovative ideas that are accepted by others (Burt, 2001). However, it is important to note that there is increasing evidence of cultural differences regarding the benefits of being a broker. For example, in a study of high-tech Chinese firms, Xiao and Tsiu (2002) found that brokering does not fit with collectivist cultures, and, when employees positioned themselves as brokers, it hampered their career aspirations and compensation packages, and hurt their relationships with others.

Past Research on Brokering

From a macro perspective, brokering creates bridging social capital by increasing community access to non-redundant resources, information, and support (Taube, 2004). Just as language brokering provides a linguistic and cultural link for families who are separated from dominant power structures, community brokers create contact with ties that cut across diverse groups and hierarchies. For example, post-Katrina surveys of New Orleans' African American/Black, White, and Vietnamese communities found that asymmetrical access to brokers who served as "social lubricants" promoting trust, information sharing, and interpretive understanding between government and civil authorities and the community accounted for radically different views of New Orleans recovery. Whereas more than 70% of White and Vietnamese New Orleanians believed that New Orleans was making a very positive recovery, only 44% of African Americans/Blacks agreed (Hamel, Firth, & Brodie, 2015). Vu, VanLandingham, Do, and Bankston (2009) also found the New Orleanian Vietnamese community's network structure included inter-group bridging and brokering that enabled a much higher level of resilience than that found in the African American/Black communities, where the lack of brokers, and thus a lack of social capital, exacerbated difficulties in accessing and understanding information about jobs, housing, and financial support.

Nevertheless, as beneficial as brokering may seem, several studies have shown that there are downsides to being a broker. Competitive advantage is based on a context in which development of other information links between disconnected clusters is inhibited (Burt, 2001). In such contexts, the broker may be enmeshed in a network of weak rather than strong ties, low-density networks in which structural holes are the source of value and network closure (i.e., cohesive ties and high network density, see Coleman, 1990) is not desired. Under these circumstances, there is a greater likelihood for burnout (Tsang, Chen, Wang, & Tai, 2012); information and emotional overload; and feelings of isolation, non-support, and high stress (House, Umberson, & Landis, 1988). Research suggests, however, that these effects can be ameliorated if the broker plays the role of connector, what has been described as *tertius iungens*, the "third who joins" (Obstfeld, 2005). In such cases the broker introduces and facilitates linkages between the two isolated groups rather than remains the sole connection between the groups. As network density increases and ties become stronger, the network becomes more cohesive, robust, trusting, and cooperative, and it provides greater relational support, legitimacy, and bonding social capital to the broker and the groups that are being connected (Stohl & Stohl, 2005).

Future Research Directions

Taken together, these studies on organizational brokering and social networks suggest several avenues for future research on language brokering. First, the cultural dynamics of families such as adherence to familism, respect, and filial piety may indeed strongly influence the child's experience of language brokering. In addition, the experience of language brokering may have long-term effects that may be seen in different types of outcomes than have been previously been considered. For example, there is are no known studies of how language brokering as a child may affect future behaviors in the workplace. Language brokering may prepare individuals for strategic networking behaviors and enhance professional advancement. Several scholars suggest that childhood psychological predispositions to achieve, develop efficacy, and exhibit control may play an important role in the entrepreneurial development of brokers (Cornwell, 2009; Kadushin, 2002). Thus, children who are language brokers may become more entrepreneurial, having experienced the autonomous and control benefits of brokering. Further, they may become more creative and innovative because they have learned to integrate multiple perspectives and bring diverse knowledge to solving problems.

Third, studies of organizational brokering point to the importance of studying the entire family network to understand the impact of brokering. The evidence suggests that children might be less likely to develop symptoms of stress when they are able to play the brokering role of *tertius iungens* (i.e., the third who joins) rather than *tertius gaudens* (i.e., the third who benefits). In such cases, brokering enables the development of social skills and the ability to induce cooperation and connections in others (Fligstein, 2001) rather than being caught in the middle between two competing and/or disparate networks. Cohesive, interconnected networks provide a sense of support, trust, and safety. Bridging structural holes provides the broker with a sense of efficacy, mastery, and success. Future studies may consider the types of brokering and strategic orientations as factors mediating the impact of brokering.

Contribution to Theory

Utilizing an interpersonal communication framework to further research and theorize about language brokering introduces unique ways of identifying complex, contextual factors that determine brokering outcomes. Interpersonal communication scholars posit that outcomes are based not only on frequently engaging in a communicative act, but also on the quality and sophistication of communication (Goldsmith, 2004). Similarly, language brokering scholars note that while frequency of brokering predicts a child's academic, relational, and health outcomes, the quality of and beliefs about brokering communication may be better determinants of the extent to which brokering episodes affect the well-being of immigrant families (Guntzviller, 2016; Kam & Lazarevic, 2014b). Parents and children with sophisticated communicative skills may be resilient to the potentially stressful nature of language brokering and may even benefit from the brokering experience, whereas unskilled communication, even with good intentions, can amplify stress and be detrimental to relationships and to health. Conceptualizing language brokering as an interpersonal process highlights different aspects of the communication process, and the application of the five theoretical frameworks outlined in this chapter provide guidance for examining communication.

Each framework can be used to elucidate specific brokering communicative processes, and applies to the description of brokering as a complex process that is social, situated, and functional. Multiple goals theories, for example, help us understand the *complex process* of language brokering, as child interaction goals influence brokering communication and messages, goal perceptions influence parent and child processing of brokering interactions, and parents and child communication is interdependent. Communication privacy management theory also draws on family coordination acts surrounding language brokering disclosures, privacy maintenance, and boundary turbulence. Message production, processing, and coordination are all markers of communication quality that may mitigate brokering stress and help develop child communicative skills. The *social* element of the brokering communicative process, highlighted in organizational brokering and social network and communal coping approaches, points to the need to examine more than just the child perspective: Parent-child dyads, brokering families, and possibly support systems surrounding the child may serve to reduce acculturation stress and appraisal of stressors through communal coping ("our problem, our responsibility"). The social network approach, which also highlights the importance of considering brokers as links between two disparate parties that over time, may facilitate a more cohesive network between family members and people from the new environment. Both interpersonal communication and language brokering are *situated* in their relational, environmental, and cultural elements. The theory of planned behavior, paired with focus theory of normative conduct, provides insight into how communication may impact beliefs, social norms, and efficacy about language brokering. Language brokering studies cannot divorce the process or the act from its situated context. Finally, all of these theoretical perspectives touch on the *functional* nature of language brokering. Multiple goals theories, for example, indicate that successful attention to and management of potentially conflicting identity goals provide more sophisticated communication and desirable relational outcomes that can reduce stress. Communication privacy management theory also considers the interplay between instrumental issues (e.g., disclosing information to get medical attention) and relational and identity aspects, as does communal coping. The proposed theoretical frameworks describe and predict ways in which the quality of brokering communication may facilitate positive outcomes or produce stress.

Apart from providing theoretical avenues for language brokering research, the interpersonal communication perspective offers a pragmatic point of entry for interventions. Communication is a controllable, changeable element of language brokering. Helping language brokering families improve their interpersonal communication skills may mitigate potential consequences of the language brokering act, but may also provide them with enhanced skills and efficacy to navigate their new environment.

References

Afifi, T. D., Hutchinson, S., & Krouse, S. (2006). Toward a theoretical model of communal coping in postdivorce families and naturally occurring groups. *Communication Theory*, *16*, 378–409.

Afifi, W. A., Felix, E. D., & Afifi, T. D. (2012). The impact of uncertainty and communal coping on mental health following natural disasters. *Anxiety, Stress, & Coping: An International Journal*, *25*, 329–347.

Ajzen, I. (1991). The theory of planned behavior. *Organizational Behavior and Human Decision Processes*, *50*, 179–211.

Baptiste, J. D. A. (1993). Immigrant families, adolescents and acculturation. *Marriage & Family Review*, *19*, 341–363.

Burleson, B. R. (2010). The nature of interpersonal communication: A message-centered approach. In C. R. Berger, M. E. Roloff, & D. R. Roskos-Ewoldsen (Eds.), *The handbook of communication science* (pp. 145–164). Los Angeles, CA: Sage.

Burt, R. S. (1992). *Structural holes*. Cambridge, MA: Harvard University Press.

Burt, R. S. (1997). The contingent value of social capital. *Administrative Science Quarterly*, *42*, 339–365.

Burt, R. S. (2001). Structural holes versus network closure as social capital. In N. Lin, K. Cook, & R. S. Burt (Eds.), *Social capital: Theory and research* (pp. 187–245). Hawthorne, NY: Aldine de Gruyter.

Caughlin, J. P. (2010). A multiple goals theory of personal relationships: Conceptual integration and program overview. *Journal of Social and Personal Relationships*, *27*, 824–848.

Chao, R. K. (2006). The prevalence and consequences of adolescents' language brokering for their immigrant parents. In M. H. Bornstein & L. R. Cote (Eds.), *Acculturation and parent-child relationships* (pp. 271–296). Mahwah, NJ: Lawrence Erlbaum.

Cialdini, R. B., Reno, R. R., & Kallgren, C. A. (1990). A focus theory of normative conduct: Recycling the concept of norms to reduce littering in public places. *Journal of Personality and Social Psychology, 58*, 1015–1026.

Cohen, S., Moran-Ellis, J., & Smaje, C. (1999). Children as informal interpreters in GP consultations: Pragmatics and ideology. *Sociology of Health and Illness, 21*, 163–186.

Coleman, J. S. (1990). *Foundations of social theory.* Cambridge, MA: Harvard University Press.

Cornwell, B. (2009). Good health and the bridging of structural holes. *Social Networks, 31*, 92–103.

Corona, R., Stevens, L. F., Halfond, R. W., Shaffer, C. M., Reid-Quiñones, K., & Gonzalez, T. (2012). A qualitative analysis of what Latino parents and adolescents think and feel about language brokering. *Journal of Children and Family Studies, 21*, 788–798.

Dorner, L. M., Orellana, M. F., & Jiménez, R. (2008). "It's one of those things that you do to help the family:" Language brokering and the development of immigrant adolescents. *Journal of Adolescent Research, 23*, 515–543.

Dorner, L. M., Orellana, M. F., & Li-Grining, C. P. (2007). "I helped my mom, and it helped me": Translating the skills of language brokers into improved standardized test scores. *American Journal of Education, 113*, 451–478. doi:0195-6744/2007/11303-0005

Elek, E., Miller-Day, M., & Hecht, M. L. (2006). Influences of personal, injunctive, and descriptive norms on early adolescent substance use. *Journal of Drug Issues, 36*, 147–172.

Fligstein, N. (2001). Social skill and the theory of fields. *Sociological Theory, 19*, 105–125.

Gabby, S. M., & Zuckerman, E. W. (1998). Social capital and opportunity in corporate R & D: The contingent effect of contact density on mobility expectations. *Social Science Research, 27*, 189–217.

Goldsmith, D. J. (2004). *Communicating social support.* New York, NY: Cambridge University Press.

Green, J., Free, C., Bhavnani, V., & Newman, T. (2005). Translators and mediators: Bilingual young people's accounts of their interpreting work in health care. *Social Science and Medicine, 60*, 2097–2110.

Guntzviller, L. M. (2015). Testing multiple goals theory with low-income, mother-child Spanish-speakers: Language brokering interaction goals and relational satisfaction. *Communication Research.* doi: 10.1177/0093650215608238

Guntzviller, L. M. (2016). Mother-child communication quality during language brokering: Validation of four measures of brokering interaction goals. *Hispanic Journal of Behavioral Sciences, 38*, 94–116. doi:10.1177/0739986315613053

Guo, Q., Johnson, C. A., Unger, J. B., Lee, L., Xie, B., Chou, C. P., Palmer, P. H., Sun, P., Gallaher, P., & Pentz, M. (2007). Utility of the theory of reasoned action and theory of planned behavior for predicting Chinese adolescent smoking. *Addictive Behaviors, 32*, 1066–1081. doi: 10.1016/j.addbeh.2006.07.015

Hall, N., & Sham, S. (2007). Language brokering as youth people's work: Evidence from Chinese adolescents in England. *Language and Education, 21*, 16–30.

Hamel, L., Firth, J., & Brodie, M. (2015). New Orleans ten years after the storm. Retrieved from http://kff.org/other/report/new-orleans-ten-years-after-the-storm-the-kaiser-family-foundation-katrina-survey-project/

House, S., Umberson, D., & Landis, K. (1988). Structures and processes of social support. *Annual Review of Sociology, 14*, 293–318.

Hua, J. M., & Costigan, C. L. (2012). The familial context of adolescent language brokering with immigrant Chinese families in Canada. *Journal of Youth and Adolescence, 41*, 894–906. doi:10.1007/s10964-011-9682-2

Jones, C., Trickett, E., & Birman, D. (2012), Determinants and consequences of child culture brokering in families from the former Soviet Union. *American Journal of Community Psychology, 50*(1/2), 182–196. doi:10.1007/s10464-012-9488-8

Kadushin, C. (2002). The motivational foundation of social networks. *Social Networks, 24*, 77–91.

Kam, J. A. (2011). The effects of language brokering frequency and feelings on Mexican-heritage youth's mental health and risky behaviors. *Journal of Communication, 61*, 455–475.

Kam, J. A., Castro, F. G., & Wang, N. (2015). Parent-child communication's attenuating effects on Mexican-heritage early-stage adolescents' depressive symptoms and substance use. *Human Communication Research, 41*, 204–225.

Kam, J. A., & Lazarevic, V. (2014a). The stressful (and not so stressful) nature of language brokering: Identifying when brokering functions as a cultural stressor for Latino immigrant children in early adolescence. *Journal of Youth and Adolescence, 43*, 1994–2011.

Kam, J. A., & Lazarevic, V. (2014b). Communicating for one's family: An interdisciplinary review of language and cultural brokering in immigrant families. *Communication Yearbook, 38*, 3–38.

Katz, V. S. (2010). How children of immigrants use media to connect their families to the community: The case of Latinos in South Los Angeles. *Journal of Children and Media, 4*, 289–315.

Katz, V. S. (2014). Communication dynamics of immigrant integration. *Communication Yearbook, 38*, 39–68.

Love, J. A., & Buriel, R. (2007). Language brokering, autonomy, parent-child bonding, biculturalism, and depression: A study of Mexican American adolescents from immigrant families. *Hispanic Journal of Behavioral Sciences, 29*, 472–291.

Lyons, R. F., Mickelson, K., Sullivan, J. L., & Coyne, J. C. (1998). Coping as a communal process. *Journal of Social and Personal Relationships, 15*, 579–607.

Martinez, C. R., McClure, H. H., & Eddy, J. M. (2009). Language brokering contexts and behavioral and emotional adjustment among Latino parents and adolescents. *The Journal of Early Adolescence, 21*, 71–98.

Mehra, A., Kilduff, M., & Brass, D. J. (2001). The social networks of high and low self-monitors: Implications for workplace performance. *Administrative Science Quarterly, 46*, 121–146.

Niehaus, K., & Kumpiene, G. (2014). Language brokering and self-concept: An exploratory study of Latino students' experiences in middle and high school. *Hispanic Journal of Behavioral Sciences, 36*, 124–143.

Obstfeld, D. (2005). Social networks, the *tertius iungens* orientation, and involvement in innovation. *Administrative Science Quarterly, 50*, 100–130.

Orellana, M. F., Dorner, L., & Pulido, L. (2003). Accessing assets: Immigrant youth's work as family translators or "para-phrasers". *Social Problems, 50*, 504–524.

Oznobishin, O., & Kurman, J. (2009). Parent–child role reversal and psychological adjustment among immigrant youth in Israel. *Journal of Family Psychology, 23*, 405–415. doi: 10.1037/a0015811

Petronio, S. (2002). *Boundaries of privacy: Dialectics of disclosure*. Albany, NY: State University of New York Press.

Petronio, S., Sargent, J., Andea, L., Reganis, P., & Cichocki, D. (2004). Family and friends as healthcare advocates: Dilemmas of confidentiality and privacy. *Journal of Social and Personal Relationships, 21*, 33–52.

Roche, K. M., Lambert, S. F., Ghazarian, S. R., & Little, T. D. (2015). Adolescent language brokering in diverse contexts: Associations with parenting and parent-youth relationships in a new immigrant destination area. *Journal of Youth and Adolescence, 44,* 77–89.

Rohrbaugh, M. J., Shoham, V., Skoyen, J. A., Jensen, M., & Mehl, M. R. (2012). We-talk, communal coping, and cessation success in a couple-focused intervention for health-compromised smokers. *Family Process, 51,* 107–121. doi: 10.1111/j.1545-5300.2012.01388.x

Shen, Y., Kim, S. Y., Wang, Y., & Chao, R. K. (2014). Language brokering and adjustment among Chinese and Korean American adolescents: A moderated mediation model of perceived maternal sacrifice, respect for the mother, and mother-child open communication. *Asian American Journal of Psychology, 5,* 86–95.

Simmel, G. ([1922] 1955). *Conflict and the web of group affiliations* (Kurt H. Wolff and Reinhard Bendix, trans.). New York, NY: Free Press.

Stohl, M., & Stohl, C. (2005). Human rights, nation states, and NGOs: Structural holes and the emergence of global regimes. *Communication Monographs, 72,* 442–467.

Taube, V. G. (2004). Measure the social capital of brokerage roles. *Connections, 26,* 29–52.

Tilghman-Osborne, E. M., Bámaca-Colbert, M., Witherspoon, D., Wadsworth, M. E., & Hecht, M. L. (2015). Longitudinal associations of language brokering and parent-adolescent closeness in immigrant Latino families. *Journal of Early Adolescence, 36,* 319–347.

Tsang, S., Chen, T., Wang, S., & Tai, H. (2012). Nursing work stress: The impacts of social network structure and organizational citizenship behavior. *Journal of Nursing Research, 20,* 9–18.

Tse, L. (1996). Language brokering in linguistic minority communities: The case of Chinese-and Vietnamese-American students. *The Bilingual Research Journal, 20,* 485–498.

Umaña-Taylor, A. J. (2003). Language brokering as a stressor for immigrant children and their families. In M. C. Coleman, & L. H. Ganong (Eds.), *Points and counterpoints: Controversial relationship and family issues in the 21st century* (pp. 157–159). Los Angeles: Roxbury, CA.

Umaña-Taylor, A. J., & Updegraff, K. A. (2007). Latino adolescents' mental health: Exploring the interrelations among discrimination, ethnic identity, cultural orientation, self-esteem, and depressive symptoms. *Journal of Adolescence, 30,* 549–567.

Umaña-Taylor, A. J., Updegraff, K. A., & Gonzales-Backen, M. A. (2011). Mexican-origin adolescent mothers' stressors and psychosocial functioning: Examining ethnic identity affirmation and familism as moderators. *Journal of Youth and Adolescence, 40*(2), 140–157.

Villanueva, C. M., & Buriel, R. (2010). Speaking on behalf of others: A qualitative study of the perceptions and feelings of adolescent Latina language brokers. *Journal of Social Issues, 66,* 197–210. doi:10.1111/j.1540-4560.2009.01640.x

Vu, L., VanLandingham, M., Do, M., & Bankston III, C. L. (2009). Evacuation and return of Vietnamese New Orleanians affected by Hurricane Katrina. *Organization and Environment, 22,* 422–436. doi: 10.1177/1086026609347187

Weisskirch, R. S. (2013). Family relationships, self-esteem, and self-efficacy among language brokering Mexican American emerging adults. *Journal of Child and Family Studies, 22,* 1147–1155. doi:10.1007/s10826-012-9678-x

Wilson, S. R. (2002). *Seeking and resisting compliance.* Thousand Oaks, CA: Sage.

Wu, N.H., & Kim, S.Y. (2009). Chinese American adolescents' perceptions of the language brokering experience as a sense of burden and sense of efficacy. *Journal of Youth and Adolescence, 38,* 703–718. DOI 10.1007/s10964-008-9379-3

Xiao, Z., & Tsui, A. (2002). When brokers may not work: The cultural contingency of social capital in Chinese high-tech firms. *Administrative Science Quarterly, 52,* 1–31.

3

OUTCOMES OF LANGUAGE BROKERING, MEDIATORS, AND MODERATORS

A Systematic Review

Yishan Shen, Kelsey E. Tilton, and Su Yeong Kim

Introduction

The demographics of the world are gradually shifting. An increasing number of people are leaving their home countries and settling down in new lands. In 2013, about 232 million people were international migrants (broadly referred to as "immigrants" hereafter; United Nations, 2013), which was an increase of 57 million since 2000. These immigrants have brought increasing linguistic and cultural diversity to host countries. For example, within the United States, the country with the largest number of immigrants in the world (46 million; United Nations, 2013), more than 20% of the population age 5 and older speaks a language other than English at home (Ryan, 2013). Other parts of the world also host large numbers of immigrants, creating rich linguistic diversity within those countries beyond the official languages. Germany, the country with the highest number of immigrants in Western Europe, has 10 million immigrants; Israel is home to more than 2 million immigrants, representing over a quarter of the country's total population (United Nations, 2013). This pattern indicates that many people have to utilize strategies for coping with cultural and linguistic changes.

In immigrant families whose heritage language is different from the language spoken in the host country, children generally learn the new language at a much faster rate than their adult family members. For this reason, they often have to serve as translators or interpreters, a process commonly referred to as *language brokering* (McQuillan & Tse, 1995). As children take on the role of language brokers, they are faced with challenges above and beyond the normative developmental issues. Children may benefit from language brokering, or they may be burdened by this extra responsibility among other potential outcomes. A growing body of research on this topic from scholars across the globe has emerged since the mid–1990s.

Thus, a systematic review of the effects of language brokering that examines the beneficial and/or harmful consequences of multiple aspects of language brokering across various adjustment domains, along with the mechanisms and conditions of such influences, is urgently needed. Such a review should be international in scope, covering research conducted on language brokering over the last two decades in multiple countries.

Summarizing the Related Research

To the authors' knowledge, there have been only two syntheses so far on language brokering. The first one was published in 2005 (Morales & Hanson, 2005) and the second one in 2014 (Kam & Lazarevic, 2014a). In this section, we summarize what has and has not been examined in these two reviews. The goal of our current review is to fill the gaps in these existing summaries and examine the influences of multiple aspects of language brokering on the brokers' well-being comprehensively across various developmental domains.

Morales and Hanson (2005) conducted the first systematic review of language brokering research within the United States and made substantial progress in synthesizing the extant knowledge about the effects of language brokering before 2005. However, as their review was limited to research within the United States, knowledge about language brokering in non-US contexts was not synthesized. Another limitation is that the quality and credibility of the documents they reviewed varied widely: Their review included all published and unpublished documents on the topic, including non-empirical book chapters that were based on personal experience or personal opinion. Of the empirical research reviewed, a high proportion was qualitative work. Although these in-depth analyses of small samples of language brokers were highly valuable, qualitative findings have less generalizability compared to quantitative work (King & Mackey, 2016), and statistical conclusions cannot be drawn about the effects of brokering. Thus, in our current systematic review, we extend beyond the US context and focus on peer-reviewed journal articles and edited book chapters that include quantitative research on the effects of language brokering.

More recently, Kam and Lazarevic (2014a) conducted a theoretical review of language and cultural brokering. Although this review is more recent, it was not conducted systematically and was not specifically about language brokering: The authors included other behaviors such as culture brokering, procedural brokering, and media brokering. Language brokering is distinct from other brokering processes in its emphasis on the linguistic component, the meaning that must be translated, and the translation process between two languages. We specifically focus on language brokering in the current review, paying special attention to the multidimensionality of language brokering and to specific domains of outcomes affected by it. When various dimensions of language brokering and multiple domains of outcomes are examined, there may be differential effects of brokering dimensions across outcome domains.

Our current review also extends beyond prior syntheses by systematically examining mediators and moderators identified, indicated, or implied in the extant literature. In the current study, mediating mechanisms are broadly reviewed to include not only statistically significant indirect effects, but also processes that are proximal outcomes of language brokering dimensions, which in turn predict distal outcomes. In addition, we also review statistically tested moderators that have been shown to interact with dimensions of language brokering to predict outcomes. By reviewing mediators and moderators of the effects of language brokering, we present synthesized knowledge of the mechanisms through which, and the circumstances under which, language brokering would have more positive versus more negative effects.

Method

Our searches for relevant journal articles and book chapters were conducted from June to September 2015. As language brokering could occur as early as middle childhood and generally continues into the broker's adolescence and emerging adulthood (Morales & Hanson, 2005), the following search terms were considered: "language broker," "language brokering," "translator AND children," "translator AND adolescents," "translator AND emerging adults," and "translator AND college students." When we searched titles and abstracts in PsycINFO, Psychology & Behavioral Sciences Collection, and PubMed databases, we found 226, 23, and 72 results, respectively. Of the initial 321 articles identified, 70 were overlapping articles, and 43 were excluded because they were not peer-reviewed or because they were published in a non-English language journal. Of these, articles that (a) included a measure of language brokering, (b) employed quantitative methodology, and (c) examined at least one outcome of language brokering were included in this review, for a total of 27 articles. Figure 3.1 provides a graphical representation of the process of determining which articles to include in this review and details the number of articles that were excluded at each step, along with the reason for their exclusion.

Results

Study and Participant Characteristics

Of the 27 articles reviewed, 25 studies had quantitative-correlational designs, and two were mixed-method studies (specifically, Dorner, Orellana, & Li-Grining, 2007 and Guan, Greenfield, & Orellana, 2014). The majority of the studies were cross-sectional, while five were longitudinal (see Benner, 2011; Dorner et al.,

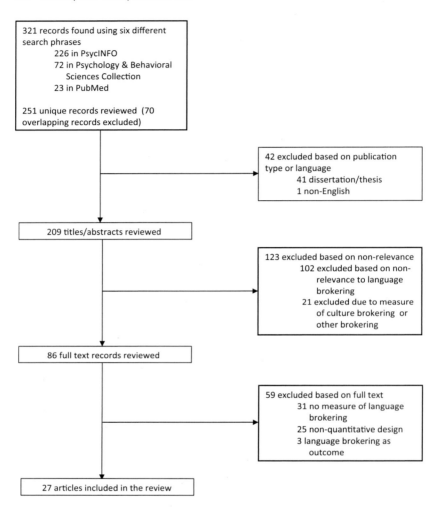

FIGURE 3.1 Inclusion/Exclusion Flow Chart

2007; Kam, 2011; Kam & Lazarevic, 2014b; Shen, Kim, Wang, & Chao, 2014). Participant characteristics are summarized in Table 3.1. Most of the studies were conducted in the United States, and more than half of the studies recruited participants residing in California. The ethnicities most represented in these studies were Latino/a (e.g., Mexican, Central American) and Asian descent (e.g., Chinese, Korean). In addition, FSU (former Soviet Union) was an immigrant ethnic group represented in studies conducted in non-US national contexts (i.e., Israel and Germany). The mean age of participants ranged from 11 to 28 years old, and most studies sampled adolescents who were attending secondary schools.

TABLE 3.1 Participant Characteristics

Ref No	Author	Country	Region	Race/Ethnicity	N	M(SD)	Range	% Female	Grade Level
1	Acoach & Webb (2004)	US	Southeastern US	Latino/a	108	—	13–18	60%	Jr. High and HS
2	Benner (2011)	US	Metropolitan Los Angeles	Latino/a	640	—	—	56%	9th–10th
3	Buriel, Perez, DeMent, Chavez, and Moran (1998)	US	Eastern Los Angeles County	Latino/a	122	14 (.7)	—	52%	9th–10th
4	Buriel, Love, and De Ment (2006)	US	Eastern Los Angeles County	Latino/a	157	15 (1.17)	—	59%	10th–11th
5	Chao (2006)	US	Los Angeles Area	Chinese, Korean, Mexican	1601	15 (.64)	—	53%	9th
6	Dorner et al. (2007)	US	Chicago, Illinois	Largely Latino/a	87	—	—	48%	5th–6th
7	Guan et al. (2014)	US	California	Latino/a, White, Russian, Asian	139	20 (2.68)	—	70%	College
8	Guan and Shen (2015)	US	Southern California	Asian, Latino/a, White	139	20 (2.43)	18–23	74%	College
9	Hua and Costigan (2012)	CAN	Western Canada	Chinese, Taiwanese	182	14 (1.69)	12–17	52%	—
10	Kam (2011)	US	Phoenix, Arizona	Mexican	684	12 (.58)	11–12	53%	7th–8th
11	Kam and Lazarevic (2014b)	US	Rural Illinois	Latino/a	234	12 (1.06)	11–13	46%	6th–8th
12	Kim, Wang, Weaver, Shen, Wu-Seibold, and Liu (2014)	US	Metropolitan Northern California	Chinese	486	17 (.8)	16–17	54%	HS
13	Love and Buriel (2007)	US	Southeastern Los Angeles County, California	Mexican	246	12 (.644)	—	57%	7th–8th
14	Martinez, McClure, and Eddy (2009)	US	Eugene–Springfield, Oregon Area	Latino/a	73	12 (1.05)	—	44%	6th–8th
15	Niehaus and Kumpiene (2014)	US	Southeastern US	Latino/a	66	—	11–16	35%	6th–11th
16	Oznobishin and Kurman (2009)	ISR	Southern Israel	Israeli FSU	180	16 (.94) 16 (.80)	15–19 15–19	59%	HS

(Continued)

TABLE 3.1 (Continued)

Ref No	Author	Country	Region	Race/Ethnicity	N	M(SD)	Range	% Female	Grade Level
17	Ponizovsky, Kurman, and Roer-Strier (2012)	ISR	Online	FSU	220	28 (3.66)	25–34	71%	College & working
18	Roche, Lambert, Ghazarian, and Little (2015)	US	Suburban Atlanta	Mexican/Central American	118	15 (.72)	12–18	53%	7th, 9th, & 11th
19	Shen et al. (2014)	US	Los Angeles Area	Chinese	237	W1:15 (.68)	—	55%	W1: 9th; W2:10th
				Korean	262	W2:15 (.69)	—		
20	Sy (2006)	US	Southern California	Latina	117	18 (.83)	—	100%	College
21	Titzmann (2012)	GER	Various German Cities	Native German	185	15 (2.5)	10–18	56%	—
				FSU	197	16 (2.6)	10–18		
22	Titzmann, Gniewosz, and Michel (2015)	GER	West German Cities in North Rhine-Westphalia	Native German	197	14 (2.5)	10–18	57%	—
				FSU	185	15 (2.7)	10–18		
23	Weisskirch (2013)	US	Western California	Mexican	75	20 (2.42)	18–25	63%	College
24	Weisskirch (2007)	US	Central California	Mexican	98	13 (.42)	12–14	48%	7th
25	Weisskirch (2005)	US	Central California	Latino/a, Mexican	55	11 (.30)	11–12	55%	6th
26	Weisskirch and Alva (2002)	US	Southern California	Mexican, African American, Indian, Multiracial	36	10 (.40)	9–11	47%	5th
27	Weisskirch, Kim, Zamboanga, Schwartz, Bersamin, and Umaña-Taylor (2011)	US	14 Universities Across the United States	African American, White, East Asian, Latino/a, South Asian, Middle Eastern	1222	19 (1.69)	—	72%	College

Note: Ref No = Reference Number; US = United States of America; Jr. High = Junior High; HS = High School; CAN = Canada; ISR = Israel; FSU = Former Soviet Union; W1 = Wave 1; W2 = Wave 2; GER = Germany

Language Brokering Dimensions and Outcomes

Table 3.2 is a summary of the relations between language brokering dimensions and outcomes. The measures used to assess language brokering experiences encompassed four dimensions of language brokering characteristics, such as frequency (e.g., how often for parents and across places), diversity of experiences (e.g., across circumstances or documents), difficulty or complexity (e.g., translating medical documents versus school assignments), and brokering norms (e.g., subjective and descriptive peer norms about language brokering). Four other dimensions were also used to assess the attitudinal and subjective experiences: positive and negative feelings, efficacy, and burden associated with language brokering. In measuring these language brokering dimensions, most studies used modifications of the early language brokering measure (Tse, 1995), which was later revised, first by Buriel and colleagues (1998) and again by Weisskirch and Alva (2002).

We then coded the associations between these language brokering dimensions and the outcomes of the language brokers or of their parents. In the current review, outcome variables are classified into the following six domains: socioemotional (e.g., depressive symptoms, internalizing symptoms), behavioral (e.g., substance use, externalizing symptoms), academic (e.g., grades, academic self-efficacy), relational (e.g., parent-child agreement, parentification), cultural (e.g., acculturation, biculturalism), and parental (e.g., parenting behaviors, parental depression) outcomes. In the rest of this section, we summarize statistically significant effects of the objective and subjective language brokering dimensions for different domains of outcomes.

Socioemotional

Much of the extant knowledge about the effects of language brokering is on brokers' socioemotional outcomes. Objective language brokering characteristics have consistently been linked to poor socioemotional outcomes. For example, brokering frequency was associated with depression (Love & Buriel, 2007), internalizing symptoms (Chao, 2006; Hua & Costigan, 2012; Martinez et al., 2009), low self-efficacy, and marginally low self-esteem (Oznobishin & Kurman, 2009). Similarly, difficulty of language brokering across different places was positively associated with depression among boys (Buriel et al., 2006). In addition, language brokers were more likely to show an increasing trajectory of loneliness across the first 2 years of high school, whereas non–language brokers were more likely to have steadily low loneliness during the same period (Benner, 2011). One exception was found for the partial relation between language brokering diversity and socioemotional outcomes: When controlling for culture brokering, the diversity of language brokering materials was negatively associated with depression and anxiety (Ponizovsky et al., 2012).

TABLE 3.2 Language Brokering Dimensions and Outcomes

Ref / No Outcomes — *Dom* — *Language Brokering Dimensions*

1 Interpersonal Perception

No / Outcomes	Dom	Jr Freq	HS Freq
1 Interpersonal Perception	A	n.s.	n.s.
Acculturation	C	n.s.	n.s.
Biculturalism	C	+	n.s.
Academic Self-Efficacy	A	n.s.	+
GPA	A	n.s.	n.s.

2 Trajectory of Loneliness

No / Outcomes	Dom	Freq
2 Trajectory of Loneliness	S	+

3 Academic Performance

No / Outcomes	Dom	Freq	Diff	Diff	Pos
3 Academic Performance	A	+	+	n.s.	n.s.

4 Parent-Child Bonding / Depression

No / Outcomes	Dom	b Freq	b Div	b Pos	g Freq	g Div	g Pos
4 Parent-Child Bonding	R	n.s.	n.s.	+	n.s.	n.s.	+
Depression	S	n.s.	+	n.s.	n.s.	n.s.	n.s.

5 Respect for Parent / Internalizing / Externalizing

No / Outcomes	Dom	M Freq—Chn	F Freq—Chn	M Freq—Kor	F Freq—Kor	F Freq—Mex	F Freq—Mex
5 Respect for Parent	R	+	n.s.	+	+	+	+
Internalizing	R	+	+	+	+	n.s.	n.s.
Externalizing	S	n.s.	n.s.	+	+	n.s.	n.s.

6 Reading Scores / Math Scores

No / Outcomes	Dom	Freq
6 Reading Scores	A	+
Math Scores	A	n.s.

			Freq	Freq	
7	Transcultural Perspective	C	+	+	
	General Perspective	R	n.s.	n.s.	
	Empathy	R	n.s.	+	
			M Freq	**F Freq**	
8	Parental Praise	P	−	−	
	Parental Criticism	P	n.s.	n.s.	
	Parental Regard	R	−	n.s.	
	Parental Support	P	−	−	
			Freq	**Freq**	
9	Internalizing	S	+	+	
	Self-Esteem	S	n.s.	n.s.	
	Parent–Child Conflict	R	+	+	
	Parent–Child Congruence	R	n.s.	n.s.	
			Freq	**Pos**	**Neg**
10	Adult Parentification	R	n.s	+	n.s.
	Problem–Solving Parent	R	n.s.	n.s.	n.s.
	Family–Based Acc. Stress	C	+	n.s.	+
	Other-based Acc. Stress	C	n.s.	n.s.	n.s.
	Alcohol Use	B	n.s.	n.s.	n.s.
	Cigarette Use	B	n.s.	−	n.s.
	Marijuana Use	B	n.s.	n.s.	n.s.
	Other Risky Behaviors	B	−	n.s.	n.s.

(Continued)

TABLE 3.2 (Continued)

Ref No Outcomes	Dom	Language Brokering Dimensions								
		P Freq	O Freq	Pos	Norm	Norm	Norm	Eff	Neg	Burd
11 Depressive Symptoms	S	n.s.	n.s.	n.s.	n.s.	n.s.	n.s.	n.s.	+	n.s.
Family-Based Acc. Stress	C	+	n.s.	n.s.	n.s.	n.s.	n.s.	n.s.	n.s.	+
Alcohol Use	B	n.s.	n.s.	n.s.	n.s.	n.s.	n.s.	n.s.	n.s.	n.s.
Cigarette Use	B	n.s.	n.s.	n.s.	n.s.	n.s.	n.s.	n.s.	n.s.	n.s.
Marijuana Use	B	n.s.	n.s.	n.s.	n.s.	n.s.	n.s.	n.s.	n.s.	n.s.
Other Risky Behaviors	B	n.s.	n.s.	n.s.	n.s.	n.s.	n.s.	n.s.	n.s.	n.s.
		M Bur	M Neg	M Eff	M Pos	F Bur	F Neg	F Eff	F Pos	
12 Parent-Child Conflict	R	+	+	n.s.	n.s.	+	+	n.s.	n.s.	
Depressive Symptoms	S	+	+	n.s.	n.s.	+	+	–	n.s.	
		b Freq	b Freq	b Freq	b Freq	g Freq	g Freq	g Freq	g Freq	
13 Depression	S	+	n.s.	n.s.	n.s.	+	+	n.s.	n.s.	
		Freq								
14 M & F Depression	P	1 n.s.; 1+								
M & F Relationship Quality	P	2 n.s.								
M & F Stress (Five Types)[a]	P	8 n.s.; 2+								
M & F Parenting (Eight Types)[a]	P	8 n.s.; 7–; 1+								
Academics (Six Types)[a]	A	4 n.s.; 2–								

		Freq	Diff	Pos
S Problems	S	1 n.s.; 1 +		
(Two Types) [a]				
Confidence	S	1 n.s.		
Ethnic	C	1 n.s.; 1−		
Identity & Belonging				
Substance	B	1 n.s.; 3 +		
Use (Four Types) [a]				
		Freq	Diff	Pos
15 Behavioral Adjustment	B	n.s.	n.s.	n.s.
Lack of Anxiety	S	n.s.	n.s.	n.s.
Happiness	S	n.s.	n.s.	n.s.
Intellectual	A	−	+	n.s.
Confidence in	S	n.s.	n.s.	+
Appearance				
Peer Acceptance	B	−	n.s.	+
Self-Concept	S	n.s.	n.s.	n.s.
		Freq		
16 Psychological Distress	S	n.s.		
Self-Efficacy	S	−		
Self-Esteem	S	−		
		Div		
17 Depression	S	−		
Anxiety	S	−		
Self-Efficacy	S	n.s.		
		Div	Div	Div
18 Parental Authority	P	n.s.	n.s.	−
Parental Knowledge	P	n.s.	n.s.	−
Mother–Child	R	n.s.	n.s.	−
Closeness				

(*Continued*)

TABLE 3.2 (Continued)

Ref No Outcomes	Dom	Language Brokering Dimensions		
		Freq	Burd	Eff
19 Maternal Sacrifice	R	+		
Respect for Mother	R	+		
Internalizing	S	n.s.		
Externalizing	B	−		
		Freq		
20 GPA	A	n.s.		
School Stress	A	+		
		Freq		
21 Instrumental Parentification	R	+		
Emotional Parentification	R	+		
Exhaustion	S	n.s.		
Self-Efficacy	S	n.s.		
		Freq		
22 Mother-child Agreement	R	−		
Conflicts	R	+		
Depressive Symptoms	S	+		
		Freq	Burd	Eff
23 Self-Esteem	S	n.s.	−	n.s.
Self-Efficacy	S	n.s.	−	n.s.

		Freq	Freq
24 Problematic Family Relationships	R	+	n.s.
Self-Esteem	S	n.s.	+
		Freq	Pos
25 Ethnic Identity	C	n.s.	+
MEIM-Search	C	+	+
MEIM-Affirmation	C	n.s.	+
Acculturation	C	n.s.	n.s.
		Freq	Pos
26 Acculturation	C	–	+
		Freq	
27 Acculturation	C	+	
Acc. Stress	C	n.s.	
Cultural Values	C	+	
Ethnic Identity	C	+	

Note: Article numbers are based on their assigned numbers in Table 3.1. A = Academic; Acc = Acculturation; b = Male Subsample; B = Behavior/Behavioral; Burd = Burden; C = Cultural; Chn = Chinese; Diff = Difficulty; Div = Diversity; Dom = Language Brokering Domain; Eff = Efficacy; F = Father; Freq = Frequency; g = Female Subsample; GPA = Grade Point Average; HS = High School Subsample; Jr = Junior High Subsample; Kor = Korean; M = Mother; Mex = Mexican; MEIM = Multigroup Ethnic Identity Measure; Neg = Negative Feelings; n.s. = not significant; Norm = Norms; o = Language Brokering for other; P = Parent/Parental; Pos = Positive Feelings; Ref No = Reference No; R = Relational; S = Socioemotional; + = significant and positive; – = significant and negative; ¹ = See Martinez et al. (2009).

With respect to the attitudinal aspects of language brokering, more positive psychological experiences of language brokering are associated with better socioemotional outcomes, whereas the opposite is found for more negative
experiences or attitudes. For example, positive language brokering feelings were
predictive of brokers' self-esteem (Weisskirch, 2007), as well as confidence in their
physical appearance (Niehaus & Kumpiene, 2014). Relatedly, a sense of efficacy in
language brokering was associated with lower levels of depressive symptoms when
brokering for fathers (Kim et al., 2014). In contrast, negative feelings about language brokering were predictive of brokers' depressive symptoms (Kam & Lazarevic, 2014b; Kim et al., 2014). Similarly, a sense of burden when brokering was
negatively associated with brokers' self-esteem and general self-efficacy (Weisskirch, 2013), and predictive of brokers' depressive symptoms (Kim et al., 2014).

Behavioral

Compared with the socioemotional outcomes of language brokering, much less
is known about behavioral outcomes. Although the extant literature is limited,
research generally seems to suggest poor behavioral outcomes for those who broker frequently. For example, frequency of language brokering for both parents
was positively related to externalizing problems among Korean American brokers
(Chao, 2006), and brokering frequency across different persons was negatively
associated with perceived peer acceptance (Niehaus & Kumpiene, 2014). Similarly, adolescents from high language brokering contexts were more engaged in
three different types of substance use than those from low brokering contexts
(Martinez et al., 2009). In a different study, after controlling for some family stressors, such as acculturation stress, brokering frequency was related to lower levels
of risky behaviors not associated with substance use (Kam, 2011). As for the attitudinal aspects of language brokering, positive feelings about language brokering
were associated with perceived peer acceptance (Niehaus & Kumpiene, 2014) and
negatively with cigarette use (Kam, 2011).

Academic

Findings on the effects of language brokering characteristics on academic outcomes are more mixed, with both positive and negative outcomes observed. Frequencies of language brokering, particularly across different places—and, more
generally, across different persons, places, and things—were positively associated with academic performance (Buriel et al., 1998), including reading scores
(Dorner et al., 2007). Language brokering frequency was positively related to
academic self-efficacy for high school students (Acoach & Webb, 2004). Difficulty
or complexity of brokering across different places was positively associated with
language brokers' beliefs about their academic abilities (Niehaus & Kumpiene,
2014). In contrast, language brokering frequency was positively associated with

school stress (Sy, 2006), and frequency of brokering across different persons was negatively associated with brokers' beliefs about their academic abilities (Niehaus & Kumpiene, 2014). In addition, adolescents from high brokering contexts showed poorer academic performance in two of six indicators, namely homework quality and language arts, compared to those from low brokering contexts (Martinez et al., 2009).

Relational

Like socioemotional well-being, the domain of interpersonal relationships has been extensively studied. Current knowledge about the effects of language brokering characteristics on brokers' interpersonal relationships indicates a mixed pattern. Higher frequency of language brokering for the mother was associated with higher perceptions of maternal sacrifice (Shen et al., 2014). Frequency of language brokering for parents was positively associated with adolescents' higher respect for at least one of the parents (Chao, 2006). Similarly, frequency of language brokering for non-parental figures was positively associated with empathetic concern (Guan et al., 2014). However, language brokering frequency was negatively associated with brokers' regard towards their mothers (Guan & Shen, 2015) and mother-child agreement (Titzmann et al., 2015), and it was positively associated with family conflict (Hua & Costigan, 2012; Titzmann et al., 2015). In addition, frequency of brokering across different materials was positively associated with instrumental parentification and emotional parentification (Titzmann, 2012). Further, diversity of home management–related language brokering materials was negatively associated with mother-child closeness (Roche et al., 2015).

In terms of the attitudinal aspects, similar to findings for socioemotional well-being, positive attitudes about brokering were associated with more positive relational outcomes, whereas negative attitudes were found to be destructive to interpersonal relationships. For example, positive language brokering feelings among boys and girls positively related to parent-child bonding (Buriel et al., 2006). In contrast, brokers' sense of burden and negative feelings about brokering for both mothers and fathers were positively associated with parent-child conflict (Kim et al., 2014). Negative feelings about language brokering were also positively associated with problematic family relationships, even controlling for brokers' self-esteem (Weisskirch, 2007). Surprisingly, positive feelings about language brokering were also positively associated with adult parentification (Kam, 2011).

Cultural

The effects of language brokering dimensions on cultural aspects of brokers' well-being vary as well. For example, frequency of language brokering for different persons was positively associated with transcultural perspective-taking (Guan et al., 2014).

In addition, language brokering frequency was positively associated with the search subscale of ethnic identity (Weisskirch, 2005), general ethnic identity and cultural values (Weisskirch et al., 2011)—and, among junior high school students (but not among high school students), with biculturalism (Acoach & Webb, 2004). In contrast, frequency of language brokering was negatively associated with acculturation (Weisskirch & Alva, 2002), and positively associated with family-based acculturative stress (Kam, 2011; Kam & Lazarevic, 2014b). Similarly, ethnic identity belonging was significantly lower, and ethnic identity search was marginally lower, for adolescents from high language brokering contexts compared to those from low brokering contexts (Martinez et al., 2009).

In terms of the attitudinal aspects of language brokering, again, positive experiences have been linked to positive indicators of cultural adjustment, whereas negative experiences have been linked to problematic cultural adjustment. Positive feelings about brokering related positively to ethnic identity search, affirmation, and overall ethnic identity (Weisskirch, 2005), as well as acculturation (Weisskirch & Alva, 2002). In addition, negative feelings about language brokering were associated with family-based acculturative stress, and marginally with other-based acculturative stress; brokering burden was also linked to family-based acculturative stress (Kam & Lazarevic, 2014b).

Parental

It seems that parenting practices and parental adjustment are generally negatively influenced by language brokering diversity and frequency. Diversity of home management–related language brokering materials was negatively associated with parenting practices, including parental decision-making authority and parental knowledge (Roche et al., 2015). Similarly, frequency of language brokering for both mothers and fathers was negatively associated with parenting practices, such as parental praise and support (Guan & Shen, 2015). Further, parents from high brokering family contexts exhibited poorer behavioral and adjustment outcomes across a constellation of indicators, including lower parental involvement and higher parental stress and depression (Martinez et al., 2009).

Mediator Variables

Table 3.3 provides information about statistically significant mediational processes and potential indirect effects. The most commonly investigated mediating processes for the influence of language brokering were relational processes, followed by cultural processes. In this section, we summarize mediational or indirect effects for these two domains. For the mediational mechanisms that involve relational processes, language brokering has been found to be indirectly related to brokers' socioemotional and behavioral well-being through promotive parent-child relationships. For example, through increased understanding of maternal sacrifice and,

TABLE 3.3 Articles with Statistically Tested or Potential Mediators

Ref No	Mediation	Mediator Variable	Domain	LB Dimension	Distal Outcome	Domain	Potential Mediating Path	Sign
1	Potential	M1: Biculturalism	C	LB1: Frequency	Y1: GPA (Jr. High)	A	LB1↑→M1↑→Y1↑	+
		M2: Academic Self–Efficacy	A	LB2: Frequency	Y2: GPA (High School)	A	LB2↑→M2↑→Y2↑	+
2	Potential	M1: Trajectory of Loneliness	S	LB1: Frequency	Y1: Academic Progress	A	LB1↑→M1↑→Y1↓	−
					Y2: Exit Exam Success	A	LB1↑→M1↑→Y2↓	−
4	Potential	M1: Parent–Child Bonding	R	LB1: Positive Feelings	Y2: Depression	S	LB1↑→M1↑→Y2↓	−
8	Tested	M1: Parental Praise	P	LB1: Frequency–mother	Y1: Maternal Regard	R	LB1↑→M1↑→Y1↓	−
				LB2: Frequency–father	Y2: Paternal Regard	R	LB1↑→M1↑→Y2↓	−
							LB2↑→M1↑→Y2↓	−
10	Tested	M1: Family–Based Acculturation Stress	C	LB1: Frequency	Y1: Alcohol Use	B	LB1↑→M1↑→Y1↑	+
				LB2: Neg. Feelings	Y2: Other Risky Behaviors	B	LB1↑→M1↑→Y2↑	+
							LB2↑→M1↑→Y1↑	+
							LB2↑→M1↑→Y2↑	+
11	Tested	M1: Family–Based Acculturation Stress	C	LB1: Frequency	Y1: Alcohol Use	B	LB1↑→M1↑→Y1↑	+
				LB2: Burden	Y2: Marijuana Use	B	LB1↑→M1↑→Y2↑	+
							LB2↑→M1↑→Y1↑	+
							LB2↑→M1↑→Y2↑	+
19	Tested	M1: Maternal Sacrifice	R	LB1: Frequency	Y1: Externalizing Problems	B	LB1↑→M1↑→M2↑→Y1↓	−
		M2: Respect for Mother	R					
21	Potential	M1: Instrumental Parentification	R	LB1: Frequency	Y1: Exhaustion	S	LB1↑→M1↑→Y1↓	−
		M2: Emotional Parentification	R		Y2: Self–Efficacy	S	LB1↑→M1↑→Y2↑	+
							LB1↑→M2↑→Y1↑	+
22	Potential	M1: Mother–Adolescent Agreement	R	LB1: Frequency	Y1: Conflicts	R	LB1↑→M1↑→Y1↑	+

Note: Article numbers are based on their assigned numbers in Table 3.1. R = Relational; P = Parental; C = Cultural; S = Socioemotional; A = Academic; Neg = Negative; M = Mediator Variable; LB = Language Brokering Dimension; Y = Outcome Variables; + = significant and positive; − = significant and negative.

in turn, more respect for the mother, language brokering frequency was associated with lower levels of adolescent externalizing problems (Shen et al., 2014). Similarly, although the indirect effect was not directly tested, positive language brokering feelings were associated with higher parent-child bonding, which was linked to lower levels of adolescent depression (Buriel et al., 2006).

In contrast, through problematic parent-child relationships, frequent language brokering seems to be indirectly related to poor socioemotional and relational adjustment. For example, frequent language brokering was associated with lower levels of mother-adolescent agreement, which was then associated with heightened family conflicts (Titzmann et al., 2015). In addition, frequent language brokering was related to both instrumental and emotional parentification; emotional parentification, in turn, was predictive of emotional exhaustion (Titzmann, 2012). Interestingly, however, when emotional parentification was controlled, instrumental parentification served as a protective mechanism, negatively predicting exhaustion and positively predicting self-efficacy (Titzmann, 2012).

Cultural processes can also serve as mediators, with protective cultural processes mediating the positive influences of brokering on brokers' academic well-being, and cultural maladjustment indicators mediating the negative influences of brokering on behavioral adjustment. For example, biculturalism served as a potential protective mechanism, through which language brokering frequency was associated with higher GPAs among junior high school students (Acoach & Webb, 2004). In contrast, language brokering frequency, negative feelings about brokering, and burden of brokering were positively associated with family-based acculturation stress, which in turn was associated with alcohol and marijuana use, as well as other risky behaviors (Kam, 2011; Kam & Lazarevic, 2014b).

Moderator Variables

Table 3.4 presents information about statistically significant moderations of the effects of language brokering. The majority of moderators fall under the domains of parenting practices or parent-child relationships. When brokers have parents who engage in problematic parenting practices, frequent language brokering has a detrimental influence on adolescents' socioemotional well-being. For example, frequent language brokering was positively associated with internalizing symptoms, low self-esteem, and low self-efficacy when adolescents perceived high parental psychological control or low parental support, but not when positive parenting practices were reported (Hua & Costigan, 2012; Oznobishin & Kurman, 2009). One exception for this pattern of moderation was that when the levels of open communication were low, language brokering frequency was positively related to adolescents' perceptions of maternal sacrifice, which then indirectly led to lower levels of externalizing problems (Shen et al., 2014).

It is less clear whether family contexts in which children and adolescents are granted more autonomy and assume more responsibilities amplify positive

TABLE 3.4 Moderators

No	Moderator Variable	Domain	LB Dimension	Impacted Outcome	Domain	Condition	Outcome	Sign
9	Mo1: Family Obligation	R	LB1: Frequency	Y1: Internalizing Symptoms	S	High Mo1	LB1↑→Y1↑	+
	Mo2: Parental Psychological Control	R		Y2: Self-Esteem	S	Low Mo1	LB1→Y1	n.s.
						High Mo2	LB1↑→Y1↑	+
						Low Mo2	LB1→Y1	n.s.
						High Mo2	LB1↑→Y2↓	−
						Low Mo2	LB1→Y2	n.s.
11	Mo1: LB Efficacy	LB	LB1: Frequency	Y1: Family−Based Acculturation Stress	C	High Mo1	LB1→Y1	n.s.
	Mo2: LB Burden	LB		Y2: Alcohol Use	B	Low Mo1	LB1↑→Y1↑→Y2↑	+
				Y3: Marijuana Use	B	High Mo2	LB1↑→Y1↑→Y2↑	+
						High Mo2	LB1↑→Y1↑→Y3↑	+
						Low Mo2	LB1→Y1	n.s.
13	Mo1: Responsibilities	P	LB1: Frequency−girls	Y1: Depression	S	High Mo1	LB1↑→Y1↑	−
						Low Mo1	Unreported	
16	Mo1: Parental Support	R	LB1: Frequency	Y2: Self−Efficacy	S	High Mo1	LB1→Y1	n.s
						Low Mo1	LB1↑→Y1↓	−
19	Mo1: Mother−Child Communication	R	LB1: Frequency	Y1: Maternal Sacrifice	R	High Mo1	LB1→Y1	n.s
				Y2: Respect for Mother	R	Low Mo1	LB1↑→Y1↓→ Y2↓→Y3↓	−
				Y3: Externalizing	B			
22	Mo1: Autonomy	R	LB1: Frequency	Y1: Mother−Adolescent Agreement	R	High Mo1	LB1→Y1	n.s.
						Low Mo1	LB1↑→Y1↓	−

Note: Article numbers are based on their assigned numbers in Table 3.1. R = Relational; P = Parental; D = Demographic Characteristic; Mo = Moderator Variable; LB = Language Brokering Dimension; Y = Outcome Variables; + = significant and positive; − = significant and negative.

influences of language brokering or exacerbate its deleterious effects. On the one hand, for girls who were allowed autonomy in the form of responsibilities, language brokering across more places was associated with lower levels of depression, although a similar pattern of associations was not found among boys (Love & Buriel, 2007). On the other hand, for adolescents who had a strong sense of family obligation—a construct related to responsibilities—frequent language brokering was associated with heightened internalizing symptoms. This relation was not found for those who had a low sense of family obligation (Hua & Costigan, 2012). Relatedly, for adolescents who had low levels of emotional autonomy, frequent language brokering negatively impacted the mother-adolescent disclosure agreement (Titzmann et al., 2015).

Conclusion

Several meaningful patterns emerge in the findings reported in this chapter. First, objective language brokering characteristics (e.g., frequency) are quite consistently linked to poor individual socioemotional and behavioral outcomes of child language brokers and their parents who receive the brokering support. In contrast, evidence is more mixed for the influences of objective language brokering characteristics on academic outcomes and interpersonal relationships, as well as cultural processes (e.g., biculturalism, ethnic identity). Second, for the attitudinal aspects, positive feelings about language brokering are generally associated with more positive outcomes across domains, whereas the opposite is true for negative feelings about brokering. Third, for mediating mechanisms, language brokering is indirectly related to positive outcomes through fostering promotive family relational and cultural processes, and to poor outcomes through problematic family relational and cultural processes. Finally, for moderating contexts, language brokering is more likely to have detrimental direct or indirect influence when there are problematic parent-child dynamics, but it is less clear whether family environments in which children are granted autonomy and are expected to fulfill more responsibilities mitigate or amplify the effects of language brokering.

Future Directions

The past two decades have witnessed a great increase in language brokering research. However, substantial gaps remain in understanding how language brokering influences adolescents' and emerging adults' well-being. The national contexts and the racial/ethnic and linguistic groups represented in the current literature on language brokering are quite limited, with the majority of research focusing on the Latino/a population in the United States. Recently, qualitative research on language brokering has emerged in other national contexts (e.g., the UK; Cline, Crafter, & Prokopiou, 2014), as well as among other racial/ethnic and linguistic groups (e.g., Arab Americans; Guan, Nash, & Orellana, 2016). However, much more work, especially quantitative research, is needed to elucidate the implications of language brokering. Future studies should investigate similarities and differences in language brokering experiences among more racial/ethnic and linguistic groups across more national and regional contexts.

On a related note, more than half of the studies reviewed in this chapter were conducted in California. Given the diversity of the population and the large number of Latino/a residents, results may be limited in their generalizability. All of these studies relied on smaller-scale, regional samples, which brings into question further the generalizability of the extant knowledge about language brokering. However, to the authors' knowledge, current large-scale, population-based datasets—at least those available in the United States—do not include language brokering scales. One way to utilize currently available population-based datasets is to follow Martinez and colleagues' (2009) approach of creating a proxy for the intensity of language brokering based on the degree of discrepancy between parents' language proficiency and that of their children. Future researchers could utilize currently available population-based datasets that assess the host language proficiency of parents and their children (e.g., the 2002 Education Longitudinal Study of the United States, a nationally representative, longitudinal study of American secondary students) to draw population-level conclusions about the effects of language brokering.

Another limitation of the extant language brokering research is that most of the quantitative studies conducted to date have been cross-sectional in their design. All of the few longitudinal studies investigated the long-term outcomes of earlier reports of language brokering. Little research has examined changes in language brokering experiences over time and the implications of such changes. A prior longitudinal qualitative study (Dorner, Orellana, & Jiménez, 2008) and a quantitative study with a three-cohort design (Buriel, Love, & Villanueva, 2011) do show some evidence that language brokering becomes more frequent in middle to late adolescence, compared to early adolescence. However, due to the limitations of qualitative and cohort designs, statistical conclusions about changes among the same group of language brokers could not be drawn. Therefore, we call for longitudinal studies that identify the stability, change, and developmental implications of long-term language brokering.

Contribution to Theory

In synthesizing research on the effects of language brokering, extant theories on conceptually relevant topics of bilingualism, acculturation gap, and youth caregiving may be considered and integrated.

First, as language brokering involves working with both the heritage and the host language, theories on bilingualism may be incorporated. For example, threshold theory (Cummins, 1976) predicts that bilingual superiority, or the cognitive benefits of bilingualism, would emerge only when bilingual children attain high linguistic proficiency in both languages. With low linguistic proficiency, bilingualism would actually have a negative effect on cognitive development. The mixed findings about language brokering, especially in the academic domain, are perhaps due to mixed linguistic abilities of the language brokers. It may be that the beneficial effects of language brokering observed in the cognitive and academic domains emerge only when language brokers are highly proficient in both languages and experience a greater sense of self-efficacy when brokering. Language brokers who are not adequately proficient in both languages may be burdened and have negative feelings about brokering, and language brokering may actually have more deleterious effects for them.

Second, language brokering is a phenomenon that occurs within immigrant families. The likelihood that children generally exhibit greater linguistic proficiency than their parents in the host language indicates that children and adults acculturate to the new society at different paces. Thus, language brokering research should be situated in the theoretical framework of intergenerational acculturation gap in immigrant families. The acculturation gap–distress model (see Lui, 2015 for a review) maintains that differing levels of acculturation between parents and children exacerbate the normative intergenerational gaps within families, resulting in problematic parent-child relationships, and, in turn, children's maladjustment. Our findings of the pernicious effects of language brokering on language brokers' socioemotional and behavioral domains of adjustment, as well as the mediational, or indirect, pathways through problematic parent-child relationships, are in line with the acculturation gap-distress model's predictions.

Finally, children's language brokering support for parents who have limited proficiency may be comparable to youth caregiving in the context of parental illness or disability. The family ecology framework (Pedersen & Revenson, 2005) in the youth caregiving literature proposes family "role redistribution," or the readjustment of roles among family members when a parent is incapable of fulfilling a role that he or she once filled, as a mediating mechanism of the effects of youth caregiving. The findings for the mediational roles of parent-child relationships may be understood within the family ecology framework. Whereas positive individual appraisal of redistribution (e.g., parent-child bonding) may serve as a promoting mechanism, negative interpretation of redistribution (e.g., emotional parentification) may serve as an inhibiting mechanism of brokering's effects. In addition, the findings suggest some moderating family contexts (e.g., supportive parenting, parental autonomy granting), although the small number of studies that examined moderators prevents us from making strong conclusions. Researchers should continue to identify both mediators and moderators of the effects of language brokering, as such efforts can further our knowledge about the complex mechanisms of the effects of language brokering, as well as how they might vary across individuals and contexts.

References

References marked with an asterisk indicate articles reviewed in this chapter.

*Acoach, C. L., & Webb, L. M. (2004). The influence of language brokering on Hispanic teenagers' acculturation, academic performance, and nonverbal decoding skills: A preliminary study. *Howard Journal of Communications, 15*, 1–19. doi:10.1080/10646170490275459

*Benner, A. D. (2011). Latino adolescents' loneliness, academic performance, and the buffering nature of friendships. *Journal of Youth and Adolescence, 40*, 556–567. doi:10.1007/s10964-010-9561-2

*Buriel, R., Love, J. A., & DeMent, T. L. (2006). The relation of language brokering to depression and parent-child bonding among Latino adolescents. In M. H. Bornstein & L. R. Cote (Eds.), *Acculturation and parent-child relationships: Measurement and development* (pp. 249–270). Mahwah, NJ: Lawrence Erlbaum.

Buriel, R., Love, J. A., & Villanueva, C. M. (2011). Language brokering in Latino immigrant families: Developmental challenges, stressors, familial supports, and adjustment. In N. J. Cabrera, F. A. Villarruel, & H. E. Fitzgerald (Eds.), *Latina and Latino children's mental health* (Vol. 1, pp. 91–116). Santa Barbara, CA: ABC-CLIO, LLC.

*Buriel, R., Perez, W., DeMent, T. L., Chavez, D. V., & Moran, V. R. (1998). The relationship of language brokering to academic performance, biculturalism, and self-efficacy among Latino adolescents. *Hispanic Journal of Behavioral Sciences, 20*, 283–297. doi:10.1177/07399863980203001

*Chao, R. K. (2006). The prevalence and consequences of adolescents' language brokering for their immigrant parents. In M. H. Bornstein & L. R. Cote (Eds.), *Acculturation and parent–child relationships: Measurement and development* (pp. 271–296). Mahwah, NJ: Lawrence Erlbaum.

Cline, T., Crafter, S., & Prokopiou, E. (2014). Child language brokering in schools: A discussion of selected findings from a survey of teachers and ex-students. *Educational & Child Psychology, 31*, 33–44.

Cummins, J. (1976). The influence of bilingualism on cognitive growth: A synthesis of research findings and explanatory hypotheses. *Working Papers on Bilingualism, 9*, 1–43.

Dorner, L. M., Orellana, M. F., & Jiménez, R. (2008). "It's one of those things that you do to help the family:" Language brokering and the development of immigrant adolescents. *Journal of Adolescent Research, 23*, 515–543. doi:10.1177/0743558408317563

*Dorner, L. M., Orellana, M. F., & Li-Grining, C. P. (2007). "I helped my mom", and it helped me: Translating the skills of language brokers into improved standardized test scores. *American Journal of Education, 113*, 451–478. doi:10.1086/512740

*Guan, S.-S. A., Greenfield, P. M., & Orellana, M. F. (2014). Translating into understanding: Language brokering and prosocial development in emerging adults from immigrant families. *Journal of Adolescent Research, 29*, 331–355. doi:10.1177/0743558413520223

Guan, S.-S. A., Nash, A., & Orellana, M. F. (2016). Cultural and social processes of language brokering among Arab, Asian, and Latin immigrants. *Journal of Multilingual and Multicultural Development, 37*, 150–166. doi:10.1080/01434632.2015.1044997

*Guan, S.-S. A., & Shen, J. (2015). Language brokering and parental praise and criticism among young adults from immigrant families. *Journal of Child & Family Studies, 24*, 1334–1342. doi:10.1007/s10826-014-9940-5

*Hua, J. M., & Costigan, C. L. (2012). The familial context of adolescent language brokering within immigrant Chinese families in Canada. *Journal of Youth and Adolescence, 41*, 894–906. doi:10.1007/s10964-011-9682-2

★Kam, J. A. (2011). The effects of language brokering frequency and feelings on Mexican heritage youth's mental health and risky behaviors. *Journal of Communication, 61*, 455–475. doi:10.1111/j.1460-2466.2011.01552.x

Kam, J. A., & Lazarevic, V. (2014a). Communicating for one's family: An interdisciplinary review of language and cultural brokering in immigrant families. In E. L. Cohen (Ed.), *Communication Yearbook 38* (pp. 3–38). London, UK: Routledge.

★Kam, J. A., & Lazarevic, V. (2014b). The stressful (and not so stressful) nature of language brokering: Identifying when brokering functions as a cultural stressor for Latino immigrant children in early adolescence. *Journal of Youth and Adolescence, 43*, 1994–2011. doi:10.1007/s10964–013–0061-z

★Kim, S.Y., Wang, Y., Weaver, S. R., Shen, Y., Wu-Seibold, N., & Liu, C. H. (2014). Measurement equivalence of the language-brokering scale for Chinese American adolescents and their parents. *Journal of Family Psychology, 28*, 180–192. doi:10.1037/a0036030

King, K. A., & Mackey, A. (2016). Research methodology in second language studies: Trends, concerns, and new directions. *The Modern Language Journal, 100*, 209–227. doi:10.1111/modl.12309

★Love, J. A., & Buriel, R. (2007). Language brokering, autonomy, parent-child bonding, biculturalism, and depression: A study of Mexican American adolescents from immigrant families. *Hispanic Journal of Behavioral Sciences, 29*, 472–491. doi:10.1177/0739986307307229

Lui, P. P. (2015). Intergenerational cultural conflict, mental health, and educational outcomes among Asian and Latino/a Americans: Qualitative and meta-analytic review. *Psychological Bulletin, 141*, 404–446. doi:10.1037/a0038449

McQuillan, J., & Tse, L. (1995). Child language brokering in linguistic minority communities: Effects on cultural interaction, cognition, and literacy. *Language and Education, 9*, 195–215. doi:10.1080/09500789509541413

★Martinez, C. R., Jr., McClure, H. H., & Eddy, J. M. (2009). Language brokering contexts and behavioral and emotional adjustment among Latino parents and adolescents. *The Journal of Early Adolescence, 29*, 71–98. doi:10.1177/0272431608324477

Morales, A., & Hanson, W. E. (2005). Language brokering: An integrative review of the literature. *Hispanic Journal of Behavioral Sciences, 27*, 471–503. doi:10.1177/0739986305281333

★Niehaus, K., & Kumpiene, G. (2014). Language brokering and self-concept: An exploratory study of Latino students' experiences in middle and high school. *Hispanic Journal of Behavioral Sciences, 36*, 124–143. doi:10.1177/0739986314524166

★Oznobishin, O., & Kurman, J. (2009). Parent–child role reversal and psychological adjustment among immigrant youth in Israel. *Journal of Family Psychology, 23*, 405–415. doi:10.1037/a0015811

Pedersen, S., & Revenson, T. A. (2005). Parental illness, family functioning, and adolescent well-being: A family ecology framework to guide research. *Journal of Family Psychology, 19*, 404–419. doi:10.1037/0893–3200.19.3.404

★Ponizovsky, Y., Kurman, J., & Roer-Strier, D. (2012). When role reversal and brokering meet: Filial responsibility among young immigrants to Israel from the former Soviet Union. *Journal of Family Psychology, 26*, 987–997. doi:10.1037/a0029913

★Roche, K. M., Lambert, S. F., Ghazarian, S. R., & Little, T. D. (2015). Adolescent language brokering in diverse contexts: Associations with parenting and parent–youth relationships in a new immigrant destination area. *Journal of Youth and Adolescence, 44*, 77–89. doi:10.1007/s10964-014-0154-3

Ryan, C. (2013). Language use in the United States: 2011. American Community Survey Reports. Retrieved from https://www.census.gov/prod/2013pubs/acs-22.pdf

*Shen, Y., Kim, S. Y., Wang, Y., & Chao, R. K. (2014). Language brokering and adjustment among Chinese and Korean American adolescents: A moderated mediation model of perceived maternal sacrifice, respect for the mother, and mother–child open communication. *Asian American Journal of Psychology*, *5*, 86–95. doi:10.1037/a0035203

*Sy, S. R. (2006). Family and work influences on the transition to college among Latina adolescents. *Hispanic Journal of Behavioral Sciences*, *28*, 368–386. doi:10.1177/0739986306290372

*Titzmann, P. F. (2012). Growing up too soon? Parentification among immigrant and native adolescents in Germany. *Journal of Youth and Adolescence*, *41*, 880–893. doi:10.1007/s10964-011-9711-1

*Titzmann, P. F., Gniewosz, B., & Michel, A. (2015). Two sides of a story: Mothers' and adolescents' agreement on child disclosure in immigrant and native families. *Journal of Youth and Adolescence*, *44*, 155–169. doi:10.1007/s10964-013-0077-4

Tse, L. (1995). Language brokering among Latino adolescents: Prevalence, attitudes, and school performance. *Hispanic Journal of Behavioral Sciences*, *17*, 180–193. doi:10.1177/07399863950172003

United Nations. (2013). International migration wallchart. Retrieved from http://www.un.org/en/development/desa/population/migration/publications/wallchart/docs/wallchart2013.pdf

*Weisskirch, R. S. (2005). The relationship of language brokering to ethnic identity for Latino early adolescents. *Hispanic Journal of Behavioral Sciences*, *27*, 286–299. doi:10.1177/0739986305277931

*Weisskirch, R. S. (2007). Feelings about language brokering and family relations among Mexican American early adolescents. *The Journal of Early Adolescence*, *27*, 545–561. doi:10.1177/0272431607302935

*Weisskirch, R. S. (2013). Family relationships, self-esteem, and self-efficacy among language brokering Mexican American emerging adults. *Journal of Child and Family Studies*, *22*, 1147–1155. doi:10.1007/s10826–012–9678-x

*Weisskirch, R. S., & Alva, S. A. (2002). Language brokering and the acculturation of Latino children. *Hispanic Journal of Behavioral Sciences*, *24*, 369–378. doi:10.1177/0739986302024003007

*Weisskirch, R. S., Kim, S. Y., Zamboanga, B. L., Schwartz, S. J., Bersamin, M., & Umaña-Taylor, A. J. (2011). Cultural influences for college student language brokers. *Cultural Diversity and Ethnic Minority Psychology*, *17*, 43–51. doi:10.1037/a0021665

PART II
Family Dynamics

4

FRIENDLY TAKEOVER

Predictors and Effects of Language Brokering Among Diaspora Immigrants in Germany

Peter F. Titzmann and Andrea Michel

Introduction

Language brokering is defined as the adolescent being the family interpreter and translator for documents, as well as the family expert for the new culture (Portes, 1997). Language brokering is a phenomenon occurring at least occasionally in almost all first-generation migrant families where heritage and host country languages differ (e.g., Jones & Trickett, 2005; Roche, Lambert, Ghazarian, & Little, 2015). For this reason, in most of the research, language brokering is regarded as a behavior that has its origins in the acculturation process, i.e., changes in the original cultural patterns of cultural groups through continuous first-hand contact with one or several other cultural group/s, e.g., after migrating to another country (Redfield, Linton, & Herskovits, 1936). Accordingly, inter-individual differences in the amount of language brokering most often are explained by differences in the acculturation process of children and their parents. Of relevance are, hence, variables such as length of residence, host and heritage language proficiency, host and heritage identity, and host and heritage culture behaviors among parents and children (Jones & Trickett, 2005; Lazarevic, Raffaelli, & Wiley, 2014).

More prevalent in this regard is, however, the intergenerational disparity in the pace of cultural adaptation between children (including adolescents) and their parents, which is also termed *acculturative dissonance* (C. Wu & Chao, 2011) or *acculturation gap* (Telzer, 2010). Children and adolescent immigrants acquire sociocultural skills (e.g., language and sociocultural behaviors) much faster than their parents by being in close contact with the new society through school experiences and frequent interactions with native peers (Pease-Alvarez, 2002; Tseng & Fuligni, 2000). For them, the process of acculturation often also comprises some degree of enculturation, i.e. acquiring, "by learning, what the culture deems necessary [by being] encompassed or surrounded by a culture" (Berry, Poortinga, Segall, & Dasen, 2002,

p. 29). Adults often are not enmeshed in the host society to the same degree. Consequently, immigrant parents often lag behind in the acquisition of sociocultural skills. The result is an acculturation gap between parents and their children, which is often discussed as a major reason for why language brokering of children and adolescents occurs (Jones & Trickett, 2005). Parents with poor host language skills are likely to rely on their children in order to translate or interpret inside and outside the home (e.g., Roche et al., 2015).

The Family Perspective

There is some research that suggests language brokering does not depend on acculturation-related variables only. Factors that are not related to acculturation, such as the individual characteristics of parents or children, also seem to play a role. For example, older children, females, first-born children, and children with a more extraverted and agreeable personality have also been found to broker more often in their families (Chao, 2006; Valdés, Chávez, & Angelelli, 2003). Because these are characteristics that also explain (acculturation-unrelated) intra-familial helping and caregiving behavior of adolescents in native samples (e.g., Crouter, Head, Bumpus, & McHale, 2001; East, 2010; Gager, Sanchez, & Demaris, 2009), family dynamics were considered in research on language brokering. Studies have begun to regard language brokering as one of many forms of provision of intra-familial care and support (e.g., Bauer, 2016). In line with these arguments, language brokering may also be framed from the perspective of theories on parent-child relations. Still, to date, few studies have examined how language brokering is related to issues of general patterns of parent-child relationships and parenting practices (Morales & Hanson, 2005).

Although studies examining the impact of parent-child relationships on the amount of language brokering done by adolescents are scant, there is some evidence that the quality of the parent-child relationship influences how language brokers feel about their task. Studies among Mexican American adolescents found, for example, that feelings and emotions that prevail during language brokering were more positive with a stronger parent-child bond (Love & Buriel, 2007), and that more problematic family relations were associated with higher ratings of negative emotions such as anxiety, nervousness, and shame during language brokering (Weisskirch, 2007). Furthermore, Buriel, Love, and DeMent (2006) found that adolescent language brokers felt emotionally more connected to their parents than non-brokers. Although these findings cannot reveal whether family variables are predictors or outcomes, these results suggest that language brokering has important connections to family dynamics.

In sum, there are good arguments to assume that language brokering should not only be seen as a result of acculturation processes in immigrant families, but also as an intra-familial process of sharing chores and tasks that need to be done. This perspective is also in line with observations that children and adolescents mostly begin to language broker in order to help their less-acculturated parents to cope with the demands of daily life in a new cultural setting (Bauer, 2016; Jones & Trickett, 2005) or, as Dorner, Orellana, and Jiménez (2008) put it "everyday language brokering may be seen as a normal expectation of the child–adult relationship" (p. 521). Consequently, language brokering adolescents might see their role as a way to fulfill their family obligations, just as they help out with other household chores like doing the dishes or taking care of siblings (Orellana, 2003; Villanueva & Buriel, 2010).

Connecting the Acculturation and the Family Dynamics Perspective

Against this background, language brokering needs to be seen as the result of two processes: acculturation-related changes and general family dynamics. From the family dynamics perspective, general theoretical models that have been developed to explain differences in parenting and parent–child-relations should not only explain general outcomes of the parent–child relations, but they should also predict inter-individual differences in language brokering among immigrant families. A useful model in this regard was developed by Belsky (e.g., 1984, 2014) and differentiates three aspects for explaining family-related behaviors: (a) characteristics of the children, (b) characteristics of the parents, and (c) characteristics of the social context. Characteristics of the children include their gender, age, temperament, and personality. Similar variables in parents are also relevant, as parents also bring their developmental history into interactions with their children. Besides parental and child characteristics, contextual variables might affect parenting and the parent–child relationship. These variables include the parents' marital relationship, their social network, and their workplace. Such general aspects until now have often been neglected in research on language brokering children and adolescents. They might nevertheless play an important role for explaining inter-individual differences in language brokering, particularly when language brokering is seen as a general aspect of the adolescent-parent relationship (Dorner et al., 2008). This model also has the advantage that these characteristics can be easily combined with acculturation-related variables in the study of immigrants (e.g., Tajima & Harachi, 2010). In our research, we wanted to know whether both acculturation- and family-related variables play a role in the extent to which adolescents language broker.

The Effects of Language Brokering for the Individual and the Family

Language Brokering and Psychological Adaptation

The expected psycho-social outcomes of language brokering depend on the theoretical perspective taken. Some researchers argue that language brokering might foster language and academic skills, as well as self-efficacy, because it entails cognitively demanding experiences and interactions with adults that promote personal and social skill development (e.g., Acoach & Webb, 2004; Buriel, Perez, DeMent, Chavez, & Moran, 1998). From a stress and coping perspective, however, other authors argue that language brokering can create stress and might overburden adolescents' social and problem-solving skills so that they experience exhaustion and may develop internalizing problems (e.g., Martinez, McClure, & Eddy, 2009). Both these perspectives may be accurate because evidence exists for both these perspectives (N.H. Wu & Kim, 2009).

This issue raises the question of whether there are potential moderators that modulate the effects of language brokering on the psychological functioning of individuals. One such moderator that comes to mind is the age of the language broker. Age is a proxy for all the developmental processes that occur through the adolescent years, which include biological (i.e., puberty), social (i.e., friendships, romantic relations, or autonomy from parents), and psychological (i.e., cognitive and planning skills) changes. From this perspective, it seems plausible that negative effects of language brokering were found primarily in younger samples (e.g., Puig, 2002; Weisskirch & Alva, 2002), whereas more positive effects were found among older adolescents (e.g., Acoach & Webb, 2004). Problem-solving and social skills increase during the adolescent years and are not yet fully developed in early adolescence (Adams, 1983; Luciana, Collins, Olson, & Schissel, 2009), so that younger adolescents in particular are more likely to lack essential strategies for dealing with their tasks of language brokering (Aneshensel & Gore, 1991). Older adolescents, on the contrary, are better prepared for dealing with brokering demands.

Language Brokering and General Family Obligations

Adolescents as language brokers come into a position with substantial responsibility for their family. They understand the spoken and written foreign language better than those for whom they translate (i.e., their parents) and have to decide what aspects are important and which words in the native language best convey the original meaning. In addition, they might come into contact with material that is beyond the scope of their age-mates' experience, such as their parents' medical diagnoses, insurance details, and bank contracts (Dorner et al., 2008). As a consequence, adolescents' support for their parents may not remain limited to translation or interpretation tasks. They may also start to take over other responsibilities related to instrumental or emotional support for their parents, so that parents start to rely on their children in other family matters. Such an involvement has been termed *parentification* and is defined as a process whereby adolescents are assigned or assume roles normally reserved for adults; for example, providing instrumental and emotional caregiving to their parents (Jurkovic, Thirkield, & Morrell, 2001; Williams & Francis, 2010). Parentification can increase adolescents' status in the family, which "undermines the traditional power relationship between parents and children and increases parental dependence on their children" (Trickett &

Jones, 2007, p. 143). This behavior was described among immigrants (e.g., Ozno-bishin & Kurman, 2009; Portes, 1997), but is well-known in other situations in which parents are incapacitated and cannot fulfill their parental role, such as families in which parents misuse drugs (Moore, McArthur, & Noble-Carr, 2011) or have mental problems (Aldridge, 2006). However, whether language brokering is associated with higher levels of acculturation-unrelated parentification behavior needs further research.

Language Brokering as Moderator of Developmental Processes

Another question concerning the effects of language brokering pertains to whether language brokering can change the normative developmental trajectories of adolescents. Such effects are particularly likely in the development of adolescents' autonomy. During adolescence, children are granted increasingly more autonomy from parents (Kerr, Stattin, & Burk, 2010; Titzmann & Silbereisen, 2012), which is defined as the freedom to self-regulate behaviors as part of the process of growing self-governance (Feldman & Wood, 1994). Both language brokering and autonomy seem to affect the expected hierarchy, role distributions, and communication in families. Further, they are likely to affect each other, and studying the interplay between them offers new insights with regard to effects on family communication, which can be a valid indicator for family dynamics and power distribution.

In particular, comparisons of associations between immigrant and native samples can highlight whether, for example, adolescent-mother communication in immigrant families is based on the same autonomy-related processes as it is in native families (with similar associations between autonomy and family communication in both groups), or whether language brokering affects the parent-child communication in immigrant families more than (normative) autonomy development. It is also possible, however, that brokering and autonomy development interact with each other in their effect on family communication. Although interactions between acculturation-related and normative developmental processes have received some attention in recent years (e.g., Michel, Titzmann, & Silbereisen, 2012), empirical results are still quite scarce. Two possible interactions of language brokering and autonomy could be expected: They may either reinforce each other or may cancel each other out. Theoretically, a reinforcement can be expected when coercive family interactions occur leading to an escalation (Granic & Patterson, 2006). Following this argument, on one hand, language brokering and autonomy may potentiate each other's effects on family communication so that autonomous adolescents who also broker communicate much less with their parents than any other group of adolescents. On the other hand, one of these processes (e.g., high levels in language brokering or high levels of autonomy) may be sufficient to change the family communication so that the effect of the other variable is eliminated. In this situation, the processes would cancel each other out.

Diaspora Migrants as a Special Case of Immigration

Most of the research on language brokering and family processes in immigrant families is conducted in North America, where, for example, about 90% of all studies on the acculturation gap originate (Telzer, 2010). Although some European studies have started to address family relations (e.g., Albert, Ferring, & Michels, 2013), more research is needed. A specific example among immigrant families in Europe is the amount of so-called diaspora migrants, such as ethnic Germans returning to Germany or Russian Jews in Israel (Tsuda, 2009). Diaspora migrants differ substantially from other immigrant groups because they lived in a diaspora "where, over lengthy time periods, they maintained their own distinct communities and dreamed of one-day returning to their ancient home" (Weingrod & Levy, 2006, p. 691). Diaspora migrants thus share ethnic, cultural, and/or religious roots with the receiving society and often also face beneficial immigration conditions, such as immediate citizenship upon arrival and social benefits. In addition, diaspora migrants often do not differ in physical appearance (e.g., skin color) from the majority of the population. Research on diaspora immigrants is still scarce, and it is an open question whether they undergo similar processes of adaptation as other immigrant groups.

Our studies have focused on the diaspora immigrant group of ethnic Germans from the former Soviet Union, the largest immigrant population in Germany. More than 2.5 million ethnic German immigrants have moved from the former Soviet Union to Germany since the fall of the Iron Curtain in 1989. Their ancestors left Germany centuries ago (mostly in the 17th or 18th century) in order to help cultivate or secure borderlands in Eastern Europe and former Russia. Until the end of the 19th century, they mostly lived in autonomous German enclaves with special rights, which allowed them to maintain their language and traditions. Nationalistic Russian ideas, however, increased the pressure on ethnic Germans to assimilate. World War II in particular changed their situation: They were deprived of their rights, subjected to severe discrimination, expelled from their regions of settlement, and deported to remote districts of the former Soviet Union in Siberia and Asia. During the Soviet era, ethnic Germans lost their German mother tongue and cultural traditions more and more, and bi-national marriages became common. The young generation grew up speaking exclusively Russian and was predominantly socialized with regard to the mainstream society (Dietz, 2003). While before 1989 emigration to Germany was restricted and ethnic Germans needed an invitation from a first-degree relative in order to leave the former Soviet Union, after the fall of the Iron Curtain many ethnic Germans and their families took the chance to migrate to Germany. "To live as German among other Germans" was an often-cited reason for their immigration (Fuchs, Schwietring, & Weiss, 1999). Although ethnic German immigrants to Germany have many commonalities with other immigrant groups—such as coming with a foreign family language— they are privileged in legal terms based on their ethnic German heritage. It was of particular interest whether language brokering is a relevant phenomenon in this group given that the immigrant parents have much better conditions to adapt to the host society than in traditional immigrant groups, and what the precursors and consequences of language brokering are for this group.

The sample for our studies was recruited in 2010 to 2011. Registry offices, where residents are recorded, in three German cities provided lists of potential participants based on the country of origin (i.e., specifically, states of the former Soviet Union or Germany) and age (between 10 and 18). Randomly selected adolescents and their mothers from this pool were invited to participate. We focused on mothers because they usually spend more time with adolescents than fathers, and often are more involved in the schooling of their children, creating more opportunities for everyday language brokering exchanges (Dubas & Gerris, 2002). Questionnaires were completed anonymously and separately sent back by mail by mothers and adolescents. In sum, 185 ethnic German and 197 native German adolescent and mother dyads responded (for details, see Titzmann, Gniewosz, & Michel, 2015). Basic characteristics of the samples are provided in Table 4.1. Both groups were rather similar on demographics, except for age and school tracks, with immigrants being older and coming more often from lower school tracks (which is not uncommon for adolescent ethnic Germans). All participating immigrant adolescents were first-generation immigrants (i.e., born in a country of the former Soviet Union) with on average 9.7 years of residence in Germany at the time of administration. Ninety percent of the adolescents in our sample performed as a language broker in the past three months before the assessment (Schulz, Titzmann, & Michel, 2013).

TABLE 4.1 Sample Characteristics

	Natives (N = 197)	Immigrants (N = 185)
	M (SD) / %	M (SD) / %
Age of adolescents	14.7 (2.5)	15.7 (2.6)
Gender (% female)	53%	60%
Adolescents in academic school track	46%	29%
Highest education of parents[a]	2.8 (1.1)	2.6 (1.2)
Family history of divorce or widowhood (single-parent families, %)	15%	21%
Length of residence (in years)	–	9.7 (4.0)

[a] *0 (no graduation), 1 (school graduation only), 2 (occupational training), 3 (college of higher education), 4 (at least one university degree);*

Language Brokering as an Acculturation-Related Phenomenon or the Result of Intra-Familial Processes

To answer our first research question, we performed a multivariate regression analysis with the level of language brokering as outcome (for a full description of the study, please see Schulz et al., 2013). For these analyses we restricted our sample to adolescents who immigrated at 4 years of age and older in order to include only adolescents who learned German as their second language ($N = 119$). Language brokering was assessed by the frequency of adolescents' translating 11 types of documents for their parents (e.g., notes or letters from school, medical forms or bills, job applications, insurance forms, or bank statements; Weisskirch & Alva, 2002). Three groups of variables were entered into the regression analysis: demographic variables (i.e., gender, age, length of residence, maternal education), variables related to the acculturation of mothers and children (i.e., maternal competence in German, adolescent competence in German, adolescents' competence in Russian, an interaction term of adolescents' competence in German and Russian), and variables related to the family environment (i.e., maternal self-efficacy, maternal employment status, two-parent versus single-parent family status, the number of German people in the mothers' network, and children's positive attitude towards language brokering); for more information on these variables, including sample items and reliability scores, see the Appendix.

Results showed that variables related to family interactions contributed to the prediction of inter-individual differences in language brokering. Among the demographic variables, age was the only significant predictor. In line with the general increase of family obligations during the adolescent years (Wilkinson-Lee, Zhang, Nuno, & Wilhelm, 2011), older adolescents reported higher levels of language brokering. Contrary to the frequent results obtained in the United States (Morales & Hanson, 2005), we found no differences in the frequency of brokering between male and female adolescents. Further research is needed on this issue, but it seems likely that gender plays a more prevalent role in immigrant groups with more differentiated gender roles, such as Latino/as (Corby, Hodges, & Perry, 2007). In this study, the adolescents were from the former Soviet Union, where gender roles are less differentiated. Empirically, this explanation is corroborated by the fact that adolescents from the former Soviet Union in the United States also reported no gender differences in language brokering (Jones & Trickett, 2005).

Somewhat surprising was the finding that mothers' lower competence in German was the only significant acculturation-related predictor for higher levels of adolescents' language brokering. Obviously, mothers rely on the children when they lack the required linguistic skills in the receiving culture, independent of the children's competence in Russian or German. A substantial share of variance in language brokering was explained by the variables usually used to predict family interactions (Belsky, 1984). Adolescents had to broker less frequently when there were two parents, when the mother had more German acquaintances in her social network, and when the adolescent had a less positive attitude towards translation. The first two of these variables demonstrate that alternative helpers in translation (such as the romantic partner, or friends) can assume some of the language broker- ing tasks from adolescents. The third significant predictor, a positive attitude of adolescents towards language brokering, was related to higher levels of brokering and represents the general motivation of adolescents to support their parents in this matter. The results, thus, support the general notion that language broker- ing, at least among diaspora immigrants in Germany, can be better understood from a family perspective, and the family interaction involved, than as purely an acculturation phenomenon, although both perspectives of acculturation and family interactions are needed for a thorough understanding of why adolescents language broker.

Effects of Language Brokering on the Individual and the Family

Our second overarching research question concerned the effects of language bro- kering. We addressed this question in three ways. First, we wanted to learn more about whether and under what circumstances language brokering was associated with better or worse psychological adaptation outcomes. Second, we wanted to see whether language brokering was associated with other acculturation-unrelated tasks. Third, we wanted to learn more about the interaction of language broker- ing with normative developmental processes (i.e., the development of autonomy).

Language Brokering and Psychological Adaptation

In order to examine whether language brokering was associated with higher lev- els of distress and a greater risk for psychological well-being, we drew on three assessments: depressive symptoms, feelings of exhaustion, and difficulties relaxing (see Appendix; for a full description of the study, see Schulz et al., 2013). Since all these assessments were highly correlated ($r > .50$), we created a latent construct termed *internalizing problems* using the three scales (depressive symptoms, exhaus- tion, difficulties relaxing) as manifest indicators for the latent construct. This latent construct was then regressed on a number of predictors, which included age, gender, family income, adolescents' externalizing behavior in childhood (retro- spective measure), and language brokering frequency. In addition, an interaction term of language brokering and age was added in order to examine whether the effects of language brokering were more or less detrimental depending on age. Only three variables reached significance. Adolescents' externalizing behavior in childhood was associated with higher levels of internalizing problems. Language brokering frequency predicted higher levels of internalizing problems, which sup- ported the general notion of language brokering being a risk rather than a pro- motive factor for adolescents' development. More important, however, was the

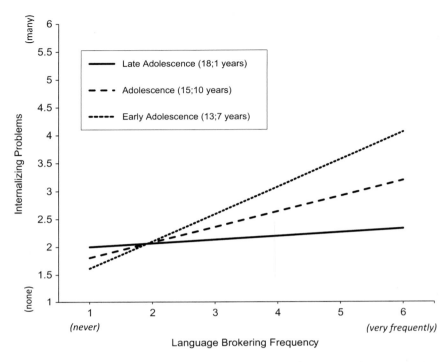

FIGURE 4.1   Moderation Effect of Age and Language Brokering Based on Regression
Results for the Prediction of Internalizing Problems

significant interaction of language brokering and age. As shown in Figure 4.1, the
detrimental effect of language brokering on internalizing problems was found
especially in the age group of younger adolescents: Simple slope analyses revealed
a significant association between language brokering and internalizing problems
in early adolescence (i.e., one standard deviation below the mean age), which
meant an age of about 13 years and 7 months (indicated by 13;7 in Figure 4.1).
In late adolescence (i.e., one standard deviation above the mean age, at an age of
18 years and 1 month, indicated by 18;1 in Figure 4.1), however, no such effect
was identified. This finding supports the supposition that language brokering may
be particularly detrimental in the early years of adolescence when individuals
have not yet developed the social and problem-solving skills that are necessary for
dealing with the demands associated with language brokering.

Language Brokering and Other Family Obligations

Another explanation for detrimental effects of language brokering could be that
adolescents acting as language brokers may also get involved in other family obligations that are not related to acculturation, so that they are not overburdened

by the language brokering but by the overall amount of responsibilities that are normally outside the scope of adolescents' lives. Hence, language brokering may be seen as a first step or an acculturation-related subcomponent of parentification. In line with earlier research (Jurkovic, 1997; Williams & Francis, 2010), we differentiated between instrumental and emotional parentification. Emotional parentification refers to support in the regulation of parental emotions and comprises behaviors such as dealing with family conflicts. Instrumental parentification refers to support in domestic-related parental responsibilities, such as financial decision-making (Hooper, Marotta, & Lanthier, 2008).

We addressed this question in two ways. First, given the fact that about 90% of immigrant adolescents language broker (e.g., Jones & Trickett, 2005; Schulz et al., 2013), we expected that the general level of instrumental and emotional parentification would be higher in immigrant as compared to native samples. Second, inter-individual differences in language brokering should be associated with inter-individual differences in instrumental and emotional parentification in the immigrant sample. Both these assumptions were supported in our past research (for a full description of the study see Titzmann, 2012).

A between-subjects multivariate analysis of variance (MANOVA) indicated that immigrant adolescents reported significantly higher levels for both types of parentification, $F(2, 337) = 7.77, p < .05$. After the control variables (i.e., parental education, age of the adolescent, academic school track of adolescents, and two-parent family) were accounted for, the mean level differences for instrumental parentification, $F(1, 338) = 4.15, p < .05$, and emotional parentification, $F(1, 338) = 15.44, p < .05$, remained significant. Ethnic German diaspora immigrants reported a mean level of 2.42 ($SD = 0.91$) for emotional parentification and 2.65 ($SD = 1.00$) for instrumental parentification, whereas native Germans reported on average a level of 2.21 ($SD = 0.92$) for instrumental and 2.22 ($SD = 0.99$) for emotional parentification. Furthermore, associations between language brokering and instrumental as well as emotional parentification were positive and significant, even after including a number of other potential predictors, such as demographic variables (age, gender, length of residence), maternal reported partnership dissatisfaction, and the share of natives in the social networks of mothers and adolescents.

Language Brokering as Moderator of Developmental Processes

Our third question on the effects of language brokering aimed at examining the communication between mothers and their children to study whether language brokering may undermine the normative developmental processes related to autonomy development (for a full description of the study see Titzmann et al., 2015). We used the concept of child disclosure to study intra-familial communication processes (see the Appendix). Child disclosure is the child's free, willing revelation of information towards parents. Past research has indicated that parents receive information about their children's whereabouts mainly through their child's willing disclosure rather than through other sources, such as control and solicitation, which are less relevant (Kerr & Stattin, 2000). High levels of child disclosure are the result of adolescents' "trust in their parents—whether they feel that their parents are willing to listen to them, are responsive, and would not ridicule or punish if they confided in them" (Stattin & Kerr, 2000, p. 1083). However, we were less interested in how much the children actually tell their parents, but focused explicitly on the agreement between mothers' and adolescents' reports on the extent of the adolescents' disclosure. In more detail, we wanted to know whether this agreement was less pronounced in immigrant as compared to native families, and whether this agreement was predicted by the amount of language brokering, by the normative developmental level of autonomy, or by the interaction of both these variables.

A general disagreement between mothers and adolescents seems to be rather normative as we found an imbalance between mothers' and adolescents' ratings in the offspring's disclosure. In both groups, mothers estimated the level of disclosure higher than the adolescents themselves did (for detailed results see Titzmann et al., 2015). More specifically, mothers from both groups did not differ in their estimation of how much their child discloses. That the mother-adolescent agreement was lower in the immigrant as compared to the native sample was, hence, mainly due to immigrant adolescents reporting lower levels of disclosure than their native age-mates. This finding strengthened the assumption that additional immigration-related predictors, such as language brokering, might play a role in the communication processes in immigrant families.

This assumption was further corroborated in multivariate regression analyses. In order to predict mother-adolescent agreement, we created a new measure that captured the profile agreement within each mother-adolescent dyad. This measure consisted of the intra-class correlation coefficient (i.e., ICC, one-way random), which is a single indicator capturing dyadic agreement in elevation, shape, and scatter/variation (Furr, 2010) across the child disclosure items used. The ICC has a Pearson correlation metric so that high positive values indicate high mother-adolescent agreement, whereas correlations close to zero point to independent disclosure ratings and thus low agreement. As each mother-adolescent dyad had a specific ICC indicating the level of agreement between mothers and adolescents, we used this indicator as outcome in the multivariate regressions.

Regressions were conducted in several steps. The first two steps (Step 1, control variables; Step 2, autonomy) were performed in both the immigrant and the native groups. In the immigrant group, an additional third step was entered consisting of the immigration-specific predictors. Results are shown in Table 4.2. First, a more general effect of growing up was observed. In both groups, the mother-adolescent agreement was lower among older adolescents—an effect that disappeared after autonomy was added as predictor in Step 2 of the regressions. These associations point out normative developmental processes of growing up. With increasing age, adolescents become more independent from parents so that parents may have

TABLE 4.2 Unstandardized regression coefficients (and standard errors) of a structural equation model predicting mother-adolescent agreement (ICC)

	Natives		Immigrants		
	Step 1	Step 2	Step 1	Step 2	Step 3
Age	−.07 (.02)**	−.02 (.03)	−.06 (.02)*	−.03 (.02)	−.02 (.02)
Gender (0 = male; 1 = female)	.35 (.12)**	.36 (.11)**	.22 (.13)	.21 (.12)	.26 (.11)*
Parental education	.06 (.05)	.07 (.05)	.07 (.05)	.12 (.05)*	.11 (.05)*
Adolescent academic track	.08 (.13)	.16 (.12)	.02 (.14)	.06 (.13)	.06 (.13)
Two parent-family (0 = yes; 1 = divorce, widowhood)	−.13 (.16)	−.13 (.15)	−.03 (.15)	−.09 (.14)	−.07 (.14)
Autonomy		−.26 (.05)***		−.23 (.05)***	−.24 (.05)***
Length of residence					.00 (.02)
Language brokering					−.16 (.07)*
Language brokering X autonomy (interaction)					.15 (.05)**
R-squared model	.10	.21	.06	.19	.26

Note: * p < .05; ** p < .01; *** p < .001. ICC = intra-class correlation coefficient.

more difficulty judging how much an adolescent actually tells them about their whereabouts. More importantly, however, language brokering and the interaction between language brokering and autonomy added to the explained variance in the immigrant group. As expected, the mother-adolescent agreement was lower in families in which adolescents broker more frequently. This finding indicates that language brokering does have similar effects as the development of autonomy. Further, the interaction of autonomy and language brokering also reached significance. As indicated in Figure 4.2, the data suggest that the processes cancel each other out. For adolescents high in autonomy, it did not matter whether they broker in their family; the mother-adolescent agreement is rather low. Similarly, for adolescents who brokered more than average, the amount of autonomy was not as strongly associated with mother-adolescent agreement than for those adolescents who brokered less frequently. This interaction between language brokering and autonomy in predicting mother-adolescent agreement in the reported level of adolescent child disclosure shows that normative development (i.e., autonomy) and immigration-specific processes (i.e., language brokering) can be competing processes for select outcomes. Research with an exclusive focus on developmental

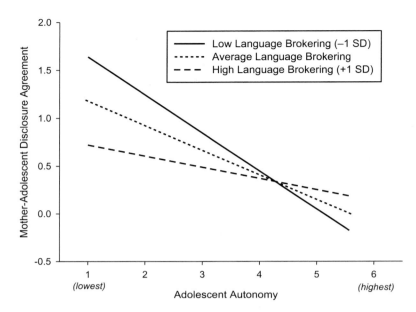

FIGURE 4.2   Interaction of Language Brokering and Autonomy in the Prediction of Mother–Adolescent Agreement on Child Disclosure (Fisher Z-Values of ICC)

aspects of immigrant adolescents' pathways may, thus, result in an oversimplification of the dynamics in immigrant families, as would be research that reduces adolescent immigrant functioning to acculturation-related processes.

Conclusion

Most of the research on language brokering has been conducted in the United States and with very specific populations, such as Hispanic families who are known to have rather high values in filial piety or familism (Kiang & Fuligni, 2009). Results, hence, may not be generalizable to other immigrant groups in other immigration contexts. Our research on diaspora immigrants is a particularly hard test for the generalizability of the existing findings, because diaspora immigrants not only have connections with the receiving society before they actually make the transition to the country, but they also receive substantial support and even citizenship rights upon entry into the country (Slonim-Nevo, Mirsky, Rubinstein, & Nauck, 2009). In our research on ethnic German diaspora immigrants from the former Soviet Union in Germany, about 90% of all adolescents performed as language brokers in the previous 3 months, although to varying degrees of involvement (Schulz et al., 2013). Indeed, language brokering is a normative experience for first-generation immigrant adolescents. However, our research also added new insights into the understanding of why adolescents act as language brokers. Language brokering is not an acculturation-related phenomenon only: Both immigration and a family-dynamics perspectives should be combined for a better understanding of inter-individual differences in the level of language brokering.

Furthermore, the effect of language brokering on the psychosocial functioning of adolescents is a consistent matter of debate, with some people expecting disad-vantageous and others expecting beneficial outcomes. Our research suggests that both these expectations may be valid depending on the age of the language broker—with younger adolescents being at a higher risk for maladjustment (Schulz et al., 2013). Negative outcomes of brokering may also be the consequence of language brokering extending to other acculturation-independent domains of adolescents' support for their parents, i.e., parentification (Titzmann, 2012). In addition, the findings showed that language brokering can interfere with normative develop-mental changes, such as changes in family communication that are normative with growing autonomy (Titzmann et al., 2015).

Future Directions

This chapter clearly shows that research has made substantial progress in the understanding of language brokering. Nevertheless, the picture is far from being complete. One challenge is that current research is often based on cross-sectional studies. What is needed is more longitudinal and experimental work, including intervention studies. Only these approaches can address issues of causality and of individual trajectories in their brokering experience. In addition, more com-parative research is needed that includes various immigrant groups. Comparative research can address the question of whether observed phenomena are universal or group specific, and it can identify similarities in adaptation, as well as group-specific aspects of adaptation (Berry, Phinney, Sam, & Vedder, 2006). However, comparisons should not be made across immigrant groups only, but also across immigrant and native populations. Although such comparisons are rarely done, our study showed that such research is informative: The association between autonomy and mother-adolescent communication was similar between native adolescents and immigrants who do not language broker.

In addition, more effort needs to be invested into the study of mechanisms that explain the developmental processes related to language brokering. For example, we found that age is a moderator for the effects of language brokering on inter-nalizing problems (Schulz et al., 2013). Unfortunately, age is only a proxy for all the processes that occur in the biological, social, and psychological domains of adolescent development. We did not include measures that allowed us to identify which competences and skills are actually relevant in this regard, although such measures may help in preparing adolescents to successfully deal with the demands of language brokering. The identification of such skills is an important step in future research.

Contribution to Theory

In our view, the most fundamental contribution of our research to the development of theories in the area of language brokering is that researchers studying immigrant adolescents' adaptation should integrate more developmental aspects and approaches into their theoretical thinking. In general, studies that combine acculturation and general developmental views reveal that immigrant adolescents are first and foremost adolescents and, only at a second glance, immigrants. Changes in autonomy expectations were, for example, best explained by normative developmental patterns rather than by acculturation-related changes (Titzmann & Silbereisen, 2012). Similarly, general predictors well-known from the research on non-immigrant samples explained a substantially higher share of variance than immigrant-specific variables in immigrant adolescents' delinquency (Titzmann, Silbereisen, & Mesch, 2014). With regard to language brokering, our results showed that a substantial share of variance can be attributed to normative developmental aspects, such as the family context.

Another theoretical implication relates to research on immigrant adolescents' civic engagement. Some studies show, for example, that immigrant adolescents are less involved in civic activities than native adolescents (e.g., Torney-Purta, Barber, & Wilkenfeld, 2006). Our findings suggest that they are not less engaged per se, but simply engaged in different domains of life. They support their family more than native adolescents and may, thus, have less time for other activities. Theory and research on adolescents' civic engagement should, therefore, include measures of family support in order to accurately assess immigrant adolescents' societal contributions to the adaptation of their immigrant families.

These approaches will not only help to understand the processes of the integration and adaptation of adolescent immigrants, but they may also reduce stereotypes and misinterpretations with regard to the behavior of adolescent immigrants. In increasingly multicultural societies, a more inclusive, problem-focused research could help in highlighting the often substantial similarities between immigrants and natives, and may thus bring different groups together. This research may also profit from looking at the interplay between native and immigrant adolescents, because the effects of immigrant adolescents' behavior may depend on how this behavior is perceived and complemented by the native peers (Titzmann & Jugert, 2015). Language brokering, for example, may not only be seen as immigration-specific and unique behavior, but more generally as part of the support one provides for others in the family that can also be observed (albeit in different form) in native families.

Acknowledgments

This study was funded by the Jacobs Foundation. We thank the Center for Applied Developmental Science (CADS), its director (Professor Rainer K. Silbereisen) and students, as well as all our participants for supporting our work.

References

Acoach, C. L., & Webb, L. M. (2004). The influence of language brokering on Hispanic teen-agers' acculturation, academic performance, and nonverbal decoding skills: A preliminary study. *Howard Journal of Communications, 15*(1), 1–19. doi:10.1080/10646170490275459

Adams, G. R. (1983). Social competence during adolescence: Social sensitivity, locus of control, empathy, and peer popularity. *Journal of Youth and Adolescence, 12*, 203–211.

Albert, I., Ferring, D., & Michels, T. (2013). Intergenerational family relations in Lux-embourg: Family values and intergenerational solidarity in Portuguese immigrant and Luxembourgish families. *European Psychologist, 18*(1), 59–69. doi:10.1027/1016–9040/a000125

Aldridge, J. (2006). The experiences of children living with and caring for parents with mental illness. *Child Abuse Review, 15*(2), 79–88. doi:10.1002/car.904

Aneshensel, C. S., & Gore, S. (1991). *Development, stress, and role restructuring: Social transitions in adolescence.* New York, NY: Plenum Press.

Bauer, E. (2016). Practising kinship care: Children as language brokers in migrant families. *Childhood 23*(1), 22–36. doi: 10.1177/0907568215574917

Belsky, J. (1984). The determinants of parenting: A process model. *Child Development, 55*(1), 83–96. doi:10.2307/1129836

Belsky, J. (2014). Social-contextual determinants of parenting. Encyclopedia on Early Childhood Development. Retrieved from http://www.child-encyclopedia.com web-site: http://www.child-encyclopedia.com/parenting-skills/according-experts

Berry, J. W., Phinney, J. S., Sam, D. L., & Vedder, P. (2006). *Immigrant youth in cultural transi-tion: Acculturation, identity, and adaptation across national contexts.* Mahwah, NJ: Lawrence Erlbaum.

Berry, J. W., Poortinga, Y. H., Segall, M. H., & Dasen, P. R. (2002). *Cross-cultural psychology: Research and applications* (2nd ed.). New York, NY: Cambridge University Press.

Buriel, R., Love, J. A., & DeMent, T. L. (2006). The relationship of language brokering to depression and parent-child bonding among Latino adolescents. In M. H. Bornstein & L. R. Cote (Eds.), *Acculturation and parent-child relationships: Measurement and development* (pp. 249–270). Mahwah, NJ: Lawrence Erlbaum.

Buriel, R., Perez, W., DeMent, T. L., Chavez, D. V., & Moran, V. R. (1998). The relation-ship of language brokering to academic performance, biculturalism, and self-efficacy among Latino adolescents. *Hispanic Journal of Behavioral Sciences, 20*(3), 283–297. doi:10.1177/07399863980203001

Chao, R. K. (2006). The prevalence and consequences of adolescents' language brokering for their immigrant parents. In M. H. Bornstein & L. R. Cote (Eds.), *Acculturation and parent-child relationships: Measurement and development* (pp. 271–296). Mahwah, NJ: Law-rence Erlbaum.

Corby, B. C., Hodges, E. V. E., & Perry, D. G. (2007). Gender identity and adjustment in black, Hispanic, and white preadolescents. *Developmental Psychology, 43*(1), 261–266. doi:10.1037/0012–1649.43.1.261

Crouter, A. C., Head, M. R., Bumpus, M. F., & McHale, S. M. (2001). Household chores: Under what conditions do mothers lean on daughters? In A. Fuligni (Ed.), *Family assis-tance and obligation during adolescence: New directions in child development* (pp. 23–41). San Francisco: Jossey-Bass. doi:10.1002/cd.29

Dietz, B. (2003). Post-Soviet youth in Germany: Group formation, values and attitudes of a new immigrant generation. In T. Horowitz, B. Kotik-Friedgut, & S. Hoffman (Eds.), *From pacesetters to dropouts: Post-Soviet youth in comparative perspective* (pp. 253–271). Lan-ham, MD: University Press of America.

Dorner, L. M., Orellana, M. F., & Jiménez, R. (2008). "It's one of those things that you do to help the family:" Language brokering and the development of immigrant adolescents. *Journal of Adolescent Research, 23*(5), 515–543. doi:10.1177/0743558408317563

Dubas, J. S., & Gerris, J. R. M. (2002). Longitudinal changes in the time parents spend in activities with their adolescent children as a function of child age, pubertal status and gender. *Journal of Family Psychology, 16*(4), 415–426. doi:10.1037/0893–3200.16.4.415

East, P. L. (2010). Children's provision of family caregiving: Benefit or burden? *Child Development Perspectives, 4*(1), doi:10.1111/j.1750–8606.2009.00118.x

Feldman, S. S., & Wood, D. N. (1994). Parents' expectations for preadolescent sons' behavioral autonomy: A longitudinal study of correlates and outcomes. *Journal of Research on Adolescence, 4*(1), 45–70. doi:10.1207/s15327795jra0401_4

Fuchs, M., Schwietring, T., & Weiss, J. (1999). Leben im Herkunftsland [Live in the heritage country]. In R. K. Silbereisen, E. D. Lantermann, & E. Schmitt-Rodermund (Eds.), *Aussiedler in Deutschland. Akkulturation von Persönlichkeit und Verhalten* (pp. 69–90). Opladen: Leske + Budrich.

Furr, R. M. (2010). The double-entry intraclass correlation as an index of profile similarity: Meaning, limitations, and alternatives. *Journal of Personality Assessment, 92*(1), 1–15. doi:10.1080/00223890903379134

Gager, C. T., Sanchez, L. A., & Demaris, A. (2009). Whose time is it? The effect of employment and work/family stress on children's housework. *Journal of Family Issues, 30*(11), 1459–1485. doi:10.1177/0192513x09336647

Goodman, R. (1997). The strengths and difficulties questionnaire: A research note. *Journal of Child Psychology and Psychiatry, 38*, 581–586.

Granic, I., & Patterson, G. R. (2006). Toward a comprehensive model of antisocial development: A dynamic systems approach. *Psychological Review, 113*(1), 101–131. doi:10.1037/0033–295x.113.1.101

Hazuda, H. P., Stern, M. P., & Haffner, S. M. (1988). Acculturation and assimilation among Mexican Americans: Scales and population-based data. *Social Science Quarterly, 69*, 687–706.

Hooper, L. M., Marotta, S. A., & Lanthier, R. P. (2008). Predictors of growth and distress following childhood parentification: A retrospective exploratory study. *Journal of Child and Family Studies, 17*(5), 693–705. doi:10.1007/s10826-007-9184-8

Jones, C. J., & Trickett, E. J. (2005). Immigrant adolescents behaving as culture brokers: A study of families from the former Soviet Union. *The Journal of Social Psychology, 145*(4), 405–428. doi:10.3200/SOCP.145.4.405–428

Jones, C. J., Trickett, E. J., & Birman, D. (2012). Determinants and consequences of child culture brokering in families from the former Soviet Union. *American Journal of Community Psychology, 50*(1–2), 182–196. doi:10.1007/s10464-012-9488-8

Jurkovic, G. J. (1997). *Lost childhoods: The plight of the parentified child.* New York, NY: Brunner Mazel.

Jurkovic, G. J., & Thirkield, A. (1998). *Parentification questionnaire.* tlanta, GA: G. J. Jurkovic, Department of Psychology, Georgia State University, University Plaza.

Jurkovic, G. J., Thirkield, A., & Morrell, R. (2001). Parentification of adult children of divorce: A multidimensional analysis. *Journal of Youth and Adolescence, 30*(2), 245–257. doi:10.1023/A:1010349925974

Kerr, M., & Stattin, H. (2000). What parents know, how they know it, and several forms of adolescent adjustment: Further support for a reinterpretation of monitoring. *Developmental Psychology, 36*(3), 366–380.

Kerr, M., Stattin, H., & Burk, W. J. (2010). A reinterpretation of parental monitoring in longitudinal perspective. *Journal of Research on Adolescence, 20*(1), 39–64. doi:10.1111/j.1532–7795.2009.00623.x

Kiang, L., & Fuligni, A. J. (2009). Ethnic identity and family processes among adolescents from Latin American, Asian, and European backgrounds. *Journal of Youth and Adolescence, 38*(2), 228–241. doi:10.1007/s10964-008-9353-0

Lazarevic, V., Raffaelli, M., & Wiley, A. (2014). Language and non-linguistic brokering: Diversity of experiences of immigrant young adults from Eastern Europe. *Journal of Comparative Family Studies, 45*(4), 517–535.

Locke, H. J., & Wallace, K. M. (1959). Short marital adjustment and prediction tests: Their reliability and validity. *Marriage and Family Living, 21*(3), 251–255. doi:19.2307/348022

Love, J. A., & Buriel, R. (2007). Language brokering, autonomy, parent-child bonding, biculturalism, and depression: A study of Mexican American adolescents from immigrant families. *Hispanic Journal of Behavioral Sciences, 29*(4), 472–491. doi:10.1177/073998 6307307229

Luciana, M., Collins, P. F., Olson, E. A., & Schissel, A. M. (2009). Tower of London performance in healthy adolescents: The development of planning skills and associations with self-reported inattention and impulsivity. *Developmental Neuropsychology, 34*(4), 461–475. doi:10.1080/87565640902964540

Martinez, C. R., McClure, H. H., & Eddy, J. M. (2009). Language brokering contexts and behavioral and emotional adjustment among Latino parents and adolescents. *The Journal of Early Adolescence, 29*(1), 71–98. doi:10.1177/0272431608324477

Michel, A., Titzmann, P. F., & Silbereisen, R. K. (2012). Psychological adaptation of adolescent immigrants from the former Soviet Union in Germany: Acculturation versus age-related time trends. *Journal of Cross-Cultural Psychology, 43*(1), 59–76. doi:10.1177/0022022111416662

Mika, P., Bergner, R. M., & Baum, M. C. (1987). The development of a scale for the assessment of parentification. *Family Therapy, 14*(3), 229–235.

Moore, T., McArthur, M., & Noble-Carr, D. (2011). Different but the same? Exploring the experiences of young people caring for a parent with an alcohol or other drug issue. *Journal of Youth Studies, 14*(2), 161–177. doi:10.1080/13676261.2010.522561

Morales, A., & Hanson, W. E. (2005). Language brokering: An integrative review of the literature. *Hispanic Journal of Behavioral Sciences, 27*(4), 471–503. doi:10.1177/0739986305281333

Orellana, M. F. (2003). Responsibilities of children in Latino immigrant homes. *New Directions for Youth Development, 100*, 25–39. doi:10.1002/yd.61

Oznobishin, O., & Kurman, J. (2009). Parent–child role reversal and psychological adjustment among immigrant youth in Israel. *Journal of Family Psychology, 23*(3), 405–415. doi:10.1037/a0015811

Pease-Alvarez, L. (2002). Moving beyond linear trajectories of language shift and bilingual language socialization. *Hispanic Journal of Behavioral Sciences, 24*(2), 114–137. doi:10.1177/ 0739986302024002002

Portes, A. (1997). Immigration theory for a new century: Some problems and opportunities. *International Migration Review, 31*(4), 799–825.

Puig, M. E. (2002). The adultification of refugee children. *Journal of Human Behavior in the Social Environment, 5*(3–4), 85–95. doi:10.1300/J137v05n03_05

Redfield, R., Linton, R., & Herskovits, M. J. (1936). Memorandum for the study of acculturation. *American Anthropologist, 38*, 149–152.

Roche, K., Lambert, S., Ghazarian, S., & Little, T. (2015). Adolescent language brokering in diverse contexts: Associations with parenting and parent–youth relationships in a new immigrant destination area. *Journal of Youth and Adolescence, 44*(1), 77–89. doi:10.1007/ s10964-014-0154-3

Schulz, S., Titzmann, P. F., & Michel, A. (2013). Jugendliche Übersetzer: Language Brokering in russischen Migrantenfamilien in Deutschland [Adolescent translators: Language brokering in Russian immigrant families in Germany]. *Zeitschrift für Entwicklungspsychologie und Pädagogische Psychologie, 45*(3), 161–171. doi:10.1026/0049–8637/a000087

Schwarzer, R., & Jerusalem, M. (1993). Cross-cultural self-efficacy research: Adaptations of the generalized self-efficacy scale. In R. Schwarzer (Ed.), *Measurement of perceived self-efficacy* (pp. 13–22). Berlin: Freie Universität.

Slonim-Nevo, V., Mirsky, J., Rubinstein, L., & Nauck, B. (2009). The impact of familial and environmental factors on the adjustment of immigrants: A longitudinal study. *Journal of Family Issues, 30*(1), 92–123. doi:10.1177/0192513X08324575

Stattin, H., & Kerr, M. (2000). Parental monitoring: A reinterpretation. *Child Development, 71*(4), 1072–1085. doi:10.1111/1467–8624.00210

Steinberg, L., & Silverberg, S. B. (1986). The vicissitudes of autonomy in early adolescence. *Child Development, 57*(4), 841–851. doi:10.2307/1130361

Tajima, E. A., & Harachi, T. W. (2010). Parenting beliefs and physical discipline practices among Southeast Asian immigrants: Parenting in the context of cultural adaptation to the United States. *Journal of Cross-Cultural Psychology, 41*(2), 212–235. doi:10.1177/0022022109354469

Telzer, E. H. (2010). Expanding the acculturation gap-distress model: An integrative review of research. *Human Development, 53*(6), 313–340.

Titzmann, P. F. (2012). Growing up too soon? Parentification among immigrant and native adolescents in Germany. *Journal of Youth and Adolescence, 41*(7), 880–893. doi:10.1007/s10964-011-9711-1

Titzmann, P. F., Gniewosz, B., & Michel, A. (2015). Two sides of a story: Mothers' and adolescents' agreement on child disclosure in immigrant and native families. *Journal of Youth and Adolescence, 44*(1), 155–169. doi:10.1007/s10964-013-0077-4

Titzmann, P. F., & Jugert, P. (2015). Acculturation in context: The moderating effects of immigrant and native peer orientations on the acculturation experiences of Immigrants. *Journal of Youth and Adolescence, 44*(11), 2079–2094. doi:10.1007/s10964-015-0314-0

Titzmann, P. F., & Silbereisen, R. K. (2012). Acculturation or development? Autonomy expectations among ethnic German immigrant adolescents and their native German agemates. *Child Development, 83*(5), 1640–1654. doi:10.1111/j.1467–8624.2012.01799.x

Titzmann, P. F., Silbereisen, R. K., & Mesch, G. (2014). Minor delinquency and immigration: A longitudinal study among male adolescents. *Developmental Psychology, 50*(1), 271–282. doi:10.1037/a0032666

Torney-Purta, J., Barber, C. H., & Wilkenfeld, B. (2006). Latino adolescents' civic development in the United States: Research results from the IEA civic education study. *Journal of Youth and Adolescence, 36*(2), 111–125. doi:10.1007/s10964–006–9121-y

Trickett, E. J., & Jones, C. J. (2007). Adolescent culture brokering and family functioning: A study of families from Vietnam. *Cultural Diversity and Ethnic Minority Psychology, 13*(2), 143–150. doi:10.1037/1099–9809.13.2.143

Tseng, V., & Fuligni, A. J. (2000). Parent-adolescent language use and relationships among immigrant families with East Asian, Filipino, and Latin American backgrounds. *Journal of Marriage and Family, 62*(2), 465–476.

Tsuda, T. (2009). *Diasporic homecomings: Ethnic return migration in comparative perspective.* Stanford, CA: Stanford University Press.

Valdés, G., Chávez, C., & Angelelli, C. (2003). A performance team: Young interpreters and their parents. In G. Valdés (Ed.), *Expanding definitions of giftedness: The case of young interpreters from immigrant communities* (pp. 63–97). Mahwah, NJ: Lawrence Erlbaum.

Villanueva, C. M., & Buriel, R. (2010). Speaking on behalf of others: A qualitative study of the perceptions and feelings of adolescent Latina language brokers. *Journal of Social Issues, 66*(1), 197–210. doi:10.1111/j.1540–4560.2009.01640.x

Weingrod, A., & Levy, A. (2006). Social thought and commentary: Paradoxes of homecoming: The Jews and their diasporas. *Anthropological Quarterly, 79*(4), 691–716.

Weisskirch, R. S. (2007). Feelings about language brokering and family relations among Mexican American early adolescents. *The Journal of Early Adolescence, 27*(4), 545–561. doi:10.1177/0272431607302935

Weisskirch, R. S., & Alva, S. A. (2002). Language brokering and the acculturation of Latino children. *Hispanic Journal of Behavioral Sciences, 24*(3), 369–378. doi:10.1177/0739986302024003007

Wilkinson-Lee, A. M., Zhang, Q., Nuno, V. L., & Wilhelm, M. S. (2011). Adolescent emotional distress: The role of family obligations and school connectedness. *Journal of Youth and Adolescence, 40*(2), 221–230. doi:10.1007/s10964-009-9494-9

Williams, K., & Francis, S. (2010). Parentification and psychological adjustment: Locus of control as a moderating variable. *Contemporary Family Therapy, 32*(3), 231–237. doi:10.1007/s10591-010-9123-5

Wu, C., & Chao, R. K. (2011). Intergenerational cultural dissonance in parent–adolescent relationships among Chinese and European Americans. *Developmental Psychology, 47*(2), 493–508. doi:10.1037/a0021063

Wu, N. H., & Kim, S. Y. (2009). Chinese American adolescents' perceptions of the language brokering experience as a sense of burden and sense of efficacy. *Journal of Youth and Adolescence, 38*(5), 703–718. doi:10.1007/s10964-008-9379-3

APPENDIX

Overview of Measures Used and Characteristics of the Immigrant and Native Group

Measure (Source)	Sample Item	Range of Scale	No. of Items (alpha-reliability)
Family Obligations			
Language brokering (Weisskirch & Alva, 2002)	During the last three months, how often have you translated *notes or letters from school* for your parents?	1 (*never*) to 6 (*very frequently*)	11 (.93)
Adolescent positive attitude towards language brokering (Weisskirch & Alva, 2002; Wu & Kim, 2009)	I feel good about myself when I translate for others.	1 (*does not apply*) to 6 (*does apply*)	8 (.80)
Emotional parentification (based on Jurkovic & Thirkield, 1998; Mika, Bergner, & Baum, 1987)	I consoled one or both of my parents when they were distressed.	1 (*does not apply*) to 6 (*does apply*)	5 (.70)
Instrumental parentification (based on Jurkovic & Thirkield, 1998; Mika et al., 1987)	My parent(s) discussed their financial issues and problems with me.	1 (*does not apply*) to 6 (*does apply*)	5 (.69)
Acculturation-Related Variables			
Maternal competence in German (Hazuda, Stern, & Haffner, 1988)	How well do you *understand* German?	1 (*not at all*) to 4 (*very good*)	4 (.77)

Measure (Source)	Sample Item	Range of Scale	No. of Items (alpha-reliability)
Adolescent competence in German (Hazuda et al., 1988)	How well do you *speak* German?	1 (*not at all*) to 4 (*very good*)	4 (.75)
Adolescent competence in Russian (Hazuda et al., 1988)	How well do you *understand* Russian?	1 (*not at all*) to 4 (*very good*)	4 (.84)
Variables Related to the Family Environment			
Maternal self-efficacy (Schwarzer & Jerusalem, 1993)	I can always manage to solve difficult problems if I try hard enough.	1 (*does not apply*) to 6 (*does apply*)	4 (.75)
Parental partnership dissatisfaction (Locke & Wallace, 1959)	My partner and I had a fight.	1 (*never*) to 6 (*very frequently*)	3 (.73)
Adolescent autonomy (based on Steinberg & Silverberg, 1986)	It's better for kids to go to their best friend than to their parents for advice on some things.	1 (*completely disagree*) to 6 (*completely agree*)	5 (.74)
Intra-familial processes			
Child disclosure (adolescent report; Kerr & Stattin, 2000)	Do you hide a lot from your parents about what you do during nights and weekends?	1 (*no, never*) to 6 (*yes, all the time*)	5 (.74)
Child disclosure (mother report; Kerr & Stattin, 2000)	Does your child hide a lot from you about what he/she does during nights and weekends?	1 (*no, never*) to 6 (*yes, all the time*)	5 (.68)
Psychological Adaptation			
Internalizing Problems (Schulz et al., 2013)	Depressive symptoms (e.g., I feel unhappy, sad or depressed.)	1 (*does not apply*) to 6 (*does apply*)	9 (.92)
	Feelings of exhaustion (e.g., I feel that I cannot cope with the many tasks I have to do.)	1 (*do not agree at all*) to 4 (*fully agree*)	10 (.88)
	Difficulties relaxing (e.g., Even on holidays I do not relax enough.)	1 (*completely disagree*) to 4 (*fully agree*)	8 (.91)
Externalizing behavior in childhood (retrospective, mother report; Goodman, 1997)	At the age of 6 or 7 years, my child often lost his/her temper.	1 (*does not apply*) to 6 (*does apply*)	5 (.56)

5

UNDERSTANDING LANGUAGE BROKERING AND SELF-PERCEPTIONS AMONG YOUNG IMMIGRANTS FROM THE FORMER SOVIET UNION IN ISRAEL

Olga Oznobishin and Jenny Kurman

Introduction

Immigrant children and adolescents often acquire the new language faster and accept the new norms and values more easily than their parents, so that the parents turn to them for assistance in understanding the new language, practices, and mores. Consequently, children often become language and culture brokers for their parents. Language brokering extends beyond face-to-face communication and may include translation and interpretation of a variety of documents, such as financial statements, medical forms, and welfare applications (Orellana, Reynolds, Dorner, & Meza, 2003). Language brokers are often involved in complex and delicate adult interactions, such as negotiating purchases, relaying sensitive medical information, and acting as "advocates" for their parents (Buriel, Perez, DeMent, Chavez, & Moran, 1998; Valenzuela, 1999). This phenomenon has been commonly found in immigrant families; however, previous research has been inconsistent concerning the effects of the language brokering role on the psychological health of language brokers and on their relationships with their parents. The aim of the present research was to investigate the relations among language brokering experiences, perceptions of parental competence, perceived pressure to assimilate into the new society, and feelings of self-efficacy and self-esteem among immigrant adolescents and young adults in Israel.

Correlates of Language Brokering

Researchers are still debating whether language brokering has positive or negative consequences for children's and adolescents' psychological development. Some propose that as a result of their interactions with adults and professionals, language brokers may develop more mature interpersonal skills and decision-making abilities as well as a sense of personal empowerment or self-efficacy. In support, several studies have reported that language brokers feel proud and believe that brokering enhances their independence and maturity as well as feelings of self-efficacy and self-esteem (McQuillan & Tse, 1995). Other studies have demonstrated quite the opposite. For instance, some adolescents reported feeling frustrated, nervous, embarrassed, and burdened when language brokering (Morales, Yakushko, & Castro, 2012). Furthermore, among adolescents from the former Soviet Union (FSU) in Israel, frequency of language brokering correlated with low self-efficacy and low self-esteem (Oznobishin & Kurman, 2009). Some researchers (e.g., Suarez-Orozco & Suarez-Orozco, 2001; Umaña-Taylor, 2003) have suggested that when the child communicates on behalf of and speaks for the parent, he or she gains power and the authority position of the parent may be suppressed as the parent becomes somewhat dependent on the child. Indeed, several studies have found more frequent language brokering associated with greater family conflict and lower levels of parenting effectiveness (Jones, Trickett, & Birman, 2012; Martinez, McClure, & Eddy, 2009).

The type of feelings and emotions youth experience when language brokering may explain such mixed results. On the one hand, dealing with broader responsibilities and adult issues may instill confidence and self-esteem, but only as long as the young person feels positively about having these responsibilities. Negative feelings toward the responsibilities, on the other hand, may result in family conflicts and problems in self-perception. In support of this assumption, in a study on language brokering among Latino/a adolescents, positive emotions when language brokering (e.g., proud and useful) were positively correlated with self-esteem, whereas negative feelings (e.g., nervous or uncomfortable) were negatively correlated with self-esteem (Weisskirch, 2007). Thus, it may be important to consider not only the frequency of language brokering but also its emotional component, which may also relate to emotional and psychological well-being.

In a study on FSU adolescents in Israel, language brokering was associated with feelings of burden when brokering for parents (Oznobishin, 2014). In contrast, Weisskirch (2013) found no significant association between language brokering frequency and feelings of burden among Mexican American emerging adults. Moreover, language brokering and feelings of language brokering efficacy were associated positively in the Mexican American adolescent sample. In the present research, we aimed at investigating which factors may be associated with negative experiences of language brokering among FSU young immigrants (adolescents and emerging adults) in Israel.

Given that most brokering activities are for parents, emotions associated with language brokering may reflect the dynamics in the parent-child relationships. For instance, if the parent is perceived as supportive and competent by the child, the outcomes may be different than for a child who perceives the opposite. Indeed, previous studies have shown that familial environments may facilitate or complicate the language brokering situation. Close relations with parents were found to be associated with child language brokers' feelings of self-efficacy and satisfaction in language brokering (Buriel, Love, & DeMent, 2006; Wu & Kim, 2009), whereas problematic family relations and negative parental practices predicted higher language brokering burden (Weisskirch, 2007, 2013). Emotional experiences of language brokering may also be influenced by the attitudes of the host society. That is, the experience may differ based on whether brokering for the parent is socially acceptable and encouraged by the society. We conducted two studies to examine the relations of both the frequency and the experience of language brokering with parental competence (Study 1) and pressure to assimilate into the new country (Study 2) as perceived by the FSU young immigrants in Israel.

Immigrants From the FSU in Israel

The FSU immigrant group is the largest immigrant population residing in Israel. Since late 1989, more than 1 million immigrants from the FSU have entered Israel and now constitute more than a fifth of the Jewish population in Israel. Overall, this particular wave of immigrants was motivated more by "push" factors (i.e., a desire to leave the FSU because of economic and social conditions) than by "pull" factors (i.e., an attraction to Israel or the seeking of a homeland; Lemish, 2000). This mass influx of immigrants has several important characteristics that may differentiate it from other waves of immigration around the world. Jewish immigration to Israel is guided by the "ingathering of the exiles" ideology (known in Hebrew as *kibbutz galuiot*) prevailing in Israel, where Jewish newcomers automatically and immediately are granted all the rights of citizenship upon their arrival in Israel. This practice may help to alleviate some of the immigration difficulties; however, at the same time, immigrants are put under great pressure to assimilate rapidly into Israeli society (Horowitz, 1996; Jasinskaja-Lahti, Liebkind, Horenczyk, & Schmitz, 2003).

The FSU immigrant group is unique due to its large percentage of highly educated people and professionals with many years of experience in science, technology, culture, and education (Remennick, 1998). This level of education and concomitant social status may provide long-standing endorsement of the heritage culture and language (Abu-Rabia, 1999). Indeed, a large part of the FSU immigrants, even after many years of living in Israel, indicate being attached to and proud of Russian culture; they continue to speak Russian at home and with their friends, read Russian literature, and expect their children to know the Russian language (Ben-Rafael, Israel, & Konigstein, 2006).

These tendencies are in some contrast with the Israeli pressures toward assimilation: Immigrants are expected to devote maximum efforts to studying Hebrew and to affiliate smoothly and fully with native Israelis at work and school (Horowitz, 1996). This pressure is indeed perceived by FSU immigrants (Roccas, Horenczyk, & Schwartz, 2000), and, as difficult as it is to manage (e.g., Berry, 2007), it may induce children to experience negative attitudes toward language brokering as a consequence. Assimilation pressure may be reflected in negative attitudes of Israelis toward parents who do not learn Hebrew proficiently as well as toward the use of the Russian language in public. Therefore, children may become angry with their parents for not assimilating quickly and making them look like "outsiders," especially in situations of language brokering for their parents.

Another reason for negative attitudes toward language brokering may be a dramatic status decline experienced by parents after immigration, given their relatively high status in the FSU (Remennick, 1998). Thus, parents from the FSU, mostly highly educated people, who were authority figures for their children in their homeland, may negatively experience their dependence on children to translate and speak for them. The frustration of parents may also contribute to a negative atmosphere involved in language brokering.

In compliance with the pressure to learn Hebrew as soon as possible, immigrant children may try to avoid using the Russian language, so that their language competence in Russian may be quite low, especially for those who immigrated at a young age. Thus, when they are required to use their mother tongue, which at some point becomes their second language, they may feel frustrated. Difficulties communicating with parents while translating for them decrease feelings of self-efficacy because the children feel inadequate personally and because their parents are dissatisfied with them (Weisskirch, 2007). Under such circumstances, language brokering in Israel may result in children's feelings of failure and embarrassment, which may be detrimental to their self-perceptions.

In sum, negative emotions and attitudes toward language brokering may be more prevalent in the Israeli context than in other countries. In the present research, we addressed both the familial context and the context of the host society in examining the relations between language brokering and self-perceptions among young immigrants from the FSU in Israel.

Study 1

In this study, we aimed to explore the relations among language brokering, emotional burden, and immigrant adolescents' perceptions of parental competence. We examined whether language brokering is related to a decline in immigrant adolescents' reported trust in parents' authority and competence. Parental competence—the belief that parents can effectively manage parenting tasks—has been found to influence various aspects of child and adolescent adjustment (Jones & Prinz, 2005). A lot of attention has been given to parents' own perceptions of competence in promoting positive and adaptive child development and outcomes (e.g., Coleman & Karraker, 2003). In the present study, we evaluated adolescents' perceptions of their parents' competence by investigating whether language brokering and negative emotions associated with it are related to perceived parental competence. We also investigated how adolescents' experience of language brokering and perceived parental competence relate to their self-perceptions—feelings of self-efficacy and self-esteem.

Our main hypotheses were that (a) a higher frequency of language brokering would be negatively related to perceived parental competence; (b) a lower level of perceived parental competence would be related to language brokering burden; and (c) language brokering burden would be related to negative self-perceptions, whereas perceptions of parental competence would be related to positive self-perceptions.

Method

Participants and Procedure

The sample was comprised of 135 immigrant adolescents from a city in the north of Israel, who immigrated with their parents from the FSU (females = 76, males = 59), aged 15 to 19 years (M = 16.13, SD = .93). Their age at arrival in Israel varied from 1 to 10 years old (M = 3.25, SD = 2.97), and they had been living in Israel from 6 to 17 years (M = 12.98, SD = 3.07). After receiving approval from the Israeli Ministry of Education and school administrations, a member of the research team recruited participants by going to classes and explaining the study to the students. Students participated on a voluntary basis (90% participation rate) and were required to bring signed parental consent forms. The self-report questionnaires were administered during the class. All questionnaires that had no prior Hebrew and/or Russian versions were back-translated by two bilingual speakers of the relevant languages. All participants answered the questionnaires in Hebrew.

Measures

Demographics

Participants reported their age, gender, immigration history, and other personal information.

Language Brokering

The Language Brokering Scale was created on the basis of the scales assessing translation among immigrant adolescents in the United States (e.g., Weisskirch, 2007; Wu & Kim, 2009). The scale included two parts. The first part referred to language brokering activities (12 items; e.g., "I translate conversations in the government offices for my parents"). Participants were requested to rate how much each item is true for them on a 5-point scale (1 = *not at all* to 5 = *very much*). In the second part, participants rated their level of agreement with five items referring to emotional burden associated with translation:"Translating is stressful";"Translating is a kind of burden (something that I prefer not to do)"; "The time that I spend translating comes at the expense of other things I prefer to do"; "I feel pressure to translate for my parents"; "When my parents ask me to translate, I feel uncomfortable." In the current sample, Cronbach's alphas were .91 for language brokering and .70 for the language brokering burden.

Perceived Parental Competence

The Perceived Parental Competence Scale was formulated for the purpose of the present study by adapting items from the Self-Efficacy Scale (Schwarzer & Jerusalem, 1995) and the Efficacy Scale from the Parenting Sense of Competence (PSOC; Gibaud-Wallston & Wandersman, 1978). The items were re-written so that adolescents could complete the measure referring to the way they perceive their parents. The adapted measure included 10 items (e.g., "My parent can deal with unexpected events"), which were answered on a 5-point scale (1 = *strongly agree* to 5 = *strongly disagree*), with higher scores indicating greater perceived parental competence. Cronbach's alpha was .82 in the current sample. Two aspects of adolescents' self-perception were assessed:

Self-Perceptions
   Self-efficacy was measured by the 10-item General Self-Efficacy Scale (Schwarzer & Jerusalem, 1995). Participants rated statements, such as "I'll always be able to solve difficult problems if I try hard enough," using a 5-point scale (1 = *not at all true* to 5 = *exactly true*), with higher scores indicating greater feelings of self-efficacy. Cronbach's alpha was .91.
   Self-esteem was assessed by the Rosenberg Self-Esteem Scale (1965). Participants rated 10 items—five positive (e.g., "Overall, I'm pleased with myself") and five negative (e.g., "I tend to think that I'm a failure"), with a 5-point scale (1 = *strongly disagree* to 5 = *strongly agree*). The total self-esteem score is obtained by summing the reversed scores of the negatively worded items and the remaining items. Cronbach's alpha was .88 for this measure.

Results and Discussion

We began by assessing if there were any demographic differences among the variables of interest. Gender comparisons for the frequency of language brokering, language brokering burden, perceived parental competence, and self-perceptions revealed a multivariate significant effect, Hotelling's $T = .19$, $F(5, 129) = 3.45$, $p < .01$, $\eta^2_p = .16$, resulting from one significant univariate difference in the frequency of language brokering, $F(1, 133) = 4.17$, $p < .05$, $\eta^2_p = .04$, with females ($M = 2.69$, $SD = 1.32$) scoring higher than males ($M = 2.19$, $SD = 1.00$). No other significant univariate effect for gender was found. Language brokering frequency was positively related to adolescents' age ($r = .28$, $p < .01$), indicating that in this sample, the older adolescents were, the more frequently they language brokered for their parents. Therefore, adolescents' age and gender were included in the main analyses as covariates.

To test the hypotheses regarding associations among language brokering, a sense of burden, and perceived parental competence, we first calculated Pearson correlations for the relevant variables. Table 5.1 presents these correlations as well as the mean scores and standard deviations of all main study variables. As expected, language brokering and perceived parental competence were significantly associated in the negative direction. These findings support our first hypothesis that parental reliance on their children as translators and interpreters may diminish their competence in the eyes of their child.

Next, we conducted a three-step hierarchical regression analysis to predict a sense of burden by language brokering frequency and perceived parental competence, controlling for age and gender (see Table 5.2). The frequency of language brokering significantly predicted language brokering burden. Perceived parental competence was negatively associated with language brokering burden and contributed

TABLE 5.1 Means, Standard Deviations, and Correlations Among Study 1 Variables

Variable	M (SD)	1	2	3	4
1. Language brokering frequency	2.49 (1.22)				
2. Language brokering burden	2.14 (.79)	.40***			
3. Perceived parental competence	4.11 (.55)	−.28**	−.28**		
4. Self-efficacy	3.61 (.64)	−.20*	−.20*	.29**	
5. Self-esteem	3.91 (.85)	−.10	−.20*	.38***	.60***

Note: N = 135. *p < .05, **p < .01, ***p < .001.

TABLE 5.2 Prediction of Language Brokering Burden by Perceived Parental Competence

	Language brokering burden		
	β	ΔR^2	F_{change}
Step 1		.01	.79
Age	−.03		
Gender	−.10		
Step 2		.11	14.91***
Age	−.10		
Gender	−.15		
Language brokering frequency	.34***		
Step 3		.03	4.26*
Age	−.08		
Gender	−.16		
Language brokering frequency	.31**		
Perceived parental competence	−.18*		
R^2		.15	

Note: N = 135. *p < .05, **p < .01, ***p < .001.

significantly to the explained variance (see Step 3 in Table 5.2). Accordingly, it seems that low perceived parental competence is related to high emotional burden when language brokering, which supports our second hypothesis.

It is worth noting that language brokering frequency was positively related to negative emotions by both simple correlations and regression analysis. These findings suggest that higher frequency of language brokering may be associated with feelings of burden and embarrassment, confirming the previous findings that FSU young immigrants feel burdened by their brokering role (Oznobishin, 2014).

To test the third hypothesis that emotional reaction to language brokering and perceived parental competence predict adolescents' self-efficacy and self-esteem, four-step hierarchical regressions were computed. In the first step, demographic indicators (i.e., age and gender) were entered as predictors. Language brokering frequency was added in the second step. In the third step, language brokering burden was added. To examine the unique contribution of perceived parental competence to prediction of self-perceptions, perceived parental competence was entered in the fourth step. The results are presented in Table 5.3.

Overall, as hypothesized, perceived parental competence and language brokering burden were predictive of self-perceptions. Feelings of burden predicted low

TABLE 5.3 Prediction of Self-Efficacy and Self-Esteem by Language Brokering, Language Brokering Burden, and Perceived Parental Competence

	Self-Efficacy			Self-Esteem		
	β	ΔR^2	F_{change}	β	ΔR^2	F_{change}
Step 1		.03	1.90		.10	7.33**
Age	.09			.16		
Gender#	−.16			−.31***		
Step 2		.004	.56		.0001	.0001
Age	.11			.16		
Gender	−.15			−.31***		
Language brokering frequency	−.07			−.001		
Step 3		.02	2.55		.03	3.87*
Age	.09			.14		
Gender	−.18			−.34***		
Language brokering frequency	−.02			.06		
Language brokering burden	−.15			−.18*		
Step 4		.06	8.14**		.10	16.49***
Age	.07			.11		
Gender	−.16			−.31***		
Language brokering frequency	.01			−.10		
Language brokering burden	−.10			−.11		
Perceived parental competence	.25**			.33***		
R^2		.11			.20	

Note: $N = 135$. *$p < .05$, **$p < .01$, ***$p < .001$.
Gender was measured as a dummy variable: male = 0, female = 1.

self-esteem and were associated with low self-efficacy and self-esteem in the simple correlations. These findings indicate that individuals who feel burdened when language brokering also have negative self-perceptions.

Perceived parental competence was positively related to self-efficacy and self-esteem by both simple correlations and regression analyses. Perceived parental competence accounted for a statistically significant unique proportion of the variance in self-perceptions (see Step 4 in Table 5.3) and emerged as the only predictor of self-efficacy. Moreover, language brokering burden ceased to be a significant predictor of self-esteem when perceived parental competence was added. These findings are in line with the notion that parental competence plays a pivotal role relative to positive individual development and well-being.

Gender was negatively associated with self-esteem, with girls revealing lower self-esteem than boys. It seems that being a boy, a lack of language brokering burden, and high perceived parental competence predict greater feelings of self-esteem.

Study 2

The main purpose of this study was to explore whether emotional experiences of language brokering relate to acculturation expectations from Israeli society as perceived by young immigrant adults. Studies have indicated that although language brokering begins in childhood, it may continue into adulthood (e.g., Weisskirch, Kim, Zamboanga, Schwartz, Bersamin, & Umaña-Taylor, 2011). Emerging adults who started language brokering at a young age may be able to provide a more reflective perspective on their current language brokering experiences. In addition, this study may extend the findings from previous studies on adolescents, which would provide support that the findings are related to the ongoing experience of language brokering and not just indicative of typical changes in parent-child relationships during adolescence.

In this study, acculturation orientations or strategies were conceptualized within the framework of Berry (1997, 2007). This framework presents two main issues facing acculturating individuals. The first of these is how important or valuable it is for the individual to maintain his or her own cultural heritage while living in the host society. The second issue relates to the importance or value of participating in the larger society. However, minority cultural groups are not always free to pursue the acculturation strategy they prefer (Berry, 1997). The prevailing multicultural ideology of a given host society sets the limits and constraints within which immigrants can pursue their own acculturation strategies. The intersection between the maintenance of one's original culture and the willingness to engage in contact with members of the host society creates four acculturation strategies of immigrants, which are also reflected in the expectations held by the host society (Bourhis & Montreuil, 2005): assimilation, segregation, integration, and marginalization. Assimilation refers to an expectation from the immigrants to interact with the new society with no maintenance of their original culture. Segregation is an expectation from the immigrants to maintain their cultural identity while avoiding involvement with others. Integration means acceptance of immigrants both maintaining their cultural identity and being involved with the new society. Marginalization (or exclusion) means that the host society does not accept immigrants' cultural maintenance or interaction with the dominant group.

As mentioned earlier, assimilation pressures prevailing in the Israeli context may be reflected in negative attitudes of Israelis toward parents who do not learn Hebrew or toward the use of Russian in public. This assimilation pressure may result in negative feelings of young immigrants who have to translate for their parents. In addition, in past research, perceived pressure to assimilate correlated negatively with well-being among immigrants from the FSU to Israel (Roccas et al., 2000). In the present study, we investigate whether perceived pressure to assimilate explains a sense of language brokering burden among young FSU immigrants in Israel.

In addition, we examined the relation of perceived assimilation pressure to self-perceptions. When immigrants experience pressure to assimilate, they are likely to understand this pressure as signaling a presumed inferiority, which may affect their well-being; however, negative social identities do not lead inevitably to low self-esteem or to low satisfaction with life (Roccas et al., 2000). Indeed, studies have shown that a majority of stigmatized individuals do not suffer from low self-esteem or life satisfaction, although some do (e.g., Crocker, Major, & Steele, 1998).

We hypothesized that perceived pressure to assimilate would be related to language brokering burden. Relations between assimilation pressure and self-perceptions were tested as an open question.

Method

Participants and Procedure

The sample included 97 immigrants from the FSU in Israel, aged 21 to 34 years ($M = 27.22$, $SD = 3.84$). Seventy-three percent of the participants were female. Participants' age at arrival in Israel varied from 4 to 17 years old ($M = 9.94$, $SD = 3.12$) and they had been living in Israel from 4 to 21 years ($M = 17.28$, $SD = 3.51$). Participants were recruited through an advertisement that was distributed on university campuses. They completed paper and pencil questionnaires on a voluntary basis. All participants responded to the questionnaires in Hebrew.

Measures

Language Brokering

Young adults' language brokering was assessed by the Frequency of Language Brokering question from Wu and Kim (2009). Participants reported their frequency of translating for their parents, using a scale of 1 (*never*) to 5 (*daily*). Language brokering burden was assessed by the same scale that was used in Study 1. Cronbach's alpha of this scale was .85 in the current sample.

Perceived Assimilation Pressure

The Host Community Acculturation Scale (HCAS; Bourhis & Dayan, 2004) and the Immigrant Acculturation Scale (Berry, Kim, Power, Young, & Bujali, 1989) were adapted to assess the four acculturation strategies of the host society: assimilation, segregation, integration, and marginalization. After pilot testing, we chose items concerning six life domains that appeared as most relevant and strong in measuring acculturation strategies in Israel: language, holidays, food, heritage culture, marriage, and housing. For each domain, all four expected acculturation strategies from the host society were rated by the participants (i.e., 24 items in total) on a 5-point scale (1 = *not at all* to 5 = *very much*), with higher scores indicating higher pressure to assimilate. A sample item is "To feel belonging, the Israeli society expects from me to give up on my original language and to speak only in Hebrew." Cronbach's alphas for assimilation, segregation, integration, and marginalization were .83, .85, .58, and .91, respectively.

Self-Perceptions

Self-perceptions were measured by the same questionnaires as in Study 1: the Self-Efficacy Scale (Schwarzer & Jerusalem, 1995) and the Self-Esteem Scale (Rosenberg, 1965). Cronbach's alphas were .89 and .81, respectively.

Results and Discussion

Data were analyzed in three steps. First, the relations between the demographic variables and all studied variables were analyzed. None of the demographic variables (i.e., age, gender, age at immigration, length of residence in Israel) were associated significantly with any studied variable. Second, correlations were computed among all variables in the study to determine if there were associations among the variables of interest. Third, hierarchical regression analyses were computed to examine the relative contribution of perceived assimilation pressure to language brokering burden and to self-perceptions. We conducted the analyses with and without including other perceived acculturation expectations; however, these factors were not significant and did not affect the results.

Table 5.4 presents the correlations, and the mean scores and standard deviations of the studied variables. Similar to Study 1, language brokering frequency was associated with negative emotions, indicating that the more the youth reported translating for their parents, the higher were their feelings of burden.

TABLE 5.4 Means, Standard Deviations, and Correlations Among Study 2 Variables

Variable	M (SD)	1	2	3	4	5	6	7
1. Language brokering frequency	3.83 (1.33)							
2. Language brokering burden	2.46 (1.28)	.35**						
3. Assimilation	2.55 (1.02)	.17	.31**					
4. Segregation	1.64 (.74)	.22*	.16	.32**				
5. Integration	2.95 (.80)	−.22*	−.15	−.01	−.10			
6. Marginalization	1.49 (.78)	.16	.17	.15	.38***	−.23*		
7. Self-efficacy	3.11 (.44)	−.01	−.22*	−.06	−.17	.03	−.26*	
8. Self-esteem	3.34 (.41)	−.13	−.30**	−.13	−.34**	.08	−.28**	.46***

Note: $N = 97$. *$p < .05$, **$p < .01$, ***$p < .001$.

TABLE 5.5 Prediction of Language Brokering Burden by Assimilation Pressure

	Language Brokering Burden		
	β	ΔR^2	F_{change}
Step 1		.04	1.96
Age	−.19		
Gender[#]	−.07		
Step 2		.02	1.52
Age	−.20		
Gender	−.06		
Language brokering frequency	.13		
Step 3		.07	6.91*
Age	−.18		
Gender	−.08		
Language brokering frequency	.08		
Assimilation pressure	.26*		
R^2		.13	

Note: $N = 97$. *$p < .05$, **$p < .01$, ***$p < .001$.

Gender was measured as a dummy variable: male = 0, female = 1.

Negative emotions when language brokering, in turn, were associated with perceived assimilation pressure and were predicted only by the assimilation pressure in the regression analysis (see Table 5.5). These findings support our hypothesis and suggest that children may negatively experience brokering activities when they are forced to be involved in cross-cultural transactions between their parents and the larger society when the society reacts negatively to parents' lack of assimilation.

As seen in Table 5.4, language brokering frequency associated positively with perceived segregation expectation and negatively with integration. In a way, this finding corresponds to the previous findings that have linked language brokering frequency with ethnic identity or heritage culture values, claiming that children who frequently engage in language brokering may demonstrate greater affiliation with cultural values (e.g., Weisskirch et al., 2011). This finding fits the segregation strategy—an orientation toward the "old," and now minority, identity. However, we focused here on perceived expectations from the society and not the strategy preferred by the individual. A speculative explanation is that individuals who perceive a pressure to assimilate may tend to prefer a segregation strategy, because perceived discrimination increases the need for support from one's own ethnic group (Jasinskaja-Lahti et al., 2003). This may result in assimilation discrepancy, when immigrants want to assimilate less than they believe the dominant society expects them to assimilate, which has been found among immigrants from the FSU in Israel (Horenczyk, 1996). The integration strategy includes elements both of assimilation and of segregation, thus, some individuals may experience an integration discrepancy as a pressure to assimilate while others experience it as a pressure to segregate.

It is interesting to note that the prevalent acculturation strategies of the host society as perceived by young immigrants were integration followed by assimilation (the means of expected segregation and marginalization were rather low). These findings may reflect that although Israel has explicitly enforced an assimilation "absorption" strategy for many decades, this approach is slowly being replaced by an integrationist policy similar to other countries (Phinney, Horenczyk, Liebkind, & Vedder, 2001). It seems that this shift is indeed being recognized and experienced by the young immigrants.

As in Study 1, feelings of burden were related to low self-efficacy and self-esteem. Language brokering frequency was not found to be related to self-perceptions. Among acculturation strategies, only marginalization was associated with low self-efficacy and self-esteem in the simple correlations. In the regression analysis, the only significant predictor of self-esteem was negative emotional reaction, $\beta = -.28, p < .01$; the model predicting self-efficacy was not significant, $F(5,91) = 1.60, ns.$

General Discussion

Research on language brokering among immigrant youth has reported both positive and negative emotional and adjustment correlates (Buriel et al., 1998; McQuillan & Tse, 1995; Oznobishin & Kurman, 2009; Ponizovsky-Bergelson, Kurman, & Roer-Strier, 2015; Weisskirch, 2007). The purpose of the present research was to investigate factors that may explain language brokering experiences and their relations with self-perceptions among young immigrants from the FSU in Israel. We examined factors within parent-child relationships—parental competence, as perceived by immigrant adolescents—and the context of the absorbing society, as reflected by perceived assimilation pressure from the dominant group.

Consistently, parental competence has been found to be an important factor in child development (Jones & Prinz, 2005); however, previous studies have mostly referred to parents' own perceptions. In this study, we addressed the perceptions of the adolescents regarding their parents' competence. The present findings support that perceived parental competence plays an important role in young immigrants' experiences of language brokering. Moreover, perceived parental competence contributes to adolescents' feelings of self-efficacy and self-esteem above and beyond emotional reactions to language brokering.

It is important to note that among both age groups studied in the present research—immigrant adolescents and young adults—the frequency of language brokering was related to negative emotions. These findings suggest that a frequent amount of language brokering may lead to feelings of burden, frustration, and embarrassment for FSU immigrant youth in Israel.

One of the major and innovative findings of the present research is the relation between perceived pressure to assimilate into the new society and negative emotions toward language brokering. Few previous studies have studied the relationship of assimilation pressure and the context of language brokering. These findings expand previous research that has considered family relations as the almost exclusive contributing setting for language brokering experience. In this study, negative emotions toward language brokering were not only related to low perceived parental competence but also to the contextual variable of pressure to assimilate into the new society. This finding may provide a possible explanation for the difference between the negative experience of language brokering and the positive experience sometimes demonstrated among Latino/a and other minority adolescents in the United States and elsewhere (e.g., Weisskirch, 2013).

A pressure to assimilate was related to feelings of burden and resentment when language brokering. It seems, therefore, that perceived acculturation attitudes of the host society toward immigrants are related to emotions associated with language brokering. The finding that language brokering was positively related to perceived segregation expectation from the host society and negatively to integration expectation corroborates the findings that language brokers who are less acculturated report more language brokering (Weisskirch, 2005). It may be that, although assimilation and segregation strategies are supposedly opposite, they are both less adaptive, whereas integration reflects a relative adaptive approach and a feeling of perceived acceptance from the dominant group.

Perceived pressure to assimilate may put a child in the middle of a conflict between the demand to assimilate into Israeli society and the wish from parents to preserve the original language and culture. There is evidence that Israeli society has developed negative stereotypes regarding immigrants from the FSU, related to their efforts to maintain their language and culture (Leshem, 2012). Therefore, children may pay an emotional price for being bilingual as they are subjected to reactions of rejection and mockery when they speak in the Russian language. On one hand, if a child chooses to give up his or her language and culture of origin, this may evolve into conflicts in family dynamics because of the need to broker on behalf of the parents, which, in turn, may result in negative emotions toward language brokering. On the other hand, if a child tries to avoid family conflicts and to preserve the original language and culture, he or she may experience a rejection from Israeli society. In both cases, the child may feel trapped "between a hammer and an anvil" and negatively experience language brokering.

Limitations and Future Directions

Several limitations of the presented studies should be noted. First of all, the studies are cross-sectional in nature, which may not capture the changes that may occur nor directionality of the variables studied. Future research that is longitudinal would help to elucidate how language brokering is experienced by individuals over time. The studies are also focused exclusively on FSU immigrants in Israel; therefore, the results may not generalize to different communities, cultural groups, or immigrant groups. Future cross-cultural research is needed to investigate how a society's pressure to assimilate, or lack thereof, affects the language brokering experience. Further research is needed to identify additional factors that can lead to positive language brokering experiences for immigrant children and adolescents, either within the family or in the context of the absorbing society.

Contribution to Theory

Although language brokering may be problematic for young immigrants' self-perceptions, the most important factors are how they experience this role. As noted in this chapter, perceived decline in parental competence as well as perceived acculturation orientation of the host society—a pressure to assimilate—may lead to negative feelings about language brokering.

The findings are consistent with previous research that has demonstrated the importance of the familial context for the language brokering experience. The studies in this chapter add an additional aspect to immigrant adolescents' relationships with their parents: perceived parental competence. The observed pattern relating negative emotional experience to perceptions of low parental competence may also be understood in terms of the theoretical implications of role reversals within the family. Authority normally reserved for parents may be granted to youth acting as language brokers (Umaña-Taylor, 2003). The risks associated with such role reversals may be particularly salient given the cultural context of the Jewish families in the FSU, where children were not encouraged to be independent, take part in family decisions, or to assume family duties (e.g., Mirsky & Prawer, 2003). Several studies have found that Soviet parents were more dominating and overbearing toward their children in comparison with parents from Western countries (e.g., Tudge, Hogan, Snezhkova, Kulakova, & Etz, 2000). Therefore, a need for language brokering by immigrant children from the FSU in Israel represents a very dramatic shift in their relationships with parents. Youth may regard this need for assistance as an indication of their parents' dependence and vulnerability, which is counter to their culture of origin. A pressure to assimilate into Israeli society may further increase youth's negative experiences of language brokering,

References

Abu-Rabia, S. (1999). Attitudes and psycholinguistic aspects of first language maintenance among Russian-Jewish immigrants in Israel. *Educational Psychology, 19*, 133–148. doi:10.1080/0144341990190202

Ben-Rafael, E., Israel, Y., & Konigstein, M. (2006). The experience of Non-Jewish "Russian" immigrants in Israel. In E. Ben-Rafael, M. Lyubansky, O. Gluckner, P. Harris, Y. Israel, W. Jasper, & J. Schoeps (Eds.), *Building a diaspora: Russian Jews in Israel, Germany, and the USA* (pp. 315–346). Leiden & Boston: Brill.

Berry, J. W. (1997). Immigration, acculturation, and adaptation. *Applied Psychology: An International Review, 46*, 5–68. doi:10.1111/j.1464-0597.1997.tb01087.x

Berry, J. W. (2007). Acculturation strategies and adaptation. In M. H. Bornstein, J. E. Lansford, & K. Deater-Deckard (Eds.), *Immigrant families in contemporary society* (pp. 69–82). New York, NY: Guilford Press.

Berry, J. W., Kim, U., Power, S., Young, M., & Bujali, M. (1989). Acculturation attitudes in plural societies. *Applied Psychology, 38*, 185–206.

Bourhis, R. Y., & Dayan, J. (2004). Acculturation orientations towards Israeli Arabs and Jewish immigrants in Israel. *International Journal of Psychology, 39*, 118–131.

Bourhis, R. Y., & Montreuil, A. (2005). *Some methodological issues related to the Host Community Acculturation Scale (HCAS).* Working Paper, LECRI, Département de Psychologie, Université du Québec à Montréal.

Buriel, R., Love, J. A., & DeMent, T. L. (2006). The relation of language brokering to depression and parent-child bonding among Latino adolescents. In M. H. Bornstein & L. R. Cote (Eds.), *Acculturation and parent-child relationships: Measurement and development* (pp. 249–270). Mahwah, NJ: Lawrence Erlbaum.

Buriel, R., Perez, W., DeMent, T. L., Chavez, D., & Moran, V. R. (1998). The relationship of language brokering to academic performance, biculturalism, and self-efficacy among Latino adolescents. *Hispanic Journal of Behavioral Sciences, 20*, 283–297. doi:10.1177/07399863980203001

Coleman, P. K., & Karraker, K. H. (2003). Maternal self-efficacy beliefs, competence in parenting, and toddlers' behavior and developmental status. *Infant Mental Health Journal, 24*, 126–148. doi:10.1002/imhj.10048

Crocker, J., Major, B., & Steele, C. (1998). Social stigma. In D. Gilbert, S. T. Fiske, & G. Lindzey (Eds.), *Handbook of Social Psychology* (pp. 504–553). Boston, MA: McGraw-Hill.

Gibaud-Wallston, J., & Wandersman, L. P. (1978). Development and validity of the Parenting Sense of Competence Scale. Paper presented at the meeting of the American Psychological Association, Toronto, Ontario.

Horenczyk, G. (1996). Migrating selves in conflict. In G. Breakwell & E. Lyons (Eds.), *Changing European identities* (pp. 241–250). Oxford: Butterworth-Heinemann.

Horowitz, R. T. (1996). Value-oriented parameters in migration policies in the 1990s: The Israeli experience. *International Migration, 34*, 513–537. doi:10.1111/j.1468-2435.1996. tb00543.x

Jasinskaja-Lahti, I., Liebkind, K., Horenczyk, G., & Schmitz, P. (2003). The interactive nature of acculturation: Perceived discrimination, acculturation attitudes and stress among young ethnic repatriates in Finland, Israel and Germany. *International Journal of Intercultural Relations, 27*, 79–97. doi:10.1016/S0147-1767(02)00061-5

Jones, C. J., Trickett, E. J., & Birman, D. (2012). Determinants and consequences of child culture brokering in families from the Former Soviet Union. *American Journal of Community Psychology, 50*, 182–196. doi:10.1007/s10464-012-9488-8

Jones, T. L., & Prinz, R. L. (2005). Potential roles of parental self-efficacy in parent and child adjustment: A review. *Clinical Psychology Review, 25*, 341–363. doi:10.1007/ s10464-012-9488-8

Lemish, D. (2000). The whole and the other: Israeli images of female immigrants from the former USSR. *Gender & Society, 14*, 333–349. doi:10.1177/089124300014002007

Leshem, E. (2012). Russian-speaking immigrants in Israel as a minority group. In D. Soen, S. Ben David & M. Shechory (Eds.) *Minority groups: Coercion, discrimination, exclusion, deviance and the quest for equality* (pp. 113–136). Hauppauge, NY: Nova Science Publishers.

McQuillan, J., & Tse, L. (1995). Child language brokering in linguistic minority communities: Effects on cultural interaction, cognition, and literacy. *Language and Education, 9*, 195–215.

Martinez, C. R., Jr., McClure, H. H., & Eddy, J. M. (2009). Language brokering contexts and behavioral and emotional adjustment among Latino parents and adolescents. *Journal of Early Adolescence, 29*, 71–98. doi:10.1177/0272431608324477

Mirsky, J., & Prawer, L. (2003). Immigrating as an adolescent. In T. Horowitz (Ed.), *Children of Perestroika in Israel* (pp. 72–118). Lanham, MD: University Press of America.

Morales, A., Yakushko, O. F., & Castro, A. J. (2012). Language brokering among Mexican-immigrant families in the Midwest: A multiple case study. *The Counseling Psychologist, 40*, 502–553. doi:10.1177/0011000011417312

Orellana, M. F., Reynolds, J., Dorner, L., & Meza, M. (2003). In other words: Translating or "para-phrasing" as a family literacy practice in immigrant households. *Reading Research Quarterly, 38*, 12–38. doi:10.1598/RRQ.38.1.2

Oznobishin, O. (2014). *Parenting immigrant parents: Role reversal, individuation, self-perception, and parenting representations toward the next generation.* Doctoral dissertation. University of Haifa, Haifa, Israel.

Oznobishin, O., & Kurman, J. (2009). Parent-child role reversal and psychological adjustment among immigrant youth in Israel. *Journal of Family Psychology, 23*, 405–415. doi:10.1037/a0015811

Phinney, J. S., Horenczyk, G., Liebkind, K., & Vedder, P. (2001). Ethnic identity, immigration, and well-being: An interactional perspective. *Journal of Social Issues, 57*, 493–510. doi:10.1111/0022-4537.00225

Ponizovsky-Bergelson, Y., Kurman, J., & Roer-Strier, D. (2015). Immigrants' emotional reactions to filial responsibilities and related psychological outcomes. *International Journal of Intercultural Relations, 45*, 104–115. doi:org/10.1016/j.ijintrel.2015.02.002

Remennick, L. I. (1998). Identity quest among Russian Jews of the 1990's: Before and after emigration. In E. Kraus & G. Tulea (Eds.), *Jewish survival: The identity problem at the close of the twentieth century* (pp. 241–258). New Brunswick & London: Transaction publisher.

Roccas, S., Horenczyk, G., & Schwartz, S. (2000). Acculturation discrepancies and well-being: The moderating role of conformity. *European Journal of Social Psychology, 30*, 323–334. doi:10.1002/(SICI)1099–0992(200005/06)30:3<323::AID-EJSP992>3.0.CO;2–5

Rosenberg, M. (1965). *Society and adolescent self-image*. Princeton, NJ: Princeton University Press.

Schwarzer, R., & Jerusalem, M. (1995). Generalized Self-Efficacy Scale. In J. Weinman, S. Wright, & M. Johnston (Eds.), *Measures in health psychology: A user's portfolio: Causal and control beliefs* (pp. 35–37). Windsor, UK: NFER-NELSON.

Suarez-Orozco, C., & Suarez-Orozco, M. M. (2001). *Children of immigration*. Cambridge, MA & London: Harvard University Press.

Tudge, J. R. H., Hogan, D. M., Snezhkova, I. A., Kulakova, N. N., & Etz, K. E. (2000). Parents' child rearing values and beliefs in the United States and Russia: The impact of culture and social class. *Infant and Child Development*, *9*, 105–121. doi:10.1002/1522-7219 (200006)9:2<105::AID-ICD222>3.0.CO;2-Y

Umaña-Taylor, A. J. (2003). Language brokering as a stressor for immigrant children and their families. In M. Coleman & L. Ganong (Eds.), *Points & counterpoints: Controversial relationship and family issues in the 21st century* (pp. 157–159). Los Angeles, CA: Roxbury.

Valenzuela, A. (1999). Gender roles and settlement activities among children and their immigrant families. *American Behavior Scientist*, *42*, 720–742. doi:10.1177/000276 4299042004009

Weisskirch, R.S. (2005). The relationship of language brokering to ethnic identity for Latino early adolescents. *Hispanic Journal of Behavioral Sciences*, *27*, 286–299. doi:10.1177/0739986305277931

Weisskirch, R. S. (2007). Feelings about language brokering and family relations among Mexican American early adolescents. *Journal of Early Adolescence*, *27*, 545–561. doi:10.1177/0272431607302935

Weisskirch, R. S. (2013). Family relationships, self-esteem, and self-efficacy among language brokering Mexican American emerging adults. *Journal of Child and Family Studies*, *22*, 1147–1155. doi:10.1007/s10826-012-9678-x

Weisskirch, R. S., Kim, S., Zamboanga, B. L., Schwartz, S. J., Bersamin, M., & Umaña-Taylor, A. J. (2011). Cultural influences for college student language brokers. *Cultural Diversity and Ethnic Minority Psychology*, *17*, 43–51. doi:10.1037/a0021665.

Wu, N. H., & Kim, S.Y. (2009). Chinese American adolescents' perceptions of the language brokering experience as a sense of burden and sense of efficacy. *Journal of Youth and Adolescence*, *38*, 703–718. doi:10.1007/s10964-008-9379-3

6

ARAB AMERICANS' BROKERING IN A CONTEXT OF TENSION AND STEREOTYPES

"It's Just a Head-Cover. Get Over It!"

Afaf Nash

Introduction

When people from diverse cultures interact, a language barrier may impede the course of interaction. In addition to language, feelings, perceptions, and knowledge play significant roles in the process of meaning making. This confluence of language, feelings, perceptions, and knowledge is the core context of language brokering. Immigrant groups and ethnic minorities often encounter stereotypes and discrimination, overtly or covertly. When these stereotypes and discrimination are revealed during language brokering, it may burden the language brokers who have to facilitate communication between the two parties in a biased atmosphere. Language brokers are truly bicultural individuals who are exposed to two world views on a daily basis: one by socialization into the heritage culture at home, and another by socialization into the dominant culture through schooling, media, and social life. This unique positioning provides them with transcultural skills (Orellana, 2009) that are helpful in facilitating intense mediating situations. Language brokering then, as a bilingual/bicultural interactional site, is important in its capacity to assist in the study of interplay between the prevailing social and political context with the local familial and heritage context.

Indeed, as a cognitive, cultural, and linguistic practice, language brokering includes a complex set of contexts, contrasted often in many ways. A socio-cognitive approach recognizes that language brokering is a dynamic and reflective process rather than a rigid structure. The socio-cognitive approach helps in the understanding of human behavior in a framework that considers the person and his or her external situations as interdependent with each other to determine a behavior. When working with this approach, attention should be brought to the linguistic, cultural, and sociopolitical matrix within which immigrant children operate during language brokering. Language brokers may have to employ specific strategies when interpreting the realities associated with being from a visible immigrant group. The strategies may differ according to the place where the brokered interaction happens, be it public or private. The linguistic and cultural contexts when language brokering may be particularly salient for young Arab Americans. As Arab Americans, and especially those wearing traditional clothing, language brokers may develop ways to ameliorate overt and covert discriminatory and demeaning interactions in public. In private settings such as the home, language brokers use strategies more responsive to their immediate familial and heritage nature. Before this chapter describes the experiences of Arab American language brokers, the next section explores the historical presence and the current sociopolitical contexts of Arab and Muslim Americans.

Arabs and Muslims on American Soil

Documentation reveals that individuals and small groups of Arabs have been present in North America before the declaration of the United States as a nation (see Orfalea, 2006; Neff, 1993). Sizable waves of inflow, however, did not arrive until the beginning of the 20th century, propelled by political crises in the Arab world, such as the Starvation of Lebanon (1915–1918), the Israel-Palestinian conflict (1948–present), the Lebanon Civil War (1975–1990), the Gulf War (1990–1991), the Invasion of Iraq (2003), and all the wars and political and social unrest that followed until the present. The coverage of these political upheavals and the representations of Arabs in political discourses and news media in association with violence and terrorism have made the Arab and Muslim communities hypervisible. In addition, a long history of offensive and racist profiling of Arabs in Hollywood has contributed a great deal to the negative stereotyping of Arabs (Shaheen, 2012). As a result, individuals in the United States may perceive Arabs as linked to violence and backward in culture. In 2014, the Pew Research Center published a large study about American attitudes towards individuals of different faith. In this study respondents used a scale of 0 to 100 (0 indicating the coldest, most negative rating and 100 the warmest, most positive rating). Muslims scored just 40 (Pew Research Center: Religion & Public Life, 2014). This disfavorable sentiment exists alongside a lack of familiarity with Muslims, as in a separate study, 74% admitted that they never worked with a Muslim and 68% said they never had a Muslim friend (YouGov US, 2015). This negative attitude has perpetuated discrimination and marginalization of Muslims and Arabs. The phenomenon known as *Islamophobia* has become a real-world concern, especially following recent terrorist attacks by fundamentalist groups claiming Islam as their religion. As these lines are being written, there are news reports of threats and attacks on Muslims and mosques across the United States and of political figures calling to ban Muslims from entering the United States. Given this focus, being Arab, speaking Arabic, and looking Arab may be seen in a negative light.

In this chapter, I explore this sociopolitical context as it is manifested during the practice of language brokering. After the methodology section, I will present the experiences of four Arab American language brokers as a sample of language brokering in the Arab American community. An analysis section follows that has two subsection: to one explain the strategies used in public and another to explain the brokering strategies in private settings. Then a concluding section situates the study within the language brokering research. Finally, I discuss how this study contributes to relevant literature, specifically that on Arab communities in the United States.

Methodology

The present study was conducted among Arab Americans in Southern California. Four qualitative interviews were conducted in an in-depth, semi-structured manner. The subjects were undergraduate students participating in an immersion Arabic-language summer program at a university on the west coast of the United States, three females and one male, aged 18 to 22. To solicit participants, program instructors announced the study in their classrooms. A larger number of students volunteered to take part, but eligibility was based on the individual's self-identification as Arab or Arab American and a family interpreter/translator, and the individual needed to consent to record the interview. The final number, four participants, was sufficient for the purpose of this study. The interview locations were chosen by the participants themselves to ensure comfort and privacy. One interview was conducted in a quiet room at the participant's home, whereas the three others took place in an empty classroom during the summer program. All interviews lasted approximately an hour to an hour and a half and were audio-recorded and transcribed by the bilingual, Arabic-speaking researcher. Participants were provided with consent forms to be signed at the outset of the interviews. Participants spoke mostly in English, but occasionally code-switched between Arabic and English. Data were elicited by questions from the interview protocol prepared for the study. The interviews were conducted in a flexible manner that allowed for changes in the order of the questions. The interview protocol contained four thematic sections:

1. Demographics
2. Language brokering experiences
3. Family dynamics
4. Social and political context

The Participants' Experiences

The following sections introduce language brokering narratives and actual statements from the four Arab American college students who participated in the study: Ali, Huda, Leila, and Salma. Pseudonyms were given to participants to protect their identities.

Ali

Ali is a 19-year-old male of Iraqi descent who escaped the Iraqi wars with his family when he was 9 years old, emigrating first to Jordan and then to the United States. He is the second child and the only boy in a family of four children. At the time of the interview, he had just graduated from high school and planned to pursue a career in medicine. Both of Ali's parents hold college degrees from their home country, but they need help with English. Ali translates for both parents, but mostly for the father, in various settings (e.g., home, school, hospital, and shopping areas). When asked who translates the most at home, he emphasized that proficiency in both Arabic and English determined that the task is shared between him and his older sister (and not the two youngest sisters, who do not speak Arabic well) but also depended on availability when brokering is needed. Ali views his language brokering as a positive experience in which he has developed a linguistic and cultural awareness as well as a sense of responsibility toward himself and his family. The difficulty of the task, according to Ali, is of a competence nature, such as "remembering the right word at the right time," rather than fulfilling family needs and expectations. He noted that he was motivated by personal concern:

> I find myself responsible because I am a member [of this family]. I am not just a translator. So, I don't find myself in the middle as an interpreter. I feel they are talking to me. I care about my family and my sisters. I like the responsibility.

In this excerpt, Ali is cognizant that the task positions him in a middle ground between two cultures, yet he clearly aligns himself with his family as a directly engaged party, and not as an impersonal intermediary. This role seems to be understood, and invoked, by all parties involved in the interaction, as he explains in the next narrative. In the next example, Ali explains that he announced his presence as a translator for his parents; however, he noticed that his role gradually changed from a broker to a central interlocutor in a parent-teacher conference that he mediated for his parents about his sister. Notwithstanding that relevant literature often presents language brokers as decision makers in certain brokering situations, Ali's next narrative shows that the role as an immediate participant rather than a translator was invoked by the principal, who recognized Ali as a mature and responsible family member rather than just a mediator:

> I told [the teacher] that I am here to translate for my parents and the talk should be directed to them. But, as we kept talking, I realized that this

was not translation. This was one-to-one conversation. The principal was talking directly to me and taking my opinion. I have to be careful the way I translate, so my parents understand the way I want them to understand. I have to concentrate and tell it the proper way, but I have to be honest too. If the teacher says she's good in this and needs help in that, so that's OK. It's a new school. But I know my parents would be "Oh, my God, she's not good."

This incident invites us further to frame and conceptualize language brokering as a process of triadic interaction, rather than an individualistic achievement. In addition, Ali interprets not only according to his understanding of the heritage culture, but also according to what he believes takes precedence in evaluating his sister's school performance in the new host culture: Well-being is more important than academic progress as his sister adjusts in a new school. Ali here adopts transcultural strategies in which he adds what is needed to convey the message. He adapts a similar brokering method in a doctor's visit when he noticed that members of Arabic culture tend to exaggerate medical diagnoses. He accordingly felt compelled to add his own words to the doctor's statement in order to calm his parents' fears:

The Iraqi people are really scared, frightened of doctors in general, they're just like "Oh, my God, maybe I have cancer." It's like the first thing they think about. I mean the doctor would say, "Maybe you have this or that; all right, it's not a big deal." The Arabs, and especially Iraqis, are so afraid. There's something about hospitals that just frighten them. I've been noticing that for many years. So, when the doctor says something . . . I would start with saying, "It's not that serious," and the doctor didn't say that, but I just have to because, if I don't and translate directly, they would misunderstand [the seriousness of the ailment].

In this example, Ali steps out of his role as a translator, playing instead the role of a cultural mediator. As a cultural broker, he reserves the option to adapt the doctor's speech to what he thinks is a more culturally fitting statement. In doing so, he also plays a role of a protector to save his parents from worrying about their health or their children's acculturation in the host country.

Ali, then, works conscientiously to alter and elaborate utterances to deliver culturally appropriate messages from one language to another. However, when faced with discrimination and stereotypes, he decides to disengage. He explains that what vexes him most is prying "curiosity and weird looks," especially surrounding his mother' appearance as a Muslim clad in a headscarf. He dismisses these intrusions, though, explaining: "I just do not deal with it and focus on the information I have to translate. I mean, get over it, it's a head-cover. What's the big deal?"

Huda

Huda is a 24-year-old Iraqi female, the oldest participant in this study, with the longest experience in language brokering. At the time of the interview, she was working as an Arabic tutor at the university from which she graduated with degrees in Chemistry and in Arabic, and she was preparing to apply for medical school. An American citizen, Huda identifies herself as an Iraqi immigrant, despite the fact that she was born in Libya after her family fled Iraq amid war, and she has never visited her Iraqi homeland. She is the only girl among her parents' four children and the only child who still lives at home (her three older brothers left for university). She recalls translating for her parents on occasion, and, soon after arriving to the United States at the age of 7, becoming their sole interpreter after her brothers moved out. When asked about her interpreting role, she spoke with a sense of commitment, albeit admitting feelings of burden and stress:

> It's a lot of weight on my shoulder, is, like, why I have to do this all the time, you know, but it's, like, you have to, and it's probably more about time. Sometimes, I need my time, like, even if I don't have school, I would like to go somewhere, not a hospital [to interpret].

Despite her busy schedule, Huda realizes the high stakes involved in brokering her mother's medical and health insurance visits, for example, and even goes as far as insisting on accompanying her mother even when restrictions against family interpreters prevail:

> Sometimes, even if my mom doesn't ask, I go with her. Sometimes, I even skip my classes, not very often, but sometimes, I do. I mostly tell her my time so she knows when to make her appointments. I went to all her interviews. That's very important because it's not just to improve her health, but also to improve her medical support. Sometimes, they don't let me translate for her because they want professional translators, but I still go with her and explain to her everything after.

Guided by a sense of confidence in her ability and the authority of an educated and experienced language broker, Huda evaluates the professional interpreter's competence, questioning her qualifications and the linguistic register in which she conducted her job:

> One time, a psychologist had to interview her [my mother]. It's a long time now, but it stuck in my mind, because I was kind of mad at my mom. They had a translator, and she was Arabic, even Iraqi, but she has nothing to do with psychology. Like I took a lot of psychology classes, and I can tell if

something make sense. She rarely translated anything, and she doesn't speak Arabic FusHa [formal Arabic], she speaks dialect.

In this excerpt, Huda expresses disappointment about the translator's choice of language form and competence to mediate so important a meeting. She suggests that communication in a standard, higher register of the language is more appropriate in a setting as formal as a medical evaluation for health coverage eligibility. Huda is also disappointed by the way her mother is treated during medical visits. She believes that her mother's appearance, distinguished as it is by the headscarf, and her lack of proficiency in English are the reasons for the substandard treatment administered during clinical visits. She notices that nurses often perform needed medical procedures, such as measuring blood pressure, without informing her mother what they are about to do. "They just move her sleeves and take her blood pressure," Huda explains. "I know that is not how it should be." Huda calls on the nurses immediately to explain what they are doing. Surprised by Huda's English skills, who also wears the headscarf, the nurses started treating Huda and her mother "with respect," as Huda claimed.

Salma

Salma is a 20-year-old college student who participated in the same Arabic language summer program as Huda. Salma's family is of Palestinian origin, but she was born and raised in Lebanon. Her family emigrated first to South America, where her mother and grandmother acquired proficiency in Spanish, and moved to the United States years later. Salma lives with her grandmother and divorced mother, three brothers, and two uncles. Salma's main language brokering experience was in the service of her grandmother, but also in helping her mother with school-related tasks since, at the interview, the mother had begun college to further her education. Salma has a close relationship with her grandmother, a circumstance that accounts for her grandmother's choice of her as the designated interpreter. "My brothers sometimes offer to take her places, and she's like, "No, it's OK. You have things to do. Salma will go with me." Salma reports being easygoing, and smiling and laughing throughout what seem to be stressful brokering incidents. She describes her grandmother as a strong, conservative, hot-tempered woman with clear religious and political views, who "does not speak a word of English, but [seems to] understand everything, or she thinks she does [laughing]." For Salma, the hardest part about brokering is contending with her neighbors' curiosity:

> The neighbors see us outside and they come and ask us questions about people visiting us because we always have my uncles and friends visiting us, so many questions. They don't understand that this's our culture. Grandma gets

annoyed and I've to translate. Sometimes, the neighbors and Grandma go on religious discussions. They ask about Quran and Islam, Grandma gets annoyed and says things like, "Well your prophet is not really the son of God, he's just a prophet like the other prophets." Can you imagine me translating that? I just say, "Aaah, Grandma, let's go inside now."

Salma also translates the news for her grandmother. Sometimes, Salma tells, the ways the news reports on political crises in the Middle East anger her grandmother, to which Salma often responds: "Why you're mad at me? I'm just telling you what they say. You know, I just translate what the news says." Salma transmits the news verbatim, as she claims, without much work on settling her grandmother's feelings, as she does when brokering in public.

Leila

Leila is an 18-year-old Palestinian American who lives with her younger sister, four older college-student brothers, and parents in Southern California. The parents, both professionals—the mother is a Sunday-school principal and the father is a pharmacist—met in New York, where they married and raised a family before moving to Southern California. The family decided to escape the rage and hate in New York directed toward Arabs and Muslims in the wake of September, 11, 2001 and moved to California. One episode Leila vividly remembers was how isolated she felt after her mother, wearing her headscarf, attended a school play Leila was taking part in: "My friends started treating me differently and saying things like: 'We didn't know you were Muslim' or 'why your mother is dressed like that?'" Yet, Leila reported it was a rather serious anti-Muslim experience that prompted the family to leave New York. While in high school, Leila's brother was confronted by a teacher who accused him of belonging to a religion that kills people and oppresses women. Leila's parents demanded an apology from the teacher and the school. In retaliation, the offending teacher gave Leila's brother a failing grade on his final project, thereby delaying his graduation and preventing him from participating in the graduation ceremony. The mother took her son's essay to a local college and asked it to be evaluated by an English professor who, in turn, judged it an A paper. After this experience, the family moved to Southern California to live close to relatives. This profound experience has influenced Leila's way of brokering, as demonstrated later, mainly, in ways to avoid confrontation.

Leila translates for her mother in a variety of settings (e.g., home, school, shopping malls, medical visits). She also works with her mother at the Sunday school where her mother, the principal of the school, depends on Leila to interpret interactions with parents and facilitate some administrative tasks. Like Salma and Huda, Leila is committed to helping her mother but also feels the demands language brokering puts on her time. She views her interpretation work as part of duties toward her mother that "never end":

> I am her office manger; I am like my mom's little assistant. She is always like: "Do this, do that." Sometimes, I have to translate instructions on the copy machine, but sometimes, it's easier just to do it. Like I work for her there, but, then, when I come home, it never ends. It's like living with your boss.

While Leila's words express a heavy sense of encumbrance, her facial expression and tone amid her narrations suggested a less stressful experience. Leila's face lit up and her voice became buoyant as she narrated an interaction with her mother around another brokering experience, and spoke of a warm relationship:

> My mother is my best friend. We are very close and we talk about everything. My mother tells me about her friends when she was my age and that helps me with my friends. We watch a lot of TV together, but then I have to translate for her and I'm like, "Mom, you're making me miss the show!" But, we watch a lot of shows together. My mom likes *Friends*, but seriously, sometimes I just want to watch, not translate [laughs]. What can I do? I love my mom.

Interestingly, it is only during conversing with the researcher that Leila came to realize how she became "mom's little helper," as she calls herself. She laughed as recalling that her parents allowed her brothers to leave home and live close to their colleges, whereas they are willing to move closer to Leila's school so she does not have to leave home. Amid narrating, she realizes "ohh yeah, I guess that is why all of a sudden I became mom's little helper, because my brothers left home, [laughing], and I always ask myself why she only wants me now. That makes sense [laughing]."

Analysis

Study participants provide unique perspectives on the Arab American language brokering experience. They display a deep sense of understanding cultural differences and social norms as they mediate their parents' interactions. They change, add, or even avoid what is necessary to ensure civil communication in public spaces whereas, at home, they seem to free themselves from bridging gaps between cultures. Further consideration of the participant's narratives bring to light the difference in the strategies used in public as apposed to those used in private space. Whereas at schools, medical facilities, and shopping centers, Arab language brokers altered received speech using selective, socializing, or omission strategies, they reported using verbatim brokering strategies and reciprocal interpretation at home, as explained with examples in the next sections.

Brokering in Public Spaces

One of the questions on the study interview protocol asks the participants to discuss memorable episodes in their language brokering experiences. Salma recalled many incidents in which she had to mediate her grandmother's traditional appearance and social norms to their modern surroundings. One in particular stands out in which Salma narrated a shopping trip with her grandmother to buy some undergarments. She recalled the saleswoman asking if they needed help and it was the saleswoman's choice of words that caught Salma's attention: "She asked us if we were 'lost' and if she could help us locate the department we need." Salma believed that by using the word "lost" the saleswoman implied that she and her grandmother did not belong there. Salma noted that, even though her grandmother did not speak or understand English, she felt uncomfortable with the way the saleswoman addressed them:

> Grandma was like, "What is wrong with this crazy woman? What does she want?" I didn't tell Grandma exactly what she said; I just told her that she is asking if we need help. But, Grandma was like, "Tell her, no thanks; we will call her when we need her."

Instead of brokering between the two parties, Salma took the opportunity to address each one directly starting with what she felt was a derogatory remark:

> So, I just said, "No thanks, we are not *lost*." But, then she came back and asked me about my grandma's dress. I told her that it is a traditional Palestinian dress, and she was like, "Are you sure your grandma wants to be here?" I was like, "This's a Palestinian customary dress, and it's for public wear, but lingerie is for private wear." So, yeah, Grandma wants to be here. She was like surprised that Grandma was shopping for that in such a nice store even though she looks traditional. And then the minute Grandma hears Palestinian, she was like, "What is wrong now? What is about Palestine?" and I was like, "Grandma, she just wants to know where your dress is from."

This encounter was further intensified after the grandmother insisted on a discount or a free gift with her purchase, to which the saleswoman replied, "Arabs, cheap and loud." This time, the saleswoman's feelings towards Arabs was overtly stated. Salma found herself in a position of standing up for her grandmother and correcting this misconception: "Grandma is not cheap; she is used to local shops where they always bargain." Salma did not translate the saleswoman's last remark but walked away with a recurrent thought, "Why do I have to deal with this?!"

One of the interesting threads in this vignette is the point when presupposed knowledge, curiosities, and ideologies interact. Salma assumed that the sales clerk's question about her grandmother's dress is an act of stereotyping in which the saleswoman seemed confused by what appeared to be a paradoxical scene: A grandmother in traditional Palestinian clothing shopping for modern under-garments in an upscale department store. Also, Salma's own interpretation of the subtle message behind using the word "lost" guided her response. In both inci-dents, Salma did not translate the remark back to her grandmother. Knowing her grandmother's "hot temper" (as noted by the fact that merely hearing the name of her home country put the grandmother in a vigilant mood), Salma avoided conflict by transferring just enough information between the two parties. In this example, when preconceived ideas and ideologies are tested and challenged, the language broker had a choice to make. By choosing the role of a not-very-literal interpreter, Salma played the role of a diplomat, controlling and judging what needs to be crossed over. Her interference was of a bidirectional manner: She modified her grandmother's as well as the saleswoman's speech. Salma used a selective brokering strategy skillfully to maintain civility in a public space.

More than playing the role of a protector and a diplomat, as Salma did, Huda positioned herself as a socializer when brokering her mother's health-related encounters. During a hospital visit, Huda narrated what she believed to be unpro-fessional patient treatment and expressed that the reason behind it was bigotry toward differences in linguistic abilities and appearances:

> Sometimes, when they measure her blood pressure, they just remove her sleeves and they order her without being nice to her, and I'm like, "Be nice to her." And, when they see me understand English, they say, "Sorry, we're in a hurry," and then they become nice. When I translate that to my mom, she's like, "No, no, no, it's OK." And I am like, "No, it's not OK." My mom thinks it's [performing the medical procedures] her work and she needs to do it, but I think it is because my mom is wearing a head covering and she doesn't speak good English they don't treat her well. They can't take advan-tage of my mom just because she dresses differently or she doesn't speak English. I can be aggressive because I want them to be nice to my parents. I want things to be right for my parents.

In this incident, Huda, unlike Salma, tries to put her mother in a real context by interpreting and commenting on all the details of the conversation. She "aggres-sively," as she puts it, noted inadequate treatment and demanded otherwise. She believed that being an immigrant and coming from different cultural values put her mother in a weak position; therefore, by leading the way, Huda tries to empower her mother to act differently:

> My mom accepts anything. So, even if I thought she doesn't need me, I go with her to make sure she is treated well. It is probably related to how they lived in Iraq, that they shouldn't complain about anything. So now my

brothers and I tell her, "Why didn't you say this and that?" So, outside, I feel I need to be more like a shell to protect my parents.

Huda realizes the need to protect her mother; furthermore, she tries to socialize her mother, through her cultural brokering, into her legal and civil rights. She does so by markedly verbalizing and modeling what needs to be said and done without much concern for her image:

> I can speak and be rude and mean, but I know I can save her from being in a bad situation. It's not fear, but my mom thinks it's not nice to talk to people like that and she doesn't like to be not nice. But I want her to understand it's not about being nice; she's not taking anything from anybody. It's our rights and they should treat us like everybody.

The process of socialization has been defined as "an interactional display (covert or overt) to a novice of expected ways of thinking, feeling, and acting through their participation in social interactions" (Ochs, 1986, p. 2). Huda, as a bicultural expert in her family, uses her linguistic and cultural brokering skills to socialize her novice mother into the norms of voicing dissatisfaction as part of her civil rights in her new home country. While the value of "being nice," is important for the mother, being treated equally "like everybody" is of a greater value to Huda; thus, Huda demands fair treatment even if that requires "not being nice." In a way, Huda is brokering the cultural expectations that are different in the host country.

As a university graduate, Huda's mother acquired moderate skills in English, which, as commonly happens, she lost after graduating and emerging into daily life dominated by the native Arabic language. In the new home country, Huda encourages her mother to regain her English skills by presenting her with opportunities to directly communicate with members of the outside world. When doing so, Huda trains her mother on what to say while at the same time stays close to take actions if needed. During a phone conversation, which ended unsuccessfully, Huda' mother, encouraged by Huda, called the pharmacy to refill her medicine. Believing her mother received unfair treatment, Huda called back and took the opportunity to demonstrate to her mother how to behave in such cases:

> I encouraged her to pick up the phone and talk to the pharmacy, but they were like, "We don't understand you," and they hung up on her. I was so mad. So, I picked up the phone and I was like, "You don't understand English? What language do you speak then? Don't blame it on the language because she was speaking English to you. I was here and I was listening. She was very clear." And then they apologized. I told my mother: "Mom, don't accept that [kind of treatment]."

Here again, Huda stands up to protect her mother, but more importantly she is socializing her mother by modeling a way of dealing with the situation. She uses both covert and overt strategies of socialization, as outlined by Ochs (1986). Through her actions (i.e., covert socialization) she shows her mother how to respond to people who mistreat her, and through her words (i.e., overt socialization) she gives direct instruction, saying in a clear and imperative sentence: "Don't accept that." In this incident, Huda is a role model for not only how to communicate in English but also for how to culturally interact in American society.

In an extreme case of selective translation, or in this case, no-translation, Leila spoke about an experience of racism she faced at her high school. Being from a Palestinian family, Leila was asked by the school administration to represent her perspective on the Israeli-Palestinian conflict. After the event, Leila's teacher spoke directly to her during the class discussion saying that her religion is backward and forces women to follow men, that her brother and father beat her, abuse her, force her into child marriage, and force her to dress differently. Afterward, Leila went to the principal and reported what had taken place in the classroom. At home, Leila did not mention what had happened at school that day:

> I know the school will take care of it. I didn't want what happened to my brother to happen to me. It is like the same thing all over again. Besides, I am graduating this year, but my sister is coming next year. It will never end.

After discussing the matter with the teacher, the principal asked the teacher to apologize to Leila in her parents' presence. The principal decided to summon all involved the next day, including Leila's parents. Leila chose not to share the entire incident with her father and shared only minimum information with her mother. At the principal's office, the mother, the principal, and Leila were present, but not the teacher. The principal explained to Leila's mother what had happened and apologized, Leila translated, but only general details of the events. Leila said the meeting was very short and her mother did not say anything:

> My mom came to school, but I only told her the teacher was saying some bad stuff about Arabs. The principal apologized. My mother did not ask anything. The teacher was not at the meeting. I didn't translate much, no need to translate rude remarks. Not a big deal, the school took care of it.

Enduring racism twice, once against her brother and another directly against her, Leila evaded disclosing details of the event, so as to save her parents and herself a repeatedly stressful experience. But, mainly, as she explained, she acted accordingly to avoid future problems with her younger sister who would enter the same school in the next year.

In these interpretation vignettes, the context of being an Arab played a pivotal role in the dynamics by which young Arab language brokers performed the act of brokering. In places within a public domain, avoidance, defiance, or socializing strategies are adopted in order to minimize or counteract the effect of stereotypes and discrimination. The brokers generally aligned themselves with their families, performing acts of protection through their choices of brokering. Through their brokering work, they represented their families in public life to support their linguistic, cultural, and religious identities. Their language brokering experiences are shaped by the way the Arab community is perceived in the United States, but simultaneously are reshaped by their agency and their own understanding of their heritage and the host culture.

Brokering in Private Spaces

When translating at home, the language brokers deal with static text (e.g., food recipes and medicine labels) and indirect connections (e.g., phone calls and TV programs), rather than direct interaction with people. Thus, they noted that it is easier for them to take a less-involved role than the one they play when brokering in public. At home, they narrated not-so-stressful brokering experiences using different strategies than those in public, and they showed less enthusiasm toward helping.

Huda, who insisted on accompanying her mother even where a professional interpreter is provided and displayed serious effort in socializing her mother into her social rights, relayed an episode that presented a different level of agency. She takes a more distancing role, claiming her right to her time and comfort when at home:

> When I come home, they know it is better not to talk to me or ask me anything. I need to eat, take my rest, drink my coffee and then I can do things for them.

Similarly, as demonstrated in the following example, Leila expresses reluctance when having to interpret for her mother at home. Leila's mother has recently started college and has been depending on Leila to interpret the American educational system and school work. Leila, who does many similar tasks at the Sunday school where she works with her mother, the principal, feels uneasy with this role reversal at home:

> It's weird that I am helping my mother with her homework. I mean she's my mother. She does things for us, and now she's depending on me to do [good] at college. It's weird because Mom never helped me with homework. She always says do your own homework and be independent. And now I am like, "Mom, I want to do my own homework."

Similarly, Ali, who puts serious efforts in bridging cultures when brokering at schools and medical visits, acts less enthusiastically at home. He talks about brokering the news for his father without much involvement, describing it as using "word-by-word" strategy:

> I actually translate exactly what they are saying, exactly. I mean when it comes to news, I have no specifics, they are saying this and that is how I say it in a different language.

Here, Ali frees himself from critically brokering the news; instead, he strictly transfers what he hears or reads to a different language. To him, the difficulty of brokering the news at home seems of a lexical nature rather than bridging cultural information as he talked about brokering in public:

> It's hard to translate the news, all these hard words. I have no idea. So, I don't have feelings when I translate the news, I just try to say it exactly word by word, whatever comes.

Ali's verbatim technique, however, is not solely due to linguistic difficulty, but also seems to free him from having to express an opinion about issues he is not ready to take a stance toward:

> I translate how it's exactly, because I don't have an opinion yet myself on many topics because I have not found myself. I mean I'm still confused about all these political problems and different perspectives and that makes me translate exactly how it is without being, I mean I'm being objective.

Ali's neutral stance, described as being "objective" and "confused," is later recognized as a place of "development": "I found good things and bad things in both cultures. So I am developing. It's a sort of changing." He provided insight into recognizing that he is still maturing as an individual and developing opinions, despite having to sometimes act adult-like in language brokering situations.

Salma, who avoided transferring remarks of hate and stereotyping to her grandmother at the shopping mall, talked about translating the news at home verbatim, even if it meant angering her grandmother. Similarly, Leila, who used selective strategies when brokering at school, work, and shopping centers, also talks about verbatim interpretation of news at home:

> When my mom watches the news about the Middle East on TV, she asks me what they're saying. She wants to know how they cover the events and what they're saying about us and I just say what they are saying exactly.

Given that in the aftermath of September 11 and the wars in the Middle East, many Arabs turned to satellite television-based or web-based Arabic media resources for the news (Shiri, 2010), many Arab American immigrants, like the participants in the study, are often exposed to two perspectives of news reporting. Leila in the following example describes the privilege of receiving diverse coverage of news events

> I feel like we just have one side of the story, one opinion from the American channels, but when we listen to Al-Jazeera [an Arab-language news channel], we hear the other side, too. So, sometimes we get to have discussions about what the Americans are saying and what the Arab world is saying.

This situation seems to provide the opportunity for parents to interpret the news from Arabic to English for their children, creating a context of reciprocal brokering to understand events:

> The best part is when we listen to Al-Jazeera; I don't understand what they are saying, Sometimes, I pick up some words, but mostly my mom translates for me.

Arabic-speaking children in diaspora are usually familiar with the home dialect (such as Iraqi, Lebanese, Egyptian, etc.) and lack competence in Modern Standard Arabic (MSA), which children learn formally at schools in Arab countries. Even when Arab children in diaspora receive language instruction at weekend schools, it is often not enough to acquire a high proficiency in the standard form. Therefore, when children engage with these programs, which are often telecasted in MSA, or encouraged by parents to do so, they will need parents' help. This situation creates a context of reciprocal translation among Arab American families in which children translate the news from English to Arabic for their parents, and parents translate for their children MSA to home dialect for understanding. A few researchers have recognized language brokering as an interactional site that has the potential for maintaining heritage languages (e.g., Dorner, Orellana, & Jiménez, 2008; Orellana et al., 2003). Acoach and Webb (2004) and Weisskirch and Alva (2002) also called for exploring the impact of language brokering on family language use. The pattern shown in this study, in which parents translate their heritage language into a colloquial form for their children, is a novel aspect of heritage language maintenance. The context of reciprocal brokering found here deserves detailed investigation in future studies. It also offers insights into the parents' role in shaping children's world views, a sentiment Ali expresses eloquently as saying: "When I enter my parents' house, I enter a whole new world."

Conclusion

Similar to their language brokering counterparts from other ethnicities, Arab American language brokers translate in different domains that include home, school, medical, and commercial settings, where they engage in a wide range of translation and interpretation activities such as medical visits, school conferences, casual conversations, phone calls, medical and insurance forms, medicine and food labels, TV shows, and news programs. In addition, two of the language brokers, Salma and Leila, also interpret by helping parents with education–related activities such as choosing and registering for courses, e-mailing professors, and working on homework, which involves language brokering and culture brokering but also knowledge of the American higher education system. Electing the designated language broker seems to be based on linguistic proficiency (e.g., Ali), availability (e.g., Huda and Leila), or favoritism (e.g., Salma). Emotionally, each of the participants expressed a sense of burden as well as a sense of responsibility toward their families; however, that burden or responsibility did not appear to transfer into negative feelings toward the parents. In fact, all four participants claimed very close parent-child bonds. They all were cognizant of the important role they play in their families' lives through the language brokering services they provide.

They are also quite aware of the stigma associated with being an Arab and Muslim in the United States. All four language brokers talked about experiences charged with stereotypes represented in reaction toward cultural and religious artifacts, such as folkloric dress or the headscarf. The language brokers' accounts, however, show that they were not passive participants in receiving this context but rather active social actors who preserve the right to shape their families' and their own experiences. When their identities and rights seemed to be threatened, as language brokers they interpreted either selectively to ensure civil engagement and protect families (as the case of Salma and her grandmother at the mall) or defiantly to counteract racism and ensure equal treatment (as the case with Huda and her mother in medical settings). In addition, in facilitating interactions, the study participants rendered personal understanding of their bicultural world, producing their versions of cultural- and situational-appropriate messages for the recipients of the communication.

The study also addressed the complex relation between context and language brokering as represented in the experience of Arab Americans. The macro-level of language brokering proved to be governed by the distressed sociopolitical context which the Arab American community in the United States negotiates. For example, cultural artifacts, such as traditional dress or the headscarf, become a focal point when brokering in public space, and political news seems to be central brokering activity at home. Through analyses of micro–language brokering settings, contextualized brokering strategies appeared. These strategies are guided by the language brokers' assumptions about their bicultural environment but are also influenced by how the language brokers are perceived by their interlocutors. For the families, their language brokering children are experts on the dominant culture, and for the representatives of the dominant culture, the language brokers are experts on their immigrant families' culture. The language brokers appeared empowered by the responsibility bestowed on them and actively navigated expectations by stepping in and out of the various roles they play. In the face of discrimination and anti-Muslim sentiments in public, language brokers often refrained from exact translation and resorted instead to selective brokering to safeguard their families from feeling marginalized.

Moreover, the language brokers, in their work, are actually paving the way for acceptance and tolerance between the two parties. Using linguistic and cultural skills, the language brokers socialize their families into the social and cultural norms of the host culture, and similarly socialize members of the dominant culture to be less apprehensive and more accepting of diverse appearances and customs. Thus, in dealing with the specific contexts of being Arab American, the study sampled selective and socializing brokering strategies accompanied with strong commitment in which the language brokers provide a safe public space for their family members to be accepted as equals.

The unthreatened spaces of private residences furnished the way for a different set of feelings, strategies, and identities to emerge. In private spaces, participants avoid deep involvement in brokering as they interpret different media outlets for their families. They resort to verbatim brokering, at least as they claimed their home brokering to be, through which they find a space for their own development and reflection on social and political problems associated with their families' original countries. Also, while they change their schedules to meet parents' broking needs outside the home, they appeared less rushed to help at home and respond more like children who are not so comfortable with role-reversal duties. In addition, a form of reciprocal brokering is used in the Arab household in which the parents embrace the chance to play the broker role for their children by transforming the formal heritage language they hear on TV to the everyday vernacular form familiar to their children.

Contribution to Theory

Broadly, this study demonstrates how the sociopolitical contexts association with the Arab American community influences the brokering methods. More studies from other immigrant communities using a similar frame of analysis may further shed light on how language brokers change their brokering strategies in different settings as effected by the dominate stereotypes related to their ethnicity, religion, race, or nationality. More specifically, the high number of Arab immigrants and the unique challenges they may face upon immigration highlight the importance of research on Arab Americans. Two variables seem to decisively influence the language brokering experience of Arab Americans: appearance and language. As such, these variables are key elements to be considered when researching language brokering or other social phenomena related to the Arab diaspora.

The first variable, appearance—which may include physical elements (e.g., skin color and facial features often associated with being an Arab or Middle Eastern) and/or cultural elements (e.g., religious and folkloric clothes)—factor a great deal in the way Arabs are perceived and in return interact with their surroundings.

The Arab Americans in this study are found to be keenly vigilant about discrimination and mistreatment by others. Consequently, they may internalize feelings of being outsiders of the society they choose to make their home. As a researcher, an educator, and a mother, I have spoke to many teens from Arab backgrounds: Without exaggeration, I have yet to meet one, even those who look and behave as any regular American teenager, who has not experienced some act of discrimination at some point in his/her life, regardless of its severity. Despite that, statistics have shown that Arab Americans generally have done well for themselves and their families in regard to economic and educational status (Shiri, 2010). However, these reports often do not explore the relation between economic or educational status and time or generation of immigration. With increased mobility due to economical and political upheavals in the Middle East, more illiterate and poor families are arriving in the United States, as well as educated and well- or moderately resourced families and individuals. One can imagine that those who already were at a disadvantage in their home country would be yet more weak and less equipped to deal with challenges faced in the host country, such as those identified in this study. Studies have shown that internalized feelings of marginalization effect mental and physical heath as well as social behavior. Therefore, this is a call not only to consider the effect of being or looking Arab as a prominent factor on Arab American interaction and well-being, but also it is to consider how we can use research outcomes to defend against racism in public and institutional contexts.

The second variable that has a wide impact on Arab American language brokering and other social and familial interaction in general is the Arabic language itself. Arabic is the language of Islam, yet is also the language used by fundamentalists and terrorists, and hence is deemed by association to be itself criminalized. Using Arabic in public settings subjects individuals to racial profiling and discrimination, such as a recent incident in which an young Iraqi college student was removed from a flight after he was heard speaking Arabic on the phone (Milman, 2016). In familial context, the rich heritage of the Arabic language in its diverse forms could have a profound influence on parent-child communication, language maintenance, and connection to identity and heritage culture, as seen in this study. The diglossia of the Arabic language and how it is manifested during interactions among different generations of Arab American should be given considerable attention.

Finally, a caveat should be warranted against generalizing the study findings. This study is limited by the small size of its participants, the gender ratio (one male as opposed to three females), and demographics (all participants are from the greater Los Angeles area, and all are college students and from educated families). For example, a study on Sudanese refugee families in Michigan (Perry, 2009) shed light on the literacy skills gained by young children brokers who were emerging into English literacy themselves, when translating and interpreting different genres of texts for their families. Another study found that gender plays a role in the language brokering experiences of Orthodox Christian Iraqi immigrants, which found that believed their daughters are empathetic about family issues (Villanueva, 2012). A larger and more diverse sample is crucial for arriving at a more comprehensive picture about Arab American language brokering experiences.

References

Acoach, C. L., & Webb, L. M. (2004). The influence of language brokering on Hispanic teenagers' acculturation, academic performance, and nonverbal decoding skills: A preliminary study. *Howard Journal of Communications, 15*, 1–19.

Baker, M. (2006). Contextualization in translator and interpreter-mediated events. *Journal of Pragmatics, 38*(3), 323–337.

DeMent, T., & Buriel, R. (1999). *Children as cultural brokers: Recollections of college students.* Paper presented at the SPSSI Conference on Immigrants and Immigration, Toronto, Ontario, Canada.

Dorner, L., Orellana, M. F., & Jiménez, R. (2008). "It's one of these things that you do to help the family:" Language brokering and the development of immigrant adolescents. *Journal of Adolescent Research, 23*(5), 515–543.

Dorner, L., Orellana M. F., & Li-Grining, C. P. (2007). "I helped my mom," and it helped me: Translating the skills of language brokers into proved standardized test score. *The American Journal of Education, 113*(3), 451–478.

Duranti, A., & Goodwin, C. (Eds.). (1992). *Rethinking context: An introduction.* Cambridge, UK: Cambridge University Press.

Fairclough, N. (1992). *Discourse and social change.* Cambridge: Polity Press.

García-Sánchez, I. M. (2009). *Moroccan immigrant children in a time of surveillance: Navigating sameness and difference in contemporary Spain.* Unpublished Doctoral dissertation. Department of Applied Linguistics, University of California, Los Angeles.

García-Sánchez, I. M., Orellana, M., & Hopkins, M. (2011). Facilitating intercultural communication in parent-teacher conferences: Lessons from child translators. *Multicultural Perspectives, 13*(3), 148–154.

Gumperz, J. J. (1992). Contextualization and understanding. In A. Duranti & C. Goodwin (Eds.), *Rethinking context: Language as an interactive phenomenon* (pp. 229–252). Cambridge, UK: Cambridge University Press.

Hanks, W. (2006). Context, communicative. In K. Brown (Ed.), *Encyclopedia of language and linguistics* (pp. 115–128). Amsterdam: Elsevier.

Hymes, D. H. (Ed.). (1964). *Language in culture and society: A reader in linguistics and anthropology.* New York, NY: Harper & Row.

Hymes, D. H. (1972). Models of interaction of language and social life. In J. J. Gumperz & D. Hymes (Eds.), *Discourse in sociolinguistics: The ethnography of communication* (pp. 35–71). New York, NY: Holt, Rinehart & Winston.

Love, J., & Buriel, R. (2007). Language brokering, autonomy, parent-child bonding, biculturalism, and depression: A study of Mexican American adolescents from immigrant families. *Hispanic Journal of Behavioral Sciences, 29*(4), 472–491.

McQuillan, J., & Tse, L. (1995). Child language brokering in linguistic minority communities: Effects on cultural interaction, cognition, and literacy. *Language and Education, 9*(3), 195–215.

Michalak, L. (1988). *Cruel and unusual: Negative images of Arabs in American popular culture.* ADC Issue Paper No. 15.

Milman, O. (2016, April 16). Southwest airlines draws outrage over man removed for speaking Arabic. *The Guardian.*

Neff, D. (1993). Jerusalem in US Policy. *Journal of Palestine Studies, 23*(1), 20–45.

Ochs, E. (1986). Introduction. In B. B. Schieffelin & E. Ochs (Eds.), *Language socialization across cultures* (pp. 1–13). New York, NY: Cambridge University Press.

Orellana, M. F. (2009). *Translating childhoods: Immigrant youth, language and culture.* Candem, NJ: Rutgers University Press.

Orellana, M. F., Dorner, L., & Pulido, L. (2003). Accessing assets: Immigrant youth's work as family translators or "para-phrasers". *Social Problems, 50*(4), 505–524.

Orfalea, G. (2006). *The Arab Americans: A history.* New York, NY: Olive Branch Press.

Perry, K. H. (2009). Genres, contexts, and literacy practices: Literacy brokering among Sudanese refugee families. *Reading Research Quarterly, 44*(3), 256–276.

Pew Research Center: Religion & Public Life (2014). How Americans feel about religious groups. Retrieved from www.pewforum.org/2014/07/16/how-americans-feel-about-religious-groups/.

Reynolds, J., & Orellana, M. F. (2009). New immigrant youth interpreting in white public space. *American Anthropologist, 111*(2), 211–222.

Sacks, H., Schegloff, E. A., & Jefferson, G. (1974). A simplest systematic for the organization of turn-taking for conversation. *Language, 50,* 696–735.

Shaheen, J. (2012). *Guilty: Hollywood's Verdict on Arabs after 9/11.* Northampton, MA: Interlink Publishing.

Shiri, S. (2010). Arabic in the USA. In K. Potowski (Ed.), *Language diversity in the USA.* (pp. 206–222). Cambridge, UK: Cambridge University Press.

Tse, L. (1995). When students translate for parents: Effects of language brokering. *Cabe Newsletter, 17*(4), 16–17.

Van Dijk, Teun A. (2009). Critical discourse studies: A sociocognitive approach. In R. Wodak & M. Meyer (Eds.), *Methods of critical discourse analysis* (pp. 62–85). London, UK: Sage.

Villanueva, S. (2012). *Cultural brokering: A qualitative exploration of orthodox Christian Iraqi immigrant families.* Doctoral dissertation, University of Illinois at Chicago.

Weisskirch, R. S. (2005). The relationship of language brokering to ethnic identity for Latino adolescents. *Hispanic Journal of Behavioral Sciences, 27,* 286–299.

Weisskirch, R. S., & Alva, S. A. (2002). Language brokering and the acculturation of Latino students. *Hispanic Journal of Behavioral Sciences, 24,* 369–378.

YouGov US. (2015). Poll Results: Islam. Retrieved from: https://today.yougov.com/news/2015/03/09/poll-results-islam/

7

ADOLESCENT LANGUAGE BROKERING FOR IMMIGRANT CHINESE PARENTS IN CANADA

Josephine M. Hua and Catherine L. Costigan

Introduction

A better understanding of the cultural-familial environments underlying the language brokering process is key to predicting the psychological adjustment of language brokers and the quality of their family relationships. This chapter examines the dynamics of language brokering by adolescents for their mothers and fathers among immigrant Chinese families in Canada. We evaluate the relative importance of language brokering frequency versus feelings about language brokering as they relate to positive and negative indicators of adolescent adjustment and to positive and negative indicators of the quality of their relationship with parents. Furthermore, we apply the theoretical lens of self-determination theory to identify potential family environments in which language brokering is associated with psychological risks for adolescents versus those in which language brokering is a neutral or even positive developmental experience for this population.

Language Brokering Within Immigrant Chinese Families Living in Canada

Canada has one of the highest rates of immigration in the world. According to the 2011 Canadian National Households Survey, 6.7 million foreign-born individuals represent 20.6% of the total population (Statistics Canada, 2013). Chinese Canadians have consistently constituted one of the largest groups of immigrants for several decades (e.g., Wang & Lo, 2004), and among the Canadian immigrant population, Chinese languages are the most commonly used in the home (Statistics Canada, 2013). Given the high rate of Chinese immigration to Canada, the study of Chinese immigrants' acculturation warrants increased attention. As is common among immigrant families, family members may learn new languages at different rates, and children may acquire the new language more quickly due to children's greater immersion into mainstream language environments such as public school settings. The large number of Chinese immigrants in Canada and their experience with acculturation makes language brokering a relevant topic in the study of Chinese families who are adjusting to life in Canada.

Language Brokering Frequency Versus Feelings

Language brokering has primarily been measured by examining either the actual behaviors involved in language brokering or the attitudes associated with language brokering (e.g., Buriel, Perez, DeMent, Chavez, & Moran, 1998; Tse, 1996). Behavioral aspects primarily include measures of language brokering frequency and are typically assessed quantitatively. Measures of language brokering frequency ask how often this form of translation and interpretation occurs across different materials (e.g., school materials, media, or immigration papers) and/or settings (e.g., home, school, or medical settings) and for whom (e.g., parents, other relatives, friends, or neighbors).

Attitudinal aspects normally refer to children's and adolescents' feelings about their language brokering experiences, prospectively and retrospectively. Some studies have documented the emotional experience of language brokering by employing qualitative interviews (e.g., Hall & Sham, 1998; Morales, Yakushko, & Castro, 2012). Other researchers have examined the extent that positive feelings (e.g., maturity, helpfulness) and negative feelings (e.g., stressed, embarrassed) about language brokering are endorsed (e.g., Buriel et al., 1998; Kam, 2011; Weisskirch, 2007; Wu & Kim, 2009).

Although language brokering frequency and feelings about language brokering are distinct constructs, they have rarely been distinguished in relation to their associations with the adjustment of family members involved in language brokering (Kam, 2011). The extent to which frequency and feelings relate similarly or uniquely to adjustment is a prime area for language brokering research (Kam & Lazarevic, 2014). Researchers who have examined language brokering frequency and feelings simultaneously have begun to shed light on how behavioral and attitudinal aspects of language brokering relate to one another and with adjustment (e.g., Kam & Lazarevic, 2014; Weisskirch, 2013). In this chapter, we evaluate whether the frequency of language brokering is more or less closely related to adjustment, compared to the feelings that adolescents experience while language brokering.

Family Dynamics Through the Lens of Self-Determination Theory

The second issue addressed in this study concerns the contexts within the family that exacerbate or minimize the relations between language brokering and adjustment. Self-determination theory (SDT; Ryan & Deci, 2000) assumes that people have a natural tendency towards curiosity, vitality, and self-motivation, and that, unthwarted, this tendency leads to well-being. At its essence, SDT focuses on the social-contextual conditions that enhance or hinder these natural tendencies and postulates autonomy as a key psychological need for optimal social development and well-being (Deci & Ryan, 2000). From a SDT perspective, autonomy is defined as volitional or self-endorsed functioning and refers to the extent that behaviors are endorsed freely, rather than motivated by pressure, control, or coercion (Deci & Ryan, 2000). Children's capacity for self-determination is optimized when parents are autonomy-supportive by encouraging their children to engage in activities with the goal of self-regulation (versus compliance), seeking to understand their children's feelings and perspectives, using reasoning in their parenting methods while minimizing the use of rewards and punishments, and offering their children choices rather than imposing their own agenda (Joussemet, Landry, & Koestner, 2008). SDT-based research has consistently found that more autonomous motives and autonomy-supportive contexts relate to positive individual and relational outcomes (Deci & Ryan, 2000, 2008a).

In contrast, parenting that seeks to manipulate children's behaviors and psychological world, such as parental psychological control, is regarded as especially undermining of children's sense of autonomy (Joussemet et al., 2008). Methods of psychological control may include the invalidation of children's feelings or perspectives, and/or the use of an existing parent-child bond as leverage for guilt induction or love withdrawal (Barber, 1996). Disciplinary actions used by psychologically controlling parents tend to be stricter and to rely on pressure, coercion, punishment, and/or restrictive rules to obtain the desired behaviors (Barber, 1996). Psychological control by parents has been associated with poorer psychological adjustment, including poorer emotional well-being, more hopelessness, fewer feelings of personal control over one's own life, lower life satisfaction, and lower self-esteem (Shek, 2008; Wang, Pomerantz, & Chen, 2007).

SDT maintains that the benefits of autonomy support and the costs associated with psychological control are universal; they apply to individuals and families from both independent and interdependent cultures (Deci & Ryan, 2008a). The theory argues that people from interdependent cultures may still feel autonomous when acting on the demands of in-group others because within an autonomy-supportive context, they are more likely to internalize those demands as their own view.

In this chapter, we hypothesized that the relations between language brokering and individual and relational adjustment would be moderated by adolescents' perceptions of autonomy-supportive parenting. Specifically, we examined adolescent reports of their parents' use of reasoning (as a positive measure that promotes autonomy development) as well as adolescent reports of parental psychological control (as a negative measure that hinders autonomy development) as potential moderators of the links between language brokering and adjustment.

Summarizing the Related Research

Language Brokering Frequency Within Asian Immigrant Families

Language brokering is a fairly common experience among children of Asian immigrants. Tse (1996), for example, reported that nearly 90% of her sample of 64 Chinese and Vietnamese American high school students had brokered at least once. Of these, 92% reportedly brokered for their parents. Chao (2006) asked 463 Mexican American, 581 Chinese American, and 557 Korean American ninth graders *how frequently* they translated for parents, across different settings and types of material. Although almost 70% reported having language brokered for a parent at least once, on average they reported language brokering quite infrequently. Similarly, in Hua and Costigan's (2012) study of 182 adolescents from Chinese immigrant families residing in Western Canada, although over 90% reported that they had language brokered at least once for their parents, the average frequency was relatively low (i.e., *a few times a year*). These findings suggest that while common among Asian immigrant families, language brokering on average may be an infrequently occurring practice. However, there is scant research to establish a consistent pattern.

The relations between language brokering frequency and adjustment are quite mixed. Most of these mixed findings have been based on samples of Latino/as in the United States (see Morales & Hanson, 2005). The smaller number of studies with Asian immigrant families also presents an inconclusive picture. For example, more frequent language brokering has been associated with more internalizing and externalizing symptoms and more parent-child conflict, but also with greater perceived parental sacrifice and greater respect for parents (Chao, 2006; Hua & Costigan, 2012; Shen, Kim, Wang, & Chao, 2014). The lack of consistent relations between language brokering frequency and adjustment highlights the complexity of this phenomenon and suggests that additional aspects of the language brokering dynamic need to be addressed.

Feelings About Language Brokering

Few studies of language brokering among children of Asian immigrants have examined aspects of language brokering other than frequency. An exception is Wu and Kim's (2009) study examining Chinese American adolescents' sense of burden and efficacy as language brokers. Specifically, they examined adolescents' orientation to Chinese culture as moderating perceptions of their language brokering experiences. Adolescents who were more strongly Chinese-oriented reported a stronger sense of family obligation, perceived that they mattered to their parents, and felt a strong sense of efficacy (i.e., feeling independent, mature, useful, competent, and capable) about language brokering. Adolescents who were less strongly

Chinese-oriented had a weaker sense of family obligation, were more likely to feel alienation from parents, and reported a stronger sense of burden and stress as language brokers. These findings provide insight into which adolescents are more likely to experience negative feelings about language brokering (i.e., those who are less heritage culture–oriented), but do not address the relations between language brokering feelings and adjustment.

Feelings about language brokering have more often been studied in Latino/a populations. For example, Weisskirch (2007) provided a list of 13 positive emotion words and 27 negative emotion words to 98 Mexican American seventh graders and had them rate the extent to which they experienced each emotion when translating. He found that language brokering evoked a range of positive and negative emotions, but most of the children reported positive feelings about language brokering more strongly (e.g., helpful and happy) than negative feelings (e.g., anxious and ashamed).

Other researchers have asked Latino/a participants to rate the degree of their agreement with various affective statements that either reflect positive (e.g., "I feel good about myself when I translate for family") or negative (e.g., "I feel embarrassed when I translate for others") feelings about their language brokering experiences (e.g., Buriel et al., 1998; Kam, 2011; Kam & Lazarevic, 2014; Neihaus & Kumpiene, 2014; Weisskirch, 2013; Wu & Kim, 2009). Negative feelings about language brokering—such as feeling embarrassed, burdened, or nervous when language brokering—have been associated with lower levels of self-esteem and self-efficacy, higher personal and family-based acculturation stress, and more problematic family relationships (Kam, 2011; Weisskirch, 2007, 2013). Positive feelings about language brokering have been associated with higher levels of self-esteem, confidence, ethnic identity, and academic self-concept, smoking fewer cigarettes, greater perceived popularity with peers, and less problematic family relationships (Buriel et al., 1998; Kam, 2011; Niehaus & Kumpiene, 2014; Weisskirch, 2007).

In the current study, we extend the study of language brokering feelings by simultaneously considering language brokering frequency, negative feelings about language brokering, and positive feelings about language brokering within a Chinese immigrant population in order to determine which of these dimensions of the language brokering experience are most strongly related to individual psychological adjustment and parent-child relationship quality. In doing so, we distinguish between language brokering for mothers versus fathers to evaluate whether the links between language brokering and adjustment depend on the recipient of language brokering assistance.

Familial Contexts of Language Brokering

Research has emphasized the importance of the contexts in which language brokering takes place as essential to understanding the links between language brokering and psychological adjustment (e.g., Hua & Costigan, 2012; Martinez, McClure, &

Eddy, 2009; Wu & Kim, 2009). This work examines the cultural-familial environments that may facilitate or complicate the language brokering process and the psychological development of children and their families. For example, Hua and Costigan (2012) considered Chinese cultural values regarding filial piety and hierarchy and examined how family obligation values and perceptions of parental psychological control shaped the way in which language brokering related to the psychological adjustment of adolescent language brokers and to the quality of parent-child relationships. They found that for language brokers who held strong values about family obligation or perceived their parents as highly controlling, more frequent language brokering was associated with higher levels of internalizing symptoms and/or lower levels of self-esteem. Shen and colleagues (2014) found that indirect relations between language brokering frequency and externalizing symptoms in Chinese and Korean American adolescents, mediated by perceived maternal sacrifice and respect for the mother, were especially pronounced in the context of less open parent-child communication. These findings highlight that the context in which language brokering takes place plays a key role in how language brokering is experienced by the youth.

In the current study, we evaluated the extent to which an autonomy-supportive context moderated the links between language brokering and adjustment. In low autonomy-supportive contexts, we expected language brokering duties would more likely be experienced as an obligation rather than as a personal choice. That is, when parents are perceived as psychologically controlling or their use of reasoning is low, the language brokering experience was hypothesized to be less likely to be in line with the adolescents' own opinions and values. Under these conditions, we expected higher language brokering frequency and more negative feelings about language brokering to be strongly associated with poorer adjustment (i.e., higher levels of distress and lower levels of well-being). In contrast, the links between positive feelings about language brokering and adjustment were expected to be attenuated in low autonomy-supportive contexts.

When adolescents experience an autonomy-supportive context, we predicted that language brokering duties would more likely to be freely endorsed and performed volitionally. Even when language brokering duties were conducted following a parent's request, language brokering was expected to be experienced positively in autonomy-supportive contexts because the rationale for providing interpretation and translation services for parents would more likely to be understood as reasonable and internalized by the language broker as his/her own view. Such instances were expected to be associated with lower distress and greater well-being in terms of psychological adjustment and parent-child relationship quality. Thus, under conditions of high autonomy support, we expected weaker relations between language brokering frequency and negative feelings and adjustment, and particularly strong relations between positive feelings and adjustment.

Method

Participants

The data used in this report were obtained in a second wave of data collection (Wave 2) from a sample of immigrant Chinese families from Hua and Costigan (2012). Unlike the first wave (Wave 1) used in Hua and Costigan's (2012) study, in Wave 2, adolescents were asked about their language brokering experiences with their mothers and fathers separately. In addition, Wave 1 did not assess adolescents' feelings about language brokering. Thus, data from Wave 2 allow for examination of the language brokering experience more deeply in terms of evaluating differences in language brokering for mothers and fathers, and exploring the relative importance of frequency versus feelings in the language brokering experience.

In Wave 2, data were collected from 152 immigrant Chinese families, typically consisting of two parents and one child. All parents emigrated voluntarily from Mainland China (63.2%), Taiwan (22.4%), or Hong Kong (13.8%). Parents had lived in Canada between 2 and 36 years (fathers, $M = 10.36$ years, $SD = 6.58$; mothers, $M = 9.86$ years, $SD = 6.02$), and first-generation adolescents had lived in Canada for an average of 5.99 years ($SD = 1.98$).

Adolescent children were between 13 and 19 years old ($M = 15.79$ years, $SD = 1.73$). There were approximately equal numbers of female (53.6%) and male (46.4%) adolescents, and approximately half came to Canada at or after the age of 6 (i.e., 55.6%), and half were born in Canada or came to Canada before the age of 6 (i.e., 44.4%). Fathers were on average 48.29 years old ($SD = 5.77$), and mothers were on average 45.76 years old ($SD = 4.48$). The majority of fathers (98.5%) and mothers (92.7%) were currently married. For these parents, the average length of marriage was 20 years (fathers = 20.27 years, $SD = 4.43$; mothers = 20.09 years, $SD = 4.52$). Most parents were well educated: 60.9% of fathers and 48.7% of mothers reported having completed a university degree or graduate work; 20.3% of fathers and 27.3% of mothers completed some college or vocational school; 9.8% of fathers and 16.7% of mothers completed high school; and 16.3% of fathers and 7.3% of mothers did not complete high school.

Procedures

To be eligible for the initial study, both parents had to have emigrated voluntarily from Mainland China, Taiwan, or Hong Kong; both parents had to immigrate to Canada after the age of 18 and identify themselves as Chinese; families had to have lived in Canada for at least 2 years; and parents had to have at least one child between the ages of 12 and 17. In Wave 1, the majority of families (78.3%) were randomly recruited from two metropolitan areas in British Columbia by randomly contacting individuals with Chinese last names by phone and screening them for eligibility. The remaining families were recruited through referrals from research assistants or participating families. Wave 2 took place 18 months after Wave 1. We retained 83.5% of the original sample in Wave 2. The families who participated in Wave 2 did not differ from those who participated in Wave 1 only in terms of parental age or education. However, Wave 2 families had lived in Canada a shorter time and had adolescents who were significantly younger than the families who participated in Wave 1 only.

During data collection, two research assistants, with at least one having bilingual Chinese and English abilities, visited each family in their homes. Although the measures used in the current study focus on adolescent reports only, both Wave 1 and 2 data collection procedures involved having fathers, mothers, and adolescents simultaneously, but independently, complete consent forms and questionnaire booklets available in the language of their choice. Prior to administration, these materials were translated into Chinese using back-translation procedures to ensure that English and Chinese versions were equivalent in meaning. This study was granted research ethics approval by the University of Victoria.

Measures

Demographic Information

A background questionnaire gathered information about participant characteristics such as age, gender, highest level of education completed, reasons for immigration, and length of residence in Canada.

Language Brokering Frequency

Adolescents reported on the frequency with which they translated or interpreted for their parents in eight situations by completing a questionnaire that was adapted from Chao's (2006) language brokering measure. The situations included materials from school, bills or financial information, household issues, medical/health information, immigration information, media (e.g., news items, TV), parents' work materials, and informal conversation. Adolescents rated the frequency of their language brokering on a 5-point scale: 0 (*never*), 1 (*a few times a year*), 2 (*about once a month*), 3 (*a few times a week*), and 4 (*daily*). They reported each item separately for their mothers and fathers. The language brokering scale, which is an average of all eight items, showed excellent internal consistency (α = .89 for mothers; α = .90 for fathers).

Language Brokering Feelings

Adolescents' positive and negative feelings about language brokering for each of their parents was examined using an 8-item scale created for this project, based on feelings reported in past studies (e.g., Chao, 2006; McQuillan & Tse, 1995). Specifically, adolescents were asked, "If you ever translate or interpret for your mother and father, how much do you feel _____ because of it?" Positive feelings included feeling proud, helpful, grown-up, and respectful, whereas negative feelings included feeling stressed, embarrassed, annoyed, and nervous. Items were rated on a 4-point scale: 1 (*not at all*), 2 (*a little*), 3 (*a fair amount*), and 4 (*a great deal*). Both the positive and negative feelings demonstrated good reliability (α = .79 positive feelings for mothers; α = .81 positive feelings for fathers; α = .73 negative feelings for mothers; α = .80 negative feelings for fathers). Items representing positive feelings and items representing negative feelings were averaged to create scales of positive and negative language brokering feelings, respectively. Higher scores indicate greater positive or negative feeling endorsement while language brokering.

Autonomy Support

Two measures were used to examine the extent of autonomy-supportive parenting practices.

Parental Reasoning

Parents' use of reasoning was assessed using the Inductive Reasoning subscale of Kim and Ge's (2000) Parenting Practices scale (e.g., "Does your mom/dad give you reasons for her/his decisions?"). This 4-item subscale was completed by adolescents with respect to their mother and father separately. All items were rated on a 7-point scale from 1 (*never*) to 7 (*always*). Good reliability was found in the current sample for adolescents' reports of their mothers' (α = .77) and fathers' (α = .76) use of reasoning.

Psychological Control

Adolescents' sense of parental psychological control was assessed using Barber's (1996) Psychological Control Scale–Youth Self Report (PCS-YSR). This 8-item scale includes measures of invalidating feelings, constraining verbal expressions, personal attack, and love withdrawal (e.g., "My mom/dad is always trying to change how I feel or think about things"), rated on a 3-point scale from 1 (*not like her/him*) to 3 (*a lot like her/him*). The current sample showed good internal consistency across both father-child (α = .79) and mother-child dyads (α = .76).

Adolescent Self-Esteem

Adolescents completed the Rosenberg Self-Esteem Scale (Rosenberg, 1965) as a measure of their psychological adjustment. This 10-item scale measures self-esteem, including concepts of personal worth, self-confidence, self-satisfaction, self-respect, and self-deprecation (e.g., "I feel that I have a number of good qualities"). Participants reported their agreement with each statement on a 4-point scale from 1 (*strongly disagree*) to 4 (*strongly agree*). The internal consistency of this scale in the current sample was good ($\alpha = .89$).

Adolescent Depressive Symptoms

The Center for Epidemiological Studies Depression Scale (CES-D; Radloff, 1977) was used to assess adolescents' depressive symptoms. The CES-D contains 20 items (e.g., "I was bothered by things that usually don't bother me"). Adolescents reported the frequency of symptoms over the past week on a 4-point scale ranging from 0 (*rarely or none of the time; less than 1 day*) to 3 (*most or all of the time; 5–7 days*). In the current sample, the internal reliability of this scale was good ($\alpha = 88$).

Parent-Adolescent Conflict Intensity

The intensity of parent-adolescent conflict was assessed using the Issues Checklist (Robin & Foster, 1989). This 26-item measure lists discussion topics that are potentially a source of parent-adolescent conflict (e.g., cleaning up the bedroom, how money is spent). Adolescents indicated separately for each parent whether each item has been a topic of discussion, and if so, how intense the discussion has been. The intensity of anger for each discussion topic was rated on a 6-point scale from 0 (*not discussed*) to 5 (*very angry*). In the current study, the Issues Checklist showed good reliability for adolescents' reports of conflict intensity with mothers ($\alpha = .86$) and fathers ($\alpha = .78$).

Intergenerational Congruence

The Intergenerational Congruence in Immigrant Families–Child Scale (ICIF-CS) was used as a positive measure of parent-child relationship quality (Ying, Lee, & Tsai, 2004). This 8-item scale assesses children's levels of understanding and satisfaction with the parent-child relationship. Because pilot data prior to Wave 1 data collection revealed high correlations between adolescents' reports of their relationship with their mothers and their fathers ($r = .93$), Wave 1 and 2 questions were re-worded for the current study to ask about adolescents' relationship with their parents collectively (e.g., "My parents and I agree on friends"). Reponses were rated on a 5-point scale that ranged from 1 (*strongly disagree*) to 5 (*strongly agree*). In the current sample, the internal reliability of this scale was good ($\alpha = .86$).

Results

Language Brokering Frequency and Feelings

Adolescents' reported language brokering on average "a few times a year" ($M = 1.24$, $SD = .83$ for mothers; $M = 1.01$, $SD = .84$ for fathers), ranging from 0 (*never*) to 4 (*daily*) for both parents. Although the average frequency was relatively low, 85.5% of adolescents reported having ever language brokered for their fathers, and 94.7% of adolescents reported having ever language brokered for their mothers. Adolescent reports of language brokering frequency for mothers and fathers were significantly positively correlated with each other, $r(139) = .75$, $p < .001$. Adolescents reported significantly more frequent language brokering for mothers compared to fathers, $t(138) = -4.76$, $p < .001$; $d = 0.28$. There were no differences between female and male adolescents in the frequency of language brokering for fathers, $t(136) = 1.08$, $p < .28$, or for mothers, $t(146) = 0.62$, $p < .53$.

There was also a wide range of responses in the extent to which adolescents endorsed positive and negative feelings about language brokering. On average, adolescents reported feeling "a little" positive ($M = 2.25$, $SD = .73$ for mothers; $M = 2.17$ $SD = .77$ for fathers) and "not at all" to "a little" negative ($M = 1.53$, $SD = .52$ for mothers; $M = 1.51$, $SD = .59$ for fathers) about language brokering for their parents. Adolescents reported more positive feelings about language brokering for mothers than fathers, $t(140) = -2.78$, $p < .006$; $d = 0.11$. No differences were observed for negative feelings. Positive feelings about language brokering for mothers and fathers were significantly correlated, $r(141) = .91$, $p < .001$, as were negative language brokering feelings for mothers and fathers, $r(141) = .84$, $p < .001$. However, positive language brokering feelings for mothers did not correlate significantly with negative language brokering feelings for mothers, $r(148) = -.003$, $p = .97$, nor did positive and negative language brokering feelings for fathers correlate significantly with each other, $r(141) = .02$, $p = .84$.

Language Brokering and Adjustment

Univariate Analyses

The zero-order correlations between language brokering constructs and adjustment variables are presented in Table 7.1. More frequent language brokering for mothers and fathers was significantly associated with higher levels of adolescent depression and parent-adolescent conflict intensity. Relations between language brokering frequency (for either parent) and positive measures of adjustment (i.e., adolescent self-esteem and parent-adolescent congruence) did not reach significance. With respect to adolescents' feelings about language brokering, adolescents' negative feelings were significantly related to all adjustment outcomes (i.e., lower

TABLE 7.1 Inter-correlations among all study variables

Variable	1	2	3	4	5	6	7	8	9	10
1. Parents' Education	.65***	−.20**	.04	−.34***	.19*	−.12	.16*	−.04	−.05	.20*
2. Language Brokering Frequency	−.34***	.75***	.40***	.35***	.07	.28***	−.09	.18*	.24**	.10
3. Positive LB Feelings	−.09	.33***	.91***	−.003	.33***	.08	.12	−.04	.09	.34***
4. Negative LB Feelings	−.37***	.36***	.02	.84***	−.19*	.28***	−.31***	.22**	.29***	−.26**
5. Parental Reasoning	.14	.13	.29***	−.19*	.70***	−.43***	.15ᵃ	−.21**	−.24**	.51***
6. Parental Psychological Control	−.15ᵃ	.28***	−.05	.39***	−.32***	.51***	−.18*	.28***	.35***	−.15ᵃ
7. Adolescent Self-Esteem	.17*	−.14	.12	−.27***	.18*	−.18*	1	−.61***	−.14	.14
8. Adolescent Depressive Symptoms	−.04	.26**	−.07	.26**	−.22**	.33***	−.61***	1	.34***	−.12
9. Parent-Adolescent Conflict Intensity	.10	.29***	.08	.19*	−.01	.39***	−.07	.27***	.48***	−.21**
10. Intergenerational Congruence	.15ᵃ	.13	.35***	−.19*	.39***	−.17*	.14	−.12	−.11	1

Note: Mother-father correlations are on the diagonal; mother correlations are above the diagonal; father correlations are below.

ᵃ $p < .10$, * $p < .05$, ** $p < .01$, *** $p < .001$

levels of adolescent self-esteem, higher levels of depressive symptoms, more intense parent–adolescent conflict, and lower levels of intergenerational congruence). In contrast, positive feelings when language brokering for mothers and fathers were significantly related to stronger feelings of intergenerational congruence only.

Multivariate Regression Analyses

Eight hierarchical regression analyses evaluated the ability of language brokering frequency and feelings to predict individual and relational adjustment, as well as to examine the proposed moderating role of autonomy-supportive contexts. The results are presented in Table 7.2 regarding fathers and Table 7.3 regarding mothers. In each regression analysis, either the mother's or the father's education was entered as a control variable in the first step. In the second step, the main effects of all language brokering constructs (i.e., frequency, positive feelings, and

TABLE 7.2 Final Step of Hierarchical Regressions Predicting Relations Between Language Brokering for Fathers, Autonomy Support Variables, and Adjustment Outcomes

Variable	Adolescent Self-Esteem n = 120			Adolescent Depressive Symptoms n = 120			Conflict Intensity With Father n = 120			Intergenerational Congruence n = 120		
	B	SE B	β	B	SE B	β	B	SE B	β	B	SE B	β
Father's education	.04	.04	.08	.68	.61	.11	.12*	.06	.19	.06	.05	.10
LB Frequency for Father	−.002	.07	−.003	2.07ᵃ	1.08	.21	.24*	.10	.26	.02	.08	.02
Positive LB Feelings for Father	.07	.07	.10	−1.56	1.07	−.14	−.02	.10	−.02	.31***	.08	.33
Negative LB Feelings for Father	−.20*	.10	−.20	2.23	1.45	.16	−.04	.13	−.03	−.23*	.11	−.19
Father's Psychological Control	−.13	.14	−.09	2.71	2.06	.14	.69***	.19	.36	−.05	.15	−.03
Father's Use of Reasoning	.02	.05	.05	−.89	.72	−.12	.07	.07	.10	.17**	.05	.28
Positive Feelings × Psychological Control	n/a			n/a			n/a			.45*	.20	.19
R^2	.10			.15			.23			.32		

Note: n/a indicates that interaction term did not enter significantly into the model.
ᵃ$p < .06$, *$p < .05$, **$p < .01$, ***$p < .001$.

negative feelings) and the two moderator variables (i.e., parental psychological control and use of reasoning) were entered. To test whether autonomy-supportive contexts interacted with language brokering constructs, each of the two-way interactions involving parental reasoning and parental psychological control with the three language brokering predictors was tested for entry at Step 3 after accounting for main effects. Significant interaction effects only were retained in the models.

Language Brokering for Fathers, Main Effects

Consistent with univariate analyses, when considered simultaneously, more frequent language brokering for fathers was significantly related to higher levels of depressive symptoms and father-adolescent conflict. In addition, adolescents' positive feelings about language brokering for fathers predicted greater relationship congruence, although this relation was moderated by perceptions of psychological control, discussed later. Finally, adolescents' negative feelings about language brokering for fathers predicted lower self-esteem and relationship congruence.

TABLE 7.3 Final Step of Hierarchical Regressions Predicting Relations Between Language Brokering for Mothers, Autonomy Support Variables, and Adjustment Outcomes

Variable	Adolescent Self-Esteem n = 138			Adolescent Depressive Symptoms n = 138			Conflict Intensity With Mother n = 137			Intergenerational Congruence n = 138		
	B	SE B	β	B	SE B	β	B	SE B	β	B	SE B	β
Mothers' education	.02	.05	.05	.55	.62	.08	.04	.04	.08	.04	.04	.07
LB Frequency for Mother	.02	.07	.03	1.42	1.03	.14	.09	.06	.12	.07	.07	.09
Positive LB Feelings for Mother	.09	.07	.12	-.99	1.10	-.08	.03	.07	.04	.16*	.07	.18
Negative LB Feelings for Mother	-.28**	.10	-.26	2.49	1.55	.15	.16	.10	.14	-.24*	.10	-.18
Mother's Psychological Control	-.19	.13	-.14	3.32	1.99	.16	.28*	.12	.21	.03	.13	.02
Mother's Use of Reasoning	-.02	.05	-.03	-.84	.78	-.11	-.11*	.05	-.20	.25***	.05	.41
Positive Feelings × Reasoning	-.11*	.05	-.16	n/a			-.14**	.05	-.20	n/a		
Negative Feelings × Reasoning	n/a			n/a			-.15*	.07	-.16	n/a		
R^2	.15			.13			.27			.34		

Note: n/a indicates that interaction term did not enter significantly into the model.

*$p < .05$, **$p < .01$, ***$p < .001$.

Language Brokering for Mothers, Main Effects

As shown in Table 7.3, controlling for mothers' education, when the language brokering constructs were considered simultaneously, language brokering frequency was unrelated to any of the four indicators of adjustment. The extent of positive feelings about language brokering predicted more positive relationship congruence. In addition, interactions with maternal reasoning showed that positive feelings were also associated with self-esteem and mother-adolescent conflict in certain conditions (discussed later). Finally, as with fathers, negative feelings about language brokering for mothers were related to lower self-esteem and lower relationship congruence. In addition, as discussed later, an interaction between negative feelings and reasoning highlighted conditions in which negative feelings were also associated with greater mother-adolescent conflict.

Autonomy Support and Adjustment

Univariate Analyses and Main Effects

At the univariate level, both indicators of autonomy-supportive contexts (i.e., high parental reasoning and low psychological control) were significantly associated with adjustment across all four indicators. In the multivariate analyses, however, adolescents' perceptions of their parents' autonomy support were stronger predictors of relational outcomes than individual outcomes. In particular, for both fathers and mothers, higher perceptions of psychological control were related to reports of more intense parent-adolescent conflict, and perceptions of greater use of parental reasoning were associated with greater relationship congruence. Greater reasoning by mothers was also associated with less intense conflict.

Autonomy-Supportive Contexts as Moderator

Contrary to expectations, there was no evidence that autonomy-supportive contexts moderated links between language brokering frequency and adjustment. However, feelings about language brokering interacted with one of the two autonomy-supportive context variables to predict adjustment in four instances. As seen in Panel A of Figure 7.1, as expected, the relation between negative feelings about language brokering for mothers and mother-adolescent conflict intensity was strongest when maternal reasoning was perceived as low, whereas negative feelings were unrelated to conflict when reasoning was high. Interestingly, the interaction between positive feelings and reasoning in the prediction of mother-adolescent conflict showed the same pattern (see Panel B of Figure 7.1). Specifically, contrary to expectations, when maternal reasoning was particularly low, higher levels of *positive* feelings were associated with higher levels of conflict intensity. In contrast, positive feelings were unrelated to conflict and levels

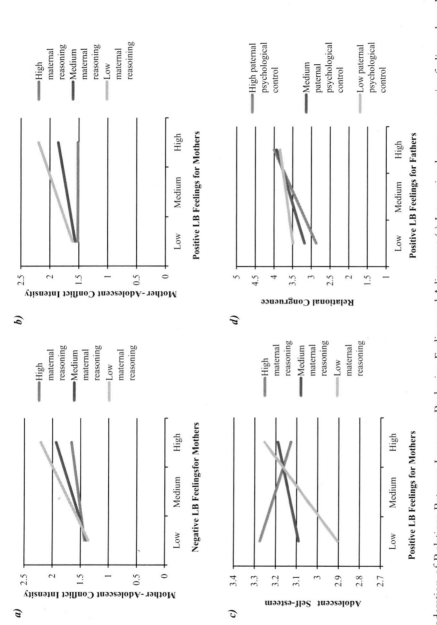

FIGURE 7.1 Moderation of Relations Between Language Brokering Feelings and Adjustment (a) Interaction between negative feelings about language brokering for mothers and maternal reasoning in the prediction of mother–adolescent conflict. (b) Interaction between positive feelings about language brokering for mothers and maternal reasoning in the prediction of mother–adolescent conflict. (c) Interaction between positive feelings about language brokering for mothers and maternal reasoning in the prediction of adolescent self-esteem. (d) Interaction between positive feelings about language brokering for fathers and paternal psychological control in the prediction of relational congruence.

of conflict were consistently low in these high autonomy-supportive contexts, regardless of the adolescents' feelings. Together, these results suggest that in low autonomy-supportive contexts, both negative and positive feelings are associated with more intense mother–child conflict.

The remaining two interactions involved the moderation of links between positive feelings and measures of positive adjustment. Specifically, positive feelings about language brokering for mothers interacted with maternal reasoning to predict adolescents' self-esteem (Panel C in Figure 7.1), and positive feelings about language brokering for fathers interacted with perceptions of psychological control to predict relationship congruence (Panel D in Figure 7.1). Inconsistent with our hypotheses, positive language brokering feelings were unrelated to self-esteem when maternal reasoning was high (instead, self-esteem was consistently high). However, in the context of low autonomy support, as measured by low maternal reasoning, when adolescents also reported higher levels of positive feelings, their report of self-esteem also tended to be higher. Similarly, more positive feelings were associated with more relationship congruence in the context of low autonomy support from fathers (as measured by high psychological control), rather than in the context of high autonomy support, which had been predicted. When adolescents perceived their fathers as low in psychological control, positive feelings were unrelated to relational congruence.

Conclusions

The results reveal a complex array of relations among language brokering frequency, feelings about language brokering, autonomy-supportive contexts, and adjustment within immigrant Chinese families in Canada. By distinguishing between language brokering for mothers versus fathers, simultaneously considering frequency and feelings, evaluating autonomy support in the family environment, and considering a range of adjustment indicators, the results provide new insights into the circumstances in which language brokering may be associated with psychological risks versus benefits.

Language Brokering Frequency and Feelings

The results suggest that language brokering for fathers may present greater challenges than language brokering for mothers. Although adolescents reported language brokering for fathers less frequently than for mothers, language brokering frequency for fathers was more predictive of adjustment difficulties (i.e., more depressive symptoms and more father-adolescent conflict). In addition, adolescents reported fewer positive feelings about language brokering for fathers compared to mothers. Because language brokering for mothers was more commonplace than for fathers, it could be that language brokering for mothers is perceived as more normative and does not significantly contribute to adolescents' sense of individual or relational well-being. In contrast, language brokering for fathers may threaten notions of family roles and hierarchy. For example, adolescents may perceive providing more frequent assistance in interpretation and translation to fathers as an indication of their father's slower acculturation in Canada or ineffectiveness in navigating issues on behalf of the family, resulting in adolescents experiencing greater conflict with fathers and feeling more depressive symptoms.

Experiencing negative feelings about language brokering for fathers and mothers was linked to less positive adjustment. That is, when language brokering for mothers and fathers evoked negative feelings, such as feeling stressed or embarrassed about providing interpretation and translation services, adolescents were more likely to report lower levels of self-esteem and poorer parent–child relational congruence. The relation between negative feelings and self-esteem is consistent with Weisskirch's (2013) study of Latino/a youth in the United States, which also found that a sense of burden when brokering was associated with lower levels of self-esteem and self-efficacy. In contrast, there was little evidence in the regression analyses that negative feelings were directly related to *negative* indicators of adjustment (i.e., adolescent depressive symptoms and parent–adolescent conflict intensity). Thus, feeling distressed about language brokering for parents may hinder personal and relational potential more than promote deleterious outcomes. Viewed in another way, this finding suggests that the less stressed, embarrassed, annoyed, and nervous adolescents feel about language brokering, the more the act of language brokering may help build their self-esteem and their emotional ties with their parents.

Positive feelings also showed an interesting pattern of relations with adjustment. With respect to mothers, more positive feelings were associated with more mother–child relationship congruence. The same was found for fathers, but only within contexts of high perceived paternal psychological control. In addition, adolescents' positive brokering feelings for mothers predicted self-esteem and mother–adolescent conflict within the context of low maternal reasoning. The patterns of these results suggest that positive feelings about language brokering for mothers are more salient for adolescents than positive feelings for fathers.

The extent to which adolescents experienced positive feelings about language brokering (i.e., helpful, grown-up, proud, and respectful) was unrelated to the extent to which they experienced negative feelings. Thus, the experience of positive feelings is not merely the absence of negative feelings; both positive and negative feelings can co-exist. These findings highlight the emotional complexity of the language brokering experience for adolescents.

When language brokering constructs were evaluated simultaneously, we found that the frequency of language brokering mattered relatively less than the emotional experience of language brokering for parents. This overall finding is consistent with previous literature examining Latino/a populations that has emphasized the relative importance of language brokering–related emotions and the time burden of language brokering compared to the frequency of language brokering (Kam & Lazarevic, 2014; Weisskirch, 2013).

Autonomy-Supportive Contexts

Consistent with SDT, the results suggest that adolescents' perceptions of autonomy support from parents were associated with positive adjustment. Autonomy support was a particularly strong predictor of relational versus individual outcomes, as low parental psychological control was significantly associated with less intense parent-adolescent conflict intensity. Similarly, mothers' and fathers' high use of reasoning was related to greater relationship congruence with their adolescent child. Higher maternal reasoning was also associated with less intense conflict. Providing an autonomy-supportive environment is inherently relational, and this may explain why there were stronger direct links with the relationship-oriented outcomes.

The prediction that autonomy-supportive contexts, as defined by SDT, would modify the relations between language brokering frequency and adjustment was largely unsupported. Similarly, there was only one instance in which autonomy-supportive contexts moderated the relations between negative feelings and adjustment. As expected, the relation between negative feelings and more intense mother-adolescent conflict was strongest when reasoning was low, and this adverse link was buffered in high autonomy-supportive (i.e., maternal reasoning) contexts. This finding supports the expectation that when adolescents do not experience an overall context that is supportive of their autonomy, the stress or pressure that they feel about language brokering spills over into more conflictual relationships with mothers, and that relationships are protected from this spillover when autonomy support is high.

With respect to significant interactions between positive language brokering feelings and autonomy-supportive contexts, we did not find support for our prediction that associations between positive feelings and adjustment would be particularly strong in autonomy-supportive contexts. Instead, self-esteem and relationship congruence were generally high in high autonomy-supportive contexts, regardless of the strength of positive feelings. Instead, it was in low autonomy-supportive contexts where the extent of positive feelings mattered most as a predictor of positive adjustment. Viewing language brokering for parents positively in terms of feeling helpful, mature, and proud in performing this form of assistance may help adolescents who experience a low autonomy-supportive context to maintain or enhance a positive connection with their parents despite the lack of autonomy support. That is, feeling positively about language brokering contributions may help adolescents compensate for a lack of an autonomy-supportive environment.

Finally, contrary to expectations, positive feelings about language brokering were significantly and positively associated with mother-adolescent conflict when maternal reasoning was particularly low. In contrast, when reasoning was high, levels of conflict intensity remained consistently low and positive feelings were unrelated to conflict. This finding suggests that adolescents who feel positive and grown-up about language brokering for their mothers, but are told what to do with little explanation (i.e., low autonomy support), experience greater conflict with their mothers. These adolescents may feel that their mothers are particularly unfair when they make rules unilaterally or do not explain the reasons for their decisions because this context of low autonomy support does not recognize the maturity and contributions the adolescents make through their language brokering assistance. As a result, these adolescents may engage in more heated disagreements with their mothers in an effort to gain more autonomy.

Future Directions

Additional research is needed to evaluate how the language brokering experience for mothers versus fathers is similar and different. In addition, the findings in this chapter were based on cross-sectional data, and thus causal conclusions cannot be drawn. Longitudinal research would be better able to assess the direction of the relations among language brokering constructs as predictors of individual and relational adjustment among Chinese Canadian immigrant families.

Additional research is also needed to better understand positive feelings about language brokering. In our study, even at the univariate level, positive feelings were significantly related to relationship congruence only, whereas negative feelings were significantly related to all four adjustment indicators, as we expected. This suggests that what we are calling "positive feelings" may not be as unqualifiedly positive as the label implies. Instead, feeling proud, helpful, grown-up, and respectful may represent more complicated emotions that include concern or pressure (e.g., getting the translation right) alongside positive affective elements. Relatedly, other studies have begun to examine additional aspects of language brokering, such as adolescents' sense of language brokering efficacy (i.e., assessing how good or confident children of immigrant parents feel about language brokering), which relate uniquely to adjustment (Kam & Lazaveric, 2014; Weisskirch, 2013). The addition of constructs such as efficacy to the study of language brokering may help clarify the nature of positive feelings specifically and further our understanding of potential benefits and risks of language brokering more generally.

Contribution to Theory

We applied SDT to predict family environments that might set the stage for language brokering constructs to be associated with positive versus negative adjustment. However, the hypothesis that contexts low in autonomy support would exacerbate poor outcomes associated with language brokering and that contexts high in autonomy support would buffer negative associations was largely unsupported. Instead, autonomy-supportive contexts showed direct main effects, particularly as predictors of parent-adolescent relationship quality. These findings are consistent with the predictions of SDT, affirming the developmental assets related to autonomy-supportive environments. In addition, the significant interactions between positive feelings and autonomy support were partially congruent with SDT in the sense that they highlighted the fact that positive developmental outcomes are more difficult to achieve in environments low in autonomy support.

The findings are also congruent with the parent-child role reversal framework, which is a prominent theoretical lens previously applied to language brokering work. This framework suggests that parents' dependence on their children for language brokering assistance may diminish parental authority and may place children in typically adult roles (McQuillan & Tse, 1995). From this deficit perspective, the unequal power relationship that is thought to accompany language brokering has negative repercussions for the child language broker and/or the parent-child relationship (Morales & Hanson, 2005).

Finally, our findings contribute to the development of a theory about language brokering specifically. Past studies have identified the act of language brokering as a stressor, but others (e.g., Kam, 2011) have emphasized the importance of how adolescents feel about language brokering. Our findings support the need to expand the lens through which language brokering experiences are viewed to incorporate multiple aspects of the experience. The context of low autonomy support may be especially undermining of children's sense of feeling authoritative in their role as language brokers and may exacerbate the complexity of feelings that may be associated with parent-child role reversals. Indeed, we found that within the strain of a low autonomy-supportive environment, also feeling less positive about language brokering is associated with developmental risk (i.e., lower self-esteem and poorer relational congruence), but in other circumstances, feeling good about language brokering can even be associated with relationship strain if the overall context undermines autonomy (i.e., low reasoning). Although our findings highlight additional contexts in which there are risks associated with language brokering, they also suggest that if parents can provide a strong autonomy-supportive environment to their children, they may directly impact well-being and potentially lessen the relative importance of how Chinese Canadian adolescents feel about language brokering.

References

Barber, B. K. (1996). Parental psychological control: Revisiting a neglected construct. *Child Development, 67*(6), 3296–3319.

Buriel, R., Perez, W., DeMent, T. L., Chavez, D. V., & Moran, V. R. (1998). The relationship of language brokering to academic performance, biculturalism, and self-efficacy among Latino adolescents. *Hispanic Journal of Behavioral Sciences, 20*(3), 283–297.

Chao, R. K. (2006). The prevalence and consequences of adolescents' language brokering for their immigrant parents. In M. H. Bornstein & L. R. Cote (Eds.), *Acculturation and parent-child relationships: Measurement and development* (pp. 271–296). Mahwah, NJ: Lawrence Erlbaum.

Deci, E. L., & Ryan, R. M. (2000). The "what" and "why" of goal pursuits: Human needs and the self-determination of behavior. *Psychological Inquiry, 11*, 227–268. doi:10.1207/S15327965PLI1104_01

Deci, E. L., & Ryan, R. M. (2008a). Self-determination theory: A macrotheory of human motivation, development, and health. *Canadian Psychology, 49*(3), 182–185. doi:10.1037/a0012801

Hall, N., & Sham, S. (1998). *Language brokering by Chinese children.* Paper presented at the Annual Conference of the British Educational Research Association, Dublin, Ireland.

Hua, J. M., & Costigan, C. L. (2012). The familial context of adolescent language brokering within immigrant Chinese families in Canada. *Journal of Youth and Adolescence, 41*(7), 894–906. doi:10.1007/s10964-011-9682-2

Joussemet, M., Landry, R., & Koestner, R. (2008). A self-determination theory perspective on parenting. *Canadian Psychology, 49*(3), 194–200.

Kam, J. A. (2011). The effects of language brokering frequency and feelings on Mexican-heritage youth's mental health and risky behaviors. *Journal of Communication, 61*(3), 455–475. doi:10.1111/j.1460–2466.2011.01552.x

Kam, J. A., & Lazarevic, V. (2014). The stressful (and not so stressful) nature of language brokering: Identifying when brokering functions as a cultural stressor for Latino immigrant children in early adolescence. *Journal of Youth and Adolescence, 43,* 1994–2011. doi:10.1007/s10964–013–0061-z

Kim, S. Y., & Ge, X. (2000). Parenting practices and adolescent depressive symptoms in Chinese American families. *Journal of Family Psychology, 14*(3), 420–435.

McQuillan, J., & Tse, L. (1995). Child language brokering in linguistic minority communities: Effects on cultural interaction, cognition, and literacy. *Language and Education, 9,* 195–215. doi:10.1080/09500789509541413

Martinez, C. R., McClure, H. H., & Eddy, J. M. (2009). Language brokering contexts and behavioral and emotional adjustment among Latino parents and adolescents. *Journal of Early Adolescence, 29*(1), 71–98.

Morales, A., & Hanson, W. E. (2005). Language brokering: An integrative review of the literature. *Hispanic Journal of Behavioral Sciences, 27,* 471–503. doi:10.1177/0739986305281333

Morales, A., Yakushko, O. F., & Castro, A. J. (2012). Language brokering among Mexican-immigrant families in the Midwest: A multiple case study. *The Counseling Psychologist, 40*(4), 520–553. doi:10.1177/0011000011417312

Niehaus, K., & Kumpiene, G. (2014). Language brokering and self-concept: An exploratory study of Latino students' experiences in middle and high school. *Hispanic Journal of Behavioral Sciences, 36*(2), 124–143. doi:10.1177/0739986314524166

Radloff, L. S. (1977). The CES-D Scale: A self-report depression scale for research in the general population. *Applied Psychological Measurement, 1,* 385–401. doi:10.1177/014662167700100306

Robin, A. L., & Foster, S. L. (1989). *Negotiating parent-adolescent conflict: A behavioral-family systems approach.* New York, NY: Guilford Press.

Rosenberg, M. (1965). *Society and the adolescent self-image.* Princeton, NJ: Princeton University Press.

Ryan, R. M., & Deci, E. L. (2000). Self-determination theory and the facilitation of intrinsic motivation, social development, and well-being. *The American Psychologist, 55*(1), 68–78.

Shek, D. T. L. (2008). Perceived parental control in Chinese adolescents in Hong Kong: A three-year longitudinal study. *The Open Family Studies Journal, 1*(1), 7–16. doi:10.2174/1874922400801010007

Shen, Y., Kim, S. Y., Wang, Y., & Chao, R. K. (2014). Language brokering and adjustment among Chinese and Korean American adolescents: A moderated mediation model of perceived maternal sacrifice, respect for the mother, and mother—child open communication. *Asian American Journal of Psychology, 5*(2), 86–95. doi:10.1037/a0035203

Statistics Canada. (2013). Immigration and ethnocultural diversity in Canada: National household survey, 2011. Catalogue no. 99–010-X201100. Retrieved from www.statcan. gc.ca

Tse, L. (1996). Language brokering in linguistic minority communities: The case of Chinese- and Vietnamese-American students. *Bilingual Research Journal, 20*, 485–498.

Wang, Q., Pomerantz, E. M., & Chen, H. (2007). The role of parents' control in early adolescents' psychological functioning: A longitudinal investigation in the United States and China. *Child Development, 78*, 1592–1610.

Wang, S., & Lo, L. (2004). Chinese immigrants in Canada: Their changing composition and economic performance. Policy Matter, No. 10, produced by the Joint Centre of Excellence for Research on Immigration and Settlement—Toronto (CERIS). Retrieved from http://www.metroplois.net

Weisskirch, R. S. (2007). Feelings about language brokering and family relations among Mexican American early adolescents. *Journal of Early Adolescence, 27*(4), 545–561.

Weisskirch, R. S. (2013). Family relationships, self-esteem, and self-efficacy among language brokering Mexican American emerging adults. *Journal of Child and Family Studies, 22*, 1147–1155. doi:10.1007/s10826–012–9678-x

Wu, N. H., & Kim, S. Y. (2009). Chinese American adolescents' perceptions of the language brokering experience as a sense of burden and sense of efficacy. *Journal of Youth and Adolescence, 38*(5), 703–18. doi:10.1007/s10964-008-9379-3

Ying, Y. W., Lee, P. A., & Tsai, J. L. (2004). Psychometric properties of the intergenerational congruence in immigrant families: Child scale in Chinese Americans. *Journal of Comparative Family Studies, 35*(1), 91–103.

PART III

Applied Contexts and Settings

8

IMMIGRANT INTERNETWORKS

Language Brokering and Internet Use

Shu-Sha Angie Guan

Introduction

Language brokering, the work done by children of immigrants, is comprised of translating "written and face-to-face communication" (Weisskirch, 2005). Given the increased prevalence of digital technologies, particularly among youth, this chapter will highlight the ways that language brokering has moved into digital spaces. Given the lack of research in this specific topic, I begin by discussing the growth of information and communication technologies (ICTs). Next, I discuss the broader literature on immigrant youth and new media use and examine how language brokers may use information and communication technologies (ICTs) in their work. I end with a discussion of how new media might affect language brokers' connection to heritage cultures based on the quantitative and qualitative findings.

Growth of Information and Communication Technologies (ICTs)

The Internet has become an important informational and social tool for young people from various socioeconomic and ethnic backgrounds (Katz & Gonzalez, 2015; Pew Research Center, 2012). ICTs include hardware such as mobile phones, smart phones, and computers as well as software such as e-mail, instant messaging (IM; e.g., Gchat), videoconferencing programs (e.g., Skype, Facetime), social networking sites (e.g., Facebook), blogs, vlogs, and forums—all of which are becoming more prevalent, nationwide and globally (Pew Research Center, 2012; World Bank, 2015). Around the world, mobile-phone use is outpacing landline usage such that, in 2002, the total number of mobiles had exceeded the number of landlines (Donner, 2008). Computer-mediated communication is also on the rise as the prevalence of computer and Internet access grows worldwide. In the most recent World Bank reports, the Internet penetration rate (number per 100 people) has risen in the United States from 69.7 in 2011 to 87.4 in 2014 (World Bank, 2015). The global trend is demonstrated by rates of individuals who have used the Internet in the last year (i.e., via computer, mobile device, etc.) rising from 2011 to 2014 in countries like Brazil (45.7 to 57.6), China (38.3 to 49.3), El Salvador (18.9 to 29.7), Iran (19.0 to 39.4), Turkey (43.1 to 51.0), and Vietnam (35.1 to 48.3). The pace of growth indicates that more people will augment their interactions with technology.

These new forms of communication technologies have unique capabilities compared to older forms of media that make them particularly useful for immigrant populations. Rogers (1986) suggests that machine-assisted interpersonal communication technologies are interactive and intelligent, allowing a back-and-forth response format similar to face-to-face conversations. In addition, in comparison to older mass media formats like radio, television, and even print, ICTs are de-massified: Individuals can choose to speak to a large audience or a select few. Finally, ICTs are asynchronous and not bound by time or geography, allowing individuals to speak to others across city, state, national, and continental borders. These capabilities make ICT an engaging, accessible, and convenient method of accessing information and communication. Immigrant populations, who often face challenges of economic survival and disconnection from established support networks, may especially benefit from these unique capabilities of new media.

Immigrant Media Use

Given the growing popularity of digital media among youth and the capacity of the Internet to provide immigrants with information and connections to host and home communities (Ito et al., 2010; Matsaganis, Katz, & Ball-Rokeach, 2010), new media use may have significant implications for children of immigrants as they adapt and help their families acculturate in new contexts. Drawing from communications work on ethnic media (mostly newspapers and television programs by and for ethnic minority groups), Matsaganis et al. (2010) suggests that the potential ways new media can meet the needs of transnational populations can be organized in three ways: orienting them toward the new culture (i.e., orientation function), representing and keeping them tied to their countries of origin (i.e., symbolic function), and connecting them to others at home and abroad (i.e., connective function).

Orientation Function

The orientation function of media has implications for acculturation processes and autonomy. Traditionally, one of the main approaches to the study of media and communication is in the study of the role of mass media and communication in the integration and acculturation processes (Kim, 1979; Meyrowitz, 1985; Skop & Adams, 2009; Weiskopf & Kissau, 2008). This approach is appropriate since one of the main tasks post-migration is acculturating to the new, host society for immigrants, foreign students, and refugees alike. Mass media and communications usually made by and in the language of the host country can be a useful tool from which to learn and adapt to the values, conventions, and governing bodies of the host society (Hwang & He, 1999; Kim, 1979). In the same way, new media, can be an important, individualized source of information about the host language and culture. There is some evidence that access to this type of information can ease the transition into new environments by increasing autonomy, teaching coping strategies, building and maintaining support, and promoting new language development (Reece & Palmgreen, 2000; Tsai, 2006; Yang, Wu, Zhu, & Brian, 2004). In a study of East Asian international students in the United States, for example, Ye (2005) found that English-language Internet access was related to increased English proficiency. In addition, in the same way that ethnic enclaves and ethnoburbs (i.e., ethnic suburbs) provide familiarity and security, diasporic websites and "cyber villages" can provide users with a sense of community and a "homelike" feeling (Benitez, 2006; Mitra, 2006; Navarrete & Huerta, 2006; Parham, 2004; Sardar & Ravetz, 1996; Weiskopf & Kissau, 2008). Just as the local, home-language media available in enclaves can work as culture brokers for their communities (Matsaganis et al., 2010), diasporic websites can draw transnational co-ethnics together in important exchanges of information. Young language brokers may also turn to digital media to find resources as they broker for their families and friends. The need for media as an acculturative tool, however, may diminish over time and generations (Chen, 2009; Ye, 2005).

Symbolic Function

The symbolic function of media may shape mainstream and ethnic identity formation among young brokers. Just as new media forms can transmit cultural information about the host country in ways that facilitate acculturation, they can also provide connection to the culture in countries of origin in ways that can shape identity formation processes, especially for second- and third-generation youth. The need to belong is a fundamental human need (Baumeister & Leary, 1995) and one of the ways individuals feel a sense of belonging is through the maintenance of emotionally significant relationships with family, friends, and romantic partners. However, individuals also gain a sense of belonging through identification with larger social groups, such as religious, cultural, ethnic, and racial groups (Phinney, 1992). Ethnic television shows, like telenovelas (Spanish-language soap operas), reflect national, ethnic, gender, and class issues that define the identities of their ethnic viewers (Mayer, 2003) and provide a way to feel a sense of belonging to the heritage group. New media spaces, such as social networking sites that allow users to personalize their pages with references to heritage cultures (e.g., using images of a Mexican flag or flag colors on a MySpace page, and sharing information about immigrant rights rallies as described in Orellana, 2009; posting links to film and songs from Indian or Pakistani films as described in Maira, 2009), also validate notions of self that may be separate from the mainstream. This ability to affiliate virtually may be especially important for second- and third-generation ethnic youth who may have less of a direct link to their countries of origin but inhabit a period of development in which they must define themselves, personally and ethnically (Erikson, 1968; Marcia, 1980; Phinney, 1992), and in particular when they reside in countries in which they may be marked as foreigners because of appearance, accent, cultural practices, or other characteristics. In this way, new media connections with people and cultures in countries of origin can serve a symbolic function in transmitting cultural values and contributing to one's developing sense of ethnic identity.

Connective Function

The connective function of new media can address issues of attachment and family cohesion post-migration. ICTs such as global e-mail, chat, social networking sites, forums, and web conferencing programs can provide immigrants access to support networks in ways that bring transnational loved ones into their homes and vice versa (Lim & Thomas, 2010; Tsai, 2006; Weiskopf & Kissau, 2008). For example, an individual can "call" home using videoconferencing and visually see and communicate with relatives in the home country and in their language of origin. In this way, ICTs can transcend borders. ICTs are often quicker, more simultaneous, and more affect-laden (in terms of being able to see and hear loved ones) than older forms of media. These new ways to connect face-to-face and in real time can have far-reaching implications for attachment and family cohesion. These connections may also bring new opportunities for cultural exchange and language brokering.

Language Brokering and Internet Use

Language brokering has orienting, symbolic, and connective functions by allowing immigrant children to maintain ties to heritage language and culture. Prior studies have found that language brokering is associated to higher heritage language aptitude and greater knowledge about heritage culture (Acoach & Webb, 2004; Buriel et al., 1998; Guan, Nash, & Orellana, 2015; Orellana, 2009; Weiskirch, 2005). In addition to language, children of immigrants also broker cultural knowledge, including knowledge about technology. As "media brokers" for their family members, children often assist their families with technology (Katz, 2010, 2014). Given that English is a prevailing language on the Internet, use of technology may further require an intermediary such as a language broker to help guide the families' computer-mediated interactions. Interviews with immigrant families suggest they also use technology to search for online resources and translation (Katz, 2014; Katz & Gonzalez, 2015). However, few studies have examined how this use of technology media among language brokers might shape acculturative and identity processes. Therefore, the current chapter will discuss the ways in which children of immigrants use ICTs. I use both qualitative and quantitative methods to assess the implications of ICT use for language brokering and cultural connection.

Method

Participants

Emerging adults from immigrant families (N = 139; female = 97; M_{age} = 20.92, SD = 2.43) from Asian (54.7%), Latino/a (19.4%), and other ethnic backgrounds (25.9%, e.g., Middle Eastern, European, mixed) completed an online survey indicating demographic information (e.g., gender, age, years in the United States, parent education), transnational Internet use, language brokering, acculturation, and ethnic identity. Participants were recruited through the Psychology Subject Pool at a large research university on the west coast of the United States. They received course credit and were included in the study if they were foreign-born or had at least one foreign-born parent. Approximately, 45.32% were first generation (i.e., they and their parents were born outside of the United States) and 54.68% were second generation (i.e., they were born in the United States, but their parents were born outside of the United States).

Measures and Procedures

ICT Use

ICT and transnational Internet use were assessed with the survey item "Do you use the Internet (Social Networking Site, Skype, etc.) to keep in touch with family in another country?" If participants responded "no," they continued to the next sections of the survey. If they answered "yes," they then described how they used the Internet to stay connected and with whom (in open-ended text boxes).

Language Brokering

Language brokering frequency (Dorner, Orellana, & Li-Grining, 2007) assessed how often participants translated and interpreted for their mother, father, grandparents, younger brothers or sisters, older brothers or sisters, other family, teachers, and friends in the past on a scale from 0 = *never* to 3 = *every day*. Cronbach's alpha indicates moderate reliability of scale, $\alpha = .67$. The number of places language brokered was assessed with a checklist of eight common places (e.g., at home, school, doctor's office, stores, on the street) and summed. The number of items brokered was assessed with a checklist of 15 common items (e.g., letters, homework, report cards, bills, phone calls, words) and summed.

Heritage and American Cultural Orientation

The degree of comfort participants felt with their native culture (i.e., heritage culture orientation) and American culture (i.e., American culture orientation) was assessed with questions modified from the Bicultural Involvement Questionnaire (BIQ; Szapocznik, Kurtines, & Fernandez, 1980). The BIQ was created based on the Behavioral Acculturation Scale (Szapocznik, Scopetta, Kurtines, & Aranalde, 1978) and developed for a primarily Latino/a population. Given the diversity of the current sample, the items were modified to generalize to broader ethnic groups. Examples of items from the heritage culture subscale are "How comfortable do you feel speaking your native language/parents' native language at home?" "How comfortable do you feel speaking your native language/parents' native language at school?" "How much do you enjoy the music of your cultural/ethnic background?" and "How much do you enjoy the T.V. programs of your cultural/ethnic background?" Examples of the American culture orientation items are "How comfortable do you feel speaking English at home?" "How comfortable do you feel speaking English at school?" "How much do you enjoy the American music?" and "How much do you enjoy American T.V. programs?" Participants used a scale from $1 = not\ at\ all\ comfortable$ to $5 = very\ comfortable$ to assess each item. Cronbach's alphas for heritage culture understanding and American culture understanding were .88 and .90, respectively.

Ethnic Identity

The Multigroup Ethnic Identity Measure (MEIM; Phinney, 1992) was used to assess the degree to which participants incorporated their ethnic group into their self-concept. The MEIM included 12 items such as "I have spent time trying to find out more about my own ethnic group, such as its history, traditions and customs," "I have a strong sense of belonging to my own ethnic group," and "I participate in cultural practices of my own group, such as special food, music, or customs" that participants rated on a scale from $1 = strongly\ disagree$ to $4 = strongly\ agree$. Cronbach's alpha for this measure was .87.

Interviews

After completing the survey, a subsample of participants were invited to participate in semi-structured, 2-hour interviews. Eight interviewees were from Asian backgrounds and two were from Latino/a backgrounds. Seven Asian American participants (one male and six females, including Li; see the case studies) and the two Latina participants (both female) were recruited for follow-up interviews after their participation in the survey portion. One Asian American participant (Chen, male; see the case studies) was an acquaintance of the author who volunteered. Participants were asked to discuss their experiences as language brokers and were asked follow-up questions about their use of the Internet to facilitate communication such as "Do you ever broker online?" and "How have you used the Internet to help you broker?" All of the interviews were conducted by the author, in English, in person, and recorded. One interview was conducted over an instant messenger program (Gchat). Interviewees were given a gift of $20. Pseudonyms are used.

Results

Survey findings

Results indicated that more than 63.3% ($n = 88$) used e-mail, instant messaging, social networking sites and videoconferencing programs to keep in touch with friends and relatives abroad. Of these participants, 29.55% reported using e-mail, 21.59% instant messenger (e.g., AOL instant messenger), 60.23% a social networking site (e.g., Facebook), 43.18% a videoconferencing program (e.g., Skype), and 12.5% other (e.g., blog comments). A majority (53.41%) used more than one communication application. The majority of participants used the Internet to connect with family (e.g., parents, siblings, cousins, aunts, uncles, grandparents; $n = 71$) and a few with friends ($n = 20$) abroad. There were no significant differences in parent education by ICT use, $t(133) = -1.25, p = .213$. Similarly, ICT use did not significantly differ by ethnic background, $\chi^2 (2) = 3.08, p = .215$. However, a greater percentage of females ($n = 66$) used ICT compared to males ($n = 16$), $\chi^2 (1) = 4.73, p = .03$. ICT users also tended to be older ($M = 21.27, SD = 2.52$) compared to non-ICT users ($M = 20.31, SD = 2.16$), $t(137) = 2.27, p = .024$.

Examination of ICT use by generational status was not significant, $\chi^2 (1) = 3.27$, $p = .071$, but suggested a trend in which second-generation participants were less likely to report ICT use to communicate with others abroad ($n = 33$) compared to first-generation participants ($n = 18$). In terms of years in the United States, those who used the Internet to keep in touch with those abroad were newer immigrants ($M = 14.98$ years in United States, $SD = 6.61$) compared to those who did not ($M = 17.52, SD = 5.27$), $t(137) = -2.39, p = .018$. Perhaps related to this, those individuals who reported ICT use had higher heritage cultural understanding on the BIQ ($M = 71.09, SD = 14.60$) compared to those who did not report using ICT ($M = 64.85, SD = 15.94$), $t(137) = 2.37, p = .019$. However, there were no differences in American culture orientation, $t(137) = -.79, p = .43$. Those individuals who used the Internet to communicate with others in a different country reported higher levels of brokering for other relatives ($M = 1.07$, $SD = .69$) compared to those who did not ($M = .80$, $SD = .66$), $t(136) = 2.33$, $p = .021$. There were no other significant differences by ICT use for any of the people for whom one could language broker, $ts(129 - 136) = -.24$–1.52, $ps = .13$–$.81$. There were also no significant differences in number of places or items brokered, $ts(136 - 137) = -.23$–1.40, $ps = .17$–$.82$.

Correlations between main study variables were examined (Table 8.1). A greater number of years in the United States was associated with lower heritage culture orientation, $r(139) = -.21$, $p = .012$; higher American culture orientation, $r(139) = .38$, $p < .001$; but was not associated with ethnic identity, $r(139) = .05$, $p = .570$; language brokering frequency, $r(138) = -.01$, $p = .928$; number of places, $r(139) = -.02$, $p = .777$; or number of items brokered, $r(139) = -.04$, $p = .611$. Language brokering frequency was associated with lower American culture orientation, $r(138) = -.17$, $p = .042$; and marginally higher ethnic identity, $r(138) = .17$, $p = .054$; but not with heritage culture orientation, $r(138) = .13$, $p = .135$. Number of places and types was associated with higher heritage culture orientation, $r(139) = .25$, $p = .003$; but not American culture orientation, $r(139) = -.11$, $p = .200$; or ethnic identity, $r(139) = .09$, $p = .278$. Number of places was associated with higher heritage culture orientation, $r(139) = .27$, $p = .001$; and lower American culture orientation, $r(139) = -.20$, $p = .018$; but not ethnic identity, $r(139) = .12$, $p = .161$.

Given the how parent education and years in the United States may affect Internet access and use, regressions were modeled to control for these covariates in examining the relationship between ICT use and cultural identity measures. As shown in Table 8.2, after controlling for parent education and years in the United States, it was found that those who used transnational connection had higher levels of heritage culture understanding ($B = 2.66$, $SE = 1.27$, $p = .038$), a trend toward higher ethnic identity ($B = .07$, $SE = .04$, $p = .062$) and language brokering frequency ($B = .07$, $SE = .04$, $p = .061$), particularly language brokering for

TABLE 8.1 Correlations Between Main Study Variables

Variables	1	2	3	4	5	6	7	8	9
1. Age	—	.01	.00	.09	−.14	.00	.04	−.02	.02
2. Years in US		—	−.04	−.21*	.38*	.05	−.01	−.02	−.04
3. Parent education			—	−.31*	.28*	−.24*	−.28*	−.34*	−.38*
4. Heritage culture				—	−.53*	.45*	.13	.25*	.27*
5. American culture					—	−.22*	−.17*	−.11	−.20*
6. Ethnic identity						—	.17†	.09	.12
7. LB frequency							—	.56*	.60*
8. LB Places								—	.77*
9. LB Items									—

Note: LB = language brokering.
†$p < .10$. *$p < .05$.

TABLE 8.2 Regression Models Predicting Cultural Orientation, Ethnic Identity, and Language Brokering Variables From ICT Use

Variable	Heritage Culture		American Culture		Ethnic Identity		LB Frequency		LB for Relatives	
	B	SE	B	SE	B	SE	B	SE	B	SE
Intercept	67.96*	1.25	81.60*	.80	3.06	.04	.77*	.04	.92*	.06
Parent education	−5.27*	1.21	3.08*	.78	−.12	.04	−.13*	.04	−.09	.06
Years in US	−3.06	1.22	3.95*	.78	.03	.04	.00	.04	.11	.06
ICT use	2.66*	1.27	−.48	.81	.07†	.04	.07†	.04	.16*	.06

Note: Standardized z-scores of parent education and years in the US centered at the mean were used to reduce multicollinearity. ICT use was effect coded with −1 = no ICT use and 1 = ICT use.

†$p < .10$. *$p < .05$.

other relatives ($B = .16$, $SE = .06$, $p = .011$), than those who did not. ICT use did not predict the number of places ($B = .04$, $SE = .19$, $p = .815$) or items ($B = .52$, $SE = .33$, $p = .12$) brokered.

Case Studies

The qualitative interviews were analyzed to contextualize the quantitative findings and the ways these relationships may emerge in the personal experiences of language brokers. When asked, all participants said they used the Internet to look up information or for translation purposes. However, only two first-generation participants, both of whom emigrated to the United States during adolescence, recalled and explicitly recounted language brokering while online. Their responses highlight ways in which all language brokers generally used technology to help them broker (e.g., accessing online dictionaries, finding document templates). The results of two interviews are summarized and given here as case studies of how language brokers are using technology.

Li

At the time of the in-person interview, Li was 20 years old. Li was born in mainland China but lived in Hong Kong most of her childhood. In Hong Kong, her father worked for the government, and she had a middle-class upbringing before moving to Chicago, Illinois when she was 14 years old. She, her parents, and her younger brother first settled with relatives in Chicago before moving to California for the warmer weather. Despite learning English in Hong Kong, Li reported that she still had difficulty understanding the language since the American accent was different from the British accent she had been exposed to in Hong Kong. However, as the eldest sibling, she remembered language brokering quite a bit. For example, she recalled helping her parents set up bank accounts and credit cards.

At first, her aunt would help language broker. However, her aunt grew impatient over time, and Li stepped in at age 14 to language broker on behalf of the family.

Although she was the preferred translator, she did not always feel her work was appreciated by her parents. She relayed that her parents would get frustrated and say things like "Oh, you're not good at translating" without sympathizing with the fact that she wasn't fully bilingual yet. She reported that her parents generally felt "disabled" in this new country without strong linguistic and cultural skills. Her father's sense of loss grew more pronounced after Li's mother died in 2009, and he had to rely on Li more. With her family's demands for language brokering, she had used an online dictionary. This was a similar approach to using a digital dictionary when she was in Hong Kong. However, she reported that, for full phrases or paperwork, the quality of the translation in these online translators are terrible "because it made me make a lot of mistakes in word choices. They always use weird words. Not the right word choice. Even though the right meaning, but not the right word choice." She recognized that the technology was imperfect, and she had to use her judgment to figure out the right words for accurate meaning.

Her recounting of interactions with friends and family in China took on a different tone. Rather than use videoconferencing, she reported most often using an instant messenger program popular in China called QQ to communicate with friends and family (e.g., cousins) in Hong Kong. She noted the dramatic change in her language abilities when she first started using the program:

> Actually, for like three months, my Chinese improved a lot because I typed in Pinyin [a system of phonetic translations into Chinese characters]. I can't remember how to type in the other type of Chinese [system used in Hong Kong]. . . . Back then I typed really slow [sic], but right now, I type really fast!

By using the technology, Li was able to maintain and further her own Chinese language and cultural understanding. Although digital media allowed Li to keep in touch with those abroad, she did not use the technology to make new friends. Rather, she used it to chat with close relatives and friends. She explained, "There is only one friend. We still keep in contact a lot. But, other friend, we are not really in contact. He's talkative also, that's why we talk more." For this friend, she reports having translated "particular idioms. You know like really specific idioms that we use in America, he might not understand." She described these interactions as reciprocal:

> [Because] his Chinese is really good, sometimes he'll explain something to me. Some really formal Chinese, he'll explain to me. And also, in a way, he's like Wikipedia [a collaborative, online encyclopedia]. So if something is more technical, or some other stuff I don't understand, I'll ask him. He's always able to give me information about a specific subject.

By interacting with this friend, Li demonstrates how her familial language brokering skills are seamlessly being used in an online environment. She is keenly aware of how she explains American idioms to her friend in a manner that must be understandable in Chinese, demonstrating a high degree of metacognitive awareness.

Chen

Chen was 28 years old at the time of the interview and living in San Francisco working as an actuarial analyst. He was given a choice of interview modalities and chose to do his interview via instant messenger (i.e., Gchat). His story is notably similar to Li's. He was also 14 years old when he arrived in the United States from China. He and his family stayed with relatives before settling elsewhere in San Francisco. His father was a wealthy businessman in China but "when he came to America, he was nothing. So, he wasn't the most patient father at the time." For some of his childhood, he misconstrued his parents' unhappiness with migration as his fault. This anxiety often spilled over into his language brokering interactions.

Like many of the language brokers interviewed, Chen recalled looking online for documents when assisting his parents. For example, when his parents asked him to contact the city to remove an overgrown tree in front of their house, he searched online for the request. When his parents wanted to rent out a room in their house, he searched online for a rental agreement template. However, unlike other brokers interviewed, he had also engaged in translation for strangers online. For a while, he was on a Chinese-language website helping to translate for unknown others. He also translated for the Chinese version of Wikipedia. Although both tasks proved to be difficult work, he found them very satisfying. He wrote:

Chen:	i perhaps made it more interesting than it sounds
	a lot of people just don't want to pay a translation agency
	it gets pretty ridiculous the kind of stuff they wanted translated.
Interviewer:	like what?
Chen:	don't remember
	some long stuff
Interviewer:	what were some of the ridiculous stuff?
Chen:	don't remember
	well some people genuinely have questions about english
	so i tried to answer those
	like how to write this sentence
	but i found that there are so many other people more capable than me
	i don't find it worth my time.
	i mean a lot of people are helping already
	. . .

Interviewer:	why did you want to do this?
	did you want to become a professional translator?
Chen:	because it makes me feel good about myself.
	it's something i can do
	if i hadn't come to america, i probably would have become an english teacher
	. . .
Interviewer:	do you think you've learned anything from your brokering experiences?
Chen:	i don't know.
	i mostly do it for fun
	i enjoy the sensation in my head when i translate things

Chen's experiences highlight how the experiences of youth in the offline world can transfer to the online environment. He had experience as a language broker with his parents, felt positively about his skills, and turned to online venues to help others and, perhaps, derive similar pleasure in helping others. The language brokering Chen performed online seemed a natural extension of his language brokering in the offline. However, for Chen, his online translation work for strangers was different in that it seemed to carry a similar level of satisfaction but less of the anxiety associated with brokering for his parents.

Conclusion

In this study and as suggested by prior research (Katz, 2014; Katz & Gonzalez, 2015), children of immigrants now use the Internet to look up information and for translation (e.g., words, templates). This resourcefulness perhaps reflects the orienting function of media, which Matsaganis et al. (2010) posit might aid immigrant youth and their families in adjusting to host countries. Children from immigrant families also may use new media to maintain transnational ties to individuals (connective function) and cultures (symbolic function). Those individuals who reported ICT use reported marginally higher levels of language brokering frequency, most likely driven by significantly higher levels of language brokering for other relatives. Although digital technology use may have detrimental effects on children's social relationships—like taking time away from family bonding experiences at home (Subrahmanyam, Kraut, Greenfield, & Gross, 2000)—it seems that ICTs may also allow immigrant children to stay connected to those who are far away. Individuals who reported transnational Internet use also showed greater understanding of heritage cultures and marginally higher levels of ethnic identity. These results suggest that these digital connections to close others in countries of origin may also serve to strengthen youth's understanding and attachment to home cultures in ways similar to language brokering (Guan et al., 2015; Weisskirch, 2005). As suggested by the literature, the results of this study indicate that ICTs have the potential to facilitate relationship formation and maintenance (Boyd, 2008; Kline & Liu, 2005; Parks & Floyd, 1996; Stafford, Kline, & Dimmick, 1999), and to provide new immigrants with resources for adjustment and information about the values of their host country (Elias, 2011; Skop & Adams, 2009). In this sense, ICTs have the capacity to be beneficial broadly to immigrant and transnational populations.

As might be expected, newer immigrants may be using ICTs to connect to home cultures at higher rates than second-generation youth. In this study, years in the United States were associated with heritage culture and American cultural understanding. The case studies suggest that this may be the situation for those who immigrated at older ages, given their literacy in the heritage language and increased opportunities pre-immigration to have formed close relationships with those in sending countries. That is, first-generation young adults are more likely to be able and motivated to communicate with those in heritage countries. Li's accounts of how her Chinese improved from her instant messaging interactions with a friend in China and how her friend learned about American idioms show how cultural exchange can be bidirectional. Prior research suggests that all of these factors, such as level of acculturation and native language aptitude, can influence ethnic identity among immigrant youth (e.g., Morales & Hanson, 2005; Phinney, Romero, Nava, & Huang, 2001).

Although the primary results are consistent with prior research, a few findings stand in contrast. Language brokering frequency was associated with lower levels of American cultural orientation, but not heritage cultural orientation. This finding is perhaps different from the literature that suggests language brokering may be associated with biculturalism (e.g., Buriel et al., 1998). However, it should be noted that acculturation was measured differently here compared to prior studies using the same scale (e.g., Acoach & Webb, 2004; Buriel et al., 1998). In the current study, heritage culture and American culture were analyzed separately rather than combined to create a biculturalism score. This separation was done with consideration of the ethnically diverse sample (relative to prior studies which had predominantly Latino/a participants) and supports the multidimensional perspective of ethnic identity development. Also, although prior research that suggests that brokering for individuals other than parents may be associated with internalizing symptoms (i.e., depression; Love & Buriel, 2007), the quantitative results did not support this finding, and the case studies suggest that, in some cases, brokering for friends and other relatives may actually be less anxiety-provoking.

Future Directions

While evidence of the potential benefits of ICTs for transnational populations is encouraging, there are several limitations to the current study. Race, class, and gender disparities in usage cannot be ignored (Boyd, 2008). For example, the two interviewees in the case studies who were able to recall brokering experiences online were first generation from pre-migration middle-class, Asian backgrounds and had friends abroad with access to technology. Further, the contexts migrants move into and from can affect media use. For example, Vietnamese immigrants abroad may have a more difficult time connecting to friends and relatives in hometowns in rural Southeast Asia given the low rates of cell phone and Internet access. Thus, future studies should explore demographic factors that contribute to issues of access. In addition, this was a largely female, young adult sample, which may skew results given that gender and age differences have been found in the language brokering literature (Buriel et al., 1998; Love & Buriel, 2007; Weisskirch, 2005). The survey and sample size of the qualitative portion makes the current study limited in scope. To increase the generalizability of these findings, future work should examine how these trends might emerge among individuals from different gender, class, and ethnic backgrounds. Given the increasing technological literacy of younger generations growing up immersed in media, it will also be interesting to examine how different cohorts of language brokers use technology in their language brokering. Some may seek out information about difficult concepts to translate and others may look for apps to assist in the translation, like Google Translate. Finally, longitudinal research would expand the present cross-sectional results and help disentangle the relationships between years in the United States, ICT use, acculturation, language brokering, and ethnic identity.

Contribution to Theory

The results in this chapter suggest that new technologies have allowed language brokering to transcend borders. That is, language brokering may not be limited to face-to-face experiences in the host country. Future conceptualizations of language brokering should include brokering that takes place in new digital spaces, given the amount of time youth spend online. On an applied level, this may mean that future assessments of language brokering consider including questions about brokering with the use of technology or brokering online for non-related others. Future work should also examine how brokering across different contexts may be unique. For example, given the negative feelings and potential detrimental effects of language brokering during high-stress and high-stakes situations, brokering in online contexts, where users have the time to formulate responses and search for more information before responding, may reduce the anxiety associated with these brokering experiences. Understanding how technology has become entwined in the practice of language brokers merits further investigation.

References

Acoach, C. L., & Webb, L. M. (2004). The influence of language brokering on Hispanic teenagers' acculturation, academic performance, and nonverbal decoding skills: A preliminary study. *Howard Journal of Communications, 15*(1), 1–19.

Baumeister, R. F., & Leary, M. R. (1995). The need to belong: Desire for interpersonal attachments as a fundamental human motivation. *Psychological Bulletin, 117*(3), 497.

Benitez, J. L. (2006). Transnational dimensions of the digital divide among Salvadoran immigrants in the Washington DC metropolitan area. *Global Networks, 6*(2), 181–199.

boyd, d. (2008). Why youth ♥ social network sites: The role of networked publics in teenage social life. In David Buckingham (Ed.), *Youth, identity, and digital media* (pp. 119–142). The John D. and Catherine T. MacArthur Foundation Series on Digital Media and Learning. Cambridge, MA: The MIT Press. doi: 10.1162/dmal.9780262524834.119

Buriel, R., Perez, W., Terri, L., Chavez, D. V., & Moran, V. R. (1998). The relationship of language brokering to academic performance, biculturalism, and self-efficacy among Latino adolescents. *Hispanic Journal of Behavioral Sciences, 20*(3), 283–297.

Chen, W. (2009). Internet-usage patterns of immigrants in the process of intercultural adaptation. *Cyberpsychology, Behavior, and Social Networking, 13*(4), 387–399.

Donner, J. (2008). Research approaches to mobile use in the developing world: A review of the literature. *The Information Society, 24*(3), 140–159.

Dorner, L. M., Orellana, M. F., & Li-Grining, C. P. (2007). "I helped my mom," and it helped me: Translating the skills of language brokers into improved standardized test scores. *American Journal of Education, 113*(3), 451–478.

Elias, N. (2011). Between Russianness, Jewishness, and Israeliness: Identity patterns and media uses of the FSU immigrants in Israel. *Journal of Jewish Identities, 4*(1), 87–104.

Erikson, E. H. (1968). *Identity: Youth and crisis.* New York, NY: Norton.

Guan, S. S. A., Greenfield, P. M., & Orellana, M. F. (2014). Translating into understanding language brokering and prosocial development in emerging adults from immigrant families. *Journal of Adolescent Research, 29*(3), 331–355.

Guan, S. S. A., Nash, A., & Orellana, M. F. (2015). Cultural and social processes of language brokering among Arab, Asian, and Latin immigrants. *Journal of Multilingual and Multicultural Development, 37*(2), 1–17.

Hwang, B., & He, Z. (1999). Media uses and acculturation among Chinese immigrants in the USA. *International Communication Gazette, 61*(1), 5.

Ito, M., Baumer, S., Bittanti, M., boyd, D., Herr-Stephenson, B., Horst, H. A., Lange, P. G., Mahendran, D., Martinez, K. Z., Pascoe, C. J., Perkel, D., Robinson, L., Sims, C., & Tripp, L. (2010). *Hanging out, messing around, and geeking out: Kids living and learning with new media.* Cambridge, MA: The MIT Press.

Katz, V. S. (2010). How children of immigrants use media to connect their families to the community: The case of Latinos in South Los Angeles. *Journal of Children and Media, 4*(3), 298–315.

Katz, V. S. (2014). *Kids in the middle: How children of immigrants negotiate community interactions for their families.* New Brunswick, NY: Rutgers University Press.

Katz, V. S., & Gonzalez, C. (2015). Community variations in low-income Latino families' technology adoption and integration, *60*(1), 59–80. *American Behavioral Scientist.* doi:0002764215601712

Kim, Y. Y. (1979). *Mass media and acculturation: Toward development of an interactive theory.* Annual meeting of the Eastern Communication Association, Philadelphia, Pennsylvania.

Kline, S. L., & Liu, F. (2005). The influence of comparative media use on acculturation, acculturative stress, and family relationships of Chinese international students. *International Journal of Intercultural Relations, 29*(4), 367–390.

Lim, S. S., & Thomas, M. (2010). *Walled-in, reaching out: Benefits and challenges of migrant workers' use of ICTs for interpersonal communication.* Suntec City, Singapore: International Communication Association.

Love, J. A., & Buriel, R. (2007). Language brokering, autonomy, parent-child bonding, biculturalism, and depression: A study of Mexican American adolescents from immigrant families. *Hispanic Journal of Behavioral Sciences, 29*(4), 472–491.

Maira, S. M. (2009). *Missing: Youth, citizenship, and empire after 9/11*. Durham, NC: Duke University Press.

Marcia, J. E. (1980). Identity in adolescence. *Handbook of Adolescent Psychology, 1*, 59–167.

Matsaganis, M. D., Katz, V. S., & Ball-Rokeach, S. J. (2010). *Understanding ethnic media: Producers, consumers, and societies*. Thousand Oaks, CA: Sage Publications.

Mayer, V. (2003). Living telenovelas/telenovelizing life: Mexican American girls' identities and transnational telenovelas. *Journal of Communication, 53*(3), 479–495.

Meyrowitz, J. (1985). *No sense of place: The impact of electronic media on social behavior*. New York, NY: Oxford University Press.

Mitra, A. (2006). Towards finding a cybernetic safe place: Illustrations from people of Indian origin. *New Media & Society, 8*(2), 251.

Morales, A., & Hanson, W. E. (2005). Language brokering: An integrative review of the literature. *Hispanic Journal of Behavioral Sciences, 27*(4), 471–503.

Navarrete, A., & Huerta, E. (2006). Building virtual bridges to home: The use of the Internet by transnational communities of immigrants. *International Journal of Communications Law & Policy, Virtual Communities* (Special Issue), 1–20.

Orellana, M. F. (2009). *Translating childhoods: Immigrant youth, language, and culture*. New York, NY: Rutgers University Press.

Parham, A. A. (2004). Diaspora, community and communication: Internet use in transnational Haiti. *Global Networks, 4*(2), 199–217.

Parks, M. R., & Floyd, K. (1996). Making friends in cyberspace. *Journal of Computer-Mediated Communication, 1*(4). doi:10.1111/j.1083–6101.1996.tb00176.x

Pew Research Center. (2012). *Teens fact sheet*. Washington, DC: Pew Research Center.

Phinney, J. S. (1992). The multigroup ethnic identity measure. *Journal of Adolescent Research, 7*(2), 156.

Phinney, J. S., Romero, I., Nava, M., & Huang, D. (2001). The role of language, parents, and peers in ethnic identity among adolescents in immigrant families. *Journal of Youth and Adolescence, 30*(2), 135–153.

Reece, D., & Palmgreen, P. (2000). Coming to America: Need for acculturation and media use motives among Indian sojourners in the US. *International Journal of Intercultural Relations, 24*(6), 807–824.

Rogers, E. M. (1986). *Communication technology: The new media in society*. New York, NY: Free Press.

Sardar, Z., & Ravetz, J. R. (1996). *Cyberfutures: Culture and politics on the information superhighway*. New York, NY: New York University Press.

Skop, E., & Adams, P. C. (2009). Creating and inhabiting virtual places: Indian immigrants in cyberspace. *National Identities, 11*(2), 127–147.

Stafford, L., Kline, S. L., & Dimmick, J. (1999). Home e-mail: Relational maintenance and gratification opportunities. *Journal of Broadcasting & Electronic Media, 43*(4), 659.

Subrahmanyam, K., Kraut, R. E., Greenfield, P. M., & Gross, E. F. (2000). The impact of home computer use on children's activities and development. *The Future of Children, 10*(2), 123–144.

Szapocznik, J., Kurtines, W., & Fernandez, T. (1980). Bicultural involvement and adjustment in Hispanic-American youths. *International Journal of Intercultural Relations, 4*, 353–365.

Szapocznik, J., Scopetta, M. A., Kurtines, W., & Aranalde, M. D. (1978). Theory and measurement of acculturation. *Revista Interamericana de Psicologia, 12*(2), 113–130.

Tsai, J. H. C. (2006). Use of computer technology to enhance immigrant families' adaptation. *Journal of Nursing Scholarship, 38*(1), 87–93.

Weiskopf, I., & Kissau, K. (2008). Internet and the integration of immigrants in Germany and Israel: Characteristics and potentials. *German Policy Studies, 4*(4), 95–124.

Weisskirch, R. S. (2005). The relationship of language brokering to ethnic identity for Latino early adolescents. *Hispanic Journal of Behavioral Sciences, 27*(3), 286–299.

World Bank. (2015). Internet users (per 100 people). World Development Indicators. Washington, DC Retrieved December 8, 2015 from http://data.worldbank.org/indicator/ IT.NET.USER.P2

Yang, C., Wu, H., Zhu, M., & Brian, G. (2004). Tuning in to fit in? Acculturation and media use among Chinese students in the United States. *Asian Journal of Communication, 14*(1), 81–94.

Ye, J. (2005). Acculturative stress and use of the Internet among East Asian international students in the United States. *CyberPsychology & Behavior, 8*(2), 154–161.

9

THEORIZING CHILD LANGUAGE BROKERING

The Example of Brokering in Health Care Settings

Guida de Abreu and Lindsay O'Dell

Introduction

In this chapter, we discuss children and young people's language brokering in health care settings. This topic is situated within the broad research field of understanding the development of young people in culturally diverse societies (Abreu & Hale, 2011; Cline, Abreu, O'Dell, & Crafter, 2010; Crafter, O'Dell, Abreu, & Cline, 2009) and our metasynthesis review of research specifically focused on health care settings. Language brokering by children and young people from immigrant families typically involves translating or interpreting on behalf of adult family members or siblings, e.g., in conversations with officials or professionals who do not speak the family's home language (Cline, Crafter, O'Dell, & Abreu, 2011). We draw on sociocultural theorizing and developmental psychology to frame conceptual and theoretical issues arising from the example of child language brokering in health care settings. We outline key features of the empirical research conducted to date and discuss conceptual and theoretical issues arising from the literature. In particular, we explore brokering in health care settings as participation in different sociocultural practices. Drawing on Goodnow, Miller, and Kessel (1995), we view practices as "meaningful actions that occur routinely in everyday life, are widely shared by members of the group, and carry normative expectations about the way things should be done" (p. 1). We view the child language broker and the other social actors involved as participants in these practices. From this perspective, we stress the need to understand the implications of these practices in new identities for child development, for families, and for health care providers.

Statements Against Child Language Brokering in Health Care Settings

Language brokering is often part of a transitional situation for migrating families. Although reliable incidence data is not available, there are indications that the activities are more prevalent in some communities than might be expected from their low profile in the research literature (Chao, 2006; Jones & Trickett, 2005; Weisskirch, 2005). Immigrant and refugee households often find themselves dependent on family members who can communicate with official channels and resources in their new country (Abreu & Hale, 2011; Candappa & Egharevba, 2003; Weisskirch, 2005). Children tend to learn languages at a faster rate than adults and receive regular exposure to the local language in schools, so that they become an invaluable resource for the survival of their families (Abreu & Hale, 2011; Suarez-Orozco & Suarez-Orozco, 2001).

Empirical evidence from our previous projects, and other published work, suggests that child language brokers are engaged often in health care settings (Abreu & Hale, 2011; Cline et al., 2011). For the purposes of this chapter, we are defining health care settings broadly to include hospitals, general practice surgeries, health care community centers, pharmacies, and other places where families may go for health care and advice. In many countries, there are highly formalized processes for managing translation for health care practitioners. In the UK, the general understanding within health care settings is that it is not acceptable to use children as translators. For example, this view has been endorsed by the British Psychological Society in the guidelines issued for psychologists on working with interpreters in health settings:

> As a general rule, it is not appropriate to ask family members or other professionals to "help out" because they appear to speak the same language as the client or have sign language skills. Interpreting is a highly skilled role and not something that any person or even any professional can just slip into [. . .]. The use of family members also creates difficulties with regard to confidentiality [. . .] although some clients may insist upon it. This should be discussed with them. Children, however, should never be used as interpreters as this places them in a difficult and prematurely adult role towards their parent or relative.
>
> *(Tribe & Thompson, 2008, p. 6)*

The view that children should not be used as language brokers has been echoed by health care practitioners who participated in research, such as doctors and nurses, in the limited UK literature in the topic (Cohen, Moran-Ellis, & Smaje, 1999; Gerrish, Chau, Sobowale, & Birks, 2004). Similar views were expressed by US providers (see for example, Giordano, 2007; Katz, 2007;

Lehna, 2005). Research undertaken by Katz (2007) in California reflects a common finding that

> The "illegality" of child brokering notwithstanding, every child I spoke with indicated that they regularly broker for their families in doctors' offices and clinics, and every health care provider confirmed that children frequently came prepared to broker for their parents, even when the office had bilingual staff.
>
> *(p. 197)*

The situations described in the research cited here document the commonplace and ongoing practice of using child language brokers in health care settings.

The realization that child language brokering will continue despite the controversy of involving children is summarized by Antonini (2010):

> Because of cultural reasons, and for a host of other motives, immigrant parents will continue to ask their children to translate and interpret for them regardless of the law and of other resources available to them, such as professional interpreters and language mediators. Therefore, before ruling out completely the possibility and appropriateness of having their children mediating for them, it would be useful for these children, for their families and for the institutions they need to communicate with, to assess how this "invisible" area of childhood affects these children.
>
> *(p. 10)*

The public concern, legislation, and prohibition of child language brokering, particularly in health care contexts, indicates that, for many people, the activities transgress assumptions about childhood and family responsibilities (Giordano, 2007; Katz, 2007, 2014). The realization that it is not for the benefit of the child, their family, and providers that the activity continues to be "invisible" has contributed to growing interest in understanding the nature of the activity and its impact considering the perspectives of children, families, and professionals.

Theoretical Framing of Child Language Brokering

The theoretical frame for our work on child language brokers draws on sociocultural theorizing and on developmental psychology. We argue that the dominant construction of child development sets up particular understandings of the capabilities and roles of children within society and that child language brokering is often viewed as problematic because it transgresses normative understandings of children and families. Rapid changes in society, including increased economic migration and the dispersal of the extended family, have created situations in which more children and young people are involved in activities that are outside of activities typically expected in mainstream British society, as well as elsewhere (Crafter et al., 2009). Children who act as language brokers are, therefore, positioned in unique circumstances due to their engagement in roles that are typically viewed as adult. For example, the dominant understanding of child development assumes that the move to adulthood is accompanied by a gradual increase in engagement in more adult-style responsibilities. In dominant understandings of childhood within Western countries such as the UK, children are assumed to be dependents within their families (Churchill & O'Dell, 2013). Furthermore, the normative expectation is that parents speak on behalf of their children, rather than children speaking for them.

The metasynthesis detailed in this chapter draws on this theoretical frame to explore the current research literature focusing on child language brokers in health care settings. Sociocultural theory offers a frame for examining the contexts within which children and families live and their engagement with each other, and others, within these contexts. Drawing on this theoretical lens enables an examination of the settings in which specific practices of language brokering take place, the sociocultural understandings of family life, and obligations to family; as well as an examination of mediation between children, their family, and the external world, in this case health care practitioners. The theory offers a frame for analyzing language brokering as a process of participation in specific social and cultural practices. Thus, brokering in medical encounters can be examined as a variety of practices, depending on the medical encounter setting and people involved: e.g., a general practitioner (GP) surgery, where people receive medical attention from a family doctor; emergency medical help (in the UK this is through accident and emergency departments of a local hospital, A&E); a specialist hospital for consultation; pharmacies; home; etc. In addition, critical developmental psychology supplements this frame by conceptualizing child development as specific to culture and society, and a time and place, as well as questioning assumptions about the child's lack of skills and dependency on others that has been evident in traditional developmental discourse. Together, the theoretical perspectives provide a frame for viewing child language brokering within specific sociocultural contexts in which family relationships and the understandings of childhood are seen as constructed and multiple.

The Literature Review

In this review, we use a metasynthesis methodological approach as our aim is to generate new insights and conceptual understandings of qualitative research on child language brokering in health settings (Thorne, Jensen, Kearney, Noblit, & Sandelowski, 2004; Walsh & Downe, 2005). A metasynthesis provides a reading of the research conducted in the field with a theoretical frame, integrating findings to reach a new theoretical or conceptual level of understanding and development. The process involved the following steps: (1) a conventional literature search; which is then provided as a conventional summary of the key papers in tables (see Tables 9.1 and 9.2); (2) an interpretative analysis looking at emerging patterns in the whole dataset; and (3) a synthesis linking and interpreting key emerging findings to sociocultural theory and critical developmental psychology.

Literature Search

A conventional literature search was carried out using the terms "language broker," "translator with child/children and health," "interpreter with child/children and health," "interpreter with child/children and medical," "cultural broker with child/children and health," and "immigrant child/children with broker/brokering." The databases searched included Academic Search Complete, Web of Science, Science Direct, and PubMed. Additional literature, identified within the reference lists of relevant papers, were also searched. Alongside the formal literature search, we also included a special issue of a European journal, *mediAzioni*, which arose from an international meeting of researchers specializing in child language brokers (edited by Antonini, 2010). In addition, we drew on two texts to provide an overview of issues relating to child language brokers: a review by Giordano (2007) that provided an overview of the advantages and disadvantages of using professional or child interpreters in health care situations, and a paper by Haffner (1992) that is an autobiographic case study of her daily experiences as a professional medical interpreter, including her encounters with child language brokers.

Initially, titles and abstracts were scrutinized to establish that the focus of the paper was on children with clear reference to health care settings. The search excluded "child protection" and studies that focus exclusively on adults translating, although we included retrospective studies where adults were discussing activities in childhood. We did not apply an age exclusion to the search. It was evident that the research undertaken to date has adopted a number of strategies, including retrospective studies of adults discussing their experiences as a child language broker, whereas other projects interviewed children and young people who were current language brokers (the age ranged from approximately 9 years to young adults up to 20 years old in these studies) as well as parents of child language brokers. We note that it is difficult to provide an accurate account of the age of children who took part in the studies because some papers did not provide the ages of their participants, and some were retrospective studies that did not provide information from the adult participants of the age at which they were child language brokers. It is clear that the research field is very recent, and there are very few published studies that focus on health settings; hence, there was no exclusion criteria relating to the date of the research papers themselves.

This initial search generated approximately 55 papers that could be accessed electronically. Further scrutiny of these papers revealed that many studies made passing references to children as informal interpreters in health care settings. Overall, the literature is dispersed and very scarce. Fourteen papers published between 1999 and 2014 were identified as having sufficient focus as to be relevant to the current review, including six papers reporting empirical studies conducted exclusively in health care settings (see Table 9.1), and eight papers that included health care jointly with other settings, such as home or school (see Table 9.2).

TABLE 9.1 Empirical Studies in Exclusively Health Care Settings

Authors	Aims	Methodology/ Design	Location	Sample Characteristics
Cohen et al. (1999)	To explore the views of GPs regarding the appropriateness of children undertaking a task of interpreting between the GP and an adult patient in primary health care consultations.	Qualitative interviews (in–depth, recorded)	London, UK, GP practices	GPs, $n = 38$ (24 had recent experience of children as informal translators in consultations with adult patients)
Free, Green, Bhavnani, and Newman (2003)	To explore bilingual young people's accounts of interpreting for family or friends in primary care settings.	Qualitative interviews (in–depth, recorded)	London, UK, community and youth groups	Young people, $n = 76$ (aged 9–18 years; 34 female, 42 male)
Green, Free, Bhavnani, and Newman (2005)	To explore mediating role of young people in health care settings as being of interest in its own right, and as "work" and therefore part of the economy of health care.	Qualitative interviews (in–depth, recorded)	London, UK, community and youth groups	Young people, $n = 76$ (aged 10–18 years; 34 female, 42 male)

(Continued)

TABLE 9.1 (Continued)

Authors	Aims	Methodology/Design	Location	Sample Characteristics
Barron, Holterman, Shipster, Batson, and Alam (2010)	To explore the views of members of ethnic minority groups regarding interpreting provision in primary health care settings.	Focus groups (recorded)	Hertfordshire, UK	24 adults (aged 35–72 years; 23 female, 1 male)
Katz (2014)	To explore providers perceptions of and interactions with child brokers and their families, taken in context of the institutions in which they work and of the intrafamily dynamics that can facilitate or constrain children's efforts.	Interviews (recorded), 18 months of field observations in two of these institutions.	South Los Angeles, US	20 parents (median age 35) 17 female and 3 male, and their primary child broker aged between 15 and 19 ($N = 19$, 17 female, 2 male), 16 formal interviews in private medical practices, community clinics, a large hospital, family counseling services, and the WIC office.
Rubio-Rico, Biosca, de Molina Fernández, and Grau (2014)	To qualitatively analyze the discourse of Maghrebi adults to the use of Maghrebi minors as translators in the health services.	Semi-structured interviews and focus group sessions.	Tarragona, Spain	12 in-depth interviews and 10 focus groups with Maghrebi adults living in Tarragona.

TABLE 9.2 Empirical Studies in *not* Exclusively Health Care Settings

Study	Aims	Methodology/Design	Location	Sample Characteristics
Orellana, Dorner, and Pulido (2003)	To demonstrate how immigrant children's work as translators	Part of a larger, multi-method program.	Los Angeles and Chicago, US	Survey of 236 Spanish-speaking

Study	Aims	Methodology/ Design	Location	Sample Characteristics
	and interpreters opens families' access to resources, knowledge, and information in a wide range of domains: educational, medical/health, commercial, legal/state, financial/ employment, housing/ residential, and cultural/ entertainment.	Interviews and focus groups with children, parents, and teachers from neighborhoods, as well as participant observation in the homes and classrooms.		children, interviews, participant observation, and audiotape data gathered in four different communities in districts of Los Angeles and Chicago
Reynolds and Orellana (2009)	To theorize child interpreters' positionalities within the interstices of several borderlands: as children; as interpreters and translators interpreting different languages, registers, and discourses; and as immigrants seeking services within White public space.	Qualitative observations recorded in field notes, youth's journal accounts, and interviews.	Chicago, US, one urban and one suburban community	Case studies with 18 young people (aged 8–13; 12 female, 6 male) Young Latino/a people, $n = 18$ (aged 10–12; 12 female, 6 male)
Villanueva and Buriel (2010)	To explore the feelings of Latina adolescents regarding child language brokering (CLB), which CLB situations	Qualitative interviews (recorded)	California, US, academic mentoring group	Young Latinas $n = 9$ (aged 13–15, female)

(Continued)

TABLE 9.2 (Continued)

Study	Aims	Methodology/ Design	Location	Sample Characteristics
	are most stressful, and the importance of their CLB activities relative to their other household responsibilities.			
Bucaria and Rossato (2010)	To provide detailed description of participants, situations and contexts of CLB; to assess the impact that CLB has on lives and development of children; To gather data on positive and negative attitudes towards CLB from former brokers; to identify potential strategies adopted by brokers when mediating for family and friends.	Individual qualitative interviews (recorded and videotaped), four focus groups (recorded and videotaped), questionnaires	Forlì-Cesena area of the Emilia-Romagna, Italy, high school, university	Young people, $n = 30$ (aged 16–30 years; 8 female, 22 male)
Degener (2010)	To assess in which situations and contexts children and youth serve as interpreters, and which topics are discussed in the interpreted talks.	Qualitative questionnaires, diaries, recorded interpreted conversations	Berlin, Germany, primary and secondary school	Young people, $n = 22$ (aged 10–20 years), $n = 8$ reported translating at doctor's appointments and hospitals

Study	Aims	Methodology/ Design	Location	Sample Characteristics
García-Sánchez (2010)	This paper is part of a larger ethnographic language socialization study, investigating the family worlds, the neighborhood peer worlds, and the school worlds of Moroccan immigrant children in a rural Spanish community, including CLB activities at the local health center, in the households, and at school.	Naturally occurring interactional routines of a target group of children were systematically observed and video/audio-recorded over a period of 16 months.	Rural town, Spain	Moroccan immigrant children ($n = 6$) and families. The age and gender of the children was not provided in the paper.
Corona, Stevens, Halfond, Shaffer, Reid-Quinones, and Gonzalez (2012)	To explore why CLB may be related to positive and negative experiences, including parental reactions to CLB.	Qualitative interviews (recorded)	Virginia, US, where there is a newly developing Latino/a community	Young people, $n = 25$ (aged 10–15 years; 14 female, 11 male) Their parents, $n = 29$ (18 mothers, 11 fathers)
Kosner, Roer-Strier, and Kurman (2014)	To examine how young immigrants to Israel from the former Soviet Union during their adolescence perceive and cope with the resulting changes in their family roles.	Qualitative interviews and focus groups (recorded)	Israel	$n = 34$, 17 adolescents (aged 15–18; 6 male and 11 female), and 17 young adults (aged 23–31; 6 male and 11 female)

Interpretative Analysis Looking at Emerging Patterns: Methodological and Sampling Issues

All of the papers included in the review used qualitative research methods (see Tables 9.1 and 9.2). Eleven out of the 14 empirical papers reported gathering data using interviews. Five papers draw on data exclusively from in-depth interviews (Cohen et al., 1999; Corona et al., 2012; Free et al., 2003; Green et al., 2005; Villanueva & Buriel, 2010). In the other six papers interviews were part of a multiple method approach that included other methods such as observations in specific settings (Katz, 2014; Orellana et al., 2003; Reynolds & Orellana, 2009), focus groups (Bucaria & Rossato, 2010; Kosner et al., 2014; Orellana et al., 2003; Rubio-Rico et al., 2014), questionnaires and survey (Bucaria & Rossato, 2010; Orellana et al., 2003). One of the remaining three papers used only focus groups (Barron et al., 2010), another used questionnaires, diaries, and recorded interpreted conversations (Degener, 2010), and the other used systematic observations, and audio and video recording of naturally occurring interactional routines of children and their families (García-Sánchez, 2010). The location of the research published in the papers reviewed varied: Four reported data from studies conducted in the UK, five in the United States, one in Israel, two in Spain, one in Italy, and one in Germany.

Overall, there is indication of a variety of methodological approaches, including ethnographic approaches with a focus on communities and specific institutional settings, and the use of retrospective biographic and narrative approaches that include recalling past experiences. In a few studies, data collection involved observations over a period of time in selected settings (e.g. García-Sánchez, 2010 recorded data over a period of 16 months). However, most studies involved only data collection at one particular time. The research by Orellana and her colleagues in the United States is an exception, as it is one of the few studies with a longitudinal dimension (Orellana et al., 2003; Reynolds & Orellana, 2009). The longitudinal dimension is important because of research findings that suggest that the nature of the child's involvement may change when the activity becomes more regular, and also when a child reaches certain steps in his or her own development. For example, GPs (family doctors) in Cohen et al. (1999) suggest that an adolescent girl who is already having periods may be acceptable to broker for her mother in conversations about sensitive reproductive issues, while a boy of the same age is not acceptable.

The sample characteristics encompassed groups of participants made up of children and young people (Bucaria & Rossato, 2010; Degener, 2010; Free et al., 2003; Green et al., 2005; Kosner et al., 2014; Orellana et al., 2003; Reynolds & Orellana, 2009; Villanueva & Buriel, 2010), of adult members of ethnic minority communities (Barron et al., 2010; Rubio-Rico et al., 2014), of doctors and other health care providers (Cohen et al., 1999; García-Sánchez, 2010; Katz, 2014), or of children and their parents (Corona et al., 2012; Katz, 2014).

It was also apparent from the other papers that were initially scrutinized but not included in this review (because they lack a sufficient focus on children) that many health care providers had encountered child language brokering in their work, such as health visitors, community nurses, midwives, and specialist nurses (see for example, Gerrish et al., 2004), and school nurses (Whitman, Davis, & Terry, 2010). The use of child language brokers in health care settings appears to be commonplace.

Children and young people become involved in language brokering not only in their homes and during their family lives, but also in formal settings and institutions, despite the formal guidelines and prohibitions, and the views of the professionals that they should not be involved. The qualitative studies reviewed in this metasynthesis, as well as other studies not included, show that often there is no immediate choice but to involve the child, as there is no one else available and sufficiently trained to help with the communication (see for example, Gerrish et al., 2004; Whitman et al., 2010). It is also apparent that the ages of the children and young people involved varied considerably. For instance, Cohen et al. (1999) report that "In one instance a GP reported having a child of five act as an informal interpreter but on average the youngest reported age was between six and eight years old" (p. 168). Other studies refer to adolescents and include children from 10 year olds (see Corona et al., 2012; Degener, 2010; Villanueva & Buriel, 2010), yet other studies include a wide range of ages, such as 9 to 17 plus (Free et al., 2003).

Conceptualizing Key Findings

A metasynthesis integrates and links the key emerging findings to theory (Thorne et al., 2004; Walsh & Downe, 2005). In the case of this review, the findings are linked back to sociocultural theory and critical developmental psychology. In particular the review focuses on conceptual issues in understanding diverse families and *different childhoods* in three key areas:

1. Placing of child language brokers within particular sociocultural settings;
2. Mediation processes in language brokering in health care encounters; and
3. Representations of childhood.

Placing of Child Language Brokers Within Particular Sociocultural Settings

Sociocultural theory emphasizes the context and settings, so the *placing*—i.e., the location of child language brokering practices—is an important element of theorizing the practice. It is clear from the research reviewed that children act as language brokers in a variety of settings. The papers reviewed show that child language brokering takes place in a variety of health care settings, including GP surgeries, hospitals, dental practices, community health centers and clinics, and family counselling services. Child language brokering is a common practice in all these settings despite the health care providers' view that it is not appropriate to use children as interpreters (see for example Barron et al., 2010; Cohen et al., 1999; Katz, 2014). One major justification given for involvement of children as interpreters in these formal settings are "deficiencies" or "limitations" in professional translation services (e.g., Barron et al., 2010; Cohen et al., 1999; Free et al., 2003). As noted by Free et al. (2003), in the UK, "Interpreting, link worker, and health advocacy services are limited in their scope in terms of the number of languages provided, the ease with which services can be accessed, and their availability for urgent appointments or outside normal working hours" (p. 7). These limitations in services are not unique to the UK. Increasing migration suggests that limitations in existing services will continue in countries with a long history of providing translation services, such as the UK (Free et al., 2003) and the United States (Katz, 2014); while in countries with a more recent history of immigration the services may not even be available, for example in Spain and Italy (see Rubio-Rico et al., 2014 and Bucaria & Rossato, 2010, respectively).

Analysis of the situations when children brokered in health care settings show a complex picture of the reasons they become involved. GPs interviewed by Cohen et al. (1999) talked about medical emergencies that required a swift response and, hence, the use of children if they were with their parents at that time. Parents also report using their children in emergency situations, such as when they had to call ambulances (e.g. Corona et al., 2012). People do not plan to get sick, and it is exactly in these hard-to-plan situations that children often end up being involved quickly. However, a preference for using a child to broker was mentioned by young people and adults from their communities, considering issues of trust in the child (Barron et al., 2010; Free et al., 2003) and their insider understanding of the parents' illness (Free et al., 2003).

Children's involvement in health related language brokering is not confined to formal settings. Studies that considered more than one setting show that these activities can take place both in formal institutional settings as well as in informal settings, such as family activities taking place in the parents' or relatives' homes (Bucaria & Rossato, 2010), or in other everyday activities. Children become involved, for example, with translating instructions for medicines, answering doctor's phone calls, and completing medical forms (Free et al., 2003). These settings pose different challenges, as routine everyday tasks can be perceived as part of a young person's normal life (Villanueva & Buriel, 2010). Orellana et al. (2003) suggest that the notion of "specialized encounters" (in formal settings) and "everyday ways" (in informal settings) can help to unpack the nature of the experiences of language brokering. They caution, however, against a rigid use of these categories as there may be fluidity between them.

In addition to brokering in both formal and informal medical settings, children are commonly involved in brokering in other settings important for their own and their family's lives. For example, Bucaria and Rossato's (2010) study of former child language brokers living in northern Italy revealed that child language brokers have been involved in translating in banks, hospitals, police headquarters, post offices, schools, and other public offices in general. Villanueva and Buriel's (2010) study with Latina adolescent language brokers in Southern California, United States also mentions school, medical, and other everyday settings where brokering experiences included translating for school-related things, medical procedures, health and insurance forms, purchases, bills, TV, phone, and newspapers.

Some of the more recent studies examined the experiences of children and young people comparing their engagement in different settings. These later studies help to provide insight into what is specific to their experiences in health care settings. Katz (2014) found that children experienced brokering in health care institutions as more difficult than in other settings, such as school, shops, or at home, which she explained in terms of:

> Their families' limited health-care access meant that brokering often occurred in emergency situations and required children to broker difficult and sometimes upsetting information very quickly. Even in nonemergency situations, health-care facilities were often unfamiliar to children. They were uncertain about norms and procedures and struggled with the complex language many providers used. As result, child brokers were most likely to recall brokering in health-care settings as times when they had experienced feelings of anxiety, helplessness, or fear of failure.
>
> *(p. 204)*

At first glance, this finding can be seen as contradicting evidence from other studies, such as Villanueva and Buriel (2010), who found that child language brokers reported that school settings were the most stressful, rather than medical settings as the authors had expected. Green et al. (2005) also found that children in their research viewed health care encounters as "easy" in comparison to other encounters, including with council officials, solicitors, and passport officers; financial encounters; encounters with the Home Office; political engagement such as registering to vote and income support. However, a closer look at the findings in both studies shows that when young people became involved in translating routine and regular situations (such as discussions about chronic health problems) they experienced it as simple and less stressful. So, these results suggest that in addition to the specific characteristic of the settings, the nature of the encounters (i.e., complexity or routine), and the roles and identities of the people involved, need closer examination. From our theoretical perspective, this links to the next major theme in our analysis: the nature of the mediation.

Mediation Processes in Language Brokering in Health Care-Encounters

The concept of mediation has been used in language brokering studies to acknowledge that the activity involves more than just *translating*, as often the broker is involved as a broader *intermediary* in interactions of a sociocultural nature. For example, Green et al. (2005) described the role of the young person as "not merely one of neutral translating, but of assertive cultural mediator for a parent he describes as unconfident about her ability to stand up for her rights in an alien country" (Green et al., 2005, p. 2105).

In our work, we have also argued that child language brokering is a process of mediation:

> In most cases children who act as family language brokers are not detached or independent in the sense that a professional interpreter would aspire to be. They are seen to be working actively to support the family's interests and are partly trusted by their parents for that reason. They are *mediators* or *advocates* on behalf of the family.
>
> *(Cline et al., 2010, p. 111)*

From a theoretical perspective, the concept of mediation has a long history within sociocultural approaches, derived primarily from Vygotsky (1978). The notion of mediation implies that the person has access to their worlds through tools provided by their culture, such as a particular language. Abreu and Elbers (2005) outline three foci of research exploring mediation that are relevant to processes of language brokering: (1) The mediating role of the cultural tool—exploring how properties of specific tools may impact on its learning, understanding and uses. For example, what is the impact of specific health and medical language, both oral (e.g., in consultations) and written (e.g., letters, prescriptions, etc.) on the experiences of language brokering? (2) The mediating role of social interactions in the way children, novices, and newcomers gain access to cultural tools—e.g., what strategies are used by parents and health providers to support the activity of language brokering? (3) The mediating role of wider social and cultural representations of parental roles, health care professional roles, and children's roles—e.g., what is the impact of representations of appropriate roles for children, parents, and professionals in the construction of the child as a language broker? As none of the studies reviewed for this chapter provides a detailed analysis of actual interactions, in the next part of this section we focus on mediation processes related to mastering the cultural tools and the representations of appropriate roles for children.

A key issue in research on language brokering in health care settings, or in communication about health-related issues, concerns children's understanding of medical vocabulary and concepts—i.e., the mediating role of the mastery of cultural tools. This is addressed in the research in terms of three main types of consultations: straightforward, complex, and sensitive consultations.

Straightforward consultations are those which, from the perspective of GPs, relate to common illnesses such as coughs, colds, sore throats, where a diagnosis is perceived as easy, with the use of simple language. Research suggests that children could make sense of these interactions because it is likely they have experienced the illness themselves, and thus it is acceptable to involve them as brokers (Cohen et al., 1999). Other situations described as straightforward included routine primary care and chronic illnesses. The young people interviewed by Free et al. (2003) in the UK described their brokering in health care settings as mostly simple, straightforward, and unproblematic. In fact, they found it easier than in other settings or saw it as "just translating" (Green et al., 2005). In contrast, young people in Katz's (2014) study conducted in the United States, reported language brokering in health care settings as more difficult than other settings. Katz argues that one of the issues is the family's limited access to health care, which resulted in brokering in mostly emergency situations. Indeed, she reports that when language brokering becomes more routine, the young people tend to find it less stressful.

Complex consultations from GPs' perspectives (Cohen et al., 1999) relate to conditions in which diagnosis is complicated to achieve, or in which the child may have difficulty in understanding the concept, such as psychosomatic or somatized illnesses. The difficulty in these circumstances can be at various levels, such as in the vocabulary, in the cultural expression of specific conditions, or in conceptual understanding (as it could involve illnesses the child has not experienced, and he or she will therefore have difficulty in making sense of the treatment or condition). Because of the risk of misdiagnosis, GPs felt that it was not appropriate to use children as language brokers in these circumstances. This view is echoed by the young people interviewed by Free et al. (2003). They reported more difficulty in translating in situations they had no direct experience, and consequently more difficulty in understanding the language and concepts. Ethnic minority adults in Barron et al.'s (2010) study also referred to the possibility of children having difficulty understanding the doctors' language. It is apparent that a key issue in language brokering is the child's mastery of the sophistication of the languages used to mediate their communication. The child's degree of mastery of these languages can be linked to several factors. It may be that the child is too young to master complex vocabulary, has little exposure to a condition and finds it difficult to understand the concept, or that the condition is in itself too complex and involves specialized medical discourses that may be difficult to grasp.

Sensitive consultations are related to areas of health considered to be sensitive to the person in terms of the location of the condition in the body and in terms of cultural taboos in relation to certain conditions. For example, sensitive consultations can include reproductive health or personal emotional difficulties, such as marital problems (e.g. Barron et al., 2010; Cohen et al., 1999; Green et al., 2005). In this case, the issue is not necessarily the complexity of the language, as the diagnosis may be achieved with simple questions and answers. The issue in sensitive consultations is judgment about the appropriateness of children gaining access to knowledge considered taboo for their age or their role. GPs in Cohen et al. (1999)'s study raised issues about gender and age—girls were potentially more acceptable in a sensitive consultation with their mothers, as they themselves could share some experiences such as menstrual periods, while boys were not acceptable. This differentiation is exemplified in a quote from one GP:

> It is problematic when I find out that the son or daughter is there and I have to ask the questions about the family planning and the cervical smear and their sexual history and personal questions which I feel myself that it is not an ideal situation where it should be conveyed through a son or daughter. I normally tell the children look I need to ask certain personal questions, could you please bring an interpreter for the next appointment . . . where they (parents) can bring somebody who speaks English and come and tell me more about their personal history.
>
> *(p. 176)*

There are particular issues encountered when brokering in health care settings that make the setting challenging for children. These include potential embarrass-ment of parents and children. Barron et al. (2010) reported that women may be embarrassed about discussing certain issues in front of their children, which can lead to further problems, particularly with regard to mental health. Several papers reported young men not wanting to translate "women's problems" (e.g. Bucaria & Rossato, 2010; Free et al., 2003; Green et al., 2005). These feelings are revealed from children's perspectives, as for example was expressed by a boy in Green et al. (2005)'s study: "Sometimes my Mum asks me to ask a question, and find it like, umm, umm, it's kind of embarrassing because like, yeah, 'cause I am a boy and my Mum is a lady. (Bm12)" (p. 2106).

Thus, in sensitive situations, there is another layer of the process of mediation. This layer is in addition to the mastery of appropriate language required for the communication, and the identity and representations of appropriate roles. Sensi-tive issues may, in fact, be a justification to use a child as a language broker. For many families, parents prefer to use their child as a language broker because of issues of trust and concern about privacy, particularly in cases of stigmatized or sensitive illnesses (e.g. Barron et al., 2010; Cohen et al., 1999). This distinction between the types of consultations is useful for examining the perspectives of the young people, their parents, and health care providers and the kind of mediation processes and skills required within the encounter.

Representations of Childhood

Understandings of the role of the family and constructions of the child's capabili-ties are implicit within the research reviewed. Critical developmental psychology argues that understandings of child development are located within specific soci-ocultural contexts (Burman, 2008). Within Western societies, childhood is viewed as a time of dependency and immaturity; children are in the process of becoming adult and are not seen to have the skills required to undertake activities viewed as adult responsibilities (Crafter et al., 2009). Language brokering by children may be deemed inappropriate because children may not have the skills or the levels of maturity required to undertake the role, and since children, because of their assumed immaturity, are viewed as dependent on adults. Hence, the assumption is that children have adults to speak on their behalf rather than speaking for adults.

The view of childhood as a time of immaturity and reliance upon adults does not correspond with the activities of child language brokers. For example, Cohen et al. (1999) report that GPs in their study questioned the appropriateness of using children as translators, drawing on the assumption that childhood is a time of innocence and freedom from worry. Reynolds and Orellana (2009) suggest that "When children speak to and for adults, they overstep the bounds of U.S. main-stream notions of childhood" (p. 123). Therefore, if childhood is constructed as a time of innocence and dependency on adults, child language brokers' activities are seen as non-normative and constructed in many research papers as burdensome for the child. For example, Barron et al.'s (2010) ethnic minority adult participants (mostly female) reported a mostly negative view of the use of children as language brokers because of the perceived burden placed on them by brokering. The burden of language brokering, particularly in health care settings, can be traumatic, especially when children are called upon to deal with sensitive or distressing issues (Haffner, 1992). For example, children may be embarrassed by discussions about intimate issues concerning reproduction or sexuality, or worried by translating information about medical conditions such as cancer.

Giordano (2007) concludes that the prevailing experience of children acting as language brokers in health care settings is a negative one, with disadvantages including the children viewing their language brokering duties as hard work that prevents them from attending school and participating in enjoyable activities more commonly associated with childhood. It can be argued that child language brokers are seen to miss out on childhood tasks by assuming the burden of adult roles of translation. Indeed, Bucaria and Rossato (2010, p. 255) reported an example of a child who said that language brokering "has taken away most of my childhood."

The burden of language brokering is thought by some to produce a role reversal where children take on an adult or parental role because of their activities. Cohen et al. (1999) and Giordano (2007) both discuss the possibility of role reversal involved in child language brokering in which children take on adult roles. They argue that role reversal could lead to conflict in the home. Haffner (1992) argued that language brokering could lead to a distortion of the parent-child relation-ship, and extended this further, observing that child language brokering can also disrupt the hierarchy of immigrant communities. This is because of the assump-tion that in translating for adults within a family, or the extended community, a child would gain a degree of power and authority, through knowing information about the adult, family, or community, that is unhelpful and threatening to the status quo of the family and community. Similarly, Degener (2010), in his research into child language brokers in Germany, noted that specific issues relating to the

German cultural context meant that "the issue is judged exclusively negatively on the German scene because of concerns that language brokering may destroy the 'natural' balance of family relations and thereby lead to cultural conflicts" (p. 354). This view of a family does not accord with many families and does not take into account the ways in which families work together to jointly care for each other. From our theoretical perspective, constructing child language brokering as a burden or a role reversal does not take into account these complexities or fully account for children's roles within their families.

An alternative view of children's engagement in language brokering is to see them as part of a family system in which children are actively engaged in their family life (Lave & Wenger, 1991; Orellana et al., 2003). Corona et al. (2012) suggests that language brokering is a team effort in which parents and children participate. Orellana et al. (2003) argue that child language brokering does not reverse the roles of parent and child, as assumed in much of the research literature that focuses on negative views of language brokering for children. They argue that in families where children are drawn on to translate, it is very frequently an adult's decision to involve children in translation, and, hence, children who are language brokers do not gain control of their family but "participate in family decisions but do not generally *make* these decisions themselves" (p. 521–522). Children continue to fulfil roles dictated by the family system.

From this perspective, child language brokering is seen as a normal part of life for many families. Villanueva and Buriel (2010) and Corona et al. (2012) both give examples of Latino/a communities in the United States where the expectation is that children are active members of their family and community, and, hence, language brokering is normal activity for many. A similar view is given by Degener (2010) in Germany who draws on a view of children as "social actors rather than as objects of adult socialization" (p. 350) and reflects the view that language brokering is a normal expectation for many children.

Furthermore, children sometimes are preferred as translators by their adult relatives because they can offer support, are convenient translators, and they have a greater understanding of the patient than a professional interpreter (Free et al., 2003; Green et al., 2005). Other research has suggested that, whilst parents may feel embarrassed at having to rely on their children, or may have mixed emotions about involving them, they were also proud that their children were able to translate for them (Corona et al., 2012). Far from being passive, children can be seen as active agents in their families and may also choose to be language brokers.

Conclusions

The metasynthesis of research focused on child language brokering in health care settings demonstrates the scarcity of research in the area. A significant issue arising from our metasynthesis is the lack of children's voices in the research into language brokering in health settings undertaken to date, and, hence, it is not known how children feel about their activities in these particular settings. Of the British empirical papers reviewed, there were few that focused exclusively on health care settings. Two studies explored the issues from the perspective of the young people themselves (see Free et al., 2003 and Green et al., 2005). Cohen et al. (1999) researched the opinions of GPs on the appropriateness of using children as informal interpreters, and Barron et al. (2010) explored the views of ethnic minority groups on interpreting provision in health care settings, where the inappropriateness of using children emerged strongly.

Very little of the research reviewed took a longitudinal perspective on language brokering. From the research evidence to date, there is strong evidence that experiences of language brokering and its efficacy may change over time and with regularity of translating. In addition, children are constantly developing; key transitions in the life of the child are also likely to impact his or her work as language brokers, such as puberty, the transition from childhood to adulthood, and moving from school to work. While a 16-year-old in some contexts may already be legally employed, a child in a primary school age bracket (i.e., 5 to 11 years old) would no doubt be in a completely different stage of his or her emotional, cognitive, and educational development.

There is scope for focused studies that target health providers (including doctors, nurses, pharmacists, dentists, etc.) in immigrant communities. As discussed earlier, Katz (2014) argued that one of the issues of concern is the family's limited access to health care, which resulted in brokering in mostly emergency situations. This suggests possible directions for future research considering the evolution of trajectories of involvement in language brokering, and also the impact of type of access to services. For example, legal immigrants have different access compared with illegal immigrants who may go to doctors only in emergencies. Examining actual encounters will help to disentangle issues that may be specific to the stage of development of a child, and issues that are related to doctor-patient communication.

Future Directions

Research is needed to explore the complexity of language brokering in health care settings to understand the following issues more fully: the variety of settings, for example, a GP/family doctor, is different from emergency treatment in a hospital in which language brokering takes place; the nature of medical conditions and the complexity (i.e., linguistic, cultural, and emotional) of the task; the relationships between actors in the language brokering situation (e.g., doctor-mother-child); identities (e.g., familial, cultural, social, etc.); resources (e.g., media, people, languages, cultural scripts); communities and neighborhoods (e.g., the idea that it is normal if one's peers also do it); understandings of childhood; children's responsibilities in their families; and the extent to which they are shared in the majority culture of the place they live.

In our previous work, we have identified two perspectives in which child language brokering has been understood. The first is a perspective in which a child's engagement in atypical activities was seen to lead to the loss of "normal" childhood. A second, more positive, perspective is that engagement in non-normative activities such as language brokering was seen as a source of pride and as providing additional skills and qualities to the child's development (Cline, Crafter, Abreu, & O'Dell, 2009). These two perspectives in child language brokering were apparent in the papers reviewed; however, we argue that child language brokering, as part of child development in culturally diverse societies, can be better understood from a third theoretical perspective that sees children's engagement in language brokering as a loss of "normal" childhood as part of a variety of positions that are available to those engaging in child language brokering. This accords with critical developmental psychology (Burman, 2008). Here, we will draw on dialogical self-theory (Hermans, 2002) to explain our theoretical thinking, but before we do that, we will elaborate how the findings of our analysis lends support to our proposed theorizing.

In the literature reviewed, engaging in child language brokering in medical settings is not only conceived as a loss of normal childhood, but also as potentially damaging and harmful to child development. This perspective is particularly dominant among health care providers and policy makers. Health care settings pose particular challenges in increasingly linguistic and culturally diverse communities, which result in children and young people getting involved in language brokering. The analysis of health care settings showed a complex picture of the reasons children become involved. For example, in routine consultations they may be involved because of a lack of translation services. In emergency situations, where a quick response is needed, and health professionals often have to prioritize the need to care for the patient over the use of the child as a translator. It is also the case that health issues are not constrained to formal settings, but also take place in the context of the home, where again children are immediately available to language broker between their families and health providers. Thus, exploring child language brokering in terms of settings, and what happens in these settings, illustrated the almost inevitability of child language brokering in linguistically diverse families and communities. The more positive perspective that engagement in language brokering could be source of pride and be seen as providing additional skills and qualities to the child's development was also evident in the analysis. This view is dominant in the perspectives of children and in parents who prefer to keep the privacy and trust of family issues by using a child as a language broker. A critical developmental psychology frame is helpful here to theorize and account for this position (see for example, Burman, 2008).

Contribution to Theory

As a strategy towards developing new theoretical ways to understand child language brokering, we drew on sociocultural and critical developmental psychology to view the data in terms of setting, mediation, and constructions of childhood. This confirmed the utility of the two perspectives we had identified in previous work, but pointed to a complexity that needed new conceptualization. Viewing child language brokering in a polarized way—i.e., that it is either a negative experience or it is beneficial, depending on the person evaluating the activity (i.e., as polarized)—is not helpful because in the everyday lives of professionals, parents, and children, language brokering can be both positive and negatively experienced by each person involved in the process. It is not possible to make a definitive decision about whether language brokering is positive *or* negative. We propose that an alternative is to draw on a dialogical self-perspective (Hermans, 2002) that enables a theorization of child language brokering not as a unified role or identity, but an understanding of the "self" (the individual child, family member, practitioner etc.) as involving many different positions or views. The positions that are brought to the fore are grounded in interactions that are dependent on the types of settings and consultations; for example, a child can be thought of (and think of him- or herself as) "I as a child language broker," but also "I as a typical child," "as a school student," "as a son/daughter," "as a member of an immigrant family," etc. These positions dialogue with other people involved in the situation. Thus, they can be in harmony, tension, or conflict. The harmony explains the child's feelings of normality, ease, and so on. The tension or conflict explains the experiences of finding language brokering difficult and stressful, among other feelings. Thus, for example, when child language brokering conflicts with duties and responsibilities of the child "as a school student" there is tension that needs to be resolved. Similarly, a parent will have a repertoire of positions; such as, "I as a mother," "as a member of my community," "as a woman," "as a novice speaker of the host language," and so on: Thus, again these positions can be harmonious when the mother perceives language brokering as a normal activity for her child. For example, the mother may feel comfortable with a child translating in routine health care, when the mother is able to schedule the activity out of school hours, but she may feel unhappy about a son being involved with issues that she feels are privy to her gender.

The close analysis of mediation in the metasynthesis showed that even those who start from the perspective that children should not be used as language brokers are faced with situations that require them to reconsider their view. From this, they start developing a complex model of what they can accept or cannot accept as a childhood activity. This dialogue, described in papers such as Cohen et al. (1999), is expressed in doctors' retrospective accounts of their experiences and shows that the "I as doctor" position interacts with more than one position of the child "as a language broker to my patient." The multiplicity of interactions is apparent when doctors start talking about the different types of consultations. A doctor can reconsider the view of the position of the child as language broker, depending on the specific identities of the child, such as their age and gender. Thus, the "I as doctor" position can conflict with or be in harmony with a child language broker position, depending on the unique situation of the child. This suggests that a polarized view between those who take a negative view of language brokering and those who take a positive view is not working in practice, as both repertoires are represented in the same person. It is the dialogue between these positions that is interesting from a theoretical point of view. We argue that the way activities in a setting (such as a health care setting) are organized, the nature of the consultations, and the norms invoked within each situation all contribute to the positions that actors in a specific situation are able to assume, or are assigned by others, and this explains how sometimes these are harmonious and at other times are in conflict. Understanding more about processes that could help to promote harmonious dialogues can contribute to better practices.

To conclude, we argue that children's language brokering activities can be better understood from perspectives that acknowledge normative childhoods are diverse (Cline et al., 2009). In order to situate child language brokering within an understanding of diverse childhoods, there is a need for approaches to the activity that can conceptualize language brokering as practices situated in sociocultural political contexts. Further, there is a need to understand normal family life in multicultural contexts in a way that recognizes multiple dialogical identities, obligations, care bonds, and dependence within families rather than assume a hierarchical model of parents who provide care for their children.

References

Abreu, G. de, & Elbers, E. (2005). Introduction: The social mediation of learning in multiethnic schools. *European Journal of Psychology of Education, 20*(1), 3–11.

Abreu, G. de, & Hale, H. (2011). Trajectories of cultural identity development of young immigrant people: The impact of family practices. *Psychological Studies, 56*(1), 53–61.

Antonini, R. (2010). The study of child language brokering: Past, current and emerging research. *MediAzioni: Journal of Interdisciplinary Studies on Language and Cultures, 10.*

Barron, D. S., Holterman, C., Shipster, P., Batson, S., & Alam, M. (2010). Seen but not heard: Ethnic minorities' views of primary health care interpreting provision: A focus group study. *Primary Health Care Research & Development, 11*(2), 132–141.

Bucaria, C., & Rossato, L. (2010). Former child language brokers: Preliminary observations on practice, attitudes and relational aspects. *MediAzioni: Journal of Interdisciplinary Studies on Language and Cultures, 10.*

Burman, E. (2008). *Developments: Child, image, nation.* London, UK: Routledge.

Candappa, M., & Egharevba, I. I. (2003). Everyday worlds of young refugees in London. *Feminist Review, 73,* 54–65.

Chao, R. K. (2006). The prevalence and consequences of adolescents' language brokering for their immigrant parents. In M. H. Bornstein & L. R. Cote (Eds.), *Acculturation and parent-child relationships: Measurement and development* (pp. 271–296). Mahwah, NJ: Lawrence Erlbaum.

Churchill, H., & O'Dell, L. (2013). Disabled parents and normative families: The obscuring of lived experiences of parents and children within policy and research accounts. In J. Ribbens, J. McCarthy, C. Hooper, & V. Gillies (Eds.), *Family troubles? Exploring changes and challenges in the family lives of children and young people.* Bristol: Policy Press.

Cline, T., Abreu, G. de, O'Dell, L., & Crafter, S. (2010). Recent research on child language brokering in the United Kingdom. *MediAzioni: Journal of Interdisciplinary Studies on Language and Cultures, 10,* 105–124.

Cline, T., Crafter, S., Abreu, G. de, & O'Dell, L. (2009). Changing families, changing childhoods—changing schools? *International Journal of Pastoral Care in Education 27*(1), 29–39.

Cline, T., Crafter, S., O'Dell, L., & Abreu, G. de. (2011). Young people's representations of language brokering. *Journal of Multilingual and Multicultural Development, 32*(3), 207–220.

Cohen, S., Moran-Ellis, J., & Smaje, C. (1999). Children as informal interpreters in GP consultations: Pragmatics and ideology. *Sociology of Health & Illness, 21*(2), 163–186.

Corona, R., Stevens, L., Halfond, R., Shaffer, C., Reid-Quiñones, K., & Gonzalez, T. (2012). A qualitative analysis of what Latino parents and adolescents think and feel about language brokering. *Journal of Child & Family Studies, 21*(5), 788–798.

Crafter, S., O'Dell, L., Abreu, G. de, & Cline, T. (2009). Young peoples' representations of "atypical" work in English society. *Children & Society, 23*(3), 176–188.

Degener, J. L. (2010). Sometimes my mother does not understand, then I need to translate. Child and youth language brokering in Berlin-Neukolin (Germany). *MediAzioni: Journal of Interdisciplinary Studies on Language and Cultures, 10.*

Free, C., Green, J., Bhavnani, V., & Newman, A. (2003). Bilingual young people's experiences of interpreting in primary care: A qualitative study. *British Journal of General Practice, 53*(492), 530–535.

García-Sánchez, I. M. (2010). (Re)shaping practices in translation: How Moroccan immigrant children and families navigate continuity and change. *MediAzioni, Journal of Interdisciplinary Studies on Languages and Cultures, 10,* 182–214.

Gerrish, K., Chau, R., Sobowale, A., & Birks, E. (2004). Bridging the language barrier: The use of interpreters in primary care nursing. *Health & Social Care in the Community, 12*(5), 407–413.

Giordano, S. (2007). Overview of the advantages and disadvantages of professional and child interpreters for limited English proficiency patients in general health care situations. *Journal of Radiology Nursing, 26*(4), 126–131.

Goodnow, J. J., Miller, P. J., & Kessel, F. (1995). *Cultural practices as contexts for development.* San Francisco, CA: Jossey-Bass.

Green, J., Free, C., Bhavnani, V., & Newman, T. (2005). Translators and mediators: Bilingual young people's accounts of their interpreting work in health care. *Social Science & Medicine, 60*(9), 2097–2110.

Haffner, L. (1992). Translation is not enough: Interpreting in a medical setting. *Western Journal of Medicine, 157*(3), 255–259.

Hermans, H. J. M. (2002). The dialogical self as a society of mind. *Theory and Psychology, 12* 147–160.

Jones, C. J., & Trickett, E. J. (2005). Immigrant adolescents behaving as culture brokers: A study of families from the former Soviet Union. *The Journal of Social Psychology, 145*(4), 405–428.

Katz, V. S. (2007). *From conversation to conversion: Children's efforts to translate their immigrant families' social networks into community connections.* Unpublished doctoral dissertation. University of Southern California, US.

Katz, V. S. (2014). Children as brokers of their immigrant families health-care connections. *Social Problems, 61*(2), 194–215.

Kosner, A., Roer-Strier, D., & Kurman, J. (2014). Changing familial roles for immigrant adolescents from the former Soviet Union to Israel. *Journal of Adolescent Research, 29*(3), 356–379.

Lave, J., & Wenger, E. (1991). *Situated learning and legitimate peripheral participation.* Cambridge, UK: Cambridge University Press.

Lehna, C. (2005). Interpreter services in pediatric nursing. *Pediatric Nursing, 31*(4), 292.

Orellana, M. F., Dorner, L., & Pulido, L. (2003). Accessing assets: Immigrant youth's work as family translators or "para-phrasers". *Social Problems, 50*(4), 505–524.

Reynolds, J. F., & Orellana, M. F. (2009). New immigrant youth interpreting in white public space. *American Anthropologist, 111*(2), 211–223.

Rubio-Rico, L., Biosca, A. R., de Molina Fernandez, I., & Grau, M. M.V. (2014). Maghrebi minors as translators in health services in Tarragona (Spain): A qualitative study of the discourse of the Maghrebi adults. *Globalization and Health, 10*(1), 1–22.

Suarez-Orozco, C., & Suarez-Orozco, M. M. (2001). *Children of immigration*. Cambridge, MA: Harvard University Press.

Thorne, S., Jensen, L., Kearney, M. H., Noblit, G., & Sandelowski, M. (2004). Qualitative metasynthesis: Reflections on methodological orientation and ideological agenda. *Qualitative Health Research, 14*(10), 1342–1365.

Tribe, R., & Thompson, K. (2008). *Working with interpreters in health settings: Guidelines for psychologists*. Leicester: British Psychology Society.

Villanueva, C. M., & Buriel, R. (2010). Speaking on behalf of others: A qualitative study of the perceptions and feelings of adolescent Latina language brokers. *Journal of Social Issues, 66*(1), 197–210.

Vygotsky, L. (1978). *Mind in society: The development of higher psychological processes*. Cambridge, MA: Harvard University Press.

Walsh, D., & Downe, S. (2005). Meta-synthesis method for qualitative research: A literature review. *Journal of Advanced Nursing, 50*(2), 204–211.

Weisskirch, R. S. (2005). The relationship of language brokering to ethnic identity for Latino early adolescents. *Hispanic Journal of Behavioral Sciences, 27*(3), 286–299.

Whitman, M.V., Davis, J. A., & Terry, A. J. (2010). Perceptions of school nurses on the challenges of service provision to ESL students. *Journal of Community Health, 35*(2), 208–213.

10

COGNITIVE, SOCIOEMOTIONAL, AND DEVELOPMENTAL NEUROSCIENCE PERSPECTIVES ON LANGUAGE BROKERING

Vanessa R. Rainey, Valerie C. Flores-Lamb, and Eva Gjorgieva

Introduction

Language brokering, a unique application of bilingualism, not only involves translating information between two different-language speakers (McQuillan & Tse, 1995; Morales & Hanson, 2005; Orellana, 2009; Tse, 1995a, 1995b), but also a deep understanding of the social ambiguities of two different cultures (Morales & Hanson, 2005; Tse, 1995a). From a national perspective, efforts to identify the strengths and risks of language brokering may be important due to the rising number of immigrants and language brokers in the United States. The number of language-minority youth and young adults who speak a language other than English at home has increased in the United States from about 6 million in 1979 to approximately 14 million in 1999 (National Center for Education Statistics, 2004). Language brokers may be different from typical bilingual children, making them a unique group to study and to inform theories of language development.

Traditional bilingual theories suggest that the management of two different language systems is beneficial to the bilingual (Bialystok, 2006, 2009; Bialystok, Craik, Klein, & Viswanathan, 2004; Costa, Hernández, & Sebastián-Gallés, 2008; Martin-Rhee & Bialystok, 2008). One of the benefits may be increases in executive function (EF) abilities. That is, strengths in EF may be a by-product of continual language separation (Bialystok, 2009). EF is a term used to describe a set of functions that oversee the cognitive control of goal-oriented actions, such as those seen when controlling impulsive responses and task switching (Best, Miller, & Jones, 2009; Diamond, 2013; Miyake et al., 2000). These functions have been localized to areas of the prefrontal cortex of the brain, suggesting that they are uniquely different from memorization and recall skills (Best & Miller, 2010; Bialystok, 2009). Consequently, EFs aid in the encoding and organization of knowledge and have emerged as an important factor in one's learning environment (Best et al., 2009; Cartwright, Marshall, Dandy, & Isaac, 2010; Deák, 2003). Bilingual theories of language development suggest that the cognitive and linguistic domains become inextricably linked for bilingual learners due to the need to continually recruit core EF skills, such as inhibition, to suppress other language interference (e.g., Baum & Titone, 2014; Bialystok & Craik, 2010; Green, 1998). The experience-dependent neuroplasticity of the brain, or the ability of the brain to accommodate challenging situations by restructuring its neural connectivity, allows for bilinguals to quickly adjust to environments with multiple languages (Baum & Titone, 2014; Knudsen, 2004).

Moreover, the sociolinguistic environment of bilinguals with significant translation experience is qualitatively different than that of non-translating bilinguals, creating a unique mixture of psychosocial forces on development. Language brokers must bridge multiple "spheres," including, for example, child language and adult language; majority values and minority values; and working class and middle class (Reynolds & Orellana, 2009). Not only are these children faced with the potential of cognitively challenging material, but they may also be faced with socially and emotionally charged information. The cumulative effects of these experiences may further shape their developing brains and neurocognitive abilities. Based on evidence from developmental neuroscience, a large portion of brain development is influenced by environmental stimulation and circumstances, such as language brokering (Andersen, 2003; Halperin & Healey, 2011; Knudsen, 2004).

Consequently, language brokers are different than their bilingual peers without translation experience because there are no constant, clear-cut boundaries between when they use one language versus the other. Bilingual children without any family language brokering duties typically use each language in certain, predictable places (Costa, Hernández, Costa-Faidella, & Sebastián-Gallés, 2009). For example, they may only use Spanish in the home and English everywhere else. They are then able to focus exclusively on one language at a time, reducing the cognitive load on the EF system. However, during translation experiences for language brokering, children must use both of their language systems in the same contexts and switch between them to be successful brokers (Tse, 1996). This type of parallel language activation may further improve aspects of EF, particularly in core areas not showing consistent advantages in the general bilingual. For instance, language brokers may display efficiencies in shifting skills because this helps them to switch rapidly between language systems (Rainey, Davidson, & Li-Grining, 2015; Soveri, Rodriguez-Fornells, & Laine, 2011).

When reviewing the literature, it is evident that language brokering children have typically been examined in segmented areas of research, either within the realm of cognitive development or socioemotional development. To further this discussion, we will incorporate evidence from developmental neuroscience examining the development of the brain and its interaction with the environment to inform these theories.

Highlights From Past Research on Cognitive Development of Language Brokers

Past research suggests that language brokers may be more advanced cognitively than non-brokering bilinguals (e.g., Buriel, Perez, DeMent, Chavez, & Moran, 1998; Christoffels, De Groot, & Kroll, 2006; Dong & Xie, 2014; Rainey et al., 2015). In a similar vein to bilingual advantages, which remain mixed in the literature (e.g., Bialystok, Craik, & Luk, 2008; Christoffels, de Haan, Steenbergen, van den Wildenberg, & Colzato, 2015), evidence has emerged for precocious cognitive abilities in young language brokers (e.g., De Groot & Christoffels, 2006; Dorner, Orellana, & Li-Grining, 2007; Rainey et al., 2015). This finding has been observed in both the academic domain and in higher-order processing abilities, such as EF. Some researchers suggest that language brokering may create the optimal environment for precocious cognitive skills because brokers must bring adult-level material to common usage and among multiple speakers (Eksner & Orellana, 2012; Gregory, Long, & Volk, 2004; Paradise & Rogoff, 2009). Often times, these children are "teaching" others and rephrasing information, so everyone in the conversation can understand the material. This exposure to sophisticated materials and conversations may help language brokers develop certain cognitive skills, such as metalinguistic awareness or switching abilities, sooner than their peers (e.g., Prior & Gollan, 2011). For example, language brokers must think more abstractly about language itself, as they switch between distinct language structures to translate parts of speech and ideas.

Some of these skills are evident in language brokers' academic performance. For example, in a sample of fifth- and sixth-grade bilingual children, those with greater levels of brokering experience had better scores on standardized reading tests (Dorner et al., 2007). Although other researchers have demonstrated similar findings, a more complex picture emerges when different age groups are examined (e.g., Acoach & Webb, 2004; Buriel et al., 1998; Orellana, 2003). For instance, junior high language brokers with greater levels of language brokering showed higher levels of acculturation and biculturalism when compared with non-brokers (Acoach & Webb, 2004), which led to greater academic self-efficacy and higher GPAs. Later in development, Acoach and Webb (2004) found that high school students with greater language brokering experience displayed higher academic self-efficacy, which positively affected their GPA. In short, cultural mediators were more salient for junior high school students' academic success, whereas only academic self-efficacy was meaningful for high schoolers' academic success. Understanding these differing pathways is essential to understanding the language broker at a more nuanced level. Research has only begun to scratch the surface on differences in adjustment depending upon the time frame in which children begin brokering duties.

To understand the biological underpinnings of these developments, researchers have begun to examine general cognitive developments in frequent language switchers (e.g., Christoffels et al., 2006; Dong & Xie, 2014; Rainey et al., 2015).

Studies have centered on developments in the realm of EF, connections between different areas of the brain, and differing neural pathways that may be present for language brokers. Indeed, in comparison to non-brokering bilinguals, recent evidence has pointed to greater connectivity in cognitive and linguistic domains among language brokers, particularly in younger populations (Hernandez, Dapretto, Mazziotta, & Bookheimer, 2001; Rainey et al., 2015; Soveri et al., 2011).

When 8- and 9-year-old English and Spanish-speaking children with high levels of language translating completed a shifting task, they were able to do this much faster, with fewer errors, than their non-brokering bilingual and monolingual peers (Rainey et al., 2015). In addition, the correlation between performance on the shifting task and a high-level language task was much stronger for the bilinguals, particularly language brokers, when compared to the monolinguals. As a result, future bilingual studies should differentiate between language brokers and bilingual non-brokers. According to Hebbian theory, language brokers' recurrent use of particular neural pathways during translation helps these pathways become more automatized and efficient (Bialystok, 2015; Christoffels et al., 2006; Hebb, 2002; Kroll, Bobb, & Hoshino, 2014; Phillips & Shonkoff, 2000). Not accounting for language brokering experience may help to explain why bilingual "advantages" are not always found in the research (e.g., Chen, Zhou, Uchikoshi, & Bunge, 2014; Morton & Harper, 2007). Should future research find that language brokering on a frequent basis automatizes particular neural pathways that are key for cognition and language, then it would be necessary for researchers to control for one's frequency of language brokering when studying a bilingual population. Not measuring and controlling for bilinguals' language brokering practice might otherwise result in the omission of a third, critical variable that may, in part, explain the mechanism responsible for bilinguals' advantage in certain domains (Cain, 1975).

Researchers have found language brokering differences to persist into adulthood, although these may be dependent upon the continued intensity of language switching on a daily basis and the type of task used during testing (Bajo, Padilla, & Padilla, 2000; García et al., 2014; Ibáñez, Macizo, & Bajo, 2010; Prior & Gollan, 2011; Soveri et al., 2011; Yudes, Macizo, Morales, & Bajo, 2012). The majority of this work has focused on frequent language switchers (i.e., those who use both languages frequently on a daily basis) and professional translators/interpreters. Although natural translation that happens during language brokering is inherently different than professional translating (Halgunseth, 2003; McQuillan & Tse, 1995), this research is at least providing preliminary evidence that parallel activation of both language systems differentiates bilinguals' brain development and could potentially last into adulthood.

There is some evidence of the long-lasting effects of bilingual language brokering into adulthood. One study examined the response times to a task-switching paradigm for two groups of bilingual emerging adults (i.e., frequent language switchers and infrequent language switchers) and monolinguals (Prior & Gollan, 2011). In this task, participants had to focus on either the shape or the color of the changing stimuli and respond as quickly as possible to the changing dimensional cue. Overall, the frequent language switchers displayed a reduced switch cost when compared to the monolinguals and the infrequent switchers, even after controlling for extraneous factors. In short, this study suggested that language brokers' cognitive strengths persist into adulthood.

In a similar vein, research focused on trained interpreters has revealed differences when compared with untrained bilinguals and monolinguals. In one particular study, trained interpreters displayed better comprehension skills overall on specific text comprehension tasks when compared to non-trained bilinguals and monolinguals (Yudes et al., 2012). It was speculated that the combination of bilingualism and a larger working memory capacity from the linguistic training set the interpreters apart from the other groups. Similar findings were displayed for interpreters when performing various comprehension, decision, and categorization tasks (Bajo et al., 2000). Although this is useful as a starting point, future researchers should continue to study language brokers as a distinct group from frequent language switchers or professional interpreters, as this may greatly affect findings.

Furthermore, other studies have not consistently identified cognitive gains among emerging adults who language brokered. For instance, a recent study examined the relations between emerging adults' language brokering practices, cognitive skills, and academic success in college (Flores, Li-Grining, Rainey, & Gjorgieva, in preparation). In particular, this study focused on comparing Spanish-English speaking brokers with non-brokering bilinguals to examine whether language brokering duties were associated with significant strengths in EFs and college GPAs. Findings from this study suggested that non-brokering bilinguals' EF skills were significantly linked to greater academic achievement, but the same link was not present for language brokers. Overall, being a language broker during college was negatively associated with students' GPA, which was also corroborated by another study conducted with Latino/a brokers in California (Shen & Guan, 2015). Unexpectedly, cognitive and academic strengths found earlier in development among language brokers (e.g., Dorner et al., 2007; Rainey et al., 2015) do not always appear to persist into emerging adulthood, or at least not in a similar way that was beneficial to their past academic successes. Nevertheless, this research underscores the importance of conducting future longitudinal studies that examine multiple aspects of language brokers' development in order to address the complexities of their adjustment in adulthood.

Overall, it appears that language brokers' parallel activation of two languages creates a unique sociolinguistic environment that should also be studied in conjunction with the effects of language brokering on socioemotional development and adjustment (Macizo & Bajo, 2004, 2006; Ruiz, Paredes, Macizo, & Bajo, 2008). As such, future studies may find that the cognitive advantages held by language brokers interact with their socioemotional skills in unexpected ways, explaining the rather inconsistent story within the socioemotional literature on language brokers.

Highlights From Past Research on Socioemotional Development of Language Brokers

Within the literature on the socioemotional development of language brokers, findings have been mixed regarding advantages and disadvantages. Overall, conclusive answers about the adjustment of language brokering children cannot be understood by merely investigating children's immediate context. Individual differences in development can be equally defined by peripheral macrosystems, such as societal cultural values or ethnic values (Bronfenbrenner, 2005).

Language brokering children grow up in unique household environments. Child language brokers are faced with challenging, adult tasks that oftentimes exceed their level of cognitive development (e.g., paying bills, applying for credit); as a result, the balance in the family can easily become unsettled (Jones, Trickett, & Birman, 2012; Morales & Hanson, 2005). Language brokers must maintain a strong bilingual balance (Halgunseth, 2003), manage time requirements of translating that take away from peer socialization (Fuligni & Pederson, 2002; Tse, 1996), and deal with family role confusion and increased conflict in the family (Martinez, McClure, & Eddy, 2009; Umaña-Taylor, 2003). In response to different stressors and protective factors, the language brokering adolescent may develop positive or negative coping mechanisms over time (Hua & Costigan, 2012). Recent research has attempted to understand brokers' overall adjustment by including familial variables that may affect relationships among family members.

Some researchers have noted that language brokering is a positive experience that forces language brokers to develop mature social mechanisms. This finding is particularly relevant when examining outcomes such as ethnic identity, confidence, and self-esteem (Buriel et al., 1998; Halgunseth, 2003; Weisskirch, 2005). Among a group of fifth- and sixth-grade Latino/a language brokers, Weisskirch (2005) found that pre-adolescents, particularly when highly acculturated, reported positive feelings toward translating and also reported higher levels of ethnic identity. Moreover, developing a strong ethnic identity may be critical for youth from immigrant families. Research has found that a strong sense of ethnic identity is a positive predictor of self-esteem and can serve as a protective factor when youth are faced with racial discrimination (Mandara, Gaylord-Harden, Richard, & Ragsdale, 2009; Neblett, Rivas-Drake, & Umaña-Taylor, 2012). Other researchers have reported similar positive findings for the effects of language brokering on biculturalism and self-confidence in children and adolescents (Buriel et al., 1998; McQuillan & Tse, 1995). Intense exposure to both languages and a greater level of biculturalism may contribute to positive feelings and a greater connection with their family. This exposure may guide adolescents into a deeper level of ethnic identity development, which may be a healthy adjustment style for children with multiple cultural backgrounds (French, Seidman, Allen, & Aber, 2006; Fuligni, Kiang, Witkow, & Baldelomar, 2008; Weisskirch, 2005).

Other studies have attempted to understand how adherence to mainstream and heritage cultures could impact development. When language brokers feel more oriented toward their heritage culture, they may feel they matter more to family members and to the overall functioning of the family. In turn, they tend not to view translating as a burden (Elliott, Kao, & Grant, 2004; Fuligni & Pederson, 2002; Love & Buriel, 2007). When investigating these linkages in Chinese American early (ages 13–14) and late (ages 17–18) adolescents, Wu and Kim (2009) found that being more Chinese-oriented led language brokers to feel a greater sense of familial obligation and ultimately led to them reporting that translating contributed to their sense of efficacy, as opposed to being a burden. Language brokering may, then, support one's understanding and adherence to heritage culture and values.

Although these findings suggest positive benefits, other studies have reported that language brokers are uncomfortable in certain translating situations, which may negatively affect well-being (e.g., Weisskirch & Alva, 2002). Negative language brokering experiences may stem from anxiety surrounding the mistranslation of information, which may negatively impact the family (Corona et al., 2012). This relation to anxiety is particularly relevant in high-stakes contexts, such as when sensitive health information needs to be conveyed to parents.

Furthermore, other research has focused on how language brokering affects the power balance within a family. Martinez and colleagues (2009) examined 73 families of 12-year-old language brokers to understand whether language brokering demands were linked to family functioning and subsequent adolescent adjustment. Families with low-frequency language brokering duties reported fewer internalizing behaviors based on parental report, higher ethnic belonging and affirmation, and less likelihood to use alcohol, tobacco, or other substances compared to the high-frequency brokers. Parents in high-brokering families may lack the ability to manage the level of autonomy that these adolescents who language broker seek, given their increased responsibility as brokers (Malakoff & Hakuta, 1991; Valdés, 2003). Overall, this research addresses the quantity or frequency of brokering on subsequent adjustment, but it does not address the quality of parent-child interactions.

Increasingly, more research has pointed toward the intensity, or quality, of language brokering duties and particular parental characteristics as key to understanding the effects of language brokering (e.g., Hua & Costigan, 2012). In general, stress in the family has been linked with greater levels of psychological dysfunction in children, such as anxiety and depression (Lupein, McEwen, Gunnar, & Heim, 2009). Parents' feelings of disempowerment likely increase the level of stress in the family and the intensity of the brokering experience for all involved. However, more research is needed to investigate the intensity of the language brokering experience and how it may affect the individuals involved. Positive, high-quality parent-child interactions may result in brokers having more advanced cognitive skills, whereas negative, low-quality brokering interactions may result in more internalizing symptoms among brokers.

Recent research has attempted to examine the impact of brokering on the psychological health and adjustment of children and adolescents (e.g., Chao, 2006; Hall & Sham, 1998; Rainey et al., 2015; Weisskirch & Alva, 2002). For instance, Hua and Costigan (2012) found frequency of language brokering to be negatively correlated with adolescents' self-esteem and linked with greater parent-child conflict. Notably, family characteristics—such as the degree of familial obligations and the level of parental psychological control—moderated these relations. That is, frequent adolescent brokers with high family obligations or high parental psychological control fared the worst when internalizing symptoms were evaluated. In addition, adolescents who frequently translated displayed lower self-esteem in the presence of high parental psychological control. In these contexts, adolescents' adjustment was not simply affected by frequency of brokering, but by the particular family context in which they were embedded.

When predicting the likelihood of internalizing disorders, other studies have begun to focus on particular time periods in which language brokering may be especially challenging (Rainey, Flores, Morrison, David, & Silton, 2014; Schulz, Titzmann, & Michel, 2013). These studies found that early adolescence (i.e., defined roughly as 9 to 13 years of age) was a particularly problematic time for language brokering youth, resulting in greater internalizing symptoms. This finding warrants greater attention to this developmental period, as such negative symptoms could create a pattern affecting one's well-being in adulthood (Rainey et al., 2014). To begin to understand why individuals within this distinct time period might be differentially affected, we will root these findings in literature on developmental neuroscience and draw from studies discussing brain maturation and environmental effects. This may help to explain why brain development during this particular developmental transition can complicate the benefits of language brokering.

Integrating the Developmental Neuroscience Perspective

Before introducing neuroscience methodology to the field of research that examines the language brokering phenomenon, it is first essential to grasp how bilingual brains are organized and operate in comparison to the monolingual brain. Some early theories suggested that bilingual brains showed more bilateral activation during tasks engaging various aspects of language (Albert & Obler, 1978). However, a comprehensive review of bilingual studies that utilized neuroscience methodologies (e.g., PET, fMRI), concluded that similar areas of the brain, notably the left prefrontal cortex, were activated for first (L1) and second languages (L2; Abutalebi, Cappa, & Perani, 2005; Chee, Caplan et al., 1999; Perani et al., 1998). Abutalebi and colleagues (2005) also pointed out that language proficiency (Chee, Tan, & Theil, 1999) as well as regular exposure to a particular language (Perani et al., 2003) play a critical role in how widespread brain activation is, with lower proficiency and less exposure correlating with a larger area of activation. Surprisingly, one's age of language acquisition was not a critical factor in bilingual individuals' brain activity (Chee, Caplan et al., 1999; Illes et al., 1999), so long as the individual was highly proficient. Moreover, it appears that more language exposure or greater proficiency in a given language were associated with linguistic networks becoming more automatized (Abutalebi et al., 2005). This means that the use of a more fluent language requires fewer neural resources, which is reflected in lessened activation overall.

As such, this research suggests one possible distinction between language brokers and non-brokering bilinguals, though research has yet to explore neural distinctions between these two populations. Assuming that language brokering is associated with greater exposure to both language environments and higher proficiency in each language, the neural networks responsible for language activation among language brokers may be more efficient and require fewer resources than those among non-brokers (Chee, Caplan et al., 1999; Perani et al., 2003). Furthermore, bilingual research has pointed to particular areas of the brain responsible for switching between languages and language selection. The dorsolateral prefrontal cortex (Hernandez et al., 2001), Broca's area, and the supramarginal gyrus (Price, Winterburn, Giraud, Moore, & Noppeney, 2003) have been implicated in bilinguals' switching between languages (Abutalebi et al., 2005). In addition, the left anterior prefrontal region (Rodriguez-Fornells, Rotte, Heinze, Nösselt, & Münte, 2002) was linked with the inhibition of a non-target language, allowing bilinguals to select the appropriate language. As both switching and inhibition of a non-target language become more automatic, such as in the case of a language broker, lesser activation of these areas may become more apparent and help distinguish between brokering and non-brokering bilinguals.

While there is a dearth of language brokering research utilizing neuroscience methodologies, a burgeoning body of literature is beginning to illuminate key differences between bilingual and monolingual brains using these methodologies. Such studies have uncovered differences in bilinguals' and monolinguals' cognitive and linguistic processing. For example, Bialystok and colleagues (2005) used magneto-encephalography (MEG) to examine bilinguals' and monolinguals' performance on cognitive tasks, which revealed more left hemispheric activity associated with bilinguals' better performance. In contrast, monolinguals' performance was correlated with general frontal activity. This suggests that bilinguals' left hemispheric specialization may help give them a cognitive edge. Another neuroscience study utilized time frequency analysis during a grammaticality judgment task that steadily increased in EF demands (Kieler, Meltzer, Moreno, Alain, & Bialystok, 2014). This study found that bilinguals, but not monolinguals, showed a decrease in their 8–30 Hz event-related dysynchronization (ERD) during syntactic violations. This suggests that this particular frequency is a marker of language processing that is distinct between these two populations.

However, this research does not always point toward advantages held by bilinguals. A recent electroencephalography (EEG) study suggested that bilinguals experience more conflict when completing tasks that require lexical selection within a single language, as exhibited by bilinguals' larger N400s (Friesen, Chung-Fat-Yim, & Bialystok, 2016). In other words, lexical selection and access may be more challenging or require more effort from bilinguals, who must always inhibit other language interference in a task involving linguistic stimuli. Yet, there remains some evidence from a recent EEG study that learning a second language can be of benefit in specific ways. For instance, a study found that even in the early stages of second language acquisition there was evidence of neural changes that are indicative of better EF skills (Sullivan, Janus, Moreno, Astheimer, & Bialystok, 2014). In this study, college students enrolled in Introductory Spanish were compared with students from an Introductory Psychology course. At the end of the semester, students in the Spanish course exhibited larger P3 amplitudes on a Go/No-Go task and smaller P6 amplitudes on a sentence judgment task. This study suggests that even 6 months of instruction in a second language could result in better cognitive functioning. In sum, cognitive neuroscience studies point to some cognitive advantages held by bilinguals, particularly in EFs, mixed with a greater level of conflict experienced by bilinguals when tasks involve language.

Now that we have a greater understanding of how neuroscience methodologies could broaden our current knowledge of the language brokering phenomenon, it is important that we also understand critical periods in development that impact brain development equally, if not more so, than bilingualism. These developmental periods can also interact with language brokering experiences to impact children in different ways.

Adolescence, a bridge between childhood and adulthood, is a distinct period in brain development during which synapses are pruned if they are not utilized (Huttenlocher, 1994). This pruning may make neural pathways more efficient, particularly those connected to the developing prefrontal cortex, so that adolescents can integrate information to think in a more intricate, adaptive manner (Blakemore & Choudry, 2006; Lenroot & Giedd, 2006). At the same time that cognitive control is maturing, neurons in the early adolescent brain are also more sensitive to excitatory neurotransmitters with the onset of puberty. This means that early adolescents may be more affected by stressful events and be more reactive, which means that feelings can be challenging for them to manage (Ernst & Spear, 2009; Sternberg, Grigorenko, & Zhang, 2008). Taken together, the streamlining of the central executive at the beginning of adolescence coupled with the greater potential for mismanaged stress suggests that language brokering may be a particularly challenging task for younger adolescents. For instance, language brokering heavily relies on one's EF system to shift between languages and communicate effectively. However, such skills are still actively developing and evolving at the beginning of adolescence, which can complicate matters. In addition, many brokering contexts may involve translation of sensitive information, such as communicating with a bank regarding parents' financial problems, which may elevate the brokers' awareness of their role and trigger emotional distress at a time in which individuals are more vulnerable to stress.

Gender coupled with the developmental time period when language brokering takes place may also influence the outcomes for the individual. According to Andersen (2003), exposure to both positive and negative experiences during puberty, and at the beginning of adolescence, may determine the prevalence of psychopathology in the future. Further, given that girls are more prone to depression than boys, the experiences of girls who language broker may have specific effects on well-being. Anderson posits that there are at least two potential explanations for females experiencing higher rates of depression. First, Andersen (2003) suggested that estrogen has both neuromodulatory and neurotrophic effects in the brain, meaning that estrogen may alter the transmission of neurotransmitters in large areas of the brain. Estrogen is essential to the growth and maintenance of neurons that help buffer the expression of depression (Grigoriadis & Seeman, 2002; Halbreich & Kahn, 2001). Second, Andersen (2003) pointed to gender differences in stress management (Klein & Corwin, 2002) and social pressures (Seeman, 2002) that might also help explain this gender discrepancy in depression.

That said, these findings are particularly salient to the language brokering literature because female adolescents may be more likely to engage in brokering (Buriel et al., 1998; Morales & Hanson, 2005; Weisskirch, 2005). If girls experience language brokering as stressful experiences during adolescence, then female brokers may be developmentally susceptible to future depression. Future studies should also evaluate whether gender differences in internalizing symptoms exist for language brokers and if these symptoms persist through adolescence and into emerging adulthood. Such research would have meaningful implications for intervention work that could, for example, target female language brokers to support their resiliency and make translation services more readily available to families that depend on young adolescent language brokers.

Moreover, the field of neuroscience guides researchers to consider multiple aspects of the brain when integrating neuroscience methods into their area of research. In the case of future cognitive neuroscience research examining language brokers, first, we must keep in mind how bilingualism might affect neural pathways and brain organization. Second, we must consider that there are many tools in neuroscience, and it is critical to select the appropriate methodology that will best address one's research question. Third, critical periods in development, such as adolescence, must be taken into consideration so that researchers understand why particular differences emerge across development as the result of pruned synapses and changing hormones. In short, the brain is very complex. Future researchers should consider the various aspects of human experience that may factor into brain development and everyday functioning.

Future Directions

In general, the language brokering literature is still evolving, with much of the early work focusing on qualitative accounts (e.g., Orellana, 2009). That said, more recent work has begun to merge both qualitative and quantitative accounts of language brokering. These studies have pointed to mixed findings, making it essential to understand these distinctions further. At first, it appears that language brokering can positively shape children's cognitive skills (Dorner et al., 2007; Rainey et al., 2015), though it is unclear whether such cognitive gains are stable over time (Flores et al., in preparation). However, at second glance the literature has linked language brokering with some negative socioemotional outcomes, such as greater anxiety (Rainey et al., 2014) and behavioral demands that distract from academics (Fuligni & Pederson, 2002). Researchers and clinicians are now tasked with developing effective interventions that would alleviate high levels of stress and conflict within immigrant families. Such research would allow for programming to target families at the greatest risk for familial stress and long-term negative outcomes.

Current research has begun to address the impact of certain family cultural values (Weisskirch, 2005; Weisskirch & Alva, 2002; Weisskirch et al., 2011) and obligations (Fuligni & Pederson, 2002) on language brokers' well-being and adjustment. Yet these studies tend to provide only a snapshot of a single developmental stage and do not capture a broader, more nuanced story across development. Such research is essential to conduct, as particular developmental outcomes may have a "sleeper effect" and manifest themselves only at a later stage in brain maturation, when the familial obligation to language broker remains (Rainey et al., 2014; Sy, 2006). Thus, future studies should extend the current approach of the language brokering literature by quantitatively tracking multiple aspects of brokers' development over time.

Finally, this review of language brokering literature draws attention to unexplored factors within children's ecosystems that should be assessed, such as family parenting style, children's personality, and children's intellectual skills (Bronfenbrenner, 2005). Integrating a greater understanding of family dynamics in future studies can only deepen the current understanding of the language brokering phenomenon. Likewise, future studies that gather more information on the individual differences across language brokers will help to differentiate outcomes for particular "types" of brokers. For instance, such studies could assess whether particular biological factors—such as personality or fluid intelligence—are associated with individuals' efficacy and self-confidence in their language brokering. It may be that individuals who are higher in extraversion and lower in neuroticism are more effective, successful brokers because they feel less threatened and more confident when interacting with adults. In regards to one's fluid intelligence, it remains unclear whether language brokering improves processing speed or whether those children with greater fluid intelligence are selected to translate for their family. Either way, such biological factors may moderate, or strengthen, the link between brokering frequency and one's effectiveness as a broker. Taken together, future studies may help identify specific characteristics that strengthen the association between language brokering and overall development.

Contribution to Theory

Although extant research has laid the foundation for this burgeoning area of research, the developmental outcomes of child translators tend to get compartmentalized and viewed with a somewhat microscopic lens. Little attention has been given to developing a macroscopic, holistic view of the language broker across childhood and adolescence. Overall, researchers should be considering the child as a holistic, multidimensional being and make efforts to incorporate cognitive, socioemotional, and biological development. A recent study examining monolingual children applies this dynamic approach, revealing that consistent, elevated stress among children was tied to lower cognitive skills later in development (Suor, Sturge-Apple, Davies, Cicchetti, & Manning, 2015). In the same way, researchers evaluating language brokers should consider the connection of multiple domains of development that will lead to a deeper understanding of the language brokering phenomenon.

References

Abutalebi, J., Cappa, S. F., & Perani, D. (2005). What can functional neuroimaging tell us about the bilingual brain. In J. F. Kroll & A. M. B. De Groot (Eds.), *Handbook of bilingualism: Psycholinguistic approaches* (pp. 497–515). New York, NY: Oxford University Press.

Acoach, C. L., & Webb, L. M. (2004). The influence of language brokering on Hispanic teenagers' acculturation, academic performance, and nonverbal decoding skills: A preliminary study. *Howard Journal of Communications, 15*(1), 1–19. doi:10.1080/10646170490275459

Albert, M. L., & Obler, L. K. (1978). *The bilingual brain: Neuropsychological and neurolinguistic aspects of bilingualism.* New York, NY: Academic Press.

Andersen, S. L. (2003). Trajectories of brain development: Point of vulnerability or window of opportunity? *Neuroscience and Biobehavioral Reviews, 27*(1), 3–18. doi:10.1016/S0149-7634(03)00005-8

Bajo, M. T., Padilla, F., & Padilla, P. (2000). Comprehension processes in simultaneous interpreting. In A. Chesterman, N. Gallardo-San Salvador, & Y. Gambier (Eds.), *Translation in context* (pp. 127–142). Amsterdam: John Benjamins.

Baum, S., & Titone, D. (2014). Moving towards a neuroplasticity view of bilingualism, executive control, and aging. *Applied Psycholinguistics, 35*(5), 857–894. doi:10.1017/S0142716414000174

Best, J. R., & Miller, P. H. (2010). A developmental perspective on executive function. *Child Development, 81*(6), 1641–1660. doi:10.1111/j.1467-8624.2010.01499

Best, J. R., Miller, P. H., & Jones, L. L. (2009). Executive functions after age 5: Changes and correlates. *Developmental Review, 29*(3), 180–200. doi:10.1016/j.dr.2009.05.002

Bialystok, E. (2006). Effect of bilingualism and computer video game experience on the Simon task. *Canadian Journal of Experimental Psychology/Revue canadienne de psychologie expérimentale, 60*(1), 68–79. doi:10.1037/cjep2006008

Bialystok, E. (2009). Bilingualism: The good, the bad, and the indifferent. *Bilingualism: Language and Cognition, 12*(1), 3–11. doi:10.1017/S1366728908003477

Bialystok, E. (2015). Bilingualism and the development of executive function: The role of attention. *Child Development Perspectives, 9*(2), 117–121. doi:10.1111/cdep.12116

Bialystok, E., & Craik, F. I. M. (2010). Cognitive and linguistic processing in the bilingual mind. *Current Directions in Psychological Science, 19*(1), 19–23. doi:10.1177/0963721409358571

Bialystok, E., Craik, F. I. M., Grady, C., Chau, W., Ishii, R., Gunji, A., & Pantev, C. (2005). Effect of bilingualism on cognitive control in the Simon task: Evidence from MEG. *NeuroImage, 24*(1), 40–49. doi:10.1016/j.neuroimage.2004.09.044

Bialystok, E., Craik, F. I. M., Klein, R., & Viswanathan, M. (2004). Bilingualism, aging, and cognitive control: Evidence from the Simon task. *Psychology and Aging, 19*(2), 290–303. doi:10.1037/0882-7974.19.2.290

Bialystok, E., Craik, F. I. M., & Luk, G. (2008). Cognitive control and lexical access in younger and older bilinguals. *Journal of Experimental Psychology: Learning, Memory, and Cognition, 34*(4), 859–873. doi:10.1037/0278-7393.34.4.859

Blakemore, S. J., & Choudhury, S. (2006). Development of the adolescent brain: Implications for executive function and social cognition. *Journal of Child Psychology and Psychiatry, 47*(3–4), 296–312. doi:10.1111/j.1469-7610.2006.01611.x

Bronfenbrenner, U. (2005). *Making human beings human: Bioecological perspectives on human development.* Thousand Oaks, CA: Sage.

Buriel, R., Perez, W., DeMent, T. L., Chavez, D. V., & Moran, V. R. (1998). The relationship of language brokering to academic performance, biculturalism, and self-efficacy among Latino adolescents. *Hispanic Journal of Behavioral Sciences, 20*(3), 283–297. doi:10.1177/07399863980203001

Cain, G. G. (1975). Regression and selection models to improve nonexperimental comparisons. In C. A. Bennett & A. A. Lumsdaine (Eds.), *Evaluation and experiment: Some critical issues in assessing social programs* (pp. 297–317). New York, NY: Academic Press.

Cartwright, K. B., Marshall, T. R., Dandy, K. L., & Isaac, M. C. (2010). The development of graphophonological-semantic cognitive flexibility and its contribution to reading comprehension in beginning readers. *Journal of Cognition and Development, 11*(1), 61–85. doi:10.1080/15248370903453584

Chao, R. K. (2006). The prevalence and consequences of adolescents' language brokering for their immigrant parents. In M. H. Bornstein & L. R. Cote (Eds.), *Acculturation and parent-child relationships: Measurement and development* (pp. 271–296). Mahwah, NJ: Lawrence Erlbaum.

Chee, M. W. L., Caplan, D., Soon, C. S., Sriram, N., Tan, E. W. L., Thiel, T., & Weekes, B. (1999). Processing of visually presented sentences in Mandarin and English studied with fMRI. *Neuron, 23*(1), 127–137. doi:10.1016/S0896-6273(00)80759-X

Chee, M. W. L., Tan, E. W. L., & Thiel, T. (1999). Mandarin and English single word processing studied with functional magnetic resonance imaging. *The Journal of Neuroscience, 19*(8), 3050–3056.

Chen, S. H., Zhou, Q., Uchikoshi, Y., & Bunge, S. A. (2014). Variations on the bilingual advantage? Links of Chinese and English proficiency to Chinese American children's self-regulation. *Frontiers in Psychology, 5*, 1–11. doi:10.3389/fpsyg.2014.01069

Christoffels, I. K., De Groot, A. M. B., & Kroll, J. F. (2006). Memory and language skills in simultaneous interpreters: The role of expertise and language proficiency. *Journal of Memory and Language, 54*(3), 324–345. doi:10.1016/j.jml.2005.12.004

Christoffels, I. K., de Haan, A. M., Steenbergen, L., van den Wildenberg, W. P. M., & Colzato, L. S. (2015). Two is better than one: Bilingual education promotes the flexible mind. *Psychological Research, 79*(3), 371–379. doi:10.1007/s00426-014-0575-3

Corona, R., Stevens, L. F., Halfond, R. W., Shaffer, C. M., Reid-Quiñones, K., & Gonzalez, T. (2012). A qualitative analysis of what Latino parents and adolescents think and feel about language brokering. *Journal of Child and Family Studies, 21*(5), 788–798. doi:10.1007/s10826-011-9536-2

Costa, A., Hernández, M., Costa-Faidella, J., & Sebastián-Gallés, N. (2009). On the bilingual advantage in conflict processing: Now you see it, now you don't. *Cognition, 113*(2), 135–149. doi:10.1016/j.cognition.2009.08.001

Costa, A., Hernández, M., & Sebastián-Gallés, N. (2008). Bilingualism aids conflict resolution: Evidence from the ANT task. *Cognition, 106*(1), 59–86. doi:10.1016/j.cognition.2006.12.013

De Groot, A. M. B., & Christoffels, I. K. (2006). Language control in bilinguals: Monolingual tasks and simultaneous interpreting. *Bilingualism: Language and Cognition, 9*(2), 189–201. doi:10.1017/S1366728906002537

Deák, G. O. (2003). The development of cognitive flexibility and language abilities. *Advances in Child Development and Behavior, 31*, 271–327. doi:10.1016/S0065-2407(03)31007-9

Diamond, A. (2013). Executive functions. *Annual Review of Psychology, 64*, 135–168. doi:10.1146/annurev-psych-113011-143750

Dong, Y., & Xie, Z. (2014). Contributions of second language proficiency and interpreting experience to cognitive control differences among young adult bilinguals. *Journal of Cognitive Psychology, 26*(5), 506–519. doi:10.1080/20445911.2014.924951

Dorner, L. M., Orellana, M. F., & Li-Grining, C. P. (2007). "I helped my mom," and it helped me: Translating the skills of language brokers into improved standardized test scores. *American Journal of Education, 113*(3), 451–478. doi:10.1086/512740

Eksner, H. J., & Orellana, M. F. (2012). Shifting in the zone: Latina/o child language brokers and the co-construction of knowledge. *Ethos, 40*(2), 196–220, doi:10.1111/j.1548-1352.2012.01246.x

Elliott, G., Kao, S., & Grant, A. M. (2004). Mattering: Empirical validation of a social-psychological concept. *Self and Identity, 3*(4), 339–354. doi:10.1080/13576500444000119

Ernst, M., & Spear, L. P. (2009). Reward systems. In M. de Hann & M. R. Gunnar (Eds.), *Handbook of developmental social neuroscience* (pp. 324–341). New York, NY: Guilford Press.

Flores, V., Li-Grining, C. P., Rainey, V. R., & Gjorgieva, E. (in preparation). *The academic achievement of Latino emerging adults: The role of language brokering, executive functions, and language proficiency.*

French, S. E., Seidman, E., Allen, L., & Aber, J. L. (2006). The development of ethnic identity during adolescence. *Developmental Psychology, 42*(1), 1–10. doi:10.1037/0012-1649.42.1.1

Friesen, D. C., Chung-Fat-Yim, A., & Bialystok, E. (2016). Lexical selection differences between monolingual and bilingual listeners. *Brain and Language, 152*, 1–13. doi:10.1016/j.bandl.2015.11.001

Fuligni, A. J., Kiang, L., Witkow, M. R., & Baldelomar, O. (2008). Stability and change in ethnic labeling among adolescents from Asian and Latin American immigrant families. *Child Development, 79*(4), 944–956. doi:10.1111/j.1467-8624.2008.01169.x

Fuligni, A. J., & Pedersen, S. (2002). Family obligation and the transition to young adulthood. *Developmental Psychology, 38*(5), 856–868. doi:10.1037//0012-1649.38.5.856

García, A. M., Ibáñez, A., Huepe, D., Houck, A. L., Michon, M., Lezama, C. G., . . . Rivera-Rei, A. (2014). Word reading and translation in bilinguals: The impact of formal and informal translation expertise. *Frontiers in Psychology, 5*, 1–14. doi:10.3389/fpsyg.2014.01302

Green, D. W. (1998). Mental control of the bilingual lexico-semantic system. *Bilingualism: Language and Cognition, 1*(2), 67–81. doi:10.1017/S1366728998000133

Gregory, E., Long, S., & Volk, D. (Eds.). (2004). *Many pathways to literacy: Young children learning with siblings, grandparents, peers, and communities.* New York, NY: RoutledgeFalmer.

Grigoriadis, S., & Seeman, M.V. (2002). The role of estrogen in schizophrenia: Implications for schizophrenia practice guidelines for women. *Canadian Journal of Psychiatry, 47*(5), 437–442. doi:10.1176/foc.4.1.134

Halbreich, U., & Kahn, L. S. (2001). Role of estrogen in the aetiology and treatment of mood disorders. *CNS Drugs, 15*(10), 797–817. doi:1172–7047/01/0010–0797

Halgunseth, L. (2003). Language brokering: Positive developmental outcomes. In M. Coleman & L. Ganong (Eds.), *Points and counterpoints: Controversial relationship and family issues in the 21st century: An anthology* (pp. 154–157). Los Angeles: Roxbury.

Hall, N., & Sham, S. (1998). *Language brokering by Chinese children.* Annual conference of the British Educational Research Association, Dublin, Ireland.

Halperin, J. M., & Healey, D. M. (2011). The influences of environmental enrichment, cognitive enhancement, and physical exercise on brain development: Can we alter the developmental trajectory of ADHD? *Neuroscience & Biobehavioral Reviews, 35*(3), 621–634. doi:10.1016/j.neubiorev.2010.07.006

Hebb, D. O. (2002). *The organization of behavior: A neuropsychological theory.* Mahwah, NJ: Lawrence Erlbaum Associates, Inc., Publishers.

Hernandez, A. E., Dapretto, M., Mazziotta, J., & Bookheimer, S. (2001). Language switching and language representation in Spanish—English bilinguals: An fMRI study. *NeuroImage, 14*(2), 510–520. doi:10.1006/nimg.2001.0810

Hua, J. M., & Costigan, C. L. (2012). The familial context of adolescent language brokering within immigrant Chinese families in Canada. *Journal of Youth and Adolescence, 41*(7), 894–906. doi:10.1007/s10964-011-9682-2

Huttenlocher, P. R. (1994). Synaptogenesis, synapse elimination, and neural plasticity in human cerebral cortex. In C. A. Nelson (Ed.), *Threats to optimal development: Integrating biological, psychological, and social risk factors, 27* (pp. 35–54). Hillsdale, NJ: Lawrence Erlbaum.

Ibáñez, A. J., Macizo, P., & Bajo, M. T. (2010). Language access and language selection in professional translators. *Acta Psychologica, 135*(2), 257–266. doi:10.1016/j.actpsy.2010.07.009

Illes, J., Francis, W. S., Desmond, J. E., Gabrieli, J. D., Glover, G. H., Poldrack, R., . . . Wagner, A. D. (1999). Convergent cortical representation of semantic processing in bilinguals. *Brain and Language, 70*(3), 347–363. doi:10.1006/brln.1999.2186

Jones, C. J., Trickett, E. J., & Birman, D. (2012). Determinants and consequences of child culture brokering in families from the former Soviet Union. *American Journal of Community Psychology, 50*(1–2), 182–196. doi:10.1007/s10464-012-9488-8

Kieler, A., Meltzer, J. A., Moreno, S., Alain, C., & Bialystok, E. (2014). Oscillatory responses to semantic and syntactic violations. *Journal of Cognitive Neuroscience, 26*(12), 2840–2862. doi:10.1162/jocn_a_00670

Klein, L. C., & Corwin, E. J. (2002). Seeing the unexpected: How sex differences in stress responses may provide a new perspective on the manifestation of psychiatric disorders. *Current Psychiatry Reports, 4*(6), 441–448. doi:10.1007/s11920–002–0072-z

Knudsen, E. I. (2004). Sensitive periods in the development of the brain and behavior. *Journal of Cognitive Neuroscience, 16*(8), 1412–1425. doi:10.1162/0898929042304796

Kroll, J. F., Bobb, S. C., & Hoshino, N. (2014). Two languages in mind: Bilingualism as a tool to investigate language, cognition, and the brain. *Current Directions in Psychological Science, 23*(3), 159–163. doi:10.1177/0963721414528511

Lenroot, R. K., & Giedd, J. N. (2006). Brain development in children and adolescents: Insights from anatomical magnetic resonance imaging. *Neuroscience and Biobehavioral Reviews, 30*(6), 718–729. doi:10.1016/j.neubiorev.2006.06.001

Love, J. A., & Buriel, R. (2007). Language brokering, autonomy, parent-child bonding, biculturalism, and depression: A study of Mexican American adolescents from immigrant families. *Hispanic Journal of Behavioral Sciences, 29*(4), 472–491. doi:10.1177/0739986307307229

Lupien, S. J., McEwen, B. S., Gunnar, M. R., & Heim, C. (2009). Effects of stress throughout the lifespan on the brain, behaviour and cognition. *Nature Reviews Neuroscience, 10*(6), 434–445. doi:10/1038/nrn2639

Macizo, P., & Bajo, M. T. (2004). When translation makes the difference: Sentence processing in reading and translation. *Psicologica: International Journal of Methodology and Experimental Psychology, 25*(1), 181–205.

Macizo, P., & Bajo, M. T. (2006). Reading for repetition and reading for translation: Do they involve the same processes? *Cognition, 99*, 1–34. doi: 10.1016/j.cognition.2004.09.012

McQuillan, J., & Tse, L. (1995). Child language brokering in linguistic minority communities: Effects on cultural interaction, cognition, and literacy. *Language and Education, 9*(3), 195–215. doi:10.1080/09500789509541413

Malakoff, M., & Hakuta, K. (1991). Translation skill and metalinguistic awareness in bilinguals. In E. Bialystok (Ed.), *Language processing in bilingual children* (pp. 141–166). Cambridge, UK: Cambridge University Press.

Mandara, J., Gaylord-Harden, N. K., Richard, M. H., & Ragsdale, B. L. (2009). The effects of changes in racial identity and self-esteem on changes in African American adolescents' mental health. *Child Development, 80*(6), 1660–1675. doi:10.1111/j.1467–8624.2009.01360.x

Martin-Rhee, M. M., & Bialystok, E. (2008). The development of two types of inhibitory control in monolingual and bilingual children. *Bilingualism: Language and Cognition, 11*(1), 81–93. doi:10.1017/S1366728907003227

Martinez, C. R., McClure, H. H., & Eddy, J. M. (2009). Language brokering contexts and behavioral and emotional adjustment among Latino parents and adolescents. *The Journal of Early Adolescence, 29*, 71–98. doi:10.1177/0272431608324477

Miyake, A., Friedman, N. P., Emerson, M. J., Witzki, A. H., Howerter, A., & Wager, T. D. (2000). The unity and diversity of executive functions and their contributions to complex frontal lobe tasks: A latent variable analysis. *Cognitive Psychology, 41*(1), 49–100. doi:10.1006/cogp.1999.0734

Morales, A., & Hanson, W. E. (2005). Language brokering: An integrative review of the literature. *Hispanic Journal of Behavioral Sciences, 27*(4), 471–503. doi:10.1177/0739986305281333

Morton, J. B., & Harper, S. N. (2007). What did Simon say? Revisiting the bilingual advantage. *Developmental Science, 10*(6), 719–726. doi:10.1111/j.1467–7687.2007.00623.x

National Center for Education Statistics. (2004). Language minorities and their educational and labor market indicators—Recent trends. Retrieved December 3, 2015, from http://nces.ed.gov/pubs2004/2004009.pdf

Neblett, E. W., Rivas-Drake, D., & Umaña-Taylor, A. J. (2012). The promise of racial and ethnic protective factors in promoting ethnic minority youth development. *Child Development Perspectives, 6*(3), 295–303. doi:10.1111/j.1750–8606.2012.00239.x

Orellana, M. F. (2003). Responsibilities of children in Latino immigrant homes. *New Directions for Youth Development, 100*, 25–39. doi:10.1002/yd.61

Orellana, M. F. (2009). *Translating childhoods: Immigrant youth, language, and culture.* Piscataway, NJ: Rutgers University Press.

Paradise, R., & Rogoff, B. (2009). Side by side: Learning by observing and pitching in. *Ethos, 37*(1), 102–138. doi:10.1111/j.1548–1352.2009.01033.x

Perani, D., Abutalebi, J., Paulesu, E., Brambati, S., Scifo, P., Cappa, S. F., & Fazio, F. (2003). The role of age of acquisition and language usage in early, high-proficient bilinguals: An fMRI study during verbal fluency. *Human Brain Mapping, 19*(3), 170–182. doi:10.1002/hbm.10110

Perani, D., Paulesu, E., Sebastián-Gallés, N., Dupoux, E., Dehaene, S., Bettinardi, V., . . . Mehler, J. (1998). The bilingual brain: Proficiency and age of acquisition of the second language. *Brain, 121*(10), 1841–1852. doi:10.1093/brain/121.10.1841

Phillips, D. A., & Shonkoff, J. P. (Eds.). (2000). *From neurons to neighborhoods: The science of early childhood development.* Washington, DC: National Academy Press.

Price, C. J., Winterburn, D., Giraud, A. L., Moore, C. J., & Noppeney, U. (2003). Cortical localisation of the visual and auditory word form areas: A reconsideration of the evidence. *Brain and Language, 85*(2), 272–286. doi:10.1016/S0093–934X(02)00544–8

Prior, A., & Gollan, T. H. (2011). Good language-switchers are good task-switchers: Evidence from Spanish-English and Mandarin-English bilinguals. *Journal of the International Neuropsychological Society, 17*(4), 682–691. doi:10.1017/S1355617711000580

Rainey, V. R., Davidson, D., & Li-Grining, C. (2015). Executive functions as predictors of syntactic awareness in English monolingual and English-Spanish bilingual language brokers and nonbrokers. *Applied Psycholinguistics, 37*(4), 1–33. doi:10.1017/S0142716415000326

Rainey, V. R., Flores, V., Morrison, R. G., David, E. J. R., & Silton, R. L. (2014). Mental health risk associated with childhood language brokering. *Journal of Multilingual and Multicultural Development, 35*(5), 463–478. doi:10.1080/01434632.2013.870180

Reynolds, J. F., & Orellana, M. F. (2009). New immigrant youth interpreting in white public space. *American Anthropologist, 111*(2), 211–223. doi:10.1111/j.1548–1433.2009.01114.x

Rodriguez-Fornells, A., Rotte, M., Heinze, H. J., Nösselt, T., & Münte, T. F. (2002). Brain potential and functional MRI evidence for how to handle two languages with one brain. *Nature, 415*(6875), 1026–1029. doi:10.1038/4151026a

Ruiz, C., Paredes, N., Macizo, P., & Bajo, M. T. (2008). Activation of lexical and syntactic target language properties in translation. *Acta Psychologica, 128*(3), 490–500. doi:10.1016/j.actpsy.2007.08.004

Schulz, S., Titzmann, P. F., & Michel, A. (2013). [Adolescent interpreter: Language brokering in migrant families in Germany]. *Zeitschrift für Entwicklungspsychologie und Pädagogische Psychologie, 45*, 161–171. doi:10.1026/0049–8637/a000087

Seeman, M. V. (2002). The role of sex hormones in psychopathology: Focus on schizophrenia. *Primary Care: Clinics in Office Practice, 29*(1), 171–182. doi:10.1016/S0095–4543(03)00080–0

Shen, J. J., & Guan, S. A. (2015). *Aspects of language brokering and academic performance among college students.* Poster presented at the 2015 Biennial Meeting of the Society for Research in Child Development, Philadelphia, PA.

Soveri, A., Rodriguez-Fornells, A., & Laine, M. (2011). Is there a relationship between bilingual language switching and executive functions in bilingualism? Introducing a within-group analysis approach. *Frontiers in Psychology, 2*(183), 1–8. doi:10.3389/fpsyg.2011.00183

Sternberg, R. J., Grigorenko, E. L., & Zhang, L. (2008). Styles of learning and thinking matter in instruction and assessment. *Perspectives on Psychological Science, 3*(6), 486–506. doi:10.1111/j.1745–6924.2008.00095.x

Sullivan, M. D., Janus, M., Moreno, S., Astheimer, L., & Bialystok, E. (2014). Early stages second-language learning improves executive control: Evidence from ERP. *Brain and Language, 139*, 84–98. doi:10.1016/j.bandl.2014.10.004

Suor, J. H., Sturge-Apple, M. L., Davies, P. T., Cicchetti, D., & Manning, L. G. (2015). Tracing differential pathways of risk: Associations among family adversity, cortisol, and cognitive functioning in childhood. *Child Development, 86*(4), 1142–1158. doi:10.1111/cdev.12376

Sy, S. R. (2006). Family and work influences on the transition to college among Latina adolescents. *Hispanic Journal of Behavioral Sciences, 28*(3), 368–386. doi:10.1177/0739986306290372

Tse, L. (1995a). Language brokering among Latino adolescents: Prevalence, attitudes, and school performance. *Hispanic Journal of Behavioral Sciences, 17*(2), 180–193. doi:10.1177/07399863950172003

Tse, L. (1995b). When students translate for parents: Effects of language brokering. *CABE Newsletter, 17*(4), 16–17.

Tse, L. (1996). Language brokering in linguistic minority communities: The case of Chinese and Vietnamese-American students. *Bilingual Research Journal, 20*(3–4), 485–498. doi:10.1080/15235882.1996.10668640

Umaña-Taylor, A. J. (2003). Language brokering as a stressor for immigrant children and their families. In M. Coleman & L. Ganong (Eds.), *Points and counterpoints: Controversial relationship and family issues in the 21st century: An anthology* (pp. 157–159). Los Angeles, CA: Roxbury.

Valdés, G. (2003). *Expanding definitions of giftedness: Young interpreters of immigrant background.* Mahwah, NJ: Lawrence Erlbaum.

Weisskirch, R. S. (2005). The relationship of language brokering to ethnic identity for Latino early adolescents. *Hispanic Journal of Behavioral Sciences, 27*(3), 286–299. doi:10.1177/0739986305277931

Weisskirch, R. S., & Alva, S. A. (2002). Language brokering and the acculturation of Latino children. *Hispanic Journal of Behavioral Sciences, 24*(3), 369–378. doi:10.1177/0739986302024003007

Weisskirch, R. S., Kim, S. Y., Zamboanga, B. L., Schwartz, S. J., Bersamin, M., & Umaña-Taylor, A. J. (2011). Cultural influences for college student language brokers. *Cultural Diversity and Ethnic Minority Psychology, 17*(1), 43–51. doi:10.1037/a0021665

Wu, N. H., & Kim, S.Y. (2009). Chinese-American adolescents' perceptions of the language brokering experience as a sense of burden and sense of efficacy. *Journal of Youth and Adolescence, 38*(5), 703–718. doi:10.1007/s10964-008-9379-3

Yudes, C., Macizo, P., Morales, L., & Bajo, M. T. (2012). Comprehension and error monitoring in simultaneous interpreters. *Applied Psycholinguistics, 34*(5), 1039–1057. doi:10.1017/S0142716412000112

11

YOUNG ADULT LANGUAGE BROKERS' AND TEACHERS' VIEWS OF THE ADVANTAGES AND DISADVANTAGES OF BROKERING IN SCHOOL

Sarah Crafter, Tony Cline, and Evangelia Prokopiou

Introduction

Schools have been cited as some of the most frequent venues where children and young people act as language brokers (Angelelli, 2014; Tse, 1996). Whilst a number of studies have used school as the access point to gather data from child language brokers (CLBs), the way in which schools might offer particular contextual challenges has been given less attention, particularly in the UK. In a past review of the literature on CLBs in the UK context (Cline, Abreu, O'Dell, & Crafter, 2010), we noted that there had been no known studies in the UK, or elsewhere, of the frequency of reliance on child language brokering activities in urban schools. In addition, there was an absence of studies of teachers' professional perspectives on language brokering and on the views of students who had undertaken language brokering while at school about their experiences in that setting. This chapter will report on a mixed-methods study involving teachers and young adults who had acted as CLBs while they were at school. In particular, we use data from an online survey of teachers and young adults who had been CLBs (teachers, $N = 63$; ex-CLBs, $N = 25$) and in-depth episodic interviews that look at teachers' ($N = 12$) and young adult language brokers' ($n = 14$) stances towards the advantages and disadvantages of students acting as language brokers in the school context. Respondents from both the two groups who were interviewed framed the advantages and disadvantages according to what they thought language brokering had offered in terms of efficiency and parental preferences. Both groups also talked about advantages and disadvantages for the future, in terms of the potential impact on young people's schooling and their social development.

The Importance of the School Context

Research studies in the United States have provided a substantial indication that school is a significant site of linguistic and cultural mediation. Evidence has shown that CLBs translate notes and letters from school for their parents more often than any other documents (Weisskirch, 2005), and the use of brokers in face-to-face meetings is not uncommon (see Orellana, Dorner, & Pulido, 2003). However, reports of language brokering activity at schools in the UK have been either anecdotal (Kaur & Mills, 1993) or have focused only on the CLB perspective (Hall & Sham, 2007) or the process of translation (Hall, 2001). There has also been a study in the UK that has explored young people's perspectives on how language brokers negotiated missing school when faced with competing family obliga-tions to undertake language brokering duties outside of school (Crafter, Abreu, Cline, & O'Dell, 2014). However, language brokering was just one aspect of that study, and school was not the main focus of interest in research that had a wider agenda. The study on which this chapter is based takes the field further by pro-viding an evidence basis for more sensitive and effective practice and articulated school policies on the use of children as language brokers in school for their own parents and others.

We had other reasons to focus on school as a particular context of inter-est. Efforts to find policy documentation or official guidance in the UK on the practice of using students to translate on behalf of their own families when the conversation with teachers is about their own or a sibling's school progress had limited success. We were not able to trace any explicit school policy statements or national policy statements by national standards bodies, and the topic is not included in initial teacher education. The lack of official policy guidelines for pro-fessionals on the use of CLBs is not unique to either the school context or the UK context. There have been similar findings, for example, from a team working in Bologna, Italy (see Cirillo, Torresi, & Valentini, 2010). There was, in the past, some official support in the UK for schemes (known as programs in the United States) in which bilingual students were trained to act as interpreters for other students' parents at the national level (QCA, 2008), and at the local level, for example, a scheme aimed more towards using young interpreters as peer support for newly arrived pupils (Hampshire Borough Council, Young Interpreter Scheme, 2014). Therefore, a wider intent for the study around which this chapter is written was to develop guidance for schools on the use of CLBs (see http://www.nuffield foundation.org/child-language-brokering-school for more information).

We have argued elsewhere (Cline, Crafter, & Prokopiou, 2014a) that the lack of official policy guidance reflects an ambivalent attitude to the practice of language brokering that permeates professional and academic commentary on the subject of second-language use and bilingualism more generally. Even within increasingly "super-diverse" locations within the UK (see Vertovec, 2005), monolingualism is still perceived as the prevailing practice, whilst multilingualism is only vaguely understood (Cline, Crafter, Abreu, & O'Dell, 2011) and, in some cases, explicitly viewed as negative (Brutt-Griffler & Varghese, 2004). In locations of high language diversity, the home languages of many immigrants are socially devalued and, in some cases, actively suppressed in institutional settings such as schools (Cummins, 2000). The lack of policy guidelines may also reflect institutional endeavors to avoid using children at all costs (Cirillo et al., 2010).

In addition, professional perspectives on using children for language brokering suggest some well-founded reticence on their behalf, particularly in the case of challenging or sensitive situations. One fundamental disadvantage to using CLBs that is often cited is that, like other non-professional interpreters, they are likely to make mistakes in their translations (Flores et al., 2003). CLBs are often asked to use the language of institutions, so it is not surprising that technical words or difficult situations lead to misunderstandings. It has also been argued that the responsibility placed on the CLBs may be stressful and excessive, and they may lose time at school (Morales & Hansen, 2005). Some commentators have advocated that children should never be used as language brokers in school settings (e.g., Linse, 2011). This view is endorsed by many other professionals who describe various types of discomfort at using children for interpreting and translating, especially when sensitive or confidential matters are to be discussed (e.g., Cirillo et al., 2010). Whilst such a perspective may be born of the best intentions, the reality is that for economic, social, migratory, and cultural reasons it is unlikely the practice will decrease. Nor does such a negative perspective take into account the potential benefits to an individual of undertaking language brokering activities in school.

The Advantages and Disadvantages to Child Language Brokering in School

In a study of dual-language immersion classes, Coyoca and Lee (2009) found that pupils who acted as language brokers to newly arrived pupils helped facilitate membership and inclusion into the classroom. In this instance, it seems likely that this was doubly enhanced by the dual-language use. However, the authors also noted that brokering in the classroom could limit children's learning and decrease autonomy and motivation. When looking specifically at a science classroom, Bayley, Hansen-Thomas, and Langman (2005) found that peer language brokering allowed pupils to follow along but was insufficient in terms of accessing the full curriculum. Further evidence demonstrates that there may be a positive link between language brokering and assessed performance in mathematics and literacy (Dorner, Orellana, & Li-Grining, 2007).

The literature on child language brokering presents a mixed picture with respect to the impacts it may have on social and emotional development. There is evidence that the activity can cause stress (see Jones & Trickett, 2005) or child distress (Jones, Trickett, & Birman, 2012). Research also points to some positive dimensions such as pride (e.g., Orellana, 2003) and to a perception in multilingual areas that such an activity is just a normal thing to do when one is bilingual (Cline et al., 2011). More recent research has taken a more nuanced approach by looking at specific activities. For example, translations around formal documents and finances were reported to put more strain on parent-child relationships than other activities (Roche, Labert, Ghazarian, & Little, 2014). In the current study, our particular focus was on the role of school and the school context, and what this might mean for the child who is language brokering.

In this study of the school context, we aimed to explore whether the stressful features of brokering—such as difficulties with technical words, levels of responsibility and significance for the outcomes of the activity—were perceived to be as great for school as in other settings such as a doctor's surgery or a bank. In addition, we were interested in exploring further the notion that CLBs are "advocates," "tutors," "surrogates" (Valenzuela, 1999), or a participated in a "performance team" with their parents (Valdés, 2003). These roles had been evidenced in an interview study with professionals in Italy (see Cirillo et al., 2010) where, in two instances, CLBs strongly advocated for their families. One situation involved a charity and the other a municipal support center. School, however, offers a wider scope for examining potential tensions between the interests of all those involved: the child, the teacher, and the parent. Our study was designed specifically to fill a gap in the published research by examining teachers' perspectives directly. We also closely examined how key stakeholders viewed the impact that engagement in child language brokering activities has on a young person's identity and social development.

Method

We collected data from two groups with difference perspectives on child language brokering activities in school: teachers who used CLBs to help communicate in school and young people with experience of language brokering in school. In this chapter, we refer to these young adults as ex-CLBs to denote that they were discussing a practice in their not-too-distant past, though many continued to language broker beyond their time in school. The study involved two phases. The first phase made use of an online survey for both the teachers and ex-CLBS that explored the frequency of child language brokering use in schools and the purposes for which it is used. The second phase involved interviews with a sample of teachers and ex-CLBs.

Participants

Twenty-five ex-CLBs participated in the online survey (female = 21, male = 4) ranging in age from 16 to 26 years. Participants were recruited from two universities in the East Midlands and two in London. We also advertised through a young interpreter network and wrote to the heads of 429 supplementary and complementary schools in London, the South East, and the East Midlands. For the interviews, 14 ex-CLBs (female = 10, male = 4) participated. Four of these were recruited from the survey phase of the study. The remaining interviewees were recruited with the help of two teacher interviewees who introduced us to older students who were about to leave their schools and had earlier experience of acting as CLBs in their schools. Their countries of origin included Austria, Hong Kong, Iceland, Lithuania, Nepal, Netherlands, Poland, Portugal, Turkey, and Venezuela. Two of our participants were born in the UK. One had parents who came from Bangladesh and the other had a mother from Mexico and a father from Italy. However, translating for their parents in school was generally more common at the secondary stage (11–16 years). Sixty percent of the young people reported that they had translated for their parents in primary school sometimes or often, a figure that rose to 88% for secondary school.

Our sample for the online survey included 63 teachers (female = 51, male = 12); 34 fell into the 24–40 age bracket and 29 were 41–60 years of age. All of them had at least one year's teaching experience with almost half the survey sample having taught for more than 10 years. The teachers in our sample held a variety of roles within schools. Some were classroom teachers and others were English as an Additional Language (EAL) teachers or coordinators. Given their professional roles, the sample shows a bias towards teachers with a specific interest in this topic. Similarly, more than a third of those teachers who completed the survey had parents who had been born overseas and over a third had been born overseas themselves. For the interviews, there were 12 teachers (female = 10, male = 2), eight were in the 41–50 age range, three were between 28 and 36 years of age, and one did not disclose his/her age. Using the UK Census categories, 10 reported their ethnic background as White British or White European, one as African Caribbean and one as Chinese. Ten worked in secondary schools and two in primary schools. In terms of their status and duties in school the sample comprised:

- Four subject/class teachers;
- Five EAL coordinators and teachers;
- Two staff with Head of Department or Senior Management Team responsibilities; and
- One teaching assistant.

On the basis of their accounts of their fluency in different languages, we judged that three members of the sample were bilingual or multilingual and nine were monolingual in English.

Measures

We used five items from Tse's (1996) Language Brokering Scale, asking about age, gender, age at which respondents began translating for others, who respondents had brokered for, and sibling information. However, we adapted some of these questions (see our website, http://tinyurl.com/j3azydt, for a copy of the full survey). For example, when we asked who the respondents had brokered for, we additionally asked how often this activity took place. In the Culture Broker Scale by Jones and Trickett (2005) participants were asked to indicate when parents relied on them to undertake particular activities such as answering the phone or the door, or filling out applications. We applied a similar type of questioning to the school context by asking our language brokers if they (or in the case of the teachers, their pupils) had translated for formal meetings or new pupils or translated school letters. The teachers in the sample were asked the same questions as the ex-CLBs, with adaptations to take their perspectives into account. For example, "When I felt comfortable translating at school it was because, (a) Lots of my friends do it." became "When I have felt comfortable asking pupils to translate at school it has been because, (a) Lots of their friends do it."

Our survey contained additional questions reviewing the range of experiences translating in school and comparing those experiences with others through the use of short vignette questions. This chapter reports on two items from the language broker and teacher surveys that were a series of statements outlining the possible advantages and disadvantages of having children act as translators on behalf of their parents (e.g., "The child understands what their parents already know and what they need extra explanation about") and possible disadvantages (e.g., "Young people may not know technical school words well enough, so that they make translation errors"). The questionnaires for teachers and ex-CLBs covered the same ground, with some variation in individual items (see here http://tinyurl.com/j3azydt). Participants indicated their agreement with each statement using a scale of 1–6, with 1 = *strongly agree* to 5 = *strongly disagree* and option 6 = *I don't know*.

We followed the online questionnaire with interviews that used the episodic approach (see Flick, 2000), with a small number of selected respondents, in order to explore issues related to the experience of language brokering in schools in greater depth. As with the survey questionnaire, the interview schedule contained many parallel topics that were applicable to both teachers and ex-CLBs. During the interview, respondents were asked to recount a situation of language brokering either with a parent or peer, to describe how this was arranged, the reactions of the people involved, the impact on relationships, and issues related to language skills and emotional responses to the situation (see http://tinyurl.com/j3azydt for a copy of the interview schedules). Both groups were asked about the advantages and disadvantages of language brokering in school and were invited to suggest recommendations that they thought would help to improve practice in schools. In addition, some questions were developed for each group separately. For example, the interviews with ex-CLBs explored their experience of the process, their own agency, their competence and effectiveness, and how the process was facilitated or obstructed by the actions and attitudes of their teachers. All of the teachers were interviewed by the third author and all of the ex-CLBs were interviewed by the first author. All the respondents' names are pseudonyms.

The interview data was subjected to a form of thematic analysis that utilized the research questions and theoretical approach as its basis. Procedurally, we followed the steps of the Framework Approach outlined by Pope, Ziebland, and Mays (2000). There was an ongoing iterative process in which successive stages of coding were informed by a regular review of the pre-determined research questions. The interviews were transcribed and coded separately and then cross-checked. Cross-case analysis then investigated patterns across the data, which were grouped together according to themes and related to the key research questions (Braun & Clarke, 2006).

Results

Outcomes from the Survey

We present the outcomes of the survey for teachers and ex-CLBs together because the comparison of responses is of interest. The table indicates the proportion of respondents in each group who indicated that they *agreed* or *strongly agreed* with each statement that highlighted what were perceived as either advantages or disadvantages of child language brokering in school.

We find it of interest that for some of the statements there is a broadly comparable level of agreement between the teachers and ex-CLBs. As mentioned previously, our sample of teachers could be viewed as somewhat biased, in that those who volunteered to be part of the study had an interest in second language learning in some capacity or were bilingual themselves. It is perhaps not surprising then, that there was a fairly equal pattern of opinions for certain responses. There was agreement about levels of understanding relating to language acquisition, language competence for technical words, and cultural understanding. Both teachers and ex-CLBs were clear that language brokering could cost children some personal time.

However, some of the statements held greater weight for the ex-CLBs than for the teachers. When looking at the statements about "advantages," where there was a difference of 15% or more, these tended to highlight the perspective of the child or parent. For example, more of the ex-CLBs either *agreed* or *strongly agreed* that parents would prefer using their own child over having a professional interpreter or a member of the school staff acting as translator. The ex-CLBs were also more likely to consider that advantages of children acting as language brokers included that the parent's own child understands what their parents already know and what they need extra explanation about. These findings support those from a study about access to professional interpreting services, which indicated that all of those sampled who had access to family or friends would use them in preference to either professional interpreters, bilingual staff, or community provision

(Alexander & Edwards, 2004). Issues of trust, not wanting others to know family business, and accessibility were cited as the main reasons in that study. In a school context, accessibility is certainly an issue, as many of the routine conversations that take place are not serious enough to require the expense of a professional interpreter. Equally, it may not be possible to have bilingual teachers or other staff that represent every language spoken in a given school.

The largest disparity between teachers and ex-CLBs, when looking at statements about "disadvantages," referred to the child feeling it is inappropriate to say boastful things about themselves, so that they do not translate accurately when teachers praise them or describe their best achievements. This sentiment has been evidenced elsewhere by Garcia-Sanchez, Orellana, and Hopkins (2011) who analyzed the audio recordings of eleven parent-teacher conferences. They found that "downgrading teachers' praise" was a dominant pattern of communication by the CLBs.

Some academic authors and media commentators have expressed concern that the CLB role gives children too much power in relation to their parents, which leads to negative feelings (Chao, 2006). The survey responses indicated that other perceived disadvantages had greater salience for both teachers and ex-CLBs than this concern about "role reversal." It is noticeable in Table 11.1 that only 44% of teachers and 46% of ex-CLBs expressed agreement or strong agreement with the proposition that acting as a translator "gives children too much power in relation to their parents." These are much lower proportions than expressed concern about such issues as children having inadequate language skills or needing to deal with sensitive issues.

TABLE 11.1 Proportion of the Sample Who Either *Agreed* or *Strongly Agreed* With Statements About Perceived Advantages and Disadvantages of School Language Brokering Arrangements

Statements Highlighting Perceived Advantages

Statement Set Out in the Survey Questionnaire	Teachers	Ex-CLBs
Parents prefer this arrangement to having a professional interpreter or a member of the school staff acting as translator.	45%	68%
Children tend to prefer this arrangement to having a professional interpreter or a member of the school staff acting as translator (ex-CLB only).	–	44%
It is better to keep things within the family.	48%	46%
The child understands what their parents already know and what they need extra explanation about.	64%	83%
The child learns both languages better.	50%	50%
The child comes to understand both cultures better.	50%	50%
The child learns social and communication skills.	77%	67%

(Continued)

TABLE 11.1 (Continued)

Statements Highlighting Perceived Disadvantages

	Teachers	Ex-CLBs
Young people may not know one of the languages well enough so that they make translation errors.	69%	68%
Young people may not know technical school words well enough so that they make translation errors (ex-CLB only).	–	58%
The meeting may cover sensitive issues so that the child or the parents may be embarrassed.	85%	88%
The child may not want their parents to know about some negative things at school so that they deliberately play down what a teacher has said.	77%	88%
The child may feel it is inappropriate to say boastful things about themselves so that they do not translate accurately when teachers praise them or describe their best achievements.	51%	67%
Translating at school for their family may impose excessive responsibilities on children so that they feel stressed or anxious.	55%	67%
Translating at school may take up children's time that would better be spent on other things.	44%	46%
The translator is in a position of power because no one else understands everything that is being said. That gives children too much power in relation to their parents.	44%	46%

Thus, the survey analysis indicated that the teachers and ex-CLBs showed agreement on many of the supposed advantages and disadvantages of having children take on this role at school. Where they disagreed, the key factor appeared to be the different experiences they had of the phenomenon, with ex-CLBs prioritizing family interests in their ratings. These trends in the data would need to be confirmed with a larger sample. However, we noted that the same broad patterns of opinion were found in the second phase of the study, in which interviews enabled us to explore the distinct perspectives of the two groups in more depth.

Responses from the Interviews

During the interviews, a question about the possible advantages and disadvantages of the child language brokering arrangements in their school stimulated extensive responses from both teachers and ex-CLBs. More participants contributed to the themes related to this question than to any other interview question. Some of their comments focused on the immediate advantages (such as cost savings and flexible timing) and disadvantages (such as a greater risk of translation errors). In this chapter, we will examine what they had to say about the longer-term impact of experiences of language brokering at school. We will present our analysis by focusing in succession on what respondents had to say about the impact of language brokering activity in three key areas: language development, school life, and identity and social development.

Impact on a Child's Language Development

It has long been asserted by some researchers and commentators that the practice of language brokering in childhood has a positive impact on the acquisition of the language that is used (Dorner et al., 2007). In our interview study, ex-CLBs discussed ways in which they felt that language brokering activities had, in their experience, led to improvements in learning English:

> For advantages I think it would, it [language brokering] also helped me with my English because obviously, because obviously at that time I like, you know, *oh I can't say it, like I know but I just can't say it,* like it was, it was useful for me being a translator because it helped my English at the time.
>
> *(Amita, ex-CLB)*

> A good thing, it improves yourself as well. . . . It makes you, as you keep on talking, as you keep on translating your, like, thinking reaction gets quicker, it increases it. So that's, that's the good thing.
>
> *(Sameer, ex-CLB)*

Some of ex-CLBs emphasized broader communication skills as well as linguistic knowledge:

> I think there has never been a disadvantage, there was always advantage because I like talking to new people, I'm learning more words and stuff and I'm getting confident which is advantage. . . . And also say like in talking with people so like eye contacts and stuff is getting better with me. And I'm not nervous. Like before if you come to me I would be like shaking and stuff but now I'm like more confident, I'm talking to you, I'm fine. Yeah.
>
> *(Anamika, ex-CLB)*

> And the advantages were that you get more confident so when you had to do presentations in class you'll feel more confident about it because you have spoken to other people and translated for other people.
>
> *(Isabel, ex-CLB)*

> I think there are more advantages than disadvantages because it makes you look more mature and grown up and you take responsibility and you kind of learn professionally how to translate and I think your language improves

a lot and you kind of learn a lot more about having proper professional conversations with grown-ups.

(Kara, ex-CLB)

In addition, some ex-CLBs mentioned improving their home language as well as English as an advantage to being a language broker. Although there could be some negative consequences to taking time in the classroom to broker for another pupil, one advantage was an opportunity to practice the home language:

> In year 8, there was a girl from Colombia who came to our country school for the first time and she was going to join the school permanently but she didn't speak a word of English so I had to, so I had to sit next to her in all her lessons to translate from Spanish to English and English to Spanish. And I personally felt I benefited from it because in a way I was practicing my Spanish but in a way it was also quite, not hard but like it was hard for me to concentrate on my work and do hers at the same time. So it was a bit difficult but overall it was, it was fine.
>
> *(Celia, ex-CLB)*

Celia weighed the time cost against the stimulus to her use of Spanish and judged the balance in the end to be "fine."

Impact on School Life

When specifically asked to talk about the advantages and disadvantages of language brokering in school, both teachers and ex-CLBs highlighted the danger of drawing pupils away from their own studies to help another pupil, perhaps putting their own progress at risk. An ex-CLB who talked about this problem highlighted the tension created by having a sense of responsibility towards the pupil who was being helped:

> I kind of like got hanged up, when, like, when I'm helping them, I couldn't take time for myself, so I sometimes get told off by my teacher as well, like "just do your work. They can do theirs." I was like "no, I have to help them because they couldn't understand you," so, yeah, so I was like, I really don't care what I'm going to do, I'm just helping them first so, yeah.
>
> *(Amita, ex-CLB)*

When teachers discussed the potential disadvantages of using language brokers to help other children in class, they sometimes also expressed concern that the pupil used as a language broker would have extra homework or work to catch up on. But, one highlighted a potential problem for the other child in the situation who might develop too strong a feeling of dependency on their brokering friend or mentor:

> We have had a case here only a couple of years ago where the, the friendship of one of the girls, she expected the other one to do all the work and she didn't speak at all and so, and when she did speak it would be in her own tongue to this other girl. And, it was putting a lot of pressure on the first student who was being the interpreter and the supporter, or the mentor, and she was feeling really, she was, it was getting her down, to put it bluntly. It was getting her down because she was getting very frustrated that the girl wouldn't talk to any of her friends, she wouldn't talk to anybody else except for her, she wouldn't do any work because all she'd do is copy this other girl's work.
>
> *(Alice, teacher)*

Observing this, teachers set up a buddy system with a different set of pupils, so that the new pupil became friends with others and gained a greater sense of independence. This arrangement helped prevent the friendship from going wrong and stimulated the new pupil to improve her command of English more rapidly than before.

The social dynamics of a school community operate in complex ways for those who accept a role that cuts across the usual networks. CLBs are simultaneously acting for the adult authorities and acting for their own family or for other pupils in the same age group. What they are asked to do will sometimes conflict with the expectations of others, creating a tension that is more difficult for them to understand and to resolve because those expectations are often unspoken. In Amita's case, she did understand what her teachers wanted, but chose to defy them: "I'm just helping them first so, yeah." Sometimes, the conflict may be with peers rather than with teachers. One ex-CLB, Isabel, described a situation of that kind to the first author.

Isabel: The disadvantages were that sometimes you could lose your friends from the translating. It's kind of horrible especially when you know the child, and it's just, like, "oh, why me," and then your friends might get cross with you, but it's not your fault, like, I can't just be, like, "oh, yeah. She's doing great" when she's really not doing great, like you need your parents to push you to do your work so yeah.

Sarah: So, you're honest. You tell them.

Isabel: Yeah, and if my friends stop talking to me, well, that's life.

Sarah: OK, has that happened?

Isabel: Yeah. But I can't do anything about it and I'm not going to lie to an adult. It's not right.

CLBs are thus set apart from their peers by taking on a semi-official role and, in Isabel's case, by taking it seriously. She went on to tell Sarah that, after losing her Spanish-speaking friends, she became close to a group that was mostly made up of pupils from England or the Philippines. Multilingual pupils are potentially members of more than one ethno-linguistic community in a school. In the next section, we will examine the broader impact of child language brokering activities on children's sense of identity and their social development.

Impact on Child's Social Development and Identity

Acting as a translator for others puts a person's language proficiency and social skills on display. He or she may feel exposed as a result and, if it proves to be a positive experience, his or her self-confidence may be enhanced. A number of teachers commented on this effect. Emma highlighted the impact of the fact that CLB activity is so visible:

> I think it [language brokering] can be a really empowering experience. I think it can because, it's, it's showing that they've learnt stuff. It's showing that they can do stuff, and, and the parent may not understand it if they see it just written on a report. They don't understand, yes, I'm working, I'm working, I'm trying to learn English but look actually I've learned some and I've learned these words because now I can tell you those in my language, in our language, and I can explain to you stuff. So, I think it can be quite empowering.
>
> *(Emma, teacher)*

Alongside the external self-confidence, a CLB is placed in a position that encourages the development of empathy and of a stance that facilitates effective social interaction:

> Yeah, yeah, it's a handy skill. Well, I think, maybe, because I can put myself in that person's situation, that I have the patience to do it. I don't know if I, if I wasn't in that situation would I have the patience to do that sometimes because, I, I could see when, especially the girl from China, I remember seeing her in science class and people would be trying to talk to her and she don't, she didn't understand what they were saying, so they'll get fed up and lose patience and go. But, I think that if I wasn't in that situation I'd probably have lost patience as well and leave, but, because I can imagine what she's going through I just stay and help her out.
>
> *(Angelica, ex-CLB)*

In contrast to these more positive perspectives was the possibility that a student would feel self-conscious and embarrassed in the role. This appeared to be more likely when language brokers were in a minority within their school or, in one case, the CLB was the only pupil from a particular country within that school.

I felt smart, gifted, and possibly embarrassed because it, like, the first two are really positive, but the last probably because it can be really embarrassing to sort of like have to translate and everyone's just like staring at you. And, as a child, you're sort of I think probably maybe more self-conscious so just kind of like "oh, my gosh, all these people are staring at me, it's like they've never heard another language before" so it did make me quite like embarrassed because it's like "oh my God," yeah. . . yeah. . . In a way, I felt sort of smart because my school, it was full of English people; so, for me to have all these languages, I felt, sort of, in a way you could say talented. But, it also did feel a bit weird because like all these other kids were like, "oh, my God, what's she saying?"

(Celia, ex-CLB)

Some teachers noted that embarrassment would be particularly likely when the setting made the child feel exposed:

I have seen situations where I got the impression that the child was feeling a bit embarrassed, because, in some cases, sometimes the parents do understand. It's just the spoken English that might, that they might be, they might not be too confident to speak, but they do understand. And I think that sometimes the child thinks, "OK, everybody's looking at me," especially if it's not private, if it's when we have Parents' Evening and we're in a hall with other parents and students and then they might think "OK, they're looking at me" so they're thinking that my parents don't speak English, so that's not good. So, I've seen that situation as well.

(Kina, teacher)

When helping a new pupil from Nepal in the classroom, Sameer felt nervous, not because of having to translate but:

Because everyone was like staring at you and like wanting to listen and I was like, "oh, please, don't look at me!"

(Sameer, ex-CLB)

For some CLBs, their obligation to translate for their parents was an embarrassing reminder of the differences between them and many of their peers. The research interview could have offered an opportunity to put this into perspective (cf. Toomey, Dorjee, & Ting-Toomey, 2013, p. 126):

It sounds like, now, more normal for me and it has refreshed my memory, how crazy I was when I was a child, and I kind of feel ashamed that I was actually embarrassed about my parents.

(Kara, ex-CLB)

The underlying source of embarrassment in those situations was the tension inherent in developing a coherent sense of identity when pulled in different directions by conflicting cultural loyalties.

> We get a situation sometimes where they've been here for 2 or 3 years and they don't want to, they want to be English, they only want to speak English, they don't want to speak their language. So, some students move away from their heritage and they want to, because they're so assimilated with their new friends, their English friends, you know, their English clothes, their English customs, they only see the language spoken at home. Whereas, they associate that this is their life here, they don't want to be, so sometimes they're not interested in, which I think is sad because it's such a skill to have the two natural languages so we have that problem sometimes.
>
> *(Tom, Teacher)*

The close alignment with English language and English culture may be a phase that a recently arrived adolescent migrant needs to work through in establishing a bicultural and bilingual identity, but there is strong evidence that an integrated bicultural or multicultural identity will be a more positive outcome in terms of their psychological health (Nguyen & Benet-Martinez, 2013). This positive outcome is associated with effective and habitual cultural frame switching and a fluid, integrative identity (Toomey et al., 2013). The informants' narrative accounts of their experiences suggested that development towards those goals can be facilitated by successful performance as a CLB. When one was asked whether she felt that she was bridging two cultural worlds, she replied:

> Yeah, in a, in a way, how do I want to say this. I don't know, I think like bringing two cultures, you know, you just feel good about yourself, you're bringing the new you and you want to, you know, participate in events here in the UK not only like bringing your culture, your home culture like your food and traditional thing, you can bring, you know, the UK culture as well, you know.
>
> *(Nathely, ex-CLB)*

Conclusion

In both parts of the study, our respondents made it clear that the context provided by a school can minimize the disadvantages of child language brokering activity and maximize its advantages. The reasons why adults (i.e., parents or teachers) arrange for children to act as language brokers are pragmatic, so as to make communication between others possible in the here-and-now. The short-term outcome and long-term impact will be more favorable if there is thoughtful staff support based on underlying attitudes that are positive. Those who had acted as

CLBs in school reported that they had found the role easier when they sensed that the staff in their school perceived bilingualism as an asset and valued the role. Situations most associated with disadvantages tended to arise if there was no one in the school monitoring and supporting the ongoing language brokering activities of the pupils.

The ultimate aim of this project was to provide an evidence base for stimulating good practice in the use of pupils as language brokers for their own parents and others in school. An Internet-based guide, *Child Interpreting in School: Supporting Good Practice*, may now be found at http://child-language-brokering.weebly.com. The guide covers four broad areas: (a) choosing the best person to act as a translator; b) involving children and young people in a formal training scheme; (c) advice about children interpreting for parents and family members; and (iv) advice about interpreters supporting peers in the classroom and around school.

All of this needs to be put into perspective. As other chapters in this volume show, child language brokering is required in many settings that offer less control and less support than are possible in schools. For the ex-CLBs in the study, the exclusive focus on school did not always make sense: Their experience of the activity was not compartmentalized, and their account of its advantages and disadvantages necessarily encompassed all the settings in which it occurred.

Future Directions

Future research on child language brokering activities in schools should aim to test the generalization of the findings from this study to larger samples in more diverse settings. Those who agreed to participate in the study may have a deeper level of interest or a relatively more positive experience of language brokering activity than those who did not take part in the study. Research is required, as ever, to explore the perspectives of those who are disinclined to participate.

Young people's language brokering experiences differed in predictable ways between multilingual inner city schools and schools in some other parts of the country where there were few pupils who spoke English as an additional language (cf. work by Cline et al., 2002) on the experiences of minority ethnic pupils in "mainly White" schools). There was also some evidence in this study of differences of perspective on language brokering activity between monolingual and bilingual teachers (see Cline et al., 2014b, pp. 40–41). In each of these areas of potential differences, it will be valuable to follow up with more detailed and targeted research on differences in language brokering experience in diverse and less diverse school settings as well as on observations of monolingual and bilingual teacher-participants.

A particular gap in this, and other, UK research is the perspectives of parents on the use of their children as language brokers at school. One significant strand of concern within the literature was whether children acting as CLBs in school would choose to translate in ways that protected their own interests or would ally themselves with their parents as either a "performance team" or "parental advocate." In contrast to meetings at a doctor's surgery or a housing office, school represents a setting where the interests of CLBs and their parents may not always be aligned. For example, Kaur and Mills (1993) reported on a child who tried to avoid trouble by making out that the report presented by his teacher was better than it was. In a different situation, Hall and Sham (2007) described a child altering notes to the school written by her father because she did not want her teachers to know that she worked in the family's café every day after school. Thus, the school setting may be a context where the family dynamics that are usually observed during child language brokering might be contested. Research to explore that issue would need to include parents. This is clearly a promising future direction for research.

A key factor in the dynamics of families' interactions with the outside world is that in most situations parents have a more sophisticated understanding of the context than their children. In our study focusing on school settings, ex-CLBs described situations where their parents had clearly lacked understanding about how particular aspects of the education system worked. The young person typically waited until he or she was home to provide in-depth explanations of this to their parents. Thus the "performance team" aspect of school brokering practice was not visible to those outside the family, and it was not cited as an advantage or a disadvantage by either CLBs or teachers. Research to investigate these processes will need to explore parents' perceptions of the dynamics of language brokering episodes in some depth, alongside those of their children.

Contribution to Theory

Our previous theorizing of child language brokering has been set against a backdrop of critical theories of child development (e.g., Rogoff, 2003). Such perspectives contest that "childhood" is necessarily bound up with assumptions about this phase of life being a time of play, formal schooling, and socialization (Jans, 2004). Childhood historians showed that not only have our ideas of childhood changed over time (Cunningham, 2006), but there are also large variations in everyday practices within families today (Rogoff, 2003). The danger lies in making assumptions about what "childhood" looks like, which then become the template for a *normal* childhood. This assumption renders a range of aspects of childhood *invisible* or *atypical* (Crafter, O'Dell, Abreu, & Cline, 2009). Sometimes, these tasks are characterized as a form of children's work (Crafter et al., 2009; Hall & Sham, 2007), Language brokering transgresses some of the characteristics of the *normal* or *ideal* childhood. For example, through the lens of Developmental Psychology (and a Western cultural context), childhood is represented by a move from dependency on adults to steadily increasing independence into early adulthood (Burman, 2008). The danger lies in assuming that the move towards independence is gradual for all children within such a society. In a globalizing world, CLBs often find themselves rapidly taking on roles and responsibilities following migration that might not be expected of an indigenous child.

In many ways, the institution of school might be seen as the central site managing that gradual move to independence as children are slowly granted access to increasing levels of knowledge and, to a lesser extent, autonomy. CLBs present school with a challenge because these children are asked to undertake tasks that sit outside the boundaries of "normal" school activities. We theorized, at the beginning of this project, that the discomfort felt by teachers towards child language brokering activities might come about because children are granted more power to affect the outcomes of interactions than is usual in teachers' dealings with parents. The picture that emerged from our informants is more complex, suggesting that perceptions and management of child language brokering vary between teachers and those with experience of the practice and (probably, though our data did not address this) between schools. There are implications for how the priorities of pastoral care in schools are evaluated (Cline et al., 2009) and for how schools ensure that their arrangements for CLBs facilitate both positive interactions with parents and positive outcomes in the long term for pupils acting as CLBs (Cline et al., 2014b).

References

Alexander, C., & Edwards, R. (2004). *Access to services with interpreters: Users view*. York: Joseph Rowntree Foundation.

Angelelli, C. (2014, May). *Looking back: A study of (non-professional/ad hoc) family interpreters*. Keynote Presentation at the 2nd non-professional interpreting and translation Germersheim, Germany.

Bayley, R., Hansen-Thomas, H., & Langman, J. (2005). Language brokering in a middle school science class. In J. Cohen, K. T. McAlister, K. Rolstad, & J. MacSwan (Eds.), *Proceedings of the 4th International Symposium on Bilingualism* (pp. 223–232). Somerville, MA: Cascadilla Press.

Braun, V., & Clarke, V. (2006). Using thematic analysis in psychology. *Qualitative Research in Psychology, 3*(2), 77–101.

Brutt-Griffler, J., & Varghese, M. (2004). Introduction. *International Journal of Bilingual Education and Bilingualism, 7*, 93–101.

Burman, E. (2008). *Deconstructing developmental psychology* (2nd ed.). Hove: Routledge.

Chao, R. K. (2006). The prevalence and consequences of adolescents' language brokering for their immigrant parents. In M. H. Bornstein & L. R. Cote (Eds.), *Acculturation and parent-child relationships: Measurement and development* (pp. 271–296). Mahwah, NJ: Lawrence Erlbaum.

Cirillo, L., Torresi, I., & Valentini, C. (2010). Institutional perceptions of child language brokering in Emilia Romagna. *MediAzioni, 10*, 269–296.

Cline, T., Abreu, G. de, Fihosy, C., Gray, H., Lambert, H., & Neale, J. (2002). *Minority ethnic pupils in mainly white schools*. London: Department for Education & Skills.

Cline, T., Abreu, G. de, O'Dell, L., & Crafter, S. (2010). Recent research on child language brokering in the United Kingdom. *MediAzioni, 10*, 105–124.

Cline, T., Crafter, S., Abreu, G. de, & O'Dell, L. (2009). Changing families, changing childhoods: Changing schools? *Pastoral Care in Education*, *27*(1), 29–39.

Cline, T., Crafter, S., Abreu, G. de, & O'Dell, L. (2011). Young peoples' representations of language brokering. *Journal of Multilingual and Multicultural Development*, *32*, 207–220.

Cline, T., Crafter, S., & Prokopiou, E. (2014a). Child language brokering in schools: A discussion of selected findings from a survey of teachers and ex-students. *Educational and Child Psychology*, *31*, 34–45.

Cline, T., Crafter, S., & Prokopiou, E. (2014b). *Child language brokering in schools: Final research report*. London: UCL. Retrieved from http://child-language-brokering.weebly.com/

Coyoca, A. M., & Lee, J. S. (2009). A typology of language-brokering events in dual-language immersion classrooms. *Bilingual Research Journal*, *32*(3), 260–279.

Crafter, S., Abreu, G. de, Cline, T., & O'Dell, L. (2014). Using the vignette methodology as a tool for exploring cultural identity positions. *Journal of Constructivist Psychology*, *28*(1), 83–96.

Crafter, S., O'Dell, L., Abreu, G. de, & Cline, T. (2009). Young peoples' representations of "atypical" work in English society. *Children and Society*, *23*, 176–188.

Cummins, J. (2000). *Language, power and pedagogy: Bilingual children in the crossfire*. Clevedon: Multilingual Matters Ltd.

Cunningham, H. (2006). *The invention of childhood*. London: BBC Books.

Dorner, L. M., Orellana, M. F., & Li-Grining, C. P. (2007). "I helped my mom," and it helped me: Translating the skills of language brokers into improved standardized test scores. *American Journal of Education*, *113*, 451–478.

Flick, U. (2000). Episodic interviewing. In M. W. Bauer & G. Gaskell (Eds.), *Qualitative research with text, image and sound* (pp. 75–92). London: Sage.

Flores, G., Laws, M. B., Mayo, S. J., Zuckerman, B., Abreu, M., Medina, L., & Hardt, E. J. (2003). Errors in medical interpretation and their potential clinical consequences in pediatric encounters. *Pediatrics*, *111*(1), 6–14.

Garcia-Sanchez, I. M., Orellana, M. F., & Hopkins, M. (2011). Facilitating intercultural communication in parent-teacher conferences: Lessons from child translators. *Multicultural Perspectives*, *13*(3), 148–154.

Hall, N. (2001). The child in the middle: Agency and diplomacy in language brokering events. In G. Hansen, K. Malmkjaer, & D. Gile (Eds.), *Claims, changes and challenges in translation studies* (pp. 285–297). Amsterdam: John Bejamins.

Hall, N., & Sham, S. (2007). Language brokering as young people's work: Evidence from Chinese adolescents in England. *Language and Education*, *21*(1), 16–30.

Hampshire. (2014). Hampshire young interpreter scheme. Retrieved from http://www3.hants.gov.uk/ema-hyis.htm

Jans, M. (2004). Children as citizens: Towards a contemporary notion of child participation. *Childhood*, *11*, 27–44.

Jones, C. J., & Trickett, E. J. (2005). Immigrant adolescents behaving as culture brokers: A study of families from the former Soviet Union. *Journal of Social Psychology*, *145*(4), 405–427.

Jones, C. J., Trickett, E. J., & Birman, D. (2012). Determinants and consequences of child culture brokering in families from the Former Soviet Union. *American Journal of Community Psychology*, *50*, 182–196.

Kaur, S., & Mills, R. (1993). Children as interpreters. In R. W. Mills & J. Mills (Eds.), *Bilingualism in the primary school: A handbook for teachers* (pp. 113–125). London, UK: Routledge.

Linse, C. T. (2011). Creating taxonomies to improve home-school connections with families of culturally and linguistically diverse learners. *Education and Urban Society*, *43*(6), 651–670.

Morales, A., & Hanson, W. E. (2005). Language brokering: An integrative review of the literature. *Hispanic Journal of Behavioral Sciences*, *27*(4), 471–503.

Nguyen, A.-M. D., & Benet-Martinez, V. (2013). Biculturalism and adjustment: A meta-analysis. *Journal of Cross-Cultural Psychology*, *44*(1), 122–159.

Orellana, M. F. (2003). Responsibilities of children in Latino immigrant homes. *New Directions for Youth Development*, *100*, 25–39.

Orellana, M. F., Dorner, L., & Pulido, L. (2003). Accessing assets: Immigrant youth's work as family translators or "para-phrasers". *Social Problems*, *50*(4), 505–524.

Pope, C., Ziebland, S., & Mays, N. (2000). Qualitative research in health care: Analysing qualitative data. *British Medical Journal*, *320*, 114–116.

Qualifications and Curriculum Authority (QCA). (2008). *Respect for all: Interpreter training*. London: Qualifications and Curriculum Authority.

Roche, K. M., Labert, S. F., Ghazarian, S. R., & Little, T. D. (2014). Adolescent language brokering in diverse contexts: Associations with parenting and parent-youth relationships in a new immigrant destination area. *Journal of Youth and Adolescence*, *44*(1), 77–89.

Rogoff, B. (2003). *The cultural nature of human development*. Oxford: Oxford University Press.

Toomey, A., Dorjee, T., & Ting-Toomey, S. (2013). Bicultural identity negotiation, conflicts, and intergroup communication strategies. *Journal of Intercultural Communication Research*, *42*(2), 112–134.

Tse, L. (1996). Language brokering in linguistic minority communities: The case of Chinese- and Vietnamese-American students. *Bilingual Research Journal*, *20*(3–4), 485–498.

Valdés, G. (2003). *Expanding definitions of giftedness: The case of young interpreters from immigrant communities*. Mahwah, NJ: Lawrence Erlbaum.

Valenzuela, A. (1999). Gender roles and settlement activities among children and their immigrant families. *The American Behavioral Scientist*, *42*, 720–742.

Vertovec, S. (2005). Super-diversity and its implications. *Ethnic and Racial Studies*, *30*, 1024–1054.

Weisskirch, R. S. (2005). The relationship of language brokering to ethnic identity for Latino early adolescents. *Hispanic Journal of Behavioral Science*, *27*, 286–200.

PART IV

Parents' Roles and Emerging Adult Language Brokers

12

IMMIGRANT PARENTS' LANGUAGE BROKERING PRACTICES

A Taxonomy of Interlingual and Intralingual Brokering Strategies

Jin Sook Lee and Meghan Corella

Introduction

Research on language brokering demonstrates the highly sophisticated language and cultural negotiations in which speakers who live at the intersections of multiple languages and cultures engage. This line of inquiry has mainly focused on the practices of children and adolescents in immigrant families, the broker's identity development, academic achievement, and affective and psychological states, and the implications of brokering for family relations (Buriel, Perez, Terri, Chavez, & Moran, 1998; Dorner, Orellana, & Jiménez, 2008; Guan, Greenfield, & Orellana, 2014; McQuillan & Tse, 1995; Morales & Hanson, 2005; Roche, Lambert, Ghazarian, & Little, 2015; Weisskirch, 2007, 2013). Although renewed interest has emerged on language brokering, earlier research recognized its complexity. For example, in studying complex group relationships in Mexico after the Mexican Revolution of 1910, Wolf (1956) described brokers who linked community-oriented individuals to nation-oriented individuals and characterized the brokers' role as one of "standing guard over the crucial junctures of synapses of relationship which connect the local system to the larger whole" (p. 1075). In 1960, Geertz introduced the role of teacher and leader as a "cultural broker" with the example of the Javanese Muslim teacher communicating Islam to the peasantry in Indonesia. Similarly, Herzog (1972) viewed brokering in the context of an anthropologist as a broker in school-community conflicts as the "attempt to articulate, explain and develop the goals, life styles and concerns of all groups within and affecting the community" (p. 9) by means of discovering shared ground. In an applied situation, Bourhis, Roth, and MacQueen (1989) used the term *brokering* to refer to how nurses interpret and translate doctors' medical language into everyday language for patients. Despite this long-standing interest in the various kinds of brokering practices, recent literature on language brokering has mainly focused on the brokering work that children and adolescents from immigrant backgrounds accomplish for their limited English proficient parents but less so on the parents themselves. In recognition of this gap in the literature, this chapter highlights the experiences of immigrant parents as they mediate linguistic and cultural norms and expectations for their children in familial, academic, and social domains. The parents in 12 Mexican immigrant families in southern California were interviewed as well as video-recorded in interactions in their home settings. A taxonomy of *interlingual brokering* practices (i.e., language brokering practices that employ paraphrasing and translating strategies across two linguistic systems, such as English and Spanish) and *intralingual brokering* practices (i.e., language brokering practices that employ paraphrasing strategies within one linguistic system) show how immigrant parents, like non-immigrant parents, broker for their children, but with the added complexity of having to cross linguistic and cultural boundaries. The analysis focuses on the communicative goals and effects of parental brokering practices and discusses the implications of such practices for the personal, social, and academic experiences of children. This chapter broadens the understanding of what constitutes language brokering and highlights the ways in which immigrant parents enact the role of strategic cultural and linguistic mediators, in spite of their limited English proficiency.

Summarizing Related Research: Language Brokering Across Settings

Language brokering often involves "[interpreting] and [translating] between culturally and linguistically different people and [mediating] interactions in a variety of situations including those found at home and school" (Tse, 1996, p. 226). Theoretically, brokering occurs when a third party, a broker (i.e., the person enacting the brokering service), facilitates communication or understanding between speakers, or between a speaker and a cultural artifact, practice, or norm (Orellana, Dorner, & Pulido, 2003a). Brokering is often viewed as involving three or more interlocutors: the speaker, the language broker, and the parent, for example (see e.g., Bolden, 2012). However, as Orellana, Reynolds, Dorner, and Meza (2003b) point out, much interpretive work in home language brokering happens dyadically, when, for example, a child is translating or paraphrasing text for his/her parents. Whether it is dyadic or triadic, brokering involves the act of mediation. In other words,

> to broker a (potential) problem of understanding is to act as an intermediary between the other participants (i.e. between the speaker of the problematic talk and his/her addressed recipient) and to attempt to resolve the problem in a way that would expose and bridge participants' divergent linguistic and/or cultural expertise—for instance, by providing a translation or a simplified paraphrase of the problematic talk.
>
> *(Bolden, 2012, p. 99)*

In the process of mediating and problem-solving, mediators can and often do alter the interpretation for a certain outcome, rather than being "neutral" (Gustafsson, Norström, & Fioretos, 2013). In addition to these strategic alterations to the interpretation of the talk or text in question, brokering also tends to involve a certain level of teaching, including correcting other parties' usage (Ikeda, 2007, as cited in Bolden, 2012).

Because of the wide range of settings in which language brokering practices have been studied, researchers have used various terms to refer to language brokering. For instance, Bourhis et al. (1989) coin the term *communication broker* to refer to nurses who act as intermediaries between doctors and their patients. Olmedo-Williams (1983) uses the term *peer teachers* to refer to bilingual children who mediate content learning and language learning strategies for their less proficient peers. Orellana et al. (2003a) propose the term *para-phrasing*, which they use interchangeably with *brokering* as a play on words that draws on the Spanish word *para* to capture the ideas of "speaking for" and "speaking in order to." The slight variances in the nuances of these terms highlight the multiple functions of and perspectives from which language brokering happens.

In this chapter, we use *language brokering* as an umbrella term that captures the complexity of the role of the broker in facilitating understandings of language and culture. The term encompasses linguistic, cultural, and communicative mediation, and its range of effects (such as teaching elements of language or culture to other parties). While the majority of recent literature on language brokering practices has focused on the role of young children as brokers for their families, our use of the term broadens its usual scope in that we turn the lens on the potentially valuable role of parents as language brokers. The only study that we have been able to identify that has focused on parental language brokering practices has been Ng's work on tri-generational family conversations of Chinese immigrant families in New Zealand (Ng, He, & Loong, 2004; Ng, 2007). In Ng's studies, parental brokering was occasioned by one of three types of goals: to facilitate communication when the broker perceived a breakdown in communication between brokerees; to sustain communication when the broker perceived the communication to come to a premature halt; and to respond to a direct request for help, as when a brokeree invites the broker to participate. Her examples, though useful, are limited in scope.

In order to better understand how parental language brokering practices are performed, in this chapter we make a distinction between interlingual brokering practices and intralingual brokering practices. We define *interlingual brokering practices* as language practices that employ paraphrasing, translating, interpreting, and/or mediating strategies across two linguistic and cultural systems, such as English and Spanish. By contrast, *intralingual brokering practices* use paraphrasing, interpretive, and mediating strategies within one linguistic system. Intralingual brokering is commonly found in many parent-child interactions in which parents explain, teach, or correct their children's understanding of a linguistic or cultural phenomenon. Analyzing intralingual brokering practices highlights the fact that immigrant parents—who are often portrayed in public discourse and popular culture as being less competent than mainstream middle-class parents—are, in actual fact, not so different from other parents in the sense that they use their real-world and life experiences to facilitate their children's understandings and communication.

A focus on interlingual brokering practices is significant in light of recent research on language brokering in family contexts, which often positions parents as being at the receiving end of assistance due to their lack of English language and cultural proficiency. Interestingly, our data show that even immigrant parents with limited English proficiency are able to engage in interlingual brokering.

Therefore, by distinguishing between interlingual and intralingual brokering, we are able to characterize the various ways in which immigrant parents—even those with limited English proficiency—may help their children in making sense of their world. Our study provides not only another lens into the parental language brokering practices from a setting different than Ng's work, but it also expands and refines the understanding of what is achieved through language brokering in general, and, notably, in parental language brokering practices.

Methods

Participants and Their Language Practices

Over a period of 18 months (2008–2010), a team of Spanish-English bilingual researchers engaged in participant observation in the homes, schools, and communities of 12 first-generation immigrant families as part of a larger qualitative study (which also included 12 Korean immigrant families) on the language practices and language development of elementary-age bilingual children living in central California (see Corella Morales & Lee, 2015; Lee, Kang, Jeong, Lopez, & Fernandez, 2010). Most families in the study were headed by two parents or parental figures. However, in most cases, the mothers were the children's primary caregivers and were most consistently present during the interviews and observational recordings; for this reason, the analyses focus somewhat more on mothers than fathers. Although the families varied widely with regard to their time in the United States, their English and Spanish proficiencies, their education levels, and other demographic characteristics, all parents were observed to engage in interlingual and intralingual brokering practices in interactions with their children. To capture the diversity of brokering practices, we analyzed approximately 100 hours of video and audio data, and selected three families who differed from one another with regard to several factors that, according to previous research (see, e.g., Ng, 2007), can impact language brokering practices: the family's amount of time in the United States, the parties' levels of proficiency in Spanish and English, and the family's home language policies and practices.

The parents of the first family, the Cepeda Díaz[1] family, had been in the United States for more than 15 years at the time of the study. Lorena Díaz and David Cepeda had two US-born children, 7-year-old Matthew (a focal child in our study) and his younger sister, Jessica. Also part of the Cepeda Díaz household were four other family members: Lorena's sister, her sister's husband, and their two small children. Lorena reported that the adults mainly spoke Spanish with one another and to their children, whereas the children spoke mainly English amongst themselves and often responded to the adults in English. Code-switching, code-mixing, and language alternation thus characterized many interactions in the Cepeda Díaz household. Focal child Matthew's first and dominant language was English; Matthew's parents had decided to teach him English first in hopes of giving him access to a wider range of communicative, socioeconomic, and educational opportunities. Although Lorena did not feel entirely confident about her English abilities, she often helped Matthew with homework in English, repeated her utterances in English when he did not understand her Spanish, and generally did whatever she could to support his English development. At the same time as somewhat prioritizing her children's English development, Lorena reported that the family valued bilingualism very highly, seeing it as a door to better educational and socioeconomic opportunities. Indeed, for this reason, she and her husband had enrolled Matthew in a dual immersion (Spanish and English) school. Like his parents, Matthew seemed invested in bilingualism. Although in his words, he knew only "a little" Spanish, and his Spanish skills were mainly receptive, he said he was eager to learn more so as to be able to talk to his family in Mexico.

The second family, the Peña family, had been in the United States for approximately 7 years at the time of the study. Vanesa, the mother, and Luis, the father, had two children: 8-year-old Gabriela (one of the focal children in our study), who was born in Mexico, and a newborn, who had been born in the United States. The parents explained that they had come to the United States to help family back in Mexico and to give Gabriela better opportunities, and they planned to stay in the United States long-term. Vanesa had occasional house-keeping work, and Luis worked as a gardener and handyman. The parents reported speaking primarily Spanish at home, largely because they both described their levels of English proficiency as relatively low. For his part, Luis reported talking with Gabriela mostly in Spanish and only a bit in English, stating, "no hablo mucho" (*I don't speak much [English]*) while also adding that his receptive skills were fairly good and that he was learning more English. Similarly, Vanesa spoke mainly Spanish to her daughter and husband, describing her English in mostly negative terms, as demonstrated by statements such as "yo lo entiendo muy poquito, y no lo hablo" (*I understand very little, and I don't speak it*). However, our observations and interviews indicated that Vanesa usually understood her daughter's English utterances and frequently code-mixed when speaking to her, often echoing her daughter's use of colloquial words such as "itchy" and "thingy" within her own Spanish utterances. In contrast to her parents, Gabriela was dominant in English, though she also had very strong language skills in Spanish. She and her mother reported that speaking Spanish was a bigger challenge for her, often causing her to feel embarrassed or shy; thus, she preferred speaking English in most contexts. On the whole, all members of the family valued bilingualism highly, and as such, the parents wanted Gabriela to continue developing in English, but they also made efforts to help Gabriela maintain and expand her Spanish, including buying her books in Spanish to teach her literacy skills and asking her to practice both languages by translating English phrases into Spanish.

Our final family, the Vega Fuentes family, had arrived in the United States only 2 years before the study began. The mother, Diana Fuentes, and stepfather, Carlos Vega, had one newborn boy together and were also raising Diana's 8-year-old daughter Flor (one of our study's focal children). Although they planned to return to Mexico eventually, the parents hoped their time in the United States would help them pursue the "American Dream," emphasizing educational opportunities and learning English as their main reasons for immigrating. Both parents had taken or were taking English classes to accomplish these goals. Carlos described his English level as intermediate, whereas Diana frequently described her English in terms of deficits (stating, for example, "no sé muchas palabras," *I don't know a lot of words*) while also noting that she was making progress in her English class and was learning English by helping Flor with homework. Both parents expressed amazement at the amount of English that Flor had learned in her short time in the United States, yet, ultimately, both Flor and her mother seemed to defer to Carlos as the strongest English speaker, asking him to provide feedback on their pronunciation or to help with translations related to homework. The family spoke primarily Spanish at home, although their family language policy was quite flexible; for instance, Carlos anticipated that they would have to start speaking more English at home as Flor learned more, and that eventually they would need to shift back to primarily speaking Spanish because he did not want Flor or his son to lose their Spanish skills. At the time of the study, Flor was dominant in Spanish, although she reported that she was starting to forget some Spanish words, and her parents likewise reported some signs of a shift to English, such as her use of English in monologues when playing by herself.

Data Collection

The analysis in this chapter is based on two types of data: observational videos in which parents engaged in brokering practices, and interview data in which parents described brokering practices. The observational videos were recorded by parents and/or children in their homes during three types of activities: mealtime interactions, playtime interactions, and homework interactions. The videos varied in duration from 20 minutes to 70 minutes. Like the observational videos, the interview videos were recorded in participants' homes so as to establish a naturalistic setting for ethnographic interviews with parents and children. During the course of the study, three to five semi-structured interviews were conducted with each focal child and parent. Bilingual Latina researchers conducted the interviews (which ranged in length from 20 to 180 minutes) in the language(s) of each participant's choice, taking an open-ended approach as they talked with participants about their home language practices, language attitudes, experiences as immigrants, and family relationships.

Data Analysis

In total, we collected more than 100 hours of interactional and interview video data (approximately 12 hours per family). These video data were then catalogued and transcribed by bilingual research assistants. For the initial phase of the present analysis, we used these logs and transcripts to identify potential language brokering events. Then, in an iterative process, we moved back and forth between videos, the written records, and the existing literature as we coded data using a combination of inductive and deductive codes (Strauss & Corbin, 1990) to better understand particular brokering devices (see Ng et al., 2004) as well as the interactional effects of brokering. During this phase of analysis, we noticed that many communicative events involved both Spanish and English, whereas others involved primarily or exclusively one language. Hence, we coded some events as interlingual and others as intralingual according to the definitions described earlier. However, depending on how each brokering exchange was defined and where analytic boundaries were drawn, we found that some events could be considered both interlingual and intralingual in that, for example, some interactional units (Bloome, Carter, Christian, Otto, & Shuart-Faris, 2005) were intralingual while the overall communicative event was interlingual. We provide an example of some of these gray areas in the analysis that follows. In describing a brokering exchange as interlingual or intralingual, we are not arguing that these are two discrete practices; rather, we aim to show the range of communicative practices involved in language brokering as well as the ways in which language brokering practices in multilingual immigrant families are both similar to and different from communicative practices in monolingual families.

Results

This section will demonstrate how interlingual and intralingual brokering are performed by parents to accomplish two of the most common communicative goals found in parent-child brokering interactions: brokering to prevent or repair interactional trouble in multi-party speech events, and brokering to facilitate a brokeree's understanding of a written text in order to complete a task.

Brokering to Facilitate Real-Time Communication

The most common function of parental language brokering appeared to be facilitating communication within multi-party interactions, often by preventing or repairing interactional trouble between two or more brokerees. In such instances, the parent broker mediates between two or more speakers, who are typically their children and one or more other interlocutors. The other interlocutors were usually adult family members or members of our research team, opening up opportunities for negotiation of meaning by the brokerees. The communicative goal in these interactions was to facilitate communication by bridging interlocutors' divergent kinds of cultural and/or linguistic knowledge. In these cases, brokerees often experienced interactional trouble because one speaker was Spanish dominant and the other was English dominant, although in other instances, the brokerees experienced interactional trouble within a single language rather than across two languages due to other communication problems. Specifically, the cause of the breakdowns generally involved a linguistic barrier between the two brokerees, divergent understandings or misunderstandings of some aspect of the context, or a physical constraint (e.g., the set-up of technical devices like computers while using Skype).

Interlingual Brokering

Example 1, which is an excerpt from an interview with 7-year-old Matthew and his mother, Lorena, highlights the multiple competencies often required in instances of multi-party interlingual brokering. In the minutes preceding this excerpt, the researcher and Lorena (along with Matthew, who often chimed in during the research team's interviews with his mother) had been discussing the challenges that English-dominant Matthew experienced when talking with his Spanish monolingual grandfather over the phone. Interestingly, in this interaction, even as Lorena is telling the researcher about the brokering role that she often takes up in these phone calls, she steps into another brokering role in order to explain to Matthew that he is getting his two grandfathers mixed up (see Appendix for transcription conventions).

Example 1

1	Matthew:	He bought me a caballo. {*horse*}
2	Lorena:	No ése, no es abuelito, ése es el de tu daddy {*No, not that one,*
3		*that's not grandpa, that's the one from your dad's side*}
4	Researcher:	You have two.
5	Lorena:	You have two grandpas and two grandmas.
6	Matthew:	Can we talk about mi {*my*} daddy's?
7	Researcher:	Qué le dices a tu daddy's dad, your grandpa? {*What do you say to*
8		*your daddy's dad, your grandpa?*}
9	Matthew:	"Qué estás haciendo? Yo estoy viendo la televisión." And then I said
10		"yo voy a pasarla* a mi mamá o papá o la Jessica. I love you, bye."
11		{*"What are you doing, I am watching television." And then I said,*
12		*"I'm going to give the phone to my mom or dad or Jessica. I love*
13		*you, bye."*}
14	Lorena:	No, no habla, o cuando quiero que hable más, yo soy la que le
15		tengo que estar diciendo las cosas para que él las repita. {*No, he*
16		*doesn't talk, or when I want him to talk more, I am the one who has*
17		*to tell him things so he can repeat after me.*}

In line 2, Lorena, apparently realizing what the researcher may be unaware of—namely, that her son is referring to his paternal grandfather—enacts the role of broker by correcting her son and clarifying that she and the researcher had been discussing his maternal grandfather. Following her lead, the researcher provides a further explanation to Matthew (line 4), and in line 5, Lorena in turn builds on the researcher's explanation, also switching to English. This shifting of the brokering role from one adult to the other highlights the fluid nature of brokering, wherein the role of broker can rapidly move across speakers.

In addition to the fluidity of the interactional role of broker, this exchange is also characterized by linguistic fluidity as all speakers code-mix and alternate languages across and within turns, a striking finding in light of Lorena's reportedly low level of proficiency in English. The kind of brokering that Lorena enacts in this interaction with her son and the researcher is thus interlingual in the sense that it requires her to have receptive and productive skills in both Spanish and English in order to be able to mediate between two brokerees and head off interactional trouble. Importantly, in this exchange, the interactional trouble is occasioned not by a linguistic difference between the two brokerees, but by different understandings of the immediate interactional context as well as their different kinds of access to key aspects of the ethnographic context, such as information about the structure of Matthew's family.

By contrast, the interlingual brokering that Lorena reports undertaking during Matthew's conversations with his grandfather is occasioned principally by linguistic differences between two parties. As is made clear by Matthew's reenactment in lines 9 to 12 of a typical conversation with his grandfather, Matthew's turns at talk in Spanish tend to be short and include English and code-mixed utterances that his Spanish monolingual grandfather is likely not able to understand. Lorena also comments elsewhere in the interview that Matthew himself sometimes has difficulties understanding his grandfather. Thus, as his mother explains in lines 14 to 16 and elsewhere in the interview, to facilitate communication between the two, she not only provides Matthew with unknown words and structures, but she also draws him out and helps him find ways of extending the conversation beyond "I'm watching TV, love you, bye" (lines 9 to 12). Such brokering requires multiple competencies: Lorena must understand Matthew's original utterances to his grandfather (i.e., whether in Spanish, English, or a mixture of the two) and must know how to translate them into Spanish, which requires lexical and grammatical knowledge; she also has to come up with potential avenues for conversation, which requires pragmatic and cultural competence to find common ground between two culturally and generationally different speakers; and she has to monitor Matthew's speech as he repeats the phrases she teaches him, which requires a complex set of pedagogical and interactional decisions (i.e., deciding how and when to intervene) as well as a range of receptive and productive competencies from grammatical to phonological to pragmatic. The brokering that Lorena frequently enacts in phone conversations between her son and his grandfather thus differs from the brokering she enacts in mediating between her son and the researcher, although both instances of brokering are interlingual in that they involve paraphrasing, interpreting, and mediating strategies across two linguistic and cultural systems.

Intralingual Brokering

As in Example 1, Example 2 is an instance of a mother brokering for her child and a grandparent, although the brokering transactions in this example occur exclusively in one language and thus call upon a rather different set of competencies. Unlike Example 1, Example 2 does not seem to be a reaction to a communication breakdown but instead highlights another kind of brokering involving technology and multi-party interactions. As shown in Example 2, brokering does not necessarily happen as a reaction to a communication breakdown or misunderstanding; rather, it can enable multi-party conversations that are otherwise constrained by the ways the interlocutors are using or set up communication technology, as in this specific case.

This excerpt is taken from a video recording of a home observation of 8-year-old Flor and her family. Flor is working on homework with her stepfather while her mother, Diana, is sitting with her baby son and talking via computer with her own mother (who lives in Mexico). Diana and her mother begin the conversation via typed instant messages and then transition to using a headset and online videoconferencing. Although the grandmother's utterances were not audible to our team's video camera, Diana's own turns at talk provide insights into when and how she steps into a brokering role to facilitate communication between her daughter, her husband (Carlos), and her mother (see Appendix for transcription conventions).

Example 2

1	Flor:	Mamá, escribe #luego de mi parte. {*Mom, write on my behalf*}
		. . .
2	Diana:	Mira a tu abue. . . Dice que no se acuerda así de nosotros @@@ {*Look at*
3		*your granny. . . She says she doesn't remember us [looking] like this*
4		@@@}
		. . .
5	Diana:	Pero yo no sé por qué allí se ve bien morenito mamá, pero no está tan
6		morenita su cara. {*But I don't know why he [her newborn son] looks so*
7		*dark there, mom, because his face isn't that dark.*}
8	Carlos:	Te dijo que está negrito? {*Did she say he's dark?*}
9	Diana:	No, no me dijo, pero yo le digo porque yo le estoy viendo allí cómo se ve
10		y se está viendo más morenito. {*No, she didn't, but I'm telling her because I see*
11		*how he looks there [on the screen], and he's looking darker.*}
		. . .

12	Diana:	Lo que pasa es que está haciendo la tarea porque el programa de ella, de la
13		escuela le mandan, le están revisando cómo hace la tarea y todo como
14		trabaja y todo eso, entonces este, le (.) le está, ya te voy a enseñar cómo
15		está la cámara filmándole. {*The thing is that she's doing homework*
16		*because her program, her school program gives them, they're checking*
17		*how she does homework and how she works and all that, so, um,*
18		*they. . . they're, I'll show you right now how the camera is filming her.*}
		. . .
19	Diana:	No, ésa se la llevan, ellos la traen. Ése es de ellos, no de nosotros. (1.0)
20		Cómo ves, mama? {*No, they take it [the camera] and bring it. It's theirs,*
21		*not ours.(1.0) What do you think, mom?*}
		. . .
22	Diana:	Flor, te habla, mira. {*Flor, she's talking to you, look.*}
23	Flor:	((turns body and head and looks toward computer))
24	Diana:	Mira a mi gordota, mamá. @@ {*Look at my chubby girl, Mom.*}
25		Di hola. {*Say hi.*}
26	Flor:	((waves toward computer)) Mira mamá, dile que ya no estoy tan gorda
27		como antes. {*Mom, tell her I'm not as fat as I was.*}
28	Diana:	Corre, que te pongas a hacer tarea. {*Come on, she says to do your*
29		*homework*}

Although Flor asks her mother some minutes before the start of Example 2 to let her talk with her grandmother, her stepfather Carlos stipulates that she finish her homework first, and this condition creates opportunities for Diana to *para-phrase*— that is, to *speak for* others and to *speak in order to* enable communication between others (see Orellana et al., 2003a). Interestingly, Flor actually makes the para-phrasing situation explicit when she asks her mother to speak for her by typing instant messages on her behalf (line 1). Then, beginning in line 2, Diana enacts a brokering role through the device of para-phrasing when she reports her mother's speech to her daughter and husband (i.e., "she says she doesn't remember us looking like this," lines 2–4). In so doing, she puts the three parties into indirect conversation with one another, thus achieving a compromise between Flor's desire to speak with her grandmother and her stepfather's stipulation that Flor focus on her homework. While the act of repeating her mother's message may appear simple, this—and any—act of reporting another's speech involves a complex set of decisions about whether, when, and how to convey one party's meanings to another. In this case, Diana's tone and laughter as she repeats or para-phrases her mother's words in lines 2 to 4 create a light-hearted context for implicitly addressing the topic of the distance between the family members, which Diana often discussed in interviews as being painful and challenging. Her decision to para-phrase her mother's words in lines 2 to 4 stands in contrast to her actions later in the conversation: for instance, despite Flor's request, she does not repeat or para-phrase Flor's statement about not being "as fat" as she once was (lines 26 to 27). Though her reasons for this decision cannot be known, the exchange reproduced in Example

2 makes clear that language brokering is not a neutral act; it involves not only choosing how to translate, para-phrase, and repeat, but also opting to do none of the above.

Throughout this exchange, Diana is able to enact a brokering role through the use of a variety of linguistic devices, including repetition or para-phrasing (e.g., "she says to do your homework," lines 28 to 29), questions that introduce a topic or focus attention on it (e.g., "What do you think?" in line 20 to 21), and instructing a brokeree what to say or do (e.g., "Say 'hi,'" line 25). These devices are key to creating an exchange that ultimately increases her brokerees' awareness or understanding of relevant aspects of several levels of context: the immediate interactional context, in which Flor is doing homework (lines 12 to 18); the interpersonal context, such as the fact that the grandmother has observed that her family looks different from the way she remembers them (lines 2 to 4); the cultural and institutional context, in which Flor is participating in a school program that evaluates her work habits while also participating in our team's study (lines 12 to 21); and embodied or physical aspects of the immediate context, such as the presence of our video camera (lines 14 to 21) and the color of Diana's son's skin (lines 5 to 11). It is important to note that it is not only Diana's verbal actions that allow her to successfully broker this complex interaction, but also her embodied actions and use of physical resources, such as her adjustments to the web camera angle to enable her mother to see her daughter and husband. Thus, language brokering is realized not just through the use of linguistic resources, but often times also through coordinated embodied action and/or integration of physical resources.

Brokering to Support the Brokeree's Accomplishment of a Given Task

In the brokering practices of parents in home settings, we also commonly observed their roles in facilitating a child's conceptual or linguistic understanding, generally of some sort of written text. Whereas the examples in the previous category involved facilitating communication between two or more brokerees so as to initiate, extend, or re-direct a conversation, this category involves instances of brokering with different types of communicative goals and interactional effects. This category is comprised of interactions in which parental brokering enabled a child to better understand a written text so as to complete a literacy-oriented task (such as doing homework or reciting bible passages). Unlike examples in the previous category, then, these brokering exchanges were occasioned not by interactional trouble among two or more brokerees, but by difficulties in understanding some aspect of a text, usually on the part of just one brokeree. In other words, in these interactions, the parent served as a broker between his or her child and an inanimate object such as a written text.

In the data, these interactions were typically dyadic exchanges, although some interactions involved more than two interlocutors (e.g., two adults co-brokering a text for a child, or one adult and a sibling co-brokering a text for one child brokeree). Interestingly, in this category, we mainly found interlingual brokering in our sample. Although it is imaginable that parents may use exclusively Spanish to simplify, explain, or interpret the meanings of unknown concepts or words that children encounter in Spanish-only texts, we found very few instances of this in the data. This may be a reflection of the tendency of children to not commonly read texts in their heritage language (Lee & Suarez, 2009) or of the limited size of our sample. Thus, the most common practices of this type involved parents brokering English texts for their children, and, hence, most of these interactions (given parents' Spanish dominance and the central role of Spanish in the homes of participants) were examples of interlingual brokering. While most examples were interlingual, we also identified some intralingual examples. This section provides an analysis of one example of each.

Interlingual Brokering

The following interaction returns to Matthew's home. Matthew is sitting on his bed working on math homework in English. He has a packet of triple-digit subtraction problems, many of which he completes on his own, often using his fingers and counting out loud in English and Spanish as he works. Occasionally he encounters a "hard" problem and asks his mom to help him, as in this brokering exchange, which highlights his own and his mother's linguistic fluidity as they work to understand the text and each other (see Appendix for transcription conventions):

Example 3

1	Matthew:	Mamá, I'm not gonna do all this. I'm not gonna do éste {*this*}. I'm gonna
2		skip these, these are hard. Because- I'm gonna skip (.) there, éste y éste
3		{*this and this*} are hard. That's why, [that's why]
4	Lorena:	[Matthew, you] have six, and you
5		take away two. How many?
6	Matthew:	Six take away two? Mm, four. (3.0) ((taking packet back, writing in
7		packet)) Five and four (.) And this'd be=
8	Lorena:	=Nn-hnn. ((taking pencil, erasing))
9	Matthew:	How did you do it then?
10	Lorena:	Nine take away nine is ze (.)? ((looking at Matthew))
11	Matthew:	Zero.
12	Lorena:	Because you don't have no number to (.) borr= <clears throat>
13	Matthew:	=Oooh, [to get] ((grabbing pencil from mom))
14	Lorena:	[You don't] have any number ((pointing at page)) to, can, borr-
15		borrow one.
16	Matthew:	=Oh, so I have to erase éste también? {*this one too*}? ((pointing at page))

17		This? Y haces una three. {*And you make a three*}.
		. . .
18		There's only (.) Mira, uno, dos, tres. {*Look, one, two, three*} ((showing her
19		each of the three pages in the packet))
20	Lorena:	Pero no vas a hacer todas ahorita, nada más haz una hoja. {*But you're not
21		gonna do everything right now, just do one page.*}
22	Matthew:	Una {*one*} page?
23	Lorena:	Uh-huh.

Throughout the hour that Matthew is working on his homework, he and his mother shift between English and Spanish as they work on math problems together. Since Matthew's utterances often include code-mixing (e.g., "I'm not gonna do éste," or *I'm not gonna do this one*, lines 1–3), Lorena is required to do receptive interlingual work in order to understand her son's questions and statements. However, most of her linguistic production while helping him with his homework is intralingual in that the majority of her own utterances are entirely in English. In this particular interaction, the only exceptions to this pattern are when she engages in other activities off-camera (e.g., talking to her daughter elsewhere in the video) or when she makes meta-discursive comments about the activity, such as encouraging her son to do one page at a time rather than trying to complete the entire packet at once (lines 20 to 21). Thus, with regard to Lorena's use of language in this interaction, code choices seem to serve a boundary-marking function wherein she uses Spanish during moments of the interaction not directly related to solving math problems and English for providing conceptual explanations to her son. She continues to speak English even when she appears to struggle with English lexical or phonological forms, as exemplified by her pauses, self-interruptions, and false starts involving *borrow* in lines 12 to 15. The reasons for her exclusive use of English even in the face of linguistic challenges appear to be related to her knowledge of what will best facilitate Matthew's comprehension; in interviews with our research team, she explained that although she often spoke to Matthew in Spanish during other interactions at home, she spoke in English when helping him with homework because otherwise "no, no puede" ('he can't [understand or complete the task]'). Thus, as part of her language brokering role in these homework-related activities, she takes on the burden of added linguistic complexity for herself for the sake of simplifying conceptual explanations for her son.

Besides the device of code choice, Lorena uses a number of other brokering devices as she explains math problems to Matthew. In lines 4 to 5, she breaks a triple-digit subtraction problem into smaller steps, first by translating one portion of the problem (i.e., six minus two) from written symbols into spoken words, and then by asking Matthew a direct question (i.e., "How many?") to prompt him to correct his answer, which he subsequently does. She also uses conventional pedagogical strategies to provide clues about the correct answer, such as uttering the first syllable of the target word and using intonational and embodied cues to prompt Matthew to orally fill in the blank (i.e., "Nine take away nine is ze(.)?"

in line 10). Even when Matthew produces the correct answer, she continues to scaffold his learning by providing explanations ("because you don't have . . ." in line 12), thereby helping him to essentially translate portions of specific math problems into more general math concepts, such as the concept of borrowing from one number to solve subtraction problems. As is the case with Diana's use of language in Example 2, Lorena's use of linguistic devices in this example is coordinated with and facilitated by her embodied actions and use of physical resources, such as pointing to specific areas of the worksheet and taking the pencil from Matthew to correct his answers (e.g., line 8), demonstrating that moments of teaching are often intertwined with the process of brokering.

Like Lorena, Diana is often called upon to do complex linguistic, conceptual, and interactional work when she helps her daughter Flor with homework in English. In Example 4, she discusses some of the challenges of this process, describing how she typically uses a dictionary to translate unknown words from English to Spanish. Diana reports that sometimes she writes the translations down for Flor and thus serves as mediator between the two texts—the homework and the dictionary. Diana also mediates during these interactions through metalinguistic comments about differences between the two linguistic systems. She explains to her daughter that some translations do not match up well because of grammatical differences and that, in these cases, the goal is to try to understand the overall sense of the word or phrase in context.

Example 4

DIANA: Incluso al principio le daban su tarea en español. Sí, se le daban traducida, y la tenía que hacer en español porque no sabía ella. Ya le daban un párrafo para que leyera, siempre le dan una historia. Y la leen y este, sobre esa historia le daban un libro, y en el libro tienen que poner "ah pues yo entendí que esto, y esto" y así. Pero eso sí siempre se la daban en inglés y tratábamos de leerla e íbamos buscando las palabras en el diccionario. Por ejemplo eran palabras sencillas como, que las entendíamos verdad y ya donde no. Incluso las escribía yo en español, y luego como que no coincidía. Le digo "pero es que la gramática pues aquí está de otra forma, hay que darle entender nosotros." Y ya le íbamos haciendo, pero ella lo tenía que poner, en inglés supuestamente como le entendía verdad.

{*In fact, at the beginning of the year, they would give her the homework in Spanish. Yes, they would give it to her translated, and she would have to do it in Spanish because she did not know [how to read in English]. They would give her a paragraph to read, they always gave her a story. And they would read it and um, they would give her a book about the story, and in the book she had to write "well I understood that this, and this," like that. But that part, they would always give it to her in English and we would try to read and look for the words in the dictionary. For example, they were simple words like, that we understood right, and then [others] we didn't. I would even write them in Spanish, and then they did not match up. I would tell* her *"but it's just that the grammar here is different. We have to try to understand it."* *And we would just keep doing it, but she had to put, supposedly in English how she understood it*}.

In such interlingual brokering interactions, Diana is required to move between two languages and two texts, all while being called upon to understand the content of the homework (in this case, a story) and to paraphrase her metalinguistic awareness of how grammatical differences between English and Spanish can affect the translation of particular lexical items as well as the overall message of the text.

Intralingual Brokering

Example 5, which also highlights the teaching functions of brokering, focuses on brokering portions of a Spanish bible in Gabriela's home. In this home observation, 8-year-old Gabriela is playing in her room as her mother Cecilia films her activities, occasionally making suggestions about what Gabriela should do next. After Gabriela has spent some time organizing her closet and telling the camera about her favorite clothes, Cecilia whispers "estudia" (*study*) to prompt her daughter to practice reading the Ten Commandments from a children's Spanish bible which, as Cecilia explained in interviews, she had recently bought in order to support the development of Gabriela's literacy skills in Spanish. Here, Gabriela reads the Ten Commandments out loud, with her mother enacting a brokering role by occasionally stepping in to help Gabriela decode the text correctly and adhere to the cultural conventions for reading the Commandments (see Appendix for transcription conventions).

Example 5

1	Gabriela:	Cuatro, (1.5) </honrea/> a tu= {*Four, honor your-*} <mispronounces
2		"honor">
3	Cecilia:	=Honra. {*honor*}
4	Gabriela:	Honra a tu padre y a tu madre. {*Honor your father and mother*}
5		. . .
6	Gabriela:	</Sies/> {*Six*} <mispronounces "six"> (.) S-, s-
7	Cecilia:	Seis= {*Six*}
8	Gabriela:	=Seis, no cometirás adulterio.
9	Cecilia:	Mm-hmm.
10		. . .
11	Gabriela:	Ocho, no di- darás falso testimonio en </cuenta/> de tu prójimo. {*Eight,*
12		*you shall not bear false witness against your neighbor*} <mispronounces
13		"against">
14		. . .
15	Gabriela:	No osierás los </buenes/> [aje] {*You shall not covet property*}
16		<mispronounces "property">
17	Cecilia:	[Los bienes=] {*Property*}
18	Gabriela:	=Los bienes ajenos. {*Others' property*}
19	Cecilia:	Ése qué número era? {*What number was that one?*}
20	Gabriela:	Diez. {*Ten*}

As Gabriela reads from her bible, she occasionally struggles to decode or pronounce certain words—or, as Cecilia put it during an interview, "se traba un poquito" *(she gets a little stuck)*. In some of these moments, Cecilia steps in to mediate between her daughter and the written text. Some of Cecilia's brokering acts seem to be prompted by prosodic features of Gabriela's speech that signal difficulties with decoding or pronouncing words, such as Gabriela's pause in line 1 and false starts in line 6. In other moments, Cecilia steps in even in the absence of such prosodic cues, such as when Gabriela mispronounces the Spanish word for "property" but continues on to the next word, apparently not noticing her mistake (lines 15 to 16). In addition to helping her daughter decode or pronounce lexical items by modeling the correct pronunciation, Cecilia also uses questions (e.g., "What number was that one?" in line 19) to ensure that her daughter adheres to the cultural convention of stating not only the Commandment itself, but also its number. However, at other times, Cecilia does not correct her daughter's errors, as is the case with her daughter's mispronunciation of the Spanish word for "against" (lines 11 to 13). Cecilia's selectivity in her acts of mediation highlights the complex nature of language brokering decisions about when and how to facilitate understanding and communication.

Although all of Cecilia's utterances during her brokering of linguistic and cultural aspects of the biblical text are in Spanish, she (like Lorena in Example 3) occasionally uses English to mark boundaries between this activity and others. For instance, following another reading of the Ten Commandments some minutes prior to Example 5, Cecilia praises her daughter by saying "good job!" in English when Gabriela finishes reading the last Commandment, after which Gabriela exclaims "I know!" and returns to organizing her closet. Similarly, when Gabriela seems to be delaying her reading of the Commandments a few moments prior to the exchange reproduced in Example 5, Cecilia prompts her daughter by saying "go." While these instances of English use do not function within this interaction to facilitate Gabriela's understanding of cultural or linguistic aspects of the text, they do help mark the beginning and end of brokering interactions. Thus, as discussed earlier, depending on how each brokering exchange is defined and where analytic boundaries are drawn, this example could be considered to involve interlingual brokering. The presence of this gray area in this brokering exchange is particularly striking in Cecilia's case in that she often reported in interviews that she did not speak English with her daughter: in her words, "no hablo inglés con ella, aparte de que no hablo" *(I don't speak English with her, since I don't speak [English])*. The discrepancies between the practices and abilities she reported in interviews versus the practices and abilities we observed in her home interactions may be related to her family language policy (which emphasized the use of Spanish in the house) as well as her own assessment of her English proficiency as fairly low. Importantly, then, it appears that even for immigrant parents who are perceived by themselves and/or others to speak little or no English, the possibility for interlingual brokering exchanges is always right around the corner.

Discussion of Overall Patterns Across Brokering Practices

The data analyzed in this study demonstrate that immigrant parents engage in intra-lingual brokering practices for their US-raised children that are similar to the practices of non-immigrant and monolingual parents, who broker understandings and communication for their children as they go about their everyday lives. However, the data indicate that immigrant parents work with the added challenges of mediating between two cultures (i.e., in both interlingual and intralingual brokering practices) and between two languages (i.e., in interlingual brokering). Moreover, we found that the parents' limited English proficiency did not deter them from engaging in brokering practices; importantly, they were able to draw on their knowledge of English and to find other strategies, such as the use of multimodal resources, to broker within and across languages. Furthermore, the analysis highlights the parents' receptive skills in English, which are often stronger than their productive skills in English. Although receptive bilingualism often goes unrecognized, it is, in fact, a strong resource that enables them to engage in brokering and other interactional practices.

In sum, based on our data, we found that the goals and/or consequences of parental language brokering are as follows:

- To support the child's linguistic development (e.g., correcting their Spanish; introducing or reinforcing vocabulary);
- To support the child's cultural development (e.g., explaining or modeling cultural values; explaining differences in cultural practices); and
- To build or maintain relationships (e.g., teaching a child how to talk to his or her grandfather; facilitating the formation of friendships with English-speaking peers).

These goals were often overlapping, which reflects the interwoven nature of language, culture, and human relationships. Furthermore, in our dataset, these goals were achieved in various interactional contexts with the following features and functions:

- Homework assistance (most often homework in English, but sometimes also in Spanish) usually involving two interlocutors (i.e., the child and the parent);
- Daily interactions among two or more family members, most often to correct, paraphrase, or teach language;
- Interactions with the researchers, often to extend the researcher's question or the child's answer or to correct the child's answer; and
- Interactions outside the home with monolinguals or those perceived to be monolingual, often to obtain information.

Conclusion

Based on parent interviews and home observations, we identified numerous moments in which parents inhabit language brokering roles. Though many of these moments are fleeting, they are significant in illuminating some of the ways in which parents support multiple linguistic and cultural dimensions of their children's development, interactions, and relationships in their often overlooked day-to-day practices. Traditional understandings of language brokering practices have emphasized the mediating roles that more linguistically proficient individuals take up in order to help less proficient individuals; however, this study demonstrates that brokering can also be enacted by individuals whose proficiency level is lower than that of their brokeree(s). This finding is explained by an examination of the various sociocultural and linguistic resources that support brokering. First, in relation to sociocultural resources, parents' life experiences, common sense, and their understandings of the world played an important role in providing resources for brokering, including both intralingual and interlingual strategies, despite their limited English proficiency. Second, in relation to linguistic resources, the data also highlight the critical role of parents' receptive English skills, which often enable them to engage in interlingual brokering practices, and yet these receptive skills are often overlooked in the assessment of their linguistic abilities. This finding in turn highlights the need for increased acceptance of receptive bilingualism and related alternative ideologies of what counts as bilingualism; even though many of the parents rated their proficiency levels in English as low, they had a high enough level of English to help their children with homework, to teach them vocabulary, to help them obtain information, and even to mediate in the development of social relationships with others. The immigrant parents in the study demonstrated strong competence and skill in brokering linguistic and cultural norms and expectations for their children.

Future Directions

Perhaps due to the limited scope of our observational data, the contexts in which parental brokering occurred were not very diverse. Hence, we were unable to confirm whether interlingual and intralingual brokering were governed by certain characteristics in each setting. However, from our initial analysis, it appears that both interlingual and intralingual brokering occur across the various settings. Further studies with a larger number of informants are warranted to determine whether certain speaker or setting variables influence the choice of interlingual or intralingual brokering and to investigate whether parental brokering occurs in other contexts.

Contribution to Theory

By drawing attention to the quotidian ways in which parents take up brokering roles for their children, this study contributes to theorization of language brokering, which in most other research is defined exclusively or primarily as a practice in which children and adolescents engage. This chapter thus broadens scholars' understanding of what constitutes language brokering and encourages a more inclusive definition of the term that can account for the fact that the language brokering role can and does shift among interlocutors within a single interaction and across interactions.

The findings are also theoretically and sociopolitically significant in that they counter widespread public discourses that characterize Latina/o and other immigrant parents as being uninvolved in their children's education and as inadequate caregivers for their children. These purported shortcomings are often attributed to immigrants' limited English proficiency and/or to other culture-of-poverty explanations (e.g., Hart & Risley, 1995; Ogbu, 1978), which, as Valencia (2015) notes, are common modes of deficit thinking. Yet, like many other monolingual and non-immigrant parents, the immigrant parents in this study were constantly engaged in mediating practices for their children through intralingual brokering, with the added complexity of having to mediate interlingually in other interactions or even in other moments within the same interaction. The examples of both interlingual and intralingual brokering that were analyzed shed light on the multiple and complex ways in which parents support their children's academic, linguistic, and cultural development. We saw considerable efforts reflected by parents' brokering practices, including sacrifices of time, undertaking of intense emotional labor, and even investment of scarce financial resources. The parents were willing to do whatever they could to help their children and seemed to view these efforts as a necessary and unremarkable part of their roles as parents. These findings thus provide further empirical challenges to deficit-based (and indeed, often racist) depictions of Latina/o immigrant parents as unwilling or unable to be involved in their children's schooling, language learning, or acculturation.

Acknowledgments

This study was funded by a grant from the Foundation of Child Development awarded to the first author. We thank the families who opened their homes to us and our research team, Jane Younga Choi, Graciela Fernandez, Piljoo Kang, Eunsook Kim, and Veronica Lopez, who assisted with the collection of the data.

Note

1 All names are pseudonyms.

References

Bloome, D., Carter, S. P., Christian, B. M., Otto, S., & Shuart-Faris, N. (2005). *Discourse analysis and the study of classroom language and literacy events: A microethnographic perspective.* Mahwah, NJ: Lawrence Erlbaum.

Bolden, G. B. (2012). Across languages and cultures: Brokering problems of understanding in conversational repair. *Language in Society, 41*(1), 97–121.

Bourhis, R.Y., Roth, S., & MacQueen, G. (1989). Communication in the hospital setting: A survey of medical and everyday language use amongst patients, nurses and doctors. *Social Science & Medicine, 28*(4), 339–346.

Buriel, R., Perez, W., Terri, L., Chavez, D.V., & Moran, V. R. (1998). The relationship of language brokering to academic performance, biculturalism, and self-efficacy among Latino adolescents. *Hispanic Journal of Behavioral Sciences, 20*(3), 283–297.

Corella Morales, M., & Lee, J. S. (2015). Stories of assessment: Spanish–English bilingual children's agency and interactional competence in oral language assessments. *Linguistics and Education, 29*, 32–45.

Dorner, L. M., Orellana, M. F., & Jiménez, R. (2008). "It's one of those things that you do to help the family:" Language brokering and the development of immigrant adolescents. *Journal of Adolescent Research, 23*, 515–543.

Geertz, C. (1960). The Javanese Kijaji: The changing role of a cultural broker. *Comparative Studies in Society and History, 2*(2), 228–249.

Guan, S. S. A., Greenfield, P. M., & Orellana, M. F. (2014). Translating into understanding language brokering and prosocial development in emerging adults from immigrant families. *Journal of Adolescent Research, 29*(3), 331–355.

Gustafsson, K., Norström, E., & Fioretos, I. (2013). The interpreter: A cultural broker? *Interpreting in a Changing Landscape: Selected Papers from Critical Link, 6*(109), 187–202.

Hart, B., & Risley, T. R. (1995). *Meaningful differences in the everyday experience of young American children*. Baltimore, MD: Paul H Brookes Publishing.

Herzog, J. D. (1972). The anthropologist as broker in community education: A case study and some general propositions. *Council on Anthropology and Education Newsletter, 3*(3), 9–14.

Lee, J. S., Kang, P., Jeong, E., Lopez, V., & Fernandez, G. (2010, May). *Understanding the influence of settings on dual language competence among Korean and Mexican immigrant children*. Paper presented at the meeting of the American Educational Research Association Denver, CO.

Lee, J. S., & Suarez, D. (2009). A synthesis of the roles of heritage languages in the lives of immigrant children. In T. Wiley, J. S. Lee, & R. Rumberger (Eds.), *The education of linguistic minority students in the United States* (pp. 136–171). Clevedon, UK: Multilingual Matters.

McQuillan, J., & Tse, L. (1995). Child language brokering in linguistic minority communities: Effects on cultural interaction, cognition, and literacy. *Language and Education, 9*(3), 195–215.

Morales, A., & Hanson, W. E. (2005). Language brokering: An integrative review of the literature. *Hispanic Journal of Behavioral Sciences, 27*(4), 471–503.

Ng, S. H. (2007). From language acculturation to communication acculturation: Addressee orientations and communication brokering in conversations. *Journal of Language and Social Psychology, 26*(1), 75–90.

Ng, S. H., He, A., & Loong, C. (2004). Tri-generational family conversations: Communication accommodation and brokering. *British Journal of Social Psychology, 43*(3), 449–464.

Ogbu, J. U. (1978). *Minority education and caste: The American system in cross-cultural perspective*. New York, NY: Academic Press.

Olmedo-Williams, I. (1983). Spanish-English bilingual children as peer teachers. In L. Elias-Olivares (Ed.), *Spanish in the U.S. setting: Beyond the Southwest* (pp. 89–106). Wheaton, MD: National Clearinghouse for Bilingual Education.

Orellana, M. F., Dorner, L., & Pulido, L. (2003a). Accessing assets: Immigrant youth's work as family translators or "para-Phrasers". *Social Problems, 50*(4), 505–524.

Orellana, M. F., Reynolds, J., Dorner, L., & Meza, M. (2003b). In other words: Translating or "para-phrasing" as a family literacy practice in immigrant households. *Reading Research Quarterly, 38*(1), 12–34.

Roche, K. M., Lambert, S. F., Ghazarian, S. R., & Little, T. D. (2015). Adolescent language brokering in diverse contexts: Associations with parenting and parent—youth relationships in a new immigrant destination area. *Journal of Youth and Adolescence, 44*(1), 77–89.

Strauss, A., & Corbin, J. (1990). *Basics of qualitative research: Grounded theory procedures and techniques.* Newbury Park, CA: Sage Publications.

Tse, L. (1996). Who decides? The effects of language brokering on home-school communication. *Journal of Educational Issues of Language Minority Students, 16*, 225–234.

Valencia, R. R. (2015). *Students of color and the achievement gap: Systemic challenges, systemic transformations.* New York, NY: Routledge.

Weisskirch, R. S. (2007). Feelings about language brokering and family relations among Mexican American early adolescents. *The Journal of Early Adolescence, 27*(4), 545–561.

Weisskirch, R. S. (2013). Family relationships, self-esteem, and self-efficacy among language brokering Mexican American emerging adults. *Journal of Child and Family Studies, 22*(8), 1147–1155.

Wolf, E. R. (1956). Aspects of group relations in a complex society: Mexico. *American Anthropologist, 58*(6), 1065–1078.

APPENDIX

Transcription Conventions

:	Speaker attribution
.	Terminative intonation
,	Continuative intonation
=	Latching
[words]	Overlapping utterances across speakers
–	Truncated/ cut-off word
@	Laughter tokens
(.)	Pause of 0.5 seconds or less
(1.1)	Measured pause of greater than 0.5 seconds
< >	Transcriber comment on manner of speech
*	Grammatically non-normative usage
#	Unintelligible syllable
#word	Uncertain transcription
((words))	Analyst comment on gestures, movements, or gaze
{words}	Translation of Spanish utterance

13

TURNING POINTS AND TENSIONS

Emerging Adulthood for Language Brokers

Lisa M. Dorner

Introduction

Although language brokering may begin in childhood, many individuals continue to broker throughout adolescence and into emerging adulthood. Little is known about how language brokering experiences may shape youths' development as emerging adults. Prior research suggests that adolescent language brokers work interdependently with others (Borrero, 2015; Cline, Crafter, O'Dell, & Abreu, 2011; Dorner, Orellana, & Jiménez, 2008) and develop pro-social capacities (Guan, Greenfield, & Orellana, 2014), as they translate and interpret not only for their families but also for members in the wider communities. However, very few studies follow adolescent brokers as they exit their teenage years, to see whether and how language brokering might continue to change over time (Bauer, 2015; Weisskirch et al., 2011). For instance, it is not known what happens during their transition to emerging adulthood, a life stage that is often characterized in the United States (and in other Western countries) as a time of self-exploration and individual growth. There is scant understanding of how language brokers balance family needs and their developed interdependence with their personal desires and opportunities. In particular, it is unclear if a new period of "self-focus" detracts from their earlier development of "helping orientations" (Dorner et al., 2008). Drawing from a longitudinal, mixed-method project that followed participants for more than 8 years, the current research sought to develop an understanding of language brokers who are no longer adolescents, but (perhaps) not quite adults—namely, those in the life phase of *emerging adulthood* (Arnett, 2015).

Framed by life-course theory, the current project developed longitudinal case studies of language brokers who averaged 22 years old at the time of the latest data collection, which included narrative interviews. Analyses explored brokers' lives in relation to their pasts and current contexts by focusing on three key principles in life course studies (Elder, Johnson, & Crosnoe, 2003).

1. Human agency: In this context, how do brokers shape their lives, through their own choices and actions, as they become adults?
2. Developmental timing: How does the timing of particular life events shape the nature and diversity of language brokering in emerging adulthood?
3. Linked lives: In these experiences, how are brokers' relationships with their parents, siblings, and communities changing throughout emerging adulthood?

This chapter will analyze the tensions and turning points of language brokering, as brokers lived in between cultures, family members, communities and their own past and future during their 20s.

Summarizing the Related Research

In the United States, "adults" are usually characterized as self-sufficient individuals who have moved away from home, started college or obtained additional vocational training, found full-time employment, found a life partner, and/or had children. For many, these transitional markers of adulthood are happening later and over a longer period of time, such that Jeffrey Arnett (2000; 2015) proposed a new stage of development that lasts from about 18 to 29 years old: *emerging adulthood*. This time period occurs between adolescence and fully realized adulthood with its concomitant independence, roles, and responsibilities. Although this life stage is a fast-growing field for study, little theorizing and scant research about emerging adulthood focus on young people from immigrant families (Syed & Mitchell, 2013), much less on language brokers (Weisskirch et al., 2011). Given that emerging adulthood has received some research attention and there is widespread growing diversity of migration worldwide, the study of language brokering in emerging adulthood merits investigation.

Emerging Adulthood

Over the second half of the 20th century in the United States, a significant number of social and cultural changes led to (1) a need for greater attainment of postsecondary education, (2) later entrance into marriage and parenthood, and (3) more work instability for people in their 20s (Arnett, 2015). Across racial-ethnic and socioeconomic groups, on average, a higher percentage of individuals continued their education beyond high school, up to nearly 70% by the 2000s; the average age of marriage increased from 20 and 22 for women and men, respectively, in the 1960s, to 26 and 28 in 2010, respectively; and stable, life-long job prospects in manufacturing or other fields no longer existed (Arnett, 2015). Jeffrey Arnett (2000) theorized that these conditions led to a new life stage for individuals previously characterized as adults: *emerging adulthood*.

Emerging adulthood has five core features that distinguish (but are not entirely unique to) this period (Arnett, 2015). Based upon research mostly in the United States, emerging adults are more likely than individuals in other life stages to experience: (1) identity exploration, (2) instability, (3) self-focus, (4) feeling in-between adulthood and adolescence, and (5) feelings of possibilities and optimism (Arnett, 2015). First, emerging adults are trying out identities and opportunities in both work and love. Second, they experience instability, not only in work and love, but also in where they live and what they do. Third, they are self-focused, more so than when they are young (i.e., when they have parents and/or siblings consistently around them) or later (i.e., when they have a stable partner or children). Fourth, they live "in between," not having reached the typical independence and self-responsibility criteria for adulthood; that is, emerging adults *are on their way toward*: (a) accepting full responsibility for oneself, (b) making independent decisions, and (c) living financially independent (Arnett, 2015, p. 15). Finally, emerging adults are generally excited and optimistic about the future and see many possibilities for their lives.

Some have argued that this life stage—which highlights exploration, individual focus, and possibility—seems particularly salient for *college-going youth* in Western societies, and less relevant for individuals from lower and working-class or immigrant backgrounds (Bynner, 2005; Katsiaficas, Suárez-Orozco, & Dias, 2015; Syed & Mitchell, 2013). Varying experiences of—or value placed on—interdependence, family obligation, and financial needs to work by certain racial and ethnic or economic groups may differentiate their transitions to adulthood (Syed & Mitchell, 2013; Vasquez-Salgado, Greenfield, & Burgos-Cienfuegos, 2015). Research has found that first-generation immigrant youth are more likely to realize the traditional markers of adulthood at earlier ages than the rest of the population (Rumbaut & Komaie, 2010), and lower-income adults may have little time for "self-focus" as they juggle multiple jobs and school (Syed & Mitchell, 2013).

In response, scholars have conceded that emerging adulthood is certainly shaped by one's cultural and historical contexts (Arnett, Kloep, Hendry, & Tanner, 2011). While they argue that some form of this life stage exists across cultures, nations, and socioeconomic groups, they admit that there is diversity in its length and nature (Arnett, 2015). Studies should explore how developmental life stages themselves are culturally defined, with indistinct boundaries that can change over time and place (Orellana & Phoenix, 2016). Researchers should also consider how individuals understand each other's diverse experiences across each of the stages (Syed & Mitchell, 2013). For example, there may be divergent outcomes when one person undergoes the core features of emerging adulthood for more than 10 years, while a friend of the same age does not.

A few studies have begun to explore these questions. Research with 17 community college students from immigrant families, ages 18 to 25, found that three tensions defined their emerging adulthood (Katsiaficas et al., 2015): (1) growing *independence* in decision-making, versus enhanced *interdependence* in contributing to society or the family's welfare; (2) living as a *child* at home, while being viewed as an *adult* in community contexts; and (3) *conflicting messages at school*, with high expectations for personal responsibility, while being treated as an immature student. Another study of college-going youth from immigrant families found that parents provided important resources for students beyond high school, perhaps demonstrating youths' continued reliance on family, rather than independence (Cooper, 2014). Thus, youth from immigrant families and lower-working-class backgrounds in their 20s seem to live "in between" (see also Vasquez-Salgado et al., 2015)—as emerging adulthood theory would predict—but perhaps with different kinds of tensions or expectations than other groups.

Other research has found that emerging adulthood for youth from immigrant families is a time for new perspective-taking. For example, emerging adults from Korean immigrant families in the United States re-interpreted childhood language barriers, academic pressures, and perceived lack of parent involvement from more sympathetic stances as they aged (Kang, Okazaki, Abelmann, Kim-Prieto, & Lan, 2010). Re-interpretations can also shift from positive to negative and back again: One emerging adult who was pleased to support her family as a child broker later resented her immigrant parents' need for assistance (Orellana & Phoenix, 2016). However, this resentment did not last long: The participant's understanding of family obligations and parent-child relationships were re-interpreted later in a more positive light, again, as her perspective was reshaped by her current context and own life course demands as a young mother.

Language Brokering in Between Adolescence and Adulthood

The majority of existing research on language brokers has focused on children and their individual development, as seen in Weisskirch (Chapter 1 in this volume); Shen, Tilton, and Kim (Chapter 3 in this volume); and prior research reviews (Morales & Hanson, 2005; Orellana, forthcoming; Orellana & Guan, 2015). Very little research—whether focused on psychological outcomes or social processes—examines these questions beyond childhood, and especially not how language brokering itself may adapt and change over time (Orellana, forthcoming; Orellana & Phoenix, 2016). Briefly, the following review of studies on language brokers from 18 to 29 years old suggests that brokering continues to be a fairly "normal," intergenerational, and shared family practice, which shapes—and is shaped by—parent-child relationships, identity experiences, and life choices.

Language brokering is a shared and distributed practice (Orellana & Guan, 2015), an "everyday expression of family obligations" (Cline et al., 2011, p. 218), whereby young people translate, interpret, and provide cultural knowledge to help their families move across contexts (Kosner, Roer-Strier, & Kurman, 2014). Studies have found that this work persists into emerging adulthood. For example, 139 Latino/a, Asian American, and White college students in southern California reported language brokering for their parents in their early 20s at only slightly lower rates in comparison to their reported "lifetime rates" (Guan et al., 2014). In another study, 63% of 1,222 college students with two immigrant parents and of various racial and ethnic backgrounds reported still language brokering for their families at the mean age of 19 years old (Weisskirch et al., 2011). While more studies need to confirm these findings, such research suggests that emerging adults in immigrant families continue brokering (Weisskirch, 2013).

Parent-Child Relationships: Tension and Understanding

Language brokering was studied early on as an activity that occurred between at least two people. Whether working to analyze a jury summons or other documents together (Orellana, Reynolds, Dorner, & Meza, 2003), or interpreting between a store clerk, medical professional, or social worker and one's mother or father, initially brokering happens within the context of a parent-child relationship, what some have defined as a "performance team" (Valdés, 2003). In turn, a few studies have considered language brokers' perceptions of parents in emerging adulthood.

First, in a diverse sample of emerging adults ($N = 139$), researchers found that higher frequencies of brokering were associated with lower levels of perceived support from parents; however, this was mediated by praise (Guan & Shen, 2015). Weisskirch (2013) found that 75 Mexican American college students who reported a lack of parental support were more likely to perceive brokering as a burden. Meanwhile, in another study, language brokers who shared activities with their parents sympathized more with their viewpoints and challenges (Guan et al., 2014). Similarly, Weisskirch et al. (2011) found that stronger cultural ties between brokers and parents helped to maintain healthy family relationships. Together, these studies suggest that tensions may arise between parents and emerging adults around brokering, but the quality of their relationships and the perceived support from parents may improve brokers' feelings about it.

Social and Cultural Processes: Being in Between

Language brokers live their lives truly *in the middle* of cultures, languages, interlocutors, and texts. A few studies have examined language brokering in relationship to emerging adults' social and cultural processes of development, especially in terms of identity development and cultural mediation.

In an interview study of 10 language brokers aged 18 to 24, researchers found two themes regarding hybrid identity/ies and transcultural competencies (Guan, Nash, & Orellana, 2015). Emerging adults in that study were aware of their families' status as immigrants in society—specifically, how others' views of their families had changed as their families moved across cultures and socioeconomic statuses—and they "displayed nuanced understanding of both heritage and host cultural norms and of the challenges in mediating between those perspectives" (Guan et al., 2015, p. 6). Similarly, Guan et al. (2014) found that language brokering for parents had a direct and positive effect on empathic concern and transcultural perspective-taking for the emerging adults in their sample. Weisskirch and colleagues (2011) found that brokering was positively related to stronger connections to one's cultural heritage (N = 1,222), and Weisskirch (2013) found that greater frequency of brokering predicted self-efficacy in a sample of Mexican American emerging adult participants (N = 75). In short, mediating between languages and cultures may help to reinforce cultural values, support brokers' positive aspects of ethnic identity development, and develop empathic perspective-taking skills.

Brokering and Changes Over Time

Only a few studies have questioned how the nature of language brokering shifts over childhood and adolescence, let alone into emerging adulthood. The extant work has highlighted that, as one moves into adolescence, brokering tasks may become more public, difficult, and consequential (Dorner et al., 2008; Orellana & Guan, 2015). By their 20s, language brokers may have been exposed to racism and discrimination in society; they may have become more aware of their ethnic identification and social stratification; and they may have started to see that what they thought was "just normal" is now perceived as deviant or wrong by others (Orellana & Guan, 2015). Even with these challenges, language brokers may continue to perceive their work positively, as needed and as valued by their families (Orellana & Phoenix, 2016). The practice may also shape their desire to help their communities through civic engagement and work in the social service sectors (Bauer, 2010; Dorner, 2010). The distribution of language brokering may change over time as well. Some easier household tasks, like answering the phone or checking the mail, may fall to younger siblings as elder children leave home, but the most difficult tasks may be reserved for the family's initial (often eldest) language broker (Weisskirch et al., 2011).

New Directions Shaped by Life-Course Studies

This review highlights that there is variation in the nature and diversity of both emerging adulthood and language brokering. Thus, with an eye on the five criteria of emerging adulthood, as well as the possibilities and tensions of language brokering, this theory-building study focused on describing and situating the practice of language brokering in the context of individuals' lives using three key principles from life-course studies: (1) *human agency*, which highlights that individuals construct their lives through their own choices and actions; (2) *developmental timing*, which argues that life events and transitions are shaped by one's age and generational status during those events; and (3) *linked lives*, which proposes that any developmental experience or transition will be shaped by—and can reshape—shared relationships (Elder et al., 2003).

Methods

The data for this chapter stem from 10 case studies (Yin, 2003) of Mexican American language brokers who were originally from the Chicago area. Drawing from a longitudinal project that collected data at three points in time (2000–2003, 2005, and 2009–2010), analyses focused on emerging adults' perspectives and experiences, in light of their childhood and adolescence. This kind of research is essential for the understanding of emerging adulthood and language brokering over time, as it allows for building and testing theory through a variety of specific cases (Robinson & McAdams, 2015).

Researcher, Participants, and Research Context

I initially met the participants for this study while working as part of a research team that used multiple methods (but mostly participant observation) to understand the cultural phenomena of language brokering in middle childhood from 2000–2003 (Orellana, Dorner, & Pulido, 2003). I led two follow-up studies with a selected group of these participants, as youth entered adolescence around 2005 (Dorner et al., 2008) and exited adolescence around 2009 (this study). Having known the youth for more than 8 years, research assistants and I had developed trusting relationships with the group, and many of them with each other. While I am not a native speaker of Spanish, my research assistants were children of recent Mexican immigrants, were bilingual, and had worked as language brokers. Throughout the research, they provided essential "member-checking," insights on migration experiences, and their knowledge of the Spanish language. The focus for this chapter is the data collected in 2009–2010.

Originally, the 10 participants were purposefully sampled from different neighborhoods across the Chicago area; about half came from ethnic enclaves in the city and half from a nearby suburb. See Table 13.1 for details about the sample. For purposes of this theory-building study, participants had diverse background experiences: They ranged from 18 to 30 years old at the time of data collection; three were born in Mexico and seven in the United States to Mexican immigrant parents. Some lived at home, some had moved out, and some planned to return to Chicago soon. Legal status varied within and across households, and their status had changed over time as some family members obtained legal residency or citizenship.

Data Collection

Data from the earlier studies included field notes, journal entries, survey responses, and audio-recordings of live spontaneous brokering interactions from 2000–2003, when most participants were in fifth or sixth grades, and semi-structured interviews from 2005, when most participants were in high school. Then, from 2009–2010,

TABLE 13.1 Participants at the Beginning of the Study in 2009

Pseudonym	Age	Immigrant Status	Household	Education	Occupation
Abe	20	US-born citizen	• Parents (recent citizens) • One sibling (US-born)	Enrolled in community college	Machine operator
Cici	30	US-born citizen	• Husband (US-born) • Three children (US-born)	Master of Public Policy	Small business owner and mother
Estela	18	Undocumented (arrived age 3)	• Parents, boyfriend (undocumented) • Three siblings (US-born) • Infant child (US-born)	High-school graduate	Fast-food employee when not on maternity leave
Josh	20	US-born citizen	• Parents (legal residents) • One sibling (US-born)	Enrolled in community college	Starbucks employee
Junior	19	Undocumented (arrived age 3)	• Parents (undocumented) • Two siblings (US-born)	High-school graduate	Janitor
Luz	28	US-born citizen	• Lives on own	Bachelor's in Education	High school teacher
María	20	US-born citizen	• Parents (legal residents) • Two siblings (US-born)	Enrolled in 4-year university for Bachelor's in Forensic Science	Work-study student and part-time in hospital food services
Nova	20	Legal resident (arrived age 10)	• Lives on own	Enrolled in 4-year college for Bachelor's in Fine Arts	Student and full-time Mac OS computer support specialist
Sammy	23	US-born citizen	• Lives on own	Master of Business Administration	Student with assistantship in finance office
Traci	22	US-born citizen	• Parents (legal residents)	Bachelor's in Communications	Customer service for Spanish newspaper, and retail job

10 of these participants took part in semi-structured narrative interviews that followed a life-story approach (McAdams, 1995). Either the researcher or a Mexican American research assistant interviewed the participants using a semi-structured interview. We began interviews by asking participants for an update about their lives and families. Then, we asked participants to describe their language brokering as a story, with a "beginning," "development," "future," "life theme," and "key scenes," including "high points" (e.g., when they felt good about their language brokering), "low points" (e.g., when translating was frustrating or difficult), and "turning points" (e.g., a change in translating, or translating that marked a significant life change). The interviews lasted from 40 minutes to 2 hours. Other data included two focus groups in 2009–2010 with six participants and a private online blog, on which three participants, who preferred to communicate in writing to others, wrote 10 posts answering questions like: "(1) How was the start of the school for you and/or for your siblings? Did you have to do any translating or helping out? (2) Describe one translation activity that happened in August. Tell us where you were, what you did, who was involved, and what they did. (3) Have you helped anyone besides your immediate family this fall? If yes, what happened, where, and how did you feel about it?" All data collection was completed in participants' choice of language, which was usually English.

Data Analysis

Analyses focused on the data collected from 2009 to 2010 and began with open-coding the transcriptions of the narrative interviews. This first step of analysis highlighted participants' descriptions of language brokering and how it had changed over time. Then, participants' responses were placed into domain charts (Spradley, 1980) using the three life-course themes: (1) **human agency**: What choices and actions shaped participants' brokering during their transition to adulthood? (2) **timing**: How did the timing of particular life events shape the nature and diversity of language brokering in emerging adulthood? and (3) **linked lives:** How was brokering implicated in their current relationships? Within each of these areas, special attention was paid to the description of "turning points" and "tensions," given the five criteria of emerging adulthood and prior research. After a summary of results, the following section presents two purposefully selected case studies to detail the *nature* and *variety* of language brokering for emerging adults across *contexts and situations.* All names used in the chapter are pseudonyms.

Results

At a glance, the participants of this study fit the definition of emerging adults: most had not yet found their full-time occupation or life partner; they were living with instability (i.e., many were in flux about career and relationships); they were looking toward the future. Almost everyone had continued language brokering for parents, but many had reached a turning point and experienced some tensions around engaging in language brokering during their early 20s. These tensions and turning points, however, were shaped by other developmental transitions and relationships in their lives. While they held their families and interdependence in high esteem, they were also making agentic and independent choices.

Overview of Emerging Adult Language Broker Lives

Given 9/11, the ensuing financial turbulence in the airline industry, and encouragement from his undergraduate professors as well as a scholarship, Sammy was delaying his dream of becoming of pilot and instead continuing his schooling in Florida to obtain a master's degree in business. Traci had just graduated with her bachelor's, was living at home, and had already left one full-time position (at the *Chicago Tribune*) to start work at a Spanish-language newspaper. Nova had just returned to college to study graphic design, after having taken time off to support his family; he also continued to work full-time in technical support at a university near home. María was living at home and working at a suburban hospital part-time while she commuted by train to the city for her first year at university. Josh and Abe were working in the service and manufacturing sectors, respectively, while living at home in the city and attending community college part-time; both hoped to obtain positions in the criminal justice system, where they expected to use their language brokering skills to help out "Hispanics" (as they said). Junior lived at home in a nearby suburb, while working full-time as a janitor and caregiving for his younger siblings. He was undocumented, and he hoped to obtain further schooling to become an auto-body mechanic. Estela also lived at home, caregiving not only for her younger siblings, but also for her newborn baby; despite her lack of "papers," she was aiming for a "brighter" future, hoping to attend college and become a nurse. The eldest participants, Cici and Luz, had moved out of their parents' households and hit other markers of adulthood: Cici was married with three children and Luz was working as a full-time teacher. However, both still felt "in between," as they worked to balance their adult responsibilities and the needs of their childhood home. See Table 13.1 for a summary of participants.

Even with the recent changes in their lives, almost all participants still supported their families through some form of language brokering, although the degree mentioned in their interviews varied. More than half of the participants chose recent emerging adult examples as their "high points" (i.e., Estela, Josh, Luz, María, Traci, Cici) and "low points" of brokering (i.e., Estela, Josh, Traci), which suggests that language brokering was still a regular part of their lives. A few reflected on their childhood experiences: i.e., Sammy, Cici, and Luz (low point only); Nova (high point only). Still others declared that it was hard to describe any particular event because it was just something that they did, woven into the fabric of their regular day: i.e., Junior, Abe, Sammy, María (low-point only).

Sammy, the third child in a family of four, and Nova, the eldest in his family, were the only two who did not mention much recent language brokering. Nova said that his low point was, in fact, his "transition" away from his family and toward his career:

> It was sort of like, you know what? I need time for myself. I need time for me to figure out things, and I'm sorry. I can't really, you know? So that could have been a low point for me and my family. . . . I sort of departed from [language brokering and] . . . me being there for them, at times. So that's when my mom started to realize that I was not going to be around all the time.

Table 13.2 demonstrates the variety and extent of language brokering that each participant reported—for families and community members—in this transitional and emerging adult time period.

TABLE 13.2 Summary of Participants and Their Language Brokering Activities in Emerging Adulthood

Abe	1. Helped parents study for citizenship exams.
	2. Translated at work.
Cici	1. Helped parents resolve identity theft; helped parents choose pension; translated occasional communications sent by fax.
	2. Translated occasionally for strangers at the grocery store; gave presentations about Catholic Charities at Spanish church services.
Estela	1. Helped father resolve an insurance issue, which had resulted in a suspension of his driver's license; called client for father's landscaping business; spoke up for mother at park; interpreted Spanish to English for her younger sister; attended parent-teacher conferences for younger siblings, in place of parents; called electric company for mother; helped pay household bills.
	2. Interpreted for a nurse at a hospital; interpreted for a stranger getting an EKG.
Josh	1. Helped translate for mother's kidney stone surgery at the hospital; helped to ask electric company to turn electricity back on; helped pay household bills.
	2. Translated for Mexican tourists at Starbucks (work).
Junior	1. Interpreted at school between teacher and mother, and at store between clerk and father; translated letters from school for younger siblings, letter from car insurance for father, and census form for mother; helped pay household bills; cared for younger siblings; answered phone calls.
	2. Interpreted between landlord and detective; interpreted at work.
Luz	1. Helped with legal case for father; provided caregiving for diabetic mother three times/week; helped pay for parents' household and younger sister's college loans; performed daily tasks like sorting mail, paying bills, reading memos from father's work, with support from younger sister
	2. Led Latino/a student group as high school history teacher.

María	1. Translated when brother broke his leg; translated mothers' annual medical exam results and other everyday activities when she was at home.
Nova	1. Interpreted at work for businessmen from Latin America; translated for the "log" at work about how he supported the men's computer/programming needs.
Sammy	(None reported.)
Traci	1. Helped parents translate pension documents; translated everyday items like the mail on semi-regular basis for parents.
	2. Helped stranger switch her cell phone settings to "Spanish;" expecting more translation work to occur at new job at Spanish newspaper

The Nature and Diversity of Emerging Adulthood for Language Brokers

Further analyses guided by three life-course principles (i.e., agency, developmental timing, and linked lives) highlight how participants experienced language brokering within their social and historical contexts. Describing two cases at opposite ends of the study time period (ages 18 and 30, respectively), who both had become mothers, but were in different socioeconomic conditions, helps to explore the nature and diversity of emerging adult experiences for language brokers from immigrant families. After drawing out these cases, the following section will review the life course principles demonstrated, in relation to data from other participants.

Cici

Cici turned 30 in 2009. She was married to a US-born White man (David) whom she had met in her early 20s. They now lived in California, near his family, raising their three children. Cici worked part-time for David's new family business, "doing their books" as needed, and as a consultant, doing public policy research and building a website and blog to support other Latina moms. However, she spent the majority of her time raising her children, who were aged 5 and under. Despite living thousands of miles away, she continued to broker for her parents, especially consequential items like picking out her father's pension or resolving his identity theft issue. That said, Cici's language brokering had changed over time, with some attempts to distance herself from this work during her 20s.

Over the years we had known Cici, she recalled a mostly happy, though not always easy, childhood in south Chicago. Her father originally came to work at the steel mills in Indiana, with legal residency. Her mother followed later, crossing the border without papers. While Cici and her two youngest siblings were born in the United States, her next youngest sister was born in Mexico, but eventually her whole family had legal residency. The children attended the nearby Catholic school, while their mother ran a small restaurant out of their house for extra money.

As the eldest of four children, Cici accomplished the majority of the translations and interpretations for her mother. She translated the mail, made appointments, spoke for family members at doctors, and interpreted at her mother's restaurant. She remembered a lot of brokering at school, before they had a bilingual secretary or offered interpreters at parent-teacher conferences (when she was in middle school). She "didn't mind" translating for her own conferences, as she noted, "because I was a pretty good student, and I trusted that the teachers probably didn't have anything really negative to say about me." However, Cici disliked translating for her sister's conferences because she did not have the "most stellar academic record."

As a young mother whose eldest was just about to enter full-time schooling, Cici recalled a childhood event as her low point of brokering, a failed interaction at school that had to do with her sister:

> My mom was so upset at the teacher because she was making my sister repeat first grade, and I felt pretty lousy because I wasn't sure how to communicate what the teacher was saying to my mom. . . . In high school, I think I came across my sister's report card? She wasn't a bad student. If I was to go in with my daughter [now], and they were going to tell me that she needed to repeat the school year, I'd be furious! My sister didn't have bad grades. So, I felt kind of bad that we never really questioned the teacher's authority. Like, "What do you mean she has to repeat this grade? Why?"

As she grew older, Cici began to travel around the city with her mother and support interactions at government offices, stores, and so on. She also supported families across the neighborhood, translating things like children's homework for parents, just as neighborhood children had done for her family when she was very young. While she felt proud of these moments, as she moved into adolescence, she also admitted wanting some of her own time:

> I remember one time, in particular, my mom was having trouble getting her property tax statement. I think she had gotten it and it was wrong, and we had called to fix it, and they had sent it to her, but the mistake was still on there. So, she was mad, and she just decided that she had enough with calling people, and she was just going to deal with it in person at city hall. And, we dealt with it. You know, we went in there, and we figured out the right people to talk to. We left with the correct amount of tax, this new receipt. And I felt pretty good about the fact that I could go in with her and figure out who to talk to and get this thing done for her. In a weird way, my mom and I weren't very close, but I could share those experiences with her and say "Look, I'm pretty smart. I did this for you." [laughter] Like, "Isn't this great? I did this for you." But, at the same time, you know, I would have liked to have just gone home and probably have done my school work.

After high school, Cici went away to a private 4-year university in the Chicago area, the first in her household to go to college. She noted that this marked a transition in her language brokering; she began to view it more as a "burden." Even though her next-youngest sibling could have supported her parents while she was away, her mother would save the mail and ask Cici to translate it every weekend:

> She would want me to sit there, and look through the mail, and basically, either, translate things she didn't understand in some letters, or determine if a piece of mail was important or junk mail. . . . So, I found that pretty annoying because I was so stressed out that I didn't want to sit there for two or three hours looking through the mail. Oh, and if a mail needed follow up, well then I had to do that. . . . So, I didn't like doing it. It got to be kind of a chore. It really went from me not caring too much [about brokering], to having to do it and really, I think, taking pride in the things that I had felt that I did a good job on, to not really wanting to do it. And I still remember, one time, it must have been one of the first few times I started to complain about it. And my mom made some funny comment about "Oh, you go off to school and you think you can't help me anymore."

There were tensions in Cici's recollections of brokering around this time point—she found it "annoying"—but she still retained a feeling of pride and accomplishment; she also understood how much her parents needed her. For example, by this point in their lives, Cici's father had acquired enough English to translate items on his own. However, she recognized that her father was not very "confident," and that both parents always wanted to "double check" if they had "done the right thing." In addition, after recalling one frustrating interaction when her mother actually hung up on her, Cici remembered: "I was the one who would help her with these things, and who was patient with her, to look at these letters with her. And I think she was realizing that I wasn't going to be home anymore." Cici may have been annoyed, yet empathetic.

Two other memories in Cici's interview demonstrate this *push and pull* that emerging adult brokers may feel about their work. Cici recalled most resenting the brokering that her mother asked her to do when she moved back home for 1 year after college at about 22 years old. At that point, her mother would simply leave letters open on the table for Cici; she expected her, at a moment's notice, to visit the apartment buildings that they owned. They had many arguments over this. Cici tried to explain that, while her current job had some flexibility, she could not "just take off a day or two every week to help." When asked to explain the high point of her language brokering, however, she recalled an experience from this exact same time period. She was translating between doctors and her mother, for an upcoming surgery for her younger brother:

I went in there very confident. I knew that I was going to be talking to . . . the surgeon and his general practitioner. . . . I just felt so confident about being a translator . . . "I already went to college. I went to [university]! I don't care. I can talk to a doctor." So, I felt really good that one time because I think I felt that I was there to really push for my brother's health. And that I *could* really push for his health because I understood what they were talking about.

By her late 20s—presumably the end of her emerging adulthood—Cici was married, fully moved out of her parents' household, and living across the country. Shortly after she had moved, she tried to keep up with the daily translating: "I wanted to, sort of show them 'I'm still here. Please don't be mad at me [because I moved away.]'" She had obtained a fax machine, so her parents could send her questionable or important items. After a frustrating event in her mid-20s, however, Cici stopped translating the everyday items. She declared:

I will triage translating for my mom. And I think . . . that was the turning point with me. I determined that if she needed my help, I was going to say to myself, "How important is this? Do I need to stop everything around me to help her with this? Or is this something that could wait a day or two?" And I think it was really healthy for me to do that because I've had to always put their needs, my [birth] family's needs, in front of what I needed to do or my priorities. And it was at a point in my life where I just decided that I was gonna do things on my timeframe and what was important to me, those were the things that were going to get done first. So in a way it was kind of selfish, but I think I needed to do it.

Cici also explained that the work was less of a team effort during emerging adulthood. For instance, in the recent case of her father's identity theft, she dealt directly with the credit companies and cut out the "middle person." She said: "It was just so much more efficient for me to do it."

In terms of her own home and life in California, Cici was not using Spanish nearly as much as she did in Chicago. She and David lived in a higher-income, mostly White neighborhood with only 20% foreign-born residents (in comparison to the rest of California, which is 27%). They spoke English with their children, and Cici only used Spanish occasionally, sometimes speaking for Catholic Charities to gather volunteers or funds, or when monolingual Spanish speakers presumed she was bilingual and asked her for assistance. Meanwhile, at home, her parents and childhood community were transitioning as well. Her father had just retired; her parents were building a house in Mexico and planned to move there soon. In addition, they relied slightly more on their children in Chicago for everyday translations, and they needed less translating overall, as businesses in the city now had more bilingual staff.

Estela

From 2009 to 2010 during our study, Estela turned 18 years old, had a baby, and graduated from high school on time, with "extra credits" and honors courses. She lived with her extended family in the small three-bedroom house that her parents had purchased when she was in upper elementary school. She, her boyfriend, and their baby shared one room; her parents slept with her three younger sisters in another room; and their cousin had the third room. The younger children in the house were born in the United States, but Estela, her parents, and her boyfriend were undocumented. Estela's parents brought her to this Chicago-area suburb when she was 3 years old; she had never been back to Mexico. Her mother worked at a fast-food restaurant and her father had two jobs: one at a company in town and one in landscaping, like many other Mexican immigrants in this mixed-income suburb. Estela's boyfriend, who had arrived in the United States a few years previously and did not speak much English, worked at a restaurant. He also did landscaping with her father; they were good friends. Estela herself had worked since she was 12 years old, first as a babysitter for "White people" in their neighborhood, and then at a fast-food restaurant. In 2009, she said it was "weird" to not have a job (because of the newborn), as she was so accustomed to working.

Over the years, Estela was an important caregiver for her family. She translated for herself and her siblings at school, helped her father build his landscaping business, arranged doctor appointments, read the mail, answered the phone, cooked dinner for her siblings, helped her siblings with homework, and generally took care of any and all paperwork for the family. Her family was often under stress, however, and this impacted her interactions with her mother, especially. Estela had had a historically tense relationship with her, for which Estela had received counseling in high school. In our 2005 interview, Estela mentioned that her mom continually cautioned her about being a teenage mother, as she herself had been, and yet this came to pass. During the 2009 interview, many of our conversations were punctuated with emotional, tear-filled memories.

Of all the participants, Estela recounted the highest number of language brokering events. Just like Cici, her earliest memory was translating at a parent-teacher conference. In addition, the more recent events were quite consequential. Unlike Cici, however, Estela had yet to recognize much change in her language brokering; at this time, she could not name a "turning point." It seemed as if translating had always been a part of her life and always would be. That said, Estela worried about the future and who would support her parents over time. The day of the interview, in fact, she reported having just asked her mom: "What's going to happen when I'm not here? Like what if I move out with the baby and my boyfriend? . . . You need to tell my sisters to try to help you."

Part of the issue, in Estela's mind, was that her sisters had yet to step up; the next youngest was now 12 years old. Since we first knew them in 2002, both she and her mother often described this sister as timid, a trait that they thought did not lend itself to language brokering: "Her personality is way different than mine. She's more, *tímida* [timid] . . . doesn't like to talk to people." In addition, Cici and Estela both told stories about how their younger siblings would try to encourage their mothers to accomplish some activities on their own. In turn, Estela worried that no one would help out her parents when she left the household.

Although Estela imagined that she had not experienced a "turning point," she was partaking in many different kinds of brokering as she aged. Estela recounted the following events from the past year; this work included everyday interpretations at home, as well as consequential, public brokering: (1) attending her siblings' parent-teacher conferences, in place of her parents; (2) translating for an "old guy" who needed an EKG at the hospital (high point); (3) asking a "kid" at the park, who bumped into her mom and siblings, to be more careful (low point); (4) interpreting for a nurse at the hospital (like Cici, she was marked as bilingual by someone in the community; the nurse saw her and asked her to translate); (5) interpreting words from Spanish to English for her sister; (6) calling a landscaping client for her father; and (7) working with officials to resolve her father's revoked driver's license issue. In fact, during the 2009 interview, both her father and mother asked her to do something. Her work seemed never-ending.

Like Cici, Estela now led brokering activities. Rather than serving "in between" two people, she simply completed the necessary tasks on her own. She continued to volunteer her language skills for her community, too. Estela described her high point of brokering like this:

> There this was old guy [in the hospital] who didn't know . . . English, and the receptionist was being really mean to him. And so she just told him to get out, to go ask someone else, and, whatever. I was getting out from my appointment, so I was going to where he was going to get an EKG. . . . So I just told him to follow me, that I was going to the same place and then, when we got there, if the lady didn't understand him . . . I could help him translate. So I told the lady that he was there to get an EKG, and he was really grateful to me. He was like, "Thank you very much. I don't know what I would have done if you wouldn't of helped me, because I don't know how to talk to them. They don't understand me."

Estela was proud and happy to help in this instance, and just like Cici, she continued to be proud of the work she completed for her family too. Despite the continued tension with her mother over the years, Estela had grown to understand her mother through her language brokering. For instance, Estela was very concerned for her parents' welfare and future. She also felt that she understood the immigrant experience, given the work she had done with her mom. Here, Estela recounted feeling positive after helping the stranger at the hospital:

> I know how it is being my mom sometimes, that people don't understand her. And she tries to tell them like, to express herself. So I'm like, I know

how it feels to be in that position, for people not to be able to understand him. So, I just, I don't know, I felt good helping him.

When we followed up with Estela in 2010, she was still living at home in similar circumstances as described earlier. Estela and her mother continued to have difficulties, much of them now surrounding her baby daughter. Estela reported her mother criticizing her choices regarding holding the baby, potty training, and reading to her (with Estela following culturally valued activities that she had learned in this US suburb from a teen-parent organization and her babysitting job). Estela had hopes to move out soon, but no definite plans, partly because of the close relationship that had developed between her dad and her boyfriend, and also because she knew the household depended upon their additional income. Estela was working 40 or more hours each week at the fast-food restaurant, while all the adults juggled day care for the younger children. Estela still had dreams to go to college, like many of her friends, and study nursing, but without a social security number and no money, that dream seemed unattainable at the moment.

Language Brokering Over the Life Course

Language brokering evolves throughout the life course. In emerging adulthood, the language brokers in this study continued to support their families—and others— but, for many, the nature and conditions of that support had shifted. Exploring the complex interactions among brokers' agency and choices, developmental timing, and relationships provides additional insights into the shifts that occur as language brokers emerge into adulthood.

Agency

Language brokers grow up making choices: They chose certain words to communicate a particular idea; they choose *not* to communicate certain emotions, such as one expressed by an angry parent; they choose which loaf of bread to buy when their mother sends them shopping; and more. As adolescents and emerging adults, brokers begin to "help out" not only their families through these choices, but also other community members (Dorner et al., 2008). Many brokers feel proud that they have a skill that can make a difference, as both Cici and Estela mentioned.

By emerging adulthood, the data suggest that brokers slowly obtain more decision-making and power over brokering interactions. First, brokers may no longer do their work situated "in between" two people, as described in the two cases. Now, they may accomplish tasks on their own, making a phone call or resolving an issue at city hall, without waiting for their mother or father to tell them what to say. They choose to act independently, finding it easier to accomplish these tasks without their parents in the background. Second, emerging adults may choose to *not* broker. Cici, Nova, and Luz each talked specifically about how they decided to control the timing and/or amount of brokering that they would provide for their families during their 20s. Luz purposefully moved out of her parents' household to gain some distance, after she helped her mother, who was battling diabetes, take more control over her own life. Nova named his turning point as separating from the family to discover "who I was and who I needed to be."

While many language brokers seemed to experience a great deal of agency, a few of our participants reminded us that some do *not* have the same range of choices to shape their own development. Estela and Junior both wanted to continue their schooling, for instance, but without social security numbers, they could not obtain financial aid. With less agency in this realm, they seemed to be tied more closely to their birth families; they did not move away or start college, like many of their peers. Instead, they continued living at home, supporting their families, performing the brokering and caregiving activities that they had done since childhood, as reported by both Estela and Junior. In turn, a range of family conditions—legal status, job opportunities, or the economic condition of their neighborhood—also shaped brokers' choices and agency.

In summary, the very nature of language brokering—the way it happens, whether it happens, and the individuals involved—changes over time and contexts, as brokers make choices given their constraints. Brokers' opportunity to choose—in their language brokering—intersects with developmental timing and linked lives, as the following sections explore.

Developmental Timing

The chronological age when an experience occurs may shape how an individual experiences it. Cici explicitly described how her perspectives on brokering had changed over time; her age and other developmental transitions shaped her reactions to it. As a very young child, she did not know anything different, so she did not care about brokering "too much," she said. As an adolescent, she felt "pride" in her work, as she had been successful at it, having developed a range of linguistic and transcultural capacities. But as an emerging adult, she called language brokering a "burden," especially right after her college years. Although she still felt valued and was proud of her work, throughout her 20s, she sometimes felt caught between the needs of her new family, as a young mother, and her own mother's demands. Language brokers may be a type of "sandwich generation," where individuals must care for parents and children at the same time (Miller, 1981). In this case, the parents are not yet elderly, but need support for other reasons. As Estela's case makes clear, especially if one still lives at home, the language brokering work may never end.

The desire for independence also shapes brokering in emerging adulthood. As Nova finished high school and started working and studying full time, he felt that he had to separate himself from his family. He wanted to pursue his schooling and future career as an artist, to focus on himself, a core feature of emerging adulthood. Similarly, Luz had obtained a full-time job north of Chicago, while her family still lived in a ethnic enclave in the far south of the city. She also felt that she had to move out to provide some distance and space as she transitioned between two different worlds daily.

Meanwhile, Junior, Abe, Josh, and María still lived at home. Although they were equally busy with work and/or school, they did not speak about brokering as a burden, nor did they actively try to do less of it. They did, however, each have younger siblings still living at home, and parents who had likewise changed and adapted over time. While this study did not measure the different needs for language brokering in each household, it could be that their families simply needed less brokering by the time these youths reached emerging adulthood. For example, at the time of the study, Abe's parents had just become US citizens, studying for the exam with Abe's help; María's mother had been working at a local school cafeteria, a job that would require using English on a more regular basis; Josh had always shared translating with his younger sister, who was close in age; and Junior reported that his mother "knows a bit of English now and she understands it . . . so she wouldn't have to rely on me, in case I move out." Luz similarly reported: "My parents are becoming a little more independent and now there's a lot more translators for services, like my dad just got the cable on his own." Their linked lives to parents and families, parents' simultaneous development, and changes in their home communities similarly shaped the nature of language brokering for those emerging adults.

Linked Lives

Language brokering occurs within relationships between parents (and others) and their children. The participants in this study continued to feel valued for their work, proud to help others, happy to advocate on behalf of their families and other immigrants, and empathetic to their parents' and others' difficult circumstances. Lives had become linked, not only parents and children, but children to their community, as suggested by our participants. In fact, Luz reported that her turning point was translating for people that her father brought home: "So I became the community translator." She accepted her role and knew it was an extension of the trust her father had in her.

That said, language brokering was not always easy. Whether translating for family members or others, certain situations were more stressful and others annoying, a finding that is consistent across life stages (Orellana, 2009). As brokers moved into emerging adulthood, it seemed that their annoyance or frustration was enhanced by the thought that parents should be able to do more of this work on their own now, at the time of the interview. Some brokers worried about their parents' own development and wanted to encourage it, as mentioned in Estela's, Luz's, and Traci's cases. Traci reported: "There are some things that she can do on her own. I think she just doubts herself." Traci's comment further demonstrates how linked brokers can be with their parents.

Brokers were also more aware of the serious consequences of their work. Josh reported interpreting at a number of medical interactions for his mother over the years. As a child, he said that he was quite emotional during these times, feeling sad for his mother; then, as an emerging adult, he was increasingly worried about her, knowing the real risks involved. Likewise, when Luz reported her low point, she spoke about working with her father when he filed a legal complaint on work-based discrimination. As an emerging adult, she knew that her father's work life was stressful and that there could be retaliation for simply filing a complaint. Because emerging adulthood also brings better understanding of consequences, language brokers may become worried about and more aligned with parents who may need their emotional support.

Future Directions

Language brokering experiences shape one's emerging adulthood, as brokers continue to support their families, linguistically, culturally, and, in some cases, financially. In contrast, a range of experiences that typically occur during emerging adulthood—moving away from home, finding and changing jobs, going to college, having children—as well as the development of other family members (e.g., siblings and parents themselves) can reshape the nature of brokering: when, how, and even if it happens.

As emerging adults, language brokers may exercise more power and decision-making over when and how they will translate or interpret, whether at home, for parents, at work, or in the community. Some, especially those living away from home, may decide to reduce their brokering for their parents, so they can turn attention to themselves and/or other people in their lives, especially their own young children. In addition, by their 20s, many language brokers have advanced skills in transcultural mediation and linguistic translation. As such, they no longer always serve "in between," but often choose to complete tasks independently; they broker without brokering, in a way. With greater capacity for empathy and perspective-taking, they show concern not only for their families, but also other immigrants in the community. Next, the nature of brokering shifts in the context of relationships. When families have a younger, willing sibling to language broker, the eldest may experience less tension around brokering as she or he moves through emerging adulthood. In contrast, if the core language broker stays living at home with parents, the parents may continue to depend upon him or her, as they always have. Families' socioeconomic condition and legal status shape these linked lives as well, with the two undocumented participants in our study reporting the most instances of brokering over the recent past. Finally, language brokers come to understand the real-world consequences of their actions to a much sharper degree, leading them to worry more significantly about the well-being of their parents and other family members.

Contribution to Theory

Emerging adulthood for many of our language brokers from immigrant families included the stage's proposed core features, especially instability in jobs (i.e., working part-time, changing jobs, continuing schooling); self-focus (e.g., especially as demonstrated by Luz, Nova, and Cici); seeing possibilities in their futures; and, for nearly everyone, feeling in-between. However, as noted by others (e.g., Syed & Mitchell, 2013), the ways of experiencing this life stage may have particular characteristics for language brokers. For instance, feeling in-between is nothing new for translators. Emerging adult language brokers may be part of another type of "sandwich generation," sharing more characteristics and experiences with elder adults in their 40s, who are caught in between caring for elderly parents and their own young children.

Future research should examine questions of agency, developmental timing, and linked lives to flesh out the experience of emerging adulthood for language brokers. Given the research evidence that language brokering does not end, further study of how this task shapes aspects of how individuals navigate this life stage are warranted. The contexts and people in the lives of emerging adult language brokers should receive further research attention. For instance, little is known about how parents develop over time, especially as their core or eldest language broker becomes an adult. Further, it is not known how siblings experience family life when language brokers move away. In addition, there is little research on the divergent experiences of emerging adult language brokers for those who remain at home in comparison to those who go away for school or work. Future studies could also examine the range and quality of brokers' life experiences beyond high school and adolescence, with an eye toward best understanding the pathways taken, and then, eventually, where those paths lead.

References

Arnett, J. J. (2000). Emerging adulthood: A theory of development from the late teens through the twenties. *American Psychologist, 55*(5), 469–480.

Arnett, J. J. (2015). *Emerging adulthood: The winding road from the late teens through the twenties* (2nd ed.). Oxford: Oxford University Press.

Arnett, J. J., Kloep, M., Hendry, L. A., & Tanner, J. L. (2011). *Debating emerging adulthood: Stage or process?* New York, NY: Oxford University Press.

Bauer, E. (2010). Language brokering: Practicing active citizenship. *MediAzioni, 10*, 125–146.

Bauer, E. (2015). Practising kinship care: Children as language brokers in migrant families. *Childhood, 23*(1), 22–36.

Borrero, N. (2015). Bilingual and proud of it: College-bound Latinos/as and the role of interpreting in their success. *Bilingual Research Journal, 38*(1), 6–22. doi:10.1080/15235 882.2015.1017027

Bynner, J. (2005). Rethinking the youth phase of the life-course: The case for emerging adulthood? *Journal of Youth Studies, 8*, 367–384.

Cline, T., Crafter, S., O'Dell, L., & Abreu, G. de. (2011). Young people's representations of language brokering. *Journal of Multilingual and Multicultural Development, 32*(3), 207–220.

Cooper, C. R. (2014). Cultural brokers: How immigrant youth in multicultural societies navigate and negotiate their pathways to college identities. *Learning, Culture, and Social Interaction, 3,* 170–176.

Dorner, L. M. (2010). *The adolescent children of immigrants, language brokering, and civic purpose.* Paper presented at the Association of Moral Education, St. Louis, MO.

Dorner, L. M., Orellana, M. F., & Jiménez, R. (2008). "It's one of those things that you do to help the family:" Language brokering and the development of immigrant adolescents. *Journal of Adolescent Research, 23*(5), 515–543.

Elder, G. H., Johnson, M. K., & Crosnoe, R. (2003). The emergence and development of life course theory. In J. T. Mortimer & M. J. Shanahan (Eds.), *Handbook of the life course* (pp. 3–22). New York, NY: Kluwer Academic.

Guan, S.-S. A., Greenfield, P. M., & Orellana, M. F. (2014). Translating into understanding: Language brokering and prosocial development in emerging adults from immigrant families. *Journal of Adolescent Research, 29*(3), 331–355.

Guan, S.-S. A., Nash, A., & Orellana, M. F. (2015). Cultural and social processes of language brokering among Arab, Asian, and Latin immigrants. *Journal of Multilingual and Multicultural Development, 37*(2), 150–166.

Guan, S.-S. A., & Shen, J. (2015). Language brokering and parental praise and criticism among young adults from immigrant families. *Journal of Child and Family Studies, 24,* 1334–1342.

Kang, H., Okazaki, S., Abelmann, N., Kim-Prieto, C., & Lan, S. (2010). Redeeming immigrant parents: How Korean American emerging adults reinterpret their childhood. *Journal of Adolescent Research, 25*(3), 441–464. doi:10.1177/0743558410361371

Katsiaficas, D., Suárez-Orozco, C., & Dias, S. I. (2015). "When do I feel like an adult?": Latino and Afro-Caribbean immigrant-origin community college students' conceptualizations and experiences of (emerging) adulthood. *Emerging Adulthood, 3*(2), 98–112.

Kosner, A., Roer-Strier, D., & Kurman, J. (2014). Changing familial roles for immigrant adolescents from the former Soviet Union to Israel. *Journal of Adolescent Research, 29*(3), 356–379.

McAdams, D. P. (1995). The life story interview. Retrieved January 9, 2009, from http://www.sesp.northwestern.edu/foley/instruments/interview/

Miller, D. (1981). The "sandwich" generation: Adult children of the aging. *Social Work, 26,* 419–423.

Morales, A., & Hanson, W. (2005). Language brokering: An integrative review of the literature. *Hispanic Journal of Behavioral Sciences, 27*(4), 471–503.

Orellana, M. F. (2009). *Translating childhoods: Immigrant youth, language and culture.* Piscataway, NJ: Rutgers University Press.

Orellana, M. F. (forthcoming). Dialoguing across differences: The past and future of language brokering research. *International Journal of Bilingualism.*

Orellana, M. F., Dorner, L. M., & Pulido, L. (2003). Accessing assets: Immigrant youth's work as family translators or "para-phrasers". *Social Problems, 50*(4), 505–524.

Orellana, M. F., & Guan, S.-S. A. (2015). Immigrant family settlement processes and the work of child language brokers: Implications for child development. In C. Suárez-Orozco, M. M. Abo-Zena, & A. K. Marks (Eds.), *Transitions: The development of children of immigrants* (pp. 184–200). New York, NY: New York University Press.

Orellana, M. F., & Phoenix, A. (2016). Re-interpreting: Narratives of childhood language brokering over time. *Childhood,* online first version. Retrieved from http://journals.sagepub.com/doi/pdf/10.1177/0907568216671178.

Orellana, M. F., Reynolds, J. F., Dorner, L. M., & Meza, M. (2003). In other words: Translating or "para-phrasing" as a family literacy practice in immigrant households. *Reading Research Quarterly, 38*(1), 12–34.

Robinson, O. C., & McAdams, D. P. (2015). Four functional roles for case studies in emerging adulthood research. *Emerging Adulthood, 3*(6), 413–420. doi:10.1177/2167696815592727

Rumbaut, R. G., & Komaie, G. (2010). Immigration and adult transitions. *Future of Children, 20*, 43–66.

Spradley, J. P. (1980). *Participant observation.* Fort Worth, TX: Harcourt Brace College Publishers.

Syed, M., & Mitchell, L. L. (2013). Race, ethnicity, and emerging adulthood: Retrospect and prospects. *Emerging Adulthood, 1*(2), 83–95.

Valdés, G. (2003). *Expanding definitions of giftedness: The case of young interpreters from immigrant families.* Mahwah, NJ: Lawrence Erlbaum.

Vasquez-Salgado, Y., Greenfield, P. M., & Burgos-Cienfuegos, R. (2015). Exploring home-school values conflicts: Implications for academic achievement and well-being among Latino first-generation college students. *Journal of Adolescent Research, 30*(3), 271–305. doi:10.1177/0743558414561297

Weisskirch, R. S. (2013). Family relationships, self-esteem, and self-efficacy among language brokering Mexican American emerging adults. *Journal of Child and Family Studies, 22*, 1147–1155. doi:10.1007/s10826–012–9678-x

Weisskirch, R. S., Zamboanga, B. L., Bersamin, M., Kim, S. Y., Schwartz, S. J., & Umaña-Taylor, A. J. (2011). Cultural influences for college student language brokers. *Cultural Diversity and Ethnic Minority Psychology, 17*(1), 43–51.

Yin, R. K. (2003). *Case study research: Design and methods.* Thousand Oaks, CA: Sage.

14

FUTURE DIRECTIONS FOR LANGUAGE BROKERING RESEARCH

Robert S. Weisskirch

Introduction

The increase in research on language brokering has offered unique insights into a commonplace phenomenon among immigrant families. Given the current worldwide increase in immigration, understanding how language brokering functions for individuals, families, institutions, and communities may provide ways to support and optimize adaptation to the host country and culture.

At its core, language brokering is an adaptive response by the individuals, the families, and the community to immigration and an outcome of the acculturation process. Language brokering as a process aligns well with Berry's (2003) concept of an acculturation strategy as individuals and families increase their acculturation. However, the individuals, the relationship dynamics, the roles, culture, and community also should be considered in investigating language brokering.

In formulating a theory or theoretical model, language brokering could be included within García Coll et al.'s (1996) integrative model for the study of developmental competencies in ethnic minority children, particularly in considering the cultural and environmental influences on minority children. In their model, developmental competencies include "linguistic" and "cognitive" competencies and "biculturalism," which align well with the construct of language brokering. Thinking of language brokering as an area of competence for children from immigrant families supports García Coll et al.'s (1996) assertion that notions of competence

> must be expanded to include a broader range of adaptive responses beyond the traditional areas of concern and to incorporate additional and alternative abilities, such as the child's ability to function in two or more difference

cultures, to cope with racism, subtle and overt discrimination, and social and psychological segregation.

(p. 1907)

The notion of language brokering being an area of competence is also consistent with Valdés's (2003) view that language brokering may be a form of giftedness. These ideas that language brokering is a competency or a form of giftedness present a stance that is asset-based and strengths-based in examining ethnic minority, immigrant children. The presumption that language brokering is a negative practice, unduly burdens the child, or "parentifies" the child within the family may demonstrate bias against what is most likely an adaptive response and may reify a deficit-based perspective towards others who are different (i.e., immigrants). There are instances where language-brokering youth may gain authority in their new role as part of the typical acculturation processes. However, these shifts in authority cannot be separated from expected gains in autonomy that may occur with development, and there is little evidence of pre-immigration family structures that may support such adaptive shifts later in immigration. Any theory or theoretical model should incorporate a strengths-based perspective and view language brokering as the adaptive, contextualized process that it is.

Further, Kam and Lazarevic (2014) provided an excellent theoretical model of language brokering's effects on youth in immigrant families. In their model, they accounted for individual, family, and community-level contexts as well as many individual factors, mediating aspects, and potential outcomes to language brokering for individuals. Their description of the model helps to capture much of the research to date on the outcomes of language brokering and various conceptual models. Here, and incorporating information from the previous chapters in this volume, I would like to propose a theoretical model of the context of language brokering with foci on developmental, familial, and cultural aspects to potential outcomes of language brokering. As Kam and Lazarevic noted, the literature has focused on three general areas of outcomes to language brokering: risky behaviors, academic performance, and individual attributes (e.g., self-esteem and self-efficacy). Parentification and positive parent-child relations are noted as mediating factors to other outcomes and as outcomes themselves. There still needs greater elucidation of the contexts or antecedents of these outcomes. The research literature is relatively limited, and there may be other outcomes that emerge, when taking into account specific developmental, familial, and cultural aspects in studying language brokering.

A New Theoretical Model

In a large framework, there are three overarching contexts that surround the potential outcomes for language brokering activities: cultural contexts, community contexts, and nature of the task. Cultural contexts include cultural norms and values of the receiving and heritage cultures. When language brokering, the child and his or her heritage cultural values, for example, may shape how the child responds to parents and other elders. At the same time, the receiving cultural norms (e.g., the United States) may support attitudes favoring individual self-sufficiency, which may make language brokering seem unwelcome. The influence of cultural contexts may relate to all aspects of language brokering.

At the same time, community contexts should be considered. The amount of community support of language brokering should be considered. This context may include the geographic location where language brokering is occurring. In places where there is a high immigrant population, members of the surrounding community may be accustomed to the presence of a child language broker and engage the language broker in conjunction with the parents. In places where there are fewer immigrants, the reception to language brokering may be more hostile. Also, the type of language and community reaction to the cultural background may influence the outcome. In this volume, Titzmann and Michel's Chapter 4, Oznobishin and Kurman's Chapter 5, Nash's Chapter 6, and Hua and Costigan's Chapter 7 provide some evidence for the importance of considering community contexts.

The nature of the language brokering task also figures prominently in the outcomes of language brokering. Past research has looked at outcomes of language brokering when the language brokering task is classified by the perceived complexity or difficulty of task (e.g., Buriel, Perez, DeMent, Chavez, & Moran, 1998). Also, the urgency of the language brokering task may shape the outcome as well. For example, a youth may be aware that immigration forms have more serious repercussions than translating the television news (e.g., Orellana, 2009). Similarly, health care settings may be experienced as more stressful because of the content and the face-to-face nature of the interaction with someone in an authority position. In this volume, see de Abreu and O'Dell's Chapter 9 and Crafter, Cline, and Prokopiou's Chapter 11 for research on the contexts and the nature of language brokering tasks. The nature of the task then may innervate the interaction and the potential outcome.

For the individual, there are many aspects that may contribute to the potential outcomes for language brokers. The individual's stage of development at the time of language brokering may affect the outcome of the experience for the individual, the family, and the relationships. In this volume, Weisskirch's Chapter 1, Rainey, Flores-Lamb, and Gjorgieva's Chapter 10, and Dorner's Chapter 13 address some aspects of developmental stages and language brokering. A young child may lack sufficient cognitive development to understand the sophisticated and nuanced concepts to translate accurately. Similarly, an adolescent may resist parents' requests for language brokering because these requests may be perceived as intruding on adolescent-focused activities.

Research has also supported the notion of personality in potentially influencing the outcome of language brokering. That is, some language brokers may be selected by parents because of their outgoing, sociable nature. Moreover, individuals who are more easygoing or more anxious than others may experience language brokering differently. Other than some comments in various qualitative studies, no systematic study of personality and language brokering could be found. Individual perception of language brokering may too affect the outcomes. In a simplistic picture, one may perceive language brokering as something one just does (i.e., neutrally), as something one enjoys, and/or as something one hates. This perception may change depending on the task (e.g., a flyer from school versus a medical appointment). Therefore, the individual perception of language brokering may contribute as well to the outcomes.

Language proficiency in both languages may also play a part in the outcomes. Most of the research relies on self-report of language proficiency. I do not know of studies in which children's and adolescents' language proficiency in both languages are assessed as means to determine the potential accuracy of the language broker's translation. Lee and Corella Chapter 12 (in this volume) provide some insights on the potential accuracy and the shared translating that occurs. Language proficiency may also contribute to the overall outcome. In addition, language proficiency ties in well with the individual's cognitive skills. Children's and adolescents' cognitive skills may not be fully developed to provide accurate translation, to understand sophisticated concepts, or to comprehend the situation. Cognitive skills extend beyond just language and vocabulary and into understanding nuanced meaning and abstract ideas required for the given language brokering task. Rainey, Flores–Lamb, and Gjorgieva's Chapter 10 (in this volume) describes the cognitive and neuroscience behind these potential limitations. Given that cognitive skills may vary from individual to individual, it may influence how one experiences language brokering.

Communication goals may also contribute to outcomes. Kam, Guntzviller, and Stohl's Chapter 2 (in this volume) discusses the role of communication goals, as do Kam and Lazarevic (2014). These researchers and others noted that parents and youth may differ in their communication goals and, when the goals are supportive of the other, there may be greater relationship satisfaction (Guntzviller, 2015). Lee and Corella's Chapter 12 (in this volume) also provides insight in how communication goals may shape the success of the language brokering as well as intercede into parent-child relations. Given that the communication exchange is fundamental in language brokering, the communication goals of the participants may be critical contributors.

Gender and gender roles further contribute to the potential outcomes for language brokers. In past research, the trend had been that female children served as designated language brokers. However, it is not clear if certain language brokering tasks were designated for female children and certain tasks for male children. This situation is further complicated by for whom the children language broker: the father or the mother. There is insufficient evidence to know if, for example, daughter–father language brokering differs from daughter–mother language brokering. Nonetheless, the influence of gender and gender roles may affect the outcomes for language brokers. More study of the effects of gender roles on language brokering would be useful.

For parents, the same issues that emanate from within the individual language broker, discussed earlier, are likely influential factors emanating from the parent as well. There is some research on parents' perception of language brokering and communication goals, and some findings around gender roles (i.e., mothers' experience versus fathers' experience in language brokering). However, consideration of the parents' stage of development, personality, and language proficiency is largely absent, despite the likelihood that these parental factors likely influence the outcome of language brokering.

There is also another component influenced by both the individual and the parent that comprises what I call the *relational component*. The relational component in the model occupies the dialectical space between what individuals and parents bring to language brokering activities. The quality of parent–child relationships may play a role in outcome of language brokering activities. Wu and Kim (2009), for example, found that family relationships were poorer when youth looked at language brokering as a burden. Similarly, Buriel, Love, and DeMent (2006) found that feelings about language brokering related to parent–child bonding. Family dynamics such as power structures, communication styles, and approaches to discipline among others may also play a role. For example, the division of labor in a household may determine who in the family and in what circumstances a language broker is solicited for a task (Katz, 2014). The feedback pattern of how parents respond to the child about language brokering may shape the child's subjective experience in doing so. There are several studies that indicate that parents who are demanding and critical about language brokering may have children who indicate more negative attitudes about language brokering and negative symptoms as outcomes (e.g., Martinez, McClure, & Eddy, 2009; Wu & Kim, 2009). At the same time, parents who provide positive feedback about language brokering and praise for the quality of language brokering have children who report more positive outcomes. These elements do not reside as a function of either the individual or the parent but rather exist within the interaction between individual and parent, the relationship.

Taken together, this theoretical model captures three structural contexts framing language brokering: community contexts, cultural contexts, and the nature of the language brokering task. Further, the model also includes the individual, parental, and relational components that influence the outcomes of language brokering. The model represents how antecedents may shape potential outcomes given the multifaceted and contextually based nature of language brokering. It is hoped the model can help frame further research on language brokering (see Figure 14.1).

Although the proposed model may help future researchers on language brokering, there are aspects of the language brokering research that remain unresolved.

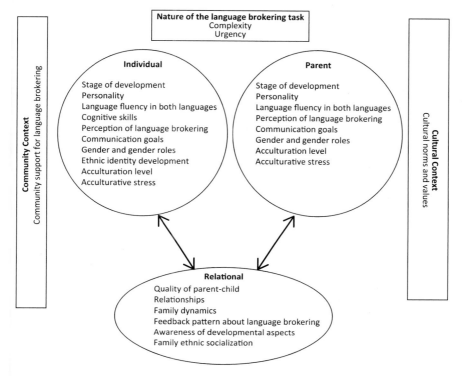

FIGURE 14.1   A Developmental-Relational-Contextual Model of Language Brokering

In order to elevate and further coalesce findings to develop stronger theoretical understanding of language brokering, better research should be conducted.

Measurement of Frequency

Measurement of language brokering continues to be challenging in advancing the field of study. Frequency of language brokering is often used as a primary indicator of engagement in language brokering. However, frequency measures of language brokering can indicate lifetime engagement in language brokering (e.g., How often have you language brokered?); recent language brokering over a specific time span such as last week, the last 30 days, the last six months, or in the last year; and with no time point such as "How often do you language broker?" The measurement of language brokering frequency is further complicated when retrospective methods are used, such as asking participants to recall the frequency with which they engaged in language brokering activities when they were younger. Typically, there is no age range given and the individual respondents have to estimate, in general, how frequently they perceived that language brokering occurred from early childhood to their current age. The retrospective nature of this approach may obscure the real frequency with which language brokering did occur because of the dependence on the individuals' perceptions of how often they had to translate. In addition, with the retrospective approach, individuals may also inflate the frequency of language brokering if language brokering pulled them away from other preferred activities as well as if the quality of the relationship with the parent colors the recollection of the frequency of language brokering.

In the future, I recommend that measurement of the frequency of language brokering include a time frame (e.g., within the last 30 days) and, specifically, that caution be taken when relating retrospective perceptions of the frequency of language brokering to current outcomes (e.g., depression, parent-child relations, etc.). Methodologically, frequency of language brokering may be well assessed in future studies by some type of diary study that would allow language brokers to report how often they translated in a given day, which then could be aggregated to determine the actual frequency with which brokering is occurring. Other types of "real time" language brokering measurement would be particularly useful for accurate assessment of frequency of language brokering.

Difficulty of Items and Situations to Translate

Several studies have investigated differences in outcomes based on the types of items translated or situations in which language brokering occurred. Buriel, Perez, DeMent, Chavez, and Moran (1998) may have been the first to weight differentially various items, situations, and experiences. However, their study weighted certain situations based on findings from a qualitative, unpublished manuscript. Valdés, Brookes, and Chávez (2003) noted that there is a continuum of language registers where high-register text (e.g., legal documents) include more sophisticated language structures and low-register text (e.g., personal letters) have reduced lexical and syntactic variety; however, there is little evidence of this level of scrutiny in language brokering research. Although logic might indicate that a rental lease might be more complicated to translate than a note home from school, there is no objective indicator of how much more complicated or sophisticated one item is than another. The same is true for situations such as translating at a school versus translating at a doctor's office. Nonetheless, there have been some significant findings based on these presumed differences. For example, Buriel et al. (2006), using the weighted language brokering scale, found that adolescent girls broker more than boys for people, for things, and in places (Buriel et al., 1998). Love and Buriel (2007) also found that brokering for many people contributed to depressive symptoms for boys and for girls. Niehaus and Kumpiene (2014) also reported how language brokering items difficulty predicted aspects of self-concept.

Given these few findings, it may be worthwhile to assess the items to determine the actual complexity of the task. For written documents, it may be possible to assess the reading level required to understand the document. For face-to-face interactions, an event recording might be useful to later transcribe to determine the complexity of the language used. Knowing the level of difficulty of the items and situations in which language brokering occurs would allow for better interpretation of outcomes. For example, if translating rental agreements, hypothetically, associates with acculturative stress, it might be partially accounted for by the language understanding required to do so exceeding the likely developmental skills of the child.

Approaches to Research

Very little research on language brokering has been experimental or in a controlled setting. Valdés, Chávez et al. (2003) is a notable exception in which high school students simulated translating for a principal and a parent based on a script provided by the researchers. They determined that the young interpreters were on average 85% accurate in reporting essential information. This finding is just one study and may be an example of how language brokers may be partially proficient as translators. Given that most of the research has been qualitative and quasi-experimental with convenience samples, it may be worthwhile to develop other simulated tasks or event sampling to determine not only how well language brokers manage their task but also if certain language brokering tasks are more challenging than others, affecting outcomes differentially.

Ethnic and Cultural Diversity of Samples

The ethnic diversity of samples in the language brokering literature has been limited. For the most part, Latino/as and Asian Americans in the United States have been the focus of several studies. As with much research that includes ethnic minorities, it would be more precise than the current general practice with much language brokering research to include the specific country and culture of origin. For example, the experiences of Latino/as in the United States may differ by country of origin, which may relate to findings. In addition, the community context may also play a part in the outcomes of research. For example, a child's experience with language brokering may differ in an urban setting where there are many immigrants—language brokering may come to be expected. However, some new research has emerged that included language brokering in recent immigrant-receiving communities and yielded novel findings (e.g., Roche, Lambert, Ghazarian, & Little, 2015). The experience of language brokers in Israel and in Germany (see Chapters 4 and 5 in this volume) may offer insights into how brokering may be experienced when the physical appearance of immigrants may be indistinguishable from that of the receiving cultural inhabitants. At the same time, Nash's Chapter 6 (in this volume) may provide some insights into how appearance and language may affect the language brokering experience with her sample of Arab Americans. Given today's highly politically reactive response to

Muslim Arabic speakers, there may be a particularly unique experience for Arab language brokers who may feel additional prejudice. It would be worthwhile to explore other immigrant ethnic groups whose receiving societies are overtly ambivalent or hostile to their ethnic group and how that may influence how language brokers experience their tasks.

Strengths-Based Approaches

Much of the research looks at language brokering as atypical activity, overly burdensome, or disequilibrating for the family among other similar sentiments. Few studies look at the resourcefulness of language brokers and their families in navigating the transition to a new country, culture, and language. Guan's Chapter 8 (in this volume) may provide a harbinger of what may further occur in the future. Other than communicating with the home culture with videoconferencing, the notion of using technology as a language brokering assistant presents a resourceful way in which language brokers and their recipients are able to compensate for the unevenness in their skills. Further, past research has indicated how family members may work together to engage in a language brokering task (Dorner, Orellana, & Jiménez, 2008). This collaborative activity may demonstrate how families may use the collective understanding for the total betterment of the family. Future research would benefit by looking at how language brokering presents a positive resource and may be a productive way in which a family manages life changes.

What Can Be Learned

The authors of each of the chapters in this book provided a section on contributions to theory as way to link how their findings may connect to larger theory. Across these sections three themes emerge that may help shape an overall theory about language brokering. These themes focus around developmental considerations in acculturation, role redistribution, contextualizing language brokering.

Several authors present findings and recommendations that individual development should be considered at the same time that acculturation as an immigrant is considered, the first theme. That is, it is keenly noted that individual development is a strong influential factor in the outcomes to language brokering. It may be more common that developmental trajectory (e.g., towards autonomy for adolescents or independence for emerging adults) may override or supersede the adjustments needed for acculturation. Developmental changes may then account for outcomes more so or equal to the contributions of aspects related to acculturation.

In addition, the second theme of role redistribution emerged as well. Shen, Tilton, and Kim in Chapter 3 (in this volume) linked language brokering to the family ecology framework and noted the need for considering how immigration and acculturation may require role redistribution within the family. The notion of role redistribution presents a more accurate and less pejorative or pathological perspective than the notions of role reversal or parentification. Role reversal emphasizes an atypical pattern, and parentification indicates that a child is in an aberrant role. Given that immigration is a non-normative and, generally, unplanned experience for most families, it may make sense for the family to redistribute roles to adapt to the new environment. Language brokering may then be a key process for adaptation, which, when acknowledged within the family, may have more positive outcomes. When families engage in language brokering, it may be how an immigrant family maintains a sense of coherence and hope, which is necessary for family resilience (Falicov, 2012).

The third emergent theme is about the importance of context in language brokering. Several authors in this volume noted that language brokering is not just a dyadic experience but must be considered with a broad societal, multidimensional, and holistic lens. The atypicality of language brokering may not be true in a given setting, for a particular family, or in a particular locale. Researchers should be aware of and note the contexts from which language brokering samples are drawn and how they may contribute to potential outcomes. In this volume, for example, former Soviet Union émigrés to Israel represent a group that are part of a large minority in a high-pressure-to-assimilate society, where there may be severe loss of status upon immigration. This combination of factors may contribute to likely outcomes that are unique but also may be similar, in some ways, to the immigration experiences of other ethnic groups in other places. Researchers should take heed to note the specific contextual contributors to the outcomes of language brokering.

Conclusion

There are three reasons for optimism about the future of language brokering research. First, language brokering research inherently gives voice to the experience of youth from immigrant families and the families themselves. This voice helps to document and disseminate the challenges and triumphs of immigrant families that may be hidden from or unknown by dominant cultures. Second, it is hoped that the research on language brokering will move towards intervention and program development. There may be opportunities to support families who use language brokers to learn ways to maintain or to create opportunities for positive outcomes. If family educators or parent educators could instruct around developmental needs and the importance of how parents provide feedback for language brokering, for instance, there may be less stress and conflict in families. Third, there is growing sophistication in methodology and measurement in language brokering that will help delineate the phenomenon. For example, Kim, Hou, Shen, and Zhang (2016) recently presented findings on the measurement equivalence of the subjective language brokering experiences scale. Their study helps to create better and psychometrically tested measures about language brokering and, hopefully, will lead to further testing of potential measures.

It is not likely that the large-scale migration occurring globally will cease. Certainly, regions, countries, and cultures that had been relatively homogenous or less attentive to immigrants' needs in the past are going to continue grappling with integrating immigrants into their societies. Language brokering has been a longstanding practice and a ready resource for immigrant families. More knowledge and understanding of language brokering can only help to optimize healthy integration into societies, amplify the resilience of families, and maximize children's, adolescents', and emerging adults' potential.

References

Berry, J. W. (2003). Conceptual approaches to acculturation. In K. M. Chun, P. Balls Organista, & G. Marín (Eds.), *Acculturation: Advances in theory, measurement, and applied research* (pp. 17–37). Washington, DC: American Psychological Association. doi:10.1037/10472–004

Buriel, R., Love, J. A., & DeMent, T. L. (2006). The relation of language brokering to depression and parent-child bonding among Latino adolescents. In M. H. Bornstein, L. R. Cote, M. H. Bornstein, & L. R. Cote (Eds.), *Acculturation and parent-child relationships: Measurement and development* (pp. 249–270). Mahwah, NJ: Lawrence Erlbaum.

Buriel, R., Perez, W., DeMent, T. L., Chavez, D. V., & Moran, V. R. (1998). The relationship of language brokering to academic performance, biculturalism, and self-efficacy among Latino adolescents. *Hispanic Journal of Behavioral Sciences, 20,* 283–297. doi:10.1177/07399863980203001

Dorner, L. M., Orellana, M. F., & Jiménez, R. (2008). "It's one of those things that you do to help the family:" Language brokering and the development of immigrant adolescents. *Journal of Adolescent Research, 23,* 515–543. doi:10.1177/0743558408317563

Falicov, C. J. (2012). Immigrant family processes: A multidimensional framework. In F. Walsh & F. Walsh (Eds.), *Normal family processes: Growing diversity and complexity* (4th ed., pp. 297–323). New York, NY: Guilford Press.

García Coll, C. G., Lamberty, G., Jenkins, R., McAdoo, H. P., Crnic, K., Wasik, B. H., & Garcia, H. V. (1996). An integrative model for the study of developmental competencies in minority children. *Child Development, 67,* 1891–1914. doi:10.2307/1131600

Guntzviller, L. M. (2015). Testing multiple goals theory with low-income, mother-child Spanish-speakers: Language brokering interaction goals and relational satisfaction. *Communication Research.* doi: 10.1177/0093650215608238

Kam, J. A., & Lazarevic, V. (2014). Communicating for one's family. *Communication Yearbook, 38,* 3–37.

Katz, V. S. (2014). *Kids in the middle: How children of immigrants negotiate community interactions for their families.* New Brunswick, NJ: Rutgers University Press.

Kim, S. Y., Hou, Y., Shen, Y., & Zhang, M. (2016). Longitudinal measurement equivalence of Subjective Language Brokering Experiences Scale in Mexican American adolescents. *Cultural Diversity and Ethnic Minority Psychology.* Retrieved from http://dx.doi.org/10.1037/cdp0000117

Love, J. A., & Buriel, R. (2007). Language brokering, autonomy, parent-child bonding, biculturalism, and depression: A study of Mexican American adolescents from immigrant families. *Hispanic Journal of Behavioral Sciences, 29,* 472–491. doi:10.1177/0739986307307229

Martinez, C. R., McClure, H. H., & Eddy, J. M. (2009). Language brokering contexts and behavioral and emotional adjustment among Latino parents and adolescents. *Journal of Early Adolescence, 29,* 71–98.

Niehaus, K., & Kumpiene, G. (2014). Language brokering and self-concept: An exploratory study of Latino students' experiences in middle and high school. *Hispanic Journal of Behavioral Sciences, 36,* 124–143. doi:10.1177/0739986314524166

Orellana, M. F. (2009). *Translating childhoods: Immigrant youth, language, and culture.* Piscataway, NJ: Rutgers University Press.

Roche, K. M., Lambert, S. F., Ghazarian, S. R., & Little, T. D. (2015). Adolescent language brokering in diverse contexts: Associations with parenting and parent—youth relationships in a new immigrant destination area. *Journal of Youth and Adolescence, 44,* 77–89. doi:10.1007/s10964-014-0154-3

Valdés, G. (2003). *Expanding definitions of giftedness: The case of young interpreters from immigrant communities.* Mahwah, NJ: Lawrence Erlbaum.

Valdés, G., Brookes, H., & Chávez, C. (2003). Bilinguals and bilingualism. In G. Valdés (Ed.), *Expanding definitions of giftedness: The case of young interpreters from immigrant communities* (pp. 25–59). Mahwah, NJ: Lawrence Erlbaum.

Valdés, G., Chávez, C., Angelelli, C., García, D., González, M., & Wyman, L. (2003). The study of young interpreters: Methods, materials, and analytical challenges. In G. Valdés (Ed.), *Expanding definitions of giftedness: The case of young interpreters from immigrant communities* (pp. 99–118). Mahwah, NJ: Lawrence Erlbaum.

Wu, N., & Kim, S. Y. (2009). Chinese American adolescents' perceptions of the language brokering experience as a sense of burden and sense of efficacy. *Journal of Youth and Adolescence, 38,* 703–718.

INDEX